Critical Literacy in Action

WRITING
WORDS,
CHANGING
WORLDS

EDITED BY

Ira Shor & Caroline Pari

Boynton/Cook
HEINEMANN
Portsmouth, NH

Boynton/Cook Publishers, Inc.
A subsidiary of Reed Elsevier Inc.
361 Hanover Street
Portsmouth, NH 03801–3912
http://www.boyntoncook.com

Offices and agents throughout the world

© 1999 by Ira Shor and Caroline Pari

The editors and publisher wish to thank those who have generously given permission to reprint borrowed material:

"Teacher, Tell Me What to Do" by Elsa Auerbach was originally published in *From the Community to the Community*. NJ: Lawrence Erlbaum: 77, 1996, 81–106. Reprinted by permission of the Publisher.

"Teaching White Students About Racism: The Search for White Allies and the Restoration of Hope" by Beverly Daniel Tatum was originally published in *Teachers College Record*. Vol 94, Summer 1995: 463–476. Reprinted by permission of the Publisher and Author.

"Basic Writing as Cultural Conflict" by Tom Fox. Reprinted from *Journal of Education*, Boston University School of Education 1990, Vol. 172, with permission from The Trustees of Boston University and the Author.

"Multicultural Classrooms Monocultural Teachers" by Terry Dean was originally published in *CCC*, 40:1 February 1989: 23–37. Copyright 1989 by the National Council of Teachers of English. Reprinted with permission.

Acknowledgments for borrowed material continue on page 324.

CIP is on file at the Library of Congress.
ISBN: 0-86709-455-9

Editor: Lisa Luedeke
Production: Vicki Kasabian
Cover design: Catherine Hawkes/Cat and Mouse
Manufacturing: Louise Richardson

Printed in the United States of America on acid-free paper
03 02 01 00 99   DA 1 2 3 4 5

Dedicated to Paulo Freire, 1921–1997, Friend and Mentor

Paulo Freire with his oldest daughter, Madalena, and youngest son, Lut.
São Paulo, Brazil, 1987.

"Experiments cannot be transplanted; they must be reinvented."
(*Pedagogy in Process,* p. 9)

"I am convinced that it is not possible to discuss language without
discussing power . . .

"My love for reading and writing . . . has to do with the creation of a
society that is less perverse, less discriminatory, less racist, less
machista than we now have . . .

"The future is something that is constantly taking place, and this constant 'taking place' means that the future only exists to the extent that
we change the present." (*Pedagogy of the City,* pp. 133, 140, 84)

"My dream is of a society in which saying the 'word' is to become
involved in the decision to transform the world." (*Omni,* p. 94)

Contents

Preface
How This Book Was Made

In 1987, Ira published *Freire for the Classroom*, a sourcebook for critical teaching. In that volume, he collected some early work in Freirean pedagogy from the 1970s and 1980s. Those decades in the United States saw Freirean critical teaching being pioneered by such educators as Nan Elsasser, Pat Irvine, Elsa Auerbach, Nancy Schniedewind, Nina Wallerstein, Marilyn Frankenstein, and others. Their valuable reports helped *Freire for the Classroom* stay in print through the years, so that early volume was apparently useful to teachers who wondered how Paulo's ideas could be adapted to their classrooms.

Since 1987, Ira has kept a folder of published material from various sources that goes beyond the early efforts in critical literacy recorded in the original volume. Ten years after *Freire for the Classroom* appeared, the folder had about a hundred items in it, a far greater collection of material than Ira had available for the first anthology. With Paulo's sad death in 1997, Ira decided to prepare a second volume as a tribute to his friend and mentor, showing the diverse growth of critical teaching. This newer material indicates Freire's wide influence on educators, even among those who do not directly cite him. Critical practice in education has been spreading despite these conservative times, so much so that Ira's folder produced enough for several volumes, of which this one on literacy and writing instruction is the first.

To select articles from the huge folder, Ira asked Caroline to join him in the project. Ira can't imagine a better coeditor than Caroline because of her intelligence and her organized approach to the mass of manuscripts. We began with a "reading marathon" in the Catskill Mountains in July 1997 to review all the materials in the folder, a process that continued for a year thereafter as we uncovered more potential essays. We hope we chose good selections from the pile. Readers will have to let us know. Our selections represent articles we thought most useful for practicing critical literacy in real classrooms, so there is a strong tilt here toward narratives of actual pedagogy derived from practical theory.

To introduce the volume, Ira wrote a new piece, "What Is Critical Literacy?" connecting Freire with Dewey and Vygotsky, and with the composition resurgence of the past thirty years. Caroline contributed an essay on reclaiming cultural and class identities in a writing classroom, while Kelly Belanger, Linda Strom, and John Russo revised and expanded earlier work on teaching writing in a union hall. Other selections are reprinted as they originally appeared. All in all, this was a great education for us, and a hopeful one as well, because of the diverse efforts under way by critical teachers. We thank the educators in this book who experimented and tested limits in these hard times for teachers and students. We also thank Lisa Luedeke of Heinemann for her wise help in bringing this material to print and Vicki Kasabian for her careful supervision of production.

Ira Shor
Caroline Pari

1

What Is Critical Literacy?

Ira Shor

We are what we say and do. The ways we speak and are spoken to help shape us into the people we become. Through speech and other actions, we build ourselves in a world that is building us. We can remake ourselves and society, if we choose, through alternative words and dissident projects. This is where critical literacy begins—words that question a world not yet finished or humane.

Critical literacy thus challenges the status quo in an effort to discover alternative paths for social and self-development. This kind of literacy—words rethinking worlds, self dissenting in society—connects the political and the personal, the public and the private, the global and the local, the economic and the pedagogical, for reinventing our lives and for promoting justice in place of inequity. Critical literacy, then, is an attitude toward history that sees language as symbolic action, as Kenneth Burke (1984) might have said; a dream of a new society against the power now in power, as Paulo Freire proposed (Shor and Freire 1987); an insurrection of subjugated knowledges, in the ideas of Michel Foucault (1980); a counterhegemonic structure of feeling, as Raymond Williams (1977) theorized; a multicultural resistance invented on the borders of identities, as Gloria Anzaldua (1990) imagined; or language used against fitting unexceptionably into the status quo, as Adrienne Rich (1979) declared.

From this perspective, *literacy* is understood as social action through language use that develops us inside a larger culture, while *critical literacy* is understood as "learning to read and write as part of the process of becoming conscious of one's experience as historically constructed within specific power relations" (Anderson and Irvine 1993, 82). Consequently, my opening question, What is critical literacy? leads me to ask, How have we been shaped by the words we use and encounter? If language helps make us, how can we use and teach oppositional discourse so as to remake ourselves and our culture?

These questions on reconstructing self in society invite each of us to examine our own development, to reveal the subjective position from which we

1

make sense of the world. All of us emerge from local cultures set in global contexts where language from multiple sources shapes us. In my case, until I left home for an elite university in 1962, I grew up in a Jewish working-class neighborhood in the South Bronx of New York City. In this treeless, teeming area, moms and dads held steady jobs but always spoke of needing money; chimneys coughed out toxic garbage smoke daily, yet no one imagined stopping it; abundant ethnic foods with names like *kishke* and *kugel* were occasions for passionate conviviality in kitchens filled with talk and stories; Eastern European accents were common and sometimes ridiculed, while non-Standard English was typical even among the native-born; televisions were always on and newspapers were delivered daily to our doors, teaching us a version of the world beyond the neighborhood; and the N-word was spoken casually on gray blocks where only whites lived and only whites operated the small stores, except for one Asian family that slept and cooked in the back of the Chinese laundry run by a mom and a dad who spoke little English, unlike the African Americans I heard who had lots of English but no stores.

In that alleged Golden Age, black families and their own English were quarantined across the Bronx River Parkway in a housing project built in 1953 along with a junior high that straddled the racial border and became a home to gangs divided by color and ethnicity. My first September day there in 1957 was memorable for a noisy knife fight at dismissal time. During the next two years, I never went to the bathroom in that building. This was a preview of the coming attraction — the even more aggressive senior high nearby, which could have been the set for *Blackboard Jungle,* a famous urban flick at the time.

Like many American places then and now across the country, these gritty streets were a suburb of Hollywood. We kids went weekly to the local Skouras movie house under the roaring Pelham Bay el, paid forty cents to see a John Wayne cowboy or war saga along with twenty cartoons, and devoured teeth-destroying candy, like a chocolate treat we called "nigger babies." It was a time when John D. Rockefeller's grandson Nelson first ran for governor of New York, and my young ears noticed a change in one of my favorite jingles: Chock Full o' Nuts, the heavenly coffee, stopped saying that "better coffee Rockefeller's money can't buy" and suddenly crooned that "better coffee a millionaire's money can't buy." Could such a change help the famous grandson get elected? Were words that important?

Rockefeller took the State House in Albany while I was afraid to use the toilet in junior high, but before I got to that gang-divided school and the accelerated "special progress" class reserved for me and some white kids, I patiently made my way up the "one" track in my all-white elementary school (1–1, 2–1, 3–1, 4–1, etc.) set aside for supposedly "smart" kids who were being divided from their "ordinary" peers very early in life. I soon learned that a handful of selected white working-class kids were supposed to leave the others behind, which I did with the push of my mother, who insisted I stop cursing like my friends and speak proper English ("he doesn't," not "he don't").

Racially, in the desegregated 1950s, my elementary school changed ever so slightly when a single, perfect black girl mysteriously appeared—Olivia was her name. One day, our third-grade teacher asked us how many of our fathers went to work in suits and ties. Few hands went up, not mine or Olivia's. The teacher's question confused and embarrassed me because my dad—a sheet-metal worker and high-school dropout—wore his only suit for special occasions, perhaps as did Olivia's father. In my neighborhood, suits were for bar mitzvahs, weddings, funerals, lodge gatherings, or union meetings. The teacher's question that morning invited me to be ashamed of my family and our clothes, which, like our thick accents and bad table manners, marked us as socially inferior, despite the white skin that gave us some decisive privileges over Olivia's family, such as my dad's union wages, apartments on the "better" side of the Parkway, segregated classes for us white kids in junior high (internal tracking), and moms who could hire black cleaning ladies on Saturdays while they went off to the local beauty parlors to get a perm.

Perms were a small weekly luxury in this neighborhood, where suits, "proper" English, and good table manners were rare. Still, I did see in those days a grown-up wearing a tie and jacket to work—the elementary school principal. One morning, this suit called me to his office to let me know he was banning the little school newspaper I had started with my best friend, Barry. We called it "The Spirit of '93" to play on "the spirit of '76" we had read about in the American Revolution unit in class, and to honor our public school that had a number but no name. When the principal abruptly ended our literate venture, I learned that eleven-year-olds in our democracy can't publish a paper without prior official approval. The suit's word was power and law. Our kid's word vanished.

Thirty years later, unfortunately, the Supreme Court's Hazelwood decision confirmed the right of public schools to censor sponsored student publications. More recently, my memory of childhood censorship was stirred when a New Jersey principal stopped my colleague Maria Sweeney's class from performing its original antisweatshop play (Nieves 1997; Karp 1997/1998). The suit this time was worn by a female who suggested that fifth graders can't really understand such issues as sweatshops, and besides, the kids weren't being fair to Nike and Disney. Maria, with some parents and theatre people, stood by the eleven-year-olds and their script, which the kids eventually performed onstage in Manhattan, so there was a happy ending to this story.

I could have used Maria Sweeney and activist parents in the '50s. Students of all ages need adult coalitions to help them win language rights to free speech and to social criticism (the presidents at two City University of New York campuses recently nullifed student government elections when dissident slates won). Adult support can keep restrictive authorities at bay, not only when a Broadway cause célèbre erupts like the sweatshop play, but also for the low-profile, everyday forms of silencing that researchers like John Goodlad (1984) and Michelle Fine (1987, 1993) found in mass schooling. Administrative rule making and top-down curricula mean that authority is unilateral, not democratic, featuring standardized tests, commercial textbooks, mandated syllabi, one-way teacher talk, and fill-in-the-blank exams. As teachers well know, silenced students find ways to make lots of noise, in the unofficial spaces of halls, toilets, lunchrooms, yards, and streets, as well as during class when teachers attempt their lesson plans (a resistance called "underlife" by Robert Brooke [1987] and "infrapolitics" by James Scott [1990]). At many sites of mass education including public colleges, a culture war of discourses is apparently under way. In wars of words, can language and literacy be innocent? Can education be neutral?

Innocent or Neutral? Literacy and Pedagogy

If language and education were innocent or neutral, I suppose my school principal would have allowed the "Spirit of '93" to circulate in the building. (Why didn't he campaign against the circulation of the N-word among us kids and our parents?) If words and schooling were unpolitical, I suppose Maria's class would have been able to perform its sweatshop play for classes at their Jersey school instead of crossing the Hudson River to do an exile gig. (Why didn't their principal support the campaign against sweatshop apparel instead of declaring the students unfair to corporate America?) All in all, if words in classrooms were in fact nonpartisan, this nation's schools and colleges would not display the conflicted histories recorded by various scholars (Ravitch 1974, 1983; Karabel and Brint 1989; Dougherty 1994; Tyack and Cuban 1995; Berliner and Biddle 1995). Consider, for example, the case of the Boston authorities in 1826, who decided to open an all-girls high school to match the all-boys one started a few years earlier. So many girls applied that the Brahmin city fathers chose to kill the project rather than to meet the demand for female equality. For the time being, patriarchy was protected. If education were indeed neutral, boys and girls of all colors and classes would have had equal access as well as equal monies invested in their development, something this democratic nation never provided and still doesn't ("Quality Counts" 1998, 20–21, 54). Racially, in fact, schools have become resegregated since the 1954 decision, according to recent studies (Orfield 1993; Orfield and Easton 1996; Orfield et al. 1997).

While segregation and unequal funding remain fixtures in American education, inequality rules daily life as well. For example, the Hunger Action Network, the Department of Agriculture, and the Food First group estimate that five million senior citizens and more than four million children go to bed hungry every day in this food-rich country (Sarasohn 1997; Lieberman 1998). Can anyone doubt that hungry students are at a disadvantage in the classroom? The response of a humane society would be to simply feed everyone with the vast food surplus already available, but distribution in a market-driven society is based on income, not need. On June 25, 1998, *Marketplace* on National Public Radio reported a "problem" for farmers in the Northwest: "too much wheat and too few customers." This sorry saga of separating hungry kids from plentiful food includes a bizarre attempt during the Reagan administration to declare ketchup a vegetable to save money on school lunch programs. You don't need a Ph.D. to know that ketchup is a condiment and not a vegetable, but such rhetorical maneuvers mark conservative politics in recent decades (Bracey 1995). Critical literacy is food for thought and feeling (symbolic nourishment), not real calories. In this wealthy society, as General Electric reports a record $8.2 billion profit (Smart 1998) and General Motors sits on $14 billion in cash (Moody 1998), should it be necessary to say that real food must be guaranteed each child to support her or his academic learning?

Food-rich America has the highest child poverty rate in the industrialized world: 20.8 percent (Bureau of the Census 1997, Table 739). Black and Hispanic kids are more than twice as likely to live in poverty as are white kids (Bureau of the Census 1997, Table 737). Conversely, in a high-tech age, white students are three times more likely to have computers at home than are black or Hispanic youth ("Technology Counts" 1997, 8, 10; Zehr 1998). A child whose parents earn $70,000 or more (top quartile) has an 80 percent chance to graduate college by age twenty-four while a child whose family earns $22,000 or less (bottom quartile) has about an 8 percent chance (Mortenson 1995; Viadero 1998). White median family income is about $41,000, which is remarkably higher than that of blacks ($24,698) or Hispanics ($24,318), indicating that white supremacy is still firmly in the saddle (Bureau of the Census 1997, Table 727). Education and literacy are situated in these larger conditions, where the economy is the "decisive" factor influencing school policy and outcomes, as John Kenneth Galbraith (1967) suggested some time ago.

The good news is that from the 1970s to mid-1980s, black students substantially narrowed test score gaps between them and their white peers (Department of Education 1997, Table 128; Williams and Ceci 1997). The bad news is that these gains slowed or stopped by the 1990s, as economic and educational policies increasing inequality gained momentum ("Quality Counts" 1998, 10–13). Further, black unemployment has remained about twice the white rate, virtually unchanged through boom and bust periods (Bureau of the Census 1997, Table 656), despite the black achievement of near-parity with whites in average levels of education (Department of Education 1997, Table 8). Similarly, the income advantage of white families over minority households mentioned above has also remained steady during this recent period of improving nonwhite educational achievement (Henwood 1997). Additionally, in higher education, black and Hispanic graduation rates severely lag behind white student rates despite a notable narrowing of the racial gap in high school completion and test scores (Gose 1998). Further, in higher education, only 3 percent of full professors are black and only 2 percent of all faculty are Hispanic

(Schneider 1998a). While the racial gap in wages has not narrowed, inner cities have become more segregated and minority families there more impoverished and isolated ("Quality Counts" 1998, 14–15; Anyon 1998).

Like black students' (stalled) test score gains, females made historic advances in college attendance and degrees, yet have not been able to translate their higher credentials into wage parity. As the Department of Education (1997) noted, "despite large gains in educational attainment and labor force participation, significant differences in earnings persist between females and males, even at similar levels of education" (18). Female high school grads earn about a third less than male grads the same age; female college grads earn about 80 percent of what their male counterparts receive. Further, few women are getting Ph.D.s in the high-paying fields of science and technology still dominated by white men, who also continue to dominate the high-salaried professions of medicine and law. Instead, women collect in low-wage doctorates and "helping" professions such as education, social work, and library science (Department of Education 1997, Tables 272, 299–304). Finally, women hold only 18 percent of high-wage full professorships but about 70 percent of low-salary schoolteacher jobs (Schneider 1998a).

Besides the race and gender divides, mass education continues to have widening gaps between social classes (Hershey 1996; Perez-Pena 1997). People of all colors and genders have gained more educational credentials every decade, yet the bottom 80 percent of wage earners saw no growth in their share of national income since the 1970s, while the top 20 percent took home higher wages (Holmes 1996; "Wealthiest Americans" 1997). In a single year, 1996–1997, the number of billionaires in the United States increased from 135 to 170, according to *Forbes* magazine's annual report on the richest Americans (Sklar and Collins 1997). The top 1 percent now control about 40 percent of the country's wealth, the highest percentage in our history even though high-school diplomas and college degrees are more widely distributed today than ever (Boutwell 1997). What Lester Faigley (1997) called "the revolution of the rich" means that class inequity is growing, not declining, at a moment when mass education is at its greatest reach.

Such inequities in school and society have been constant sources of critique as well as conflict. For example, Christopher Jencks (1972) concluded in a landmark study that progress toward equality would occur at the speed of *glaciers* (his metaphor) if we depended on education to level disparities. What would move equality faster? Jencks proposed reducing wage differences and rotating jobs within occupations to give all people access to all competencies in a field or industry. An income/employment policy plus progressive taxation to redistribute wealth would be far swifter equity mechanisms than mass education, he argued, because they would directly create more wages from the bottom up. Shortly after Jencks proposed changing the economic system to achieve equities impossible from school reform, Bowles and Gintis (1976) agreed in their own monumental study that "Education over the years has never been a potent force for economic equality. . . . Schools foster types of personal development compatible with the relationships of dominance and subordinacy in the economic sphere" (8, 11). Several decades later, as I write, Jencks' original analysis still holds, I would argue, insofar as economic inequality is the primary problem needing change to build community foundations for school achievement (Anyon 1998; Mickelson and Smith 1998).

All in all, perhaps these are a few good reasons to question the status quo, including the myth of education as a "great equalizer," Horace Mann's hope, which I discuss further shortly. Critical literacy is a pedagogy for those teachers and students morally disturbed by the above "savage inequalities," as Jonathan Kozol (1991) named them, for those who wish to act against the violence of imposed hierarchy, restrictedness, and forced hunger.

Literacy for Equity:
Transforming Words in the World

In many ways, the project of critical literacy fits the savage and hopeful time in which it emerged. In recent decades, America has been moving left and right at the same time, though not in the same way or at the same speed, I would say. In this long period of polarization, when the liberal "center" declined dramatically, Democrats and Republicans virtually fused on the right. Humane hope has resided in challenges to inequality made on various fronts of the left—challenges that have been met by powerful reactionary efforts to maintain tradition and privilege (Faludi 1991; Ingalls 1998; Morris 1998; Shepard 1998). To state the obvious, the past thirty years have witnessed intense culture wars in school and society over gender, race, class, and sexual preference. Since the 1960s, these culture wars—a long-term questioning of the unequal status quo—have disturbed traditional language arts (phonics and grammar drills) and mainstream discourse (such as the practice of only using the masculine pronoun *he* to refer to people in general). In response to egalitarian pressures from below, "political correctness" charges and other conservative education projects have attempted to turn back the clock through various mechanisms: career education, back-to-basics, the literacy crisis, steep tuition increases, public sector budget cuts, increased testing at all levels, restrictions on open access to higher education, "cultural literacy" proposals steeped in Eurocentric facts and didactic lecturing (Hirsch 1987, 1989; Hirsch, Kett, and Trefil 1988), and "bell curve" arguments justifying the subordination of minorities (Herrnstein and Murray 1994; Gould 1995; Williams and Ceci 1997). This counteroffensive to defend the status quo, which I call "the conservative restoration" against the democratic opening of the 1960s (see Shor 1992a), included corporate conglomeration of the mass media as well as high-profile attempts to muzzle criticism, such as progressive Jim Hightower's removal from national talk radio; *Time* magazine's refusal to run essays on welfare reform, militarism, and the death penalty by its own columnist Barbara Ehrenreich; Oprah Winfrey's famous "free speech" beef case in Texas; and the industry lawsuit against Cornell researcher Professor Kate Bronfenbrenner, who publicly criticized labor-law violations of Beverly Enterprises, a health-care provider. The broad defense of the status quo also brought attacks on affirmative action, which had begun in earnest with the 1978 Bakke case in California (see Sandman [1998] and Hill [1997] for more recent events); on welfare, best epitomized by the punitive W-2 program in Wisconsin and cheap-labor "workfare" in New York (see Coniff [1998] on the "mirage" of welfare reform and Gordon [1994] on "how welfare became a dirty word"); on labor unions, such as the 1998 corporate attempt to end labor financing of political campaigns through Proposition 226 in California; on abortion rights, such as restrictive access sanctioned by the Supreme Court and vandalism, murders, and bombings; on school-equity, including the refusal of states like New Jersey and Texas to equalize student funding despite three decades of lawsuits and one court order after another; and on gay rights, like the banning of the Indigo Girls from some high school concerts because of their lesbian identification (Strauss 1998) and the attempt to drive Terrence McNally's new play *Corpus Christi* out of the Manhattan Theater Club (Blumenthal 1998).

In this embattled period, when the status quo mobilized to defend tradition, hierarchy, and the market system, culture wars have been particularly sharp in the field of English. Consider the bitter conflict fought by Linda Brodkey (1996) at Austin when she tried to redesign freshman comp with diversity issues; Maxine Hairston's (1992a) denunciation of critical theorists in composition and the responses it provoked; the growing dispute between entrenched literary study and subordinated writing instruction (the "comp-lit split" [Schneider 1998b]); the rescue of the SAT as a tool for measuring literacy despite twenty years of criticism against its cultural bias (Weissglass 1998); and the long-term contention between phonics and whole language (Daniels, Zemelman, and Bikar 1998).

The specific area of culture war relevant to this book involves literacy and pedagogy in the field of writing instruction. The papers in this volume ask, What methods help develop students as critically thinking citizens who use language to question knowledge, experience, and power in society? This social context for education joins a long discussion dating back to John Dewey and in some ways to Horace Mann before him.

(Briefly) Looking Back: Reform and Reformers

In the year John Dewey was born in Vermont—1859—an ailing sixty-three-year-old Horace Mann delivered his final commencement address as president of Antioch, which he had helped found six years earlier as the first coed college in the country. It also admitted blacks as well as whites, though Oberlin broke the race barrier a decade before. Mann, known as the Father of the Common

School for his prodigious efforts to set up free public schooling in Massachusetts from 1837 to 1849, had helped rescue Antioch from near bankruptcy soon after it opened (Williams 1937). Now, on a June day in Ohio, he ended his last address with an extraordinary challenge to students, "Be ashamed to die until you have won some victory for humanity." A zealous reformer, he succumbed to illness that August, ending a controversial career primarily devoted to mass education, which he hoped, in part, would solve growing class divisions in nineteenth-century America. If education remained private, Mann thought, "Intellectual castes would inevitably be followed by castes in privilege, in honor, in property" (188).

Dewey, more secular than Mann, argued in *Democracy and Education* ([1916] 1966) that the curricular split between elite and mass education was passed down from the class divisions of ancient Greece, where leisured rulers could study philosophy and evade useful labor, supported by the majority who were marked inferior precisely because they worked with their hands. A class-based curriculum deemed subject matters dealing with utility and labor lesser than those relating to philosophy. Dewey thus saw the new mass curriculum of his own time (the three Rs and job training) deriving from ancient class inequities, where the study of abstract liberal arts remained a leisure class privilege, while basic skills and occupationalism were relegated to society's subordinates:

> The idea still prevails that a truly cultural or liberal education cannot have anything in common, directly at least, with industrial affairs, and that the education which is fit for the masses must be a useful or practical education in a sense which opposes useful and practical to nurture of appreciation and liberation of thought. . . . The notion that the "essentials" of elementary education are the three Rs mechanically treated, is based upon ignorance of the essentials needed for realization of democratic ideals. (257, 192)

Education separated from experience and usefulness on the one hand, and from philosophy on the other, was a dead end for learning in a democracy, he argued. Dewey thus affirmed a holistic curriculum based simultaneously in experience and philosophy, in working and thinking, in action and reflection.

Accordingly, from such an integrated curriculum, Deweyan education seeks the construction of a reflective democratic citizen. In this curriculum, the class-based division between the ideal and the real, the liberal arts and the vocations, is collapsed into a unified learning field. Language use in such an egalitarian field is the vehicle for making knowledge and for nurturing democratic citizens through a philosophical approach to experience. For Dewey, language use is a social activity where theory and experience meet for the discovery of meaning and purpose. In this curricular theory and practice, discourse in school is not a one-way, teacher-centered conduit of class-restricted materials and "language arts" is not a separate subject for the transfer of correct usage or grammar skills to students. "Think of the absurdity of having to teach language as a thing by itself," Dewey proposed in *The School and Society* ([1900] 1971c). To him, children are born language users, naturally and eagerly talking about the things they do and are interested in. He continued,

> But when there are no vital interests appealed to in the school, when language is used simply for the repetition of lessons, it is not surprising that one of the chief difficulties of school work has come to be instruction in the mother-tongue. Since the language taught is unnatural, not growing out of the real desire to communicate vital impressions and convictions, the freedom of children in its use gradually disappears. (55–56)

With vital interests disconnected from classroom discourse, the students lose touch with the purpose of human communication. When they lose touch with purpose in speaking or writing, they struggle to mobilize their inherent language competencies. They lose their articulateness along with their motivation, Dewey suggested, compelling the teacher "to invent all kinds of devices to assist in getting any spontaneous and full use of speech" (56).

Dewey's hundred-year-old observations remain relevant today for the ongoing campaign against drilling in grammar and rhetorical forms (like comparison and contrast, description, narration, and so on), and against "cultural literacy" transmission models that E. D. Hirsch has promoted (see also Stunkel [1998] for a traditional defense of "the lecture"). Since the 1960s, dialogic and student-centered methods from expressivist, feminist, and other critical teachers have foregrounded the personal and the social as the subject matters Dewey called for in his reference to "vital impressions and convictions." The remarkable growth of composition studies in the last few decades has led to substantial alternatives to skill drills, such as writing across the curriculum, ethnography as syllabus, writing process methods, service learning, journal writing, community literacy approaches, literacy narratives, mainstreaming basic writers, portfolio assessment, and collaborative learning, with many classrooms redesigned as writing workshops. These forward-looking developments in language arts coexist with the regressive dominance of grammar books and workbooks, and the rise of more standardized testing and more mandated syllabi in public schools, as well as the greater exploitation of adjunct teachers in higher education (Shor 1997). Top-down authority in school and society has aggressively reasserted itself against bottom-up efforts for democratic language arts.

In this conflicted milieu, recent developments include the emergence of critical literacy as one approach to pedagogy and language use. Critical literacy can be thought of as a social practice in itself and as a tool for the study of other social practices. That is, critical literacy is reflective and reflexive: Language use and education are social practices used to critically study all social practices including the social practices of language use and education. Globally, this literate practice situates discourse in the larger cultural context of any specific situation. "Only as we interpret school activities with reference to the larger circle of social activities to which they relate do we find any standard for judging their moral significance," Dewey wrote ([1909] 1975, 13). Oriented toward self in social context, critical literacy involves questioning received knowledge and immediate experience with the goals of challenging inequality and developing an activist citizenry. The two foundational thinkers in this area are certainly Dewey and Freire, but the work of Lev Vygotsky is also central. Some contemporary critical educators have made exceptional contributions: theorists and practitioners like Elsa Auerbach, Jim Berlin, Bill Bigelow, Patricia Bizzell, Stephen Brookfield, Linda Christensen, Jim Cummins, Nan Elsasser, Marilyn Frankenstein, Moacir Gadotti, Henry Giroux, Patricia Irvine, Donaldo Macedo, Peter Mayo, Peter McLaren, Richard Ohmann, Bob Peterson, Arthur Powell, Peter Roberts, Roger Simon, and Nina Wallerstein; feminists like Carmen Luke, Jennifer Gore, and Kathleen Weiler; and multiculturalists like Alma Flor Ada, Jim Banks, Antonia Darder, Deborah Menkart, Sonia Nieto, Nancy Schniedewind, Christine Sleeter, and Carlos Torres.

The diverse paths to critical literacy represent it as a discourse and pedagogy that can be configured in feminist, multicultural, queer, and neo-Marxist approaches. As mentioned earlier, it invites students and teachers to consider options to fitting quietly into the way things are. Disturbing the status quo is certainly not easy, transparent, or risk-free—for example, try questioning Nike's use of sweatshop labor to students who are "Nike'd" from head to toe and for whom Michael Jordan is an airborne god or questioning such ventures as the Gulf War of 1991 among students with military relatives ordered to the front in Iraq. Coming to critical literacy is a rather unpredictable and even contentious process filled with surprises, resistances, breakthroughs, and reversals (Shor 1996). It's no easy or open road for a number of reasons that I've been defining in various books. The forces that need questioning are very old and deeply entrenched, while student experience is remarkably complex, sometimes too complicated for the interventions of critical pedagogy in a single semester. But, as Horton and Freire (1990) put it, we make the road by walking, and for teachers reporting in this volume, the critical road has produced some very interesting results and some still unresolved problems.

Do Not Walk Gently into That Status Quo: Alternative Roads for Development

As I've been arguing, critical literacy belongs to Deweyan constructivist education, which has also been associated with *activity theory*. As David Russell (1995) defined it in a masterful essay:

Activity theory analyzes human behavior and consciousness in terms of *activity systems:* goal-directed, historically situated, cooperative human interactions, such as a child's attempt to reach an out-of-reach toy, a job interview, a "date," a social club, a classroom, a discipline, a profession, an institution, a political movement, and so on. The activity system is the basic unit of analysis for both cultures' and individuals' psychological and social processes. . . . Activity systems are historically developed, mediated by tools, dialectically structured, analyzed as the relationship of participants and tools, and changed through *zones of proximal development.* (54–55)

Activity theory in general, and the "zone of proximal development" specifically, derive from cognitivist Lev Vygotsky (1962, 1978), who proposed that such zones exist when a less developed individual or student interacts with a more advanced person or teacher, allowing the student to achieve things not possible when acting on her or his own. The relationship with the more developed person pulls the less developed one forward, a dynamic similar to the curriculum Dewey described that began from student experience and was structured forward into organized reflective knowledge of the kind teachers have. In posing experience as the starting point of a reflective process, Dewey asked, "What is the place and meaning of subject-matter and of organization within experience? How does subject-matter function? Is there anything inherent in experience which tends towards progressive organization of its contents?" ([1938] 1963, 19).

A critical writing class is a zone where teachers invite students to move into deepening interrogations of knowledge in its global contexts. The main differences between critical literacy as I propose it here and Vygotsky's zone of proximal development are first that critical literacy is an activity that reconstructs and develops *all* parties involved, pulling teachers forward as well as students (whereas Vygotsky focused on student development), and second that dissident politics is foregrounded in a critical literacy program, inviting democratic relations in class and democratic action outside class (whereas Vygotsky did not foreground power relations as the social context for learning). I want here to emphasize the mutual and dissident orientations of critical literacy's zone compared to the ZPD of Vygotsky. Again, one key departure is that *all* participants in a critical process become redeveloped as democratic agents and social critics. Critical teaching is not a one-way development, not "something done for students or to them" for their own good (Freire 1989, 34). It's not a paternal campaign of clever teachers against defenseless students. Rather, a critical process is driven and justified by mutuality. This ethic of mutual development can be thought of as a Freirean addition to the Vygotskian zone. By inviting students to develop critical thought and action on various subject matters, the teacher herself develops as a critical-democratic educator who becomes more informed of the needs, conditions, speech habits, and perceptions of the students, from which knowledge she designs activities and integrates her special expertise. Besides learning in-process how to design a course *for* the students, the critical teacher also learns how to design the course *with* the students (cogovernance). A mutual learning process develops the teacher's democratic competence in negotiating the curriculum and in sharing power. Overall, then, regarding the Freirean addition to the Vygotskian zone, the mutual development ethic constructs students as authorities, agents, and unofficial teachers who educate the official teacher while also getting educated by each other and by the teacher.

Though he highlighted mutuality in his two foundational works, Freire (1970, 1973) was not a libertarian educator of the "Summerhill" kind. He believed in rigor and structure. For Freire, critical education as a group process was neither permissive nor agnostic (Shor and Freire 1987, 75–96). That is, on the one hand, students and teachers were not free to do whatever they wanted whenever they wanted, and on the other hand, the conceptual knowledge of the teacher was not denied but rather posed as a necessary element. The teacher must be expert and knowledgeable to be a responsible critical-democratic educator, Freire thought.

Yet, teacher knowledge and authority could also contradict dialogue and thus destroy mutuality in this critical process. A central problem for Freirean mutuality is how and when a teacher should use authority and expertise to promote rather than to silence student agency. Saying too much or too little too soon or too late can damage the group process. The problem of adjusting to dialogic practice is complicated because students and teachers have already been deeply socialized by prior "banking" models, that is, one-way teacher talk and nonnegotiable syllabi. Critical literacy has to develop mutual inquiry in a field already crowded with anticritical monologue. No wonder, then, that in Freire's "culture circle," the first problem of education was reconciling the student-teacher dichotomy (1970, 57–60). Freire (1973) complained early on that "liberatory" educators were themselves too often poor practitioners of dialogue and too infected with the old habits of one-way communication:

> A major problem in setting up the program is instructing the teams of coordinators. Teaching the purely technical aspects of the procedure is not difficult. The difficulty lies rather in the creation of a new attitude—that of dialogue, so absent in our upbringing and education. (52; see also Shor [1992b, 85–111])

While being a democratic authority is a teacher's challenge in a dialogic program, there is also the opposite dilemma, that is, of the teacher *not* having enough authority. In some cases, the *lack* of authority interferes with a teacher's ability to initiate a critical and power-sharing process. On the one hand, there are classrooms where some students' disruptive behavior overwhelms other students and the teacher's authority, making control the issue instead of power sharing. On the other hand, the authority teachers bring to class varies according to the teacher's gender, race, age, condition of employment (full- or part-time), physical stature and ability, regional location, grade level, discipline or subject matter, type of institution (elite or mass), and other factors. Similarly, the students' varying ages, genders, races, classes, ethnicities, and so forth, equally affect their authority as well as that of the teacher. Students who develop socially subordinate identities can possess too little authority for them to join an unfamiliar critical process. Put simply, there is no universal teacher authority uniformly empowered in front of standard students. Teachers, students, and settings differ. The same teacher can have more authority in one class and less in another because few classes are alike. In sum, difference in an unequal society means that teachers possess uneven authority when they address students. Consequently, while all teachers need to establish their authority in class, some are at a distinct advantage both in taking charge and in sharing power: White males who are tall, older, full-time, long-employed, and able-bodied generally have the most authority, though teachers of color tend to have more authority than whites in inner-city schools with minority populations.

These differences complicate the mutual ethic of critical literacy. The risk and difficulty of democratizing education should be apparent to those who read these lines or to those who have attempted critical literacy, perhaps encountering the awkward position of distributing authority to students who often do not want it or know how to use it. Still, the long history of this mutual ethic makes it a landmark responsibility of democratic teachers. Mutuality certainly goes back to Dewey ([1938] 1963), who was preoccupied with the cooperative development of social feeling and with the democratic involvement of students:

> There is, I think, no point in the philosophy of progressive education which is sounder than its emphasis upon the importance of the participation of the learner in the formation of the purposes which direct his activities in the learning process, just as there is no defect in traditional education greater than its failure to secure the active cooperation of the pupil in construction of the purposes involved in his studying. (67)

Dewey saw cooperative relations central to democratic education and society. To him, any social situation where people could not consult, collaborate, or negotiate was an activity of slaves rather than of free people. Freedom and liberty are high-profile "god-words" in American life, but, traditionally, teachers are trained and rewarded as unilateral authorities who transmit expert skills and information, who not only take charge but stay in charge. At the same time, students are trained to be authority-dependent, waiting to be told what things mean and what to do, an alienating position that encourages passive-aggressive submission and sabotage.

In this difficult project, I knew Freire as an optimist aware of the limits. His was a pedagogy of hope that saw critical action bringing the future to life in the present (Shor and Freire 1987, 184–87). Before Freire, Dewey was himself optimistically focused on pragmatic "agencies for doing" ([1916] 1966, 38). Dewey proposed that a curriculum must have "the intention of improving the life we live in common so that the future shall be better than the past" (191). As did Freire, he recognized the power embedded in the ordinary to impede change as well as to promote it. Dewey even quantified this everyday power with a metaphor by saying that "An ounce of experience is better than a ton of theory" (144), certainly a strong statement for this man of sober words. Only in experience, Dewey argued, does theory have any "vital and verifiable significance." Reflection on experience, he thought, could yield extensive theory while theory alone was "a mere verbal formula, a set of catchwords" that obscured critical thinking. Freire later agreed, referring to theory-based action/ action-based theorizing as "praxis."

The notion of praxis—reflective action—works off the difference between *theorizing practice* and *theorizing theory*. Consider the phrase "theorizing practice" and how it can be reversed to "practicing theory." This is what praxis meant to Freire: a close relationship between words and action, between the symbolic and the concrete—theorizing practice/practicing theory. If we try this linguistic reversal with the phrase "theorizing theory," we lose praxis; we wind up with the same phrase we began with—"theorizing theory"—because the participle and the noun in that phrase have the same root, referring to the same thing, theory alone, words without the world (as Freire might have said). Beginning and staying in theory keeps the word and the world abstractly apart, making discourse into a "conceptual ballet" or "dance of the concepts," as Freire called it (Shor and Freire 1987, 147). Yet, in elite academic life, the more abstract a discourse, the more prestige the speaker represents. However, from Freire and from Dewey before him, the praxis of critical literacy involves language in and for action beginning from the everyday words and knowledge students bring to class, an approach shared with expressivism (see Elbow [1991] on the students' need to use their own language for writing development).

Praxis that begins from student themes and connects to the global evolves what I have called "the third idiom," that is, a local critical discourse synthesized in the immediate zone for the purposes undertaken there, different from the everyday language of students and from the academic language of the teacher (Shor 1992, 169–99). The emergence of a situated third idiom indicates that some of the power conflicts between students and teacher are being worked through. In this regard, Patricia Bizzell's forthcoming work in "hybrid discourses" is very helpful in identifying new idioms as egalitarian options to traditional academic discourse.

Working Through the Writing Class

As I have argued, discourse in general, education in particular, and literacy classes specifically are agencies for making self in society. Kenneth Burke's (1966) notion of language as symbolic action not only defined discourse as a material force in history, but also that language is "suasive," that is, a force that socially pulls individuals to develop one way or another. On the one hand, we make ourselves in the world according to the way we learn to think and talk about society and our place in it. On the other hand, however, thought, language, and action are never fully under control, never fully determined by the status quo. The opposite to determinism is the potential for alternative agency; we can speak and act critically to change ourselves and the world. We can critique the way things are, imagine alternatives, hypothesize ways to get there, act from these plans, evaluate and adjust our actions. Consider Dewey's problem-solving method ([1933] 1971a); Stephen Brookfield's (1987) social theory of critical thinking; and Freire's connection to Gramsci and activist adult education (Mayo 1994), which suggest the potential of critical discourse for alternative growth.

Because critical writing classes propose social and personal alternatives to the status quo, the stakes are high. Why else would so much controlling regulation and administration be directed at writing and reading practices in school and society? Power is obviously involved in the "sponsorship of literacy," as Deborah Brandt (1998) wrote:

> everybody's literacy practices are operating in differential economies, which supply different access routes, different degrees of sponsoring power, and different scales of monetary worth to the practices in use. In fact, the interviews I conducted are filled with examples of how economic and political forces, some of them originating in quite distant corporate and government policies, affect people's day-to-day ability to seek out and practice literacy. (172)

The power issues specifically circulating in language education were described like this by John Rouse (1979):

> language learning is the process by which a child comes to acquire a specific social identity. What kind of person should we help bring into being? . . . [E]very vested interest in the community is concerned with what is to happen during those years, with how language training is to be organized and evaluated, for the continued survival of any power structure requires the production of certain personality types. The making of an English program becomes, then, not simply an educational venture but a political act. (1)

Rouse noted that a writing program can help produce people "acceptable to those who would maintain things as they are, who already have power," which Dick Ohmann ([1976] 1996, 1987) saw as the official function of composition. Ohmann and Rouse anticipated Jim Berlin's idea that when we teach writing we are teaching a version of the world and the students' places in it. Berlin (1996) said that a curriculum

> is a device for encouraging the production of a certain kind of graduate, in effect, a certain kind of person. In directing what courses will be taken in what order, the curriculum undertakes the creation of consciousness. The curriculum does not do this on its own, free of outside influence. It instead occupies a position between the conditions of the larger society it is serving—the economic, political, and cultural sectors—and the work of teacher-scholars within the institution. (17)

Berlin's orientation was concretely tied to a pedagogy for critical consciousness by Tom Fox (1993), who proposed a composition class that interrogates cultural and political commonplaces . . . refuses to repeat cliched explanations for poverty, racism, sexism, homophobia . . . explores and embodies conflicts . . . critiques institutional inequities, especially in the immediate context of the classroom, the writing program, the department, the university, but also in the institutions that have played an important role in students' lives . . . demonstrates successful practices of resistance, that seeks historical evidence for possibilities and promise . . . self-consciously explores the workings of its own rhetoric . . . and seeks to reduce the deafening violence of inequality. (43–44)

While Fox stipulated goals for questioning the status quo, Robert Brooke (1987) defined writing per se as an act of resistance:

[Writing] necessarily involves standing outside the roles and beliefs offered by a social situation—it involves questioning them, searching for new connections, building ideas that may be in conflict with accepted ways of thinking and acting. Writing involves being able to challenge one's assigned roles long enough that one can think originally; it involves living in conflict with accepted (expected) thought and action. (141)

Brooke offered an intelligent argument that writing itself was synonymous with divergent thinking. Still, I doubt this direct link of composing with resisting. Some kinds of writing and pedagogy consciously disconfirm the status quo, but not composing and instruction in general. Think of all the books written from and for the status quo. Further, it is also easy to find composition classes that reflect traditional values and encourage status quo writing ("current-traditional rhetoric"; see Ohmann [(1976) 1996] as well as Crowley [1996]). Human beings are certainly active when writing, and all action involves development and agency of some kind, but not all agency or development is critical. Critical agency and writing are self-conscious positions of questioning the status quo and imagining alternative arrangements for self and society (Brookfield 1987).

This perspective on literacy for questioning society is markedly different from Erika Lindemann's (1995) definition of writing as "a process of communication that uses a conventional graphic system to convey a message to a reader" (11). From a different point of view than Lindemann's rhetorical functionalism, Louise Phelps (1988) acknowledged writing as a rich cultural activity, not a set of basic skills: "the potential for composing becomes the principle of reflection . . . and especially the critical spirit" (67), echoing Brooke above and endorsing Shirley Brice Heath's (1983) idea of writing as a complex social activity. Phelps also embraced Ann Berthoff's (1981) notion, which was taken up as well by Knoblauch and Brannon (1984) and John Mayher (1990), that "Writing is an act of making meaning for self and for others" (70). Related to activity theory and to cultural context, Marilyn Cooper and Michael Holtzman (1989) proposed that "Writing is a form of social action. It is part of the way in which some people live in the world. Thus, when thinking about writing, we must also think about the way that people live in the world" (xii). They reflected Brian Street's (1984) and Harvey Graff's (1987) arguments that all language use is socially situated, against what Street called the myth of autonomous literacy, that is, language use falsely posed as techniques independent of social context. One of the more complex and ambitious efforts to place language learning in a social context is the community literacy project organized by Linda Flower, which seeks an "alternative discourse" for "social change, . . . intercultural conversation, . . . new strategies for decision making, . . . [and] inquiry" (Peck, Flower, and Higgins 1995, 205; Flower 1998).

The social context and making-of-meaning schools of literacy go back not only to Vygotsky's activity theory but also to Dewey's definition of "education" as increasing the ability to perceive and act on meaning in one's society (Dewey [1916] 1966, 76ff). To Dewey, the goal of education was to advance students' ability to understand, articulate, and act democratically in their social experiences. This definition of education as meaning-making social action prefigures the epistemic approach to composition, which Kenneth Dowst (1980) described as "the activity of making some sense out of an extremely complex set of personal perceptions and experiences of an infinitely complex world. . . . A writer (or other language-user), in a sense, composes the world in which he or she lives" (66). Maxine Hairston (1992b) also featured the epistemic nature of "writing as a way of learning" (reiterating Brooke's ideal that writing per se is critical): "Writing helps us absorb new information . . . discover new information . . . [and] promotes critical thinking" (1).

Berlin, Ohmann, and Fox would agree with the epistemic definition of writing as a way of making meaning, but they distinguish their critical position by foregrounding and historicizing the power relations at any site where meaning is made. Specifying the political forces in any rhetorical setting is a key distinction of critical literacy, separating it from other writing-to-learn proponents and epistemic rhetoricians. Critical literacy, then, is a discourse that foregrounds and questions power relations; such a discourse was called "social-epistemic rhetoric" by Berlin (1988, 1996). Foregrounding and questioning the ideologies in any setting links critical educators who may be feminists, multiculturalists, queer theorists, or neo-Marxists. These various dissident approaches expose and disconfirm dominant ideologies in the rhetorical settings that construct self in society. Because there are multiple ideologies informing dominant culture and converging in experience (for example, male supremacy, white supremacy, corporate supremacy, heterosexism), the positions or identities for contesting the status quo also need to be appropriately multiple. Critical literacy not only embraces and examines identity differences but also acknowledges that every difference will be used against us in a society where an elite minority maintains power by a divide-and-conquer strategy, among other mechanisms.

Identity, Difference, and Power: Literacy in Contact Zones

Critical literacy classes focused on difference have also been construed as "contact zones" by Mary Louise Pratt (1991): "social spaces where cultures meet, clash, and grapple with each other, often in contexts of highly asymmetrical relations of power . . . " (34). Pratt proposed rhetorical arts in a critical pedagogy to explore difference and resist dominant culture, including two useful alternatives to mimicking elite discourse in writing classes. These two alternatives for producing texts offer students and teachers options to assimilating uncritically into academic discourse:

> Autoethnography: a text in which people undertake to describe themselves in ways that engage with representations others have made of them. . . .
>
> Transculturation: the processes whereby members of subordinated or marginal groups select and invent from materials transmitted by a dominant or metropolitan culture. . . . While subordinate peoples do not usually control what emanates from the dominant culture, they do determine to varying extents what gets absorbed into their own and what it gets used for. (35, 36)

These literate practices ask students to take critical postures toward their own language uses as well as toward the discourses dominating school and society. Further, from Pratt's contact zone theory, we can extract and summarize more pedagogy that questions power relations and encourages critical literacy:

1. Structure the class to include "safe houses" (group caucuses within the larger class where marginalized "others" can develop autonomous positions).

2. Offer exercises in oral and written storytelling and in identifying with the ideas, interests, histories, and attitudes of "others."

3. Give special attention to the rhetorical techniques of parody, comparison, and critique so as to strengthen students' abilities to resist their immersion in the literate products of the dominant culture.

4. Explore suppressed aspects of history (what Foucault referred to as "disqualified" or "unqualified" narratives relating popular resistance).

5. Define ground rules for communication across differences and in the midst of existing hierarchies of authority.

6. Do systematic studies of cultural mediation, or how cultural material is produced, distributed, received, and used.

Finally, Pratt enumerated other "critical arts" of the contact zone that could encourage a rhetoric of resistance: doing imaginary dialogues to develop student ability to create diverse subjectivities in history, writing in multiple dialects and idioms to avoid privileging one dominant form, and addressing diverse audiences with discourses of resistance to invite students to imagine themselves speaking to empowered and disempowered groups both. Pratt's contact zone approach has been extensively developed for writing classes by Patricia Bizzell and Bruce Herzberg (1996). In general, contact zone theory has a friendly fit with the critical literacy I defined elsewhere as

> Habits of thought, reading, writing, and speaking which go beneath surface meaning, first impressions, dominant myths, official pronouncements, traditional cliches, received wisdom, and mere opinions, to understand the deep meaning, root causes, social context, ideology, and personal consequences of any action, event, object, process, organization, experience, text, subject matter, policy, mass media, or discourse. (1992b, 129)

My definition is also consistent with Aronowitz and Giroux's (1985) notion that

> critical literacy would make clear the connection between knowledge and power. It would present knowledge as a social construction linked to norms and values, and it would demonstrate modes of critique that illuminate how, in some cases, knowledge serves very specific economic, political, and social interests. Moreover, critical literacy would function as a theoretical tool to help students and others develop a critical relationship to their own knowledge. (132)

With this kind of literacy, students "learn how to read the world and their lives critically and relatedly . . . and, most important, it points to forms of social action and collective struggle" (132). This activist agenda was also central to Joe Kretovics' (1985) definition:

> Critical literacy . . . points to providing students not merely with functional skills, but with the conceptual tools necessary to critique and engage society along with its inequalities and injustices. Furthermore, critical literacy can stress the need for students to develop a collective vision of what it might be like to live in the best of all societies and how such a vision might be made practical. (51)

Critical Literacy and Visions for Change

Envisioning and realizing change were key goals of Freire's literacy teams in Brazil before they were destroyed by the military coup of April 1964.

> From the beginning, we rejected . . . a purely mechanistic literacy program and considered the problem of teaching adults how to read in relation to the awakening of their consciousness. . . . We wanted a literacy program which would be an introduction to the democratization of culture, a program with human beings as its subjects rather than as patient recipients, a program which itself would be an act of creation, capable of releasing other creative acts, one

in which students would develop the impatience and vivacity which characterize search and invention. (Freire 1973, 43)

Freire's method included trisyllabic exercises for decoding and encoding. Even though this project had explicit political intentions, Freire's culture circles deployed a practical pedagogy focused on writing, reading, and dialogue, not on didactic lectures. Freire thus developed pragmatic "agencies for doing," to use Dewey's phrase. The students' literacy skills emerged through concrete exercises on generative themes displayed in drawings, or "codifications," from their lives (Dewey's vital subject matter as the context for developing language abilities).

Freire's much-read reports of dialogic pedagogy for illiterate Brazilian peasants and workers offer an instructive comparison to the inspiring literacy narrative of Mike Rose (1990), who chronicled his life and work among basic writers at UCLA and elsewhere. Rose, based at a high-profile campus dominated by academic discourse, developed and taught a rhetorical form of critical literacy: "framing an argument or taking someone else's argument apart, systematically inspecting a document, an issue, or an event, synthesizing different points of view, applying theory to disparate phenomena . . . comparing, synthesizing, analyzing . . . summarizing, classifying . . . " (188, 194, 138). Rose's definition of critical literacy echoes Mina Shaughnessy's (1977) earlier advice for teaching rhetorical habits to basic writers. By naming these literate habits and by asking students to learn them through complex cases drawn from across the curriculum, Rose responded to the academic needs of basic writers at UCLA. In Freire's case, even before he became secretary of education for the city of Sao Paulo in 1989 and responsible for an impoverished school system of about seven hundred thousand students, he too proposed that standard forms be taught to nonelite Brazilian students in the context of democratizing schools and integrating the themes of their lives:

> Finally, teachers have to say to students, Look, in spite of being beautiful, this way you speak also includes the question of *power.* Because of the political problem of power, you need to learn how to command the dominant language, in order for you to survive in the struggle to transform society. (Shor and Freire 1987, 73)

Freire reiterated this point a few years later in *Pedagogy of the City* (1993): "The need to master the dominant language is not only to survive but also better to fight for the transformation of an unjust and cruel society where the subordinate groups are rejected, insulted, and humiliated" (135). In the United States, the argument for teaching standard usage to black youth has been taken up strenuously by Lisa Delpit, who also produced a special anthology defending ebonics in the classroom (*The Real Ebonics Debate,* with coeditor Theresa Perry), which includes an essay by Geneva Smitherman, the longtime proponent for using African American English in writing and teaching. A bidialectal or contrastive rhetoric approach is being suggested here, for honoring and using the students' community language while also studying Standard English. However, for Freire, standard usage, rhetorical forms, and academic discourse make democratic sense only when taught in a critical curriculum explicitly posing problems about experience and power. In such a program, clearly against inequality, many tools and resources can be useful, including standard usage, bidialectalism, bilingualism, contrastive translations of texts from community language into academic discourse, and so on. In a critical program, the teaching of standard form is thus embedded in a thematic curriculum oriented toward social questioning for democratic development. By themselves, taught in a curriculum that emphasizes isolated skills and rhetorical forms, academic discourse and Standard English are certainly not democratic roads to critical consciousness or oppositional politics, as Pat Bizzell (1992) recognized after her long attempt to connect the teaching of formal technique with the development of social critique.

Another oppositional approach merging technique and critique is Gerald Graff's (1992) "teach the conflicts" method, which has been developed thoughtfully for writing classes by Don Lazere (see Chapter 16 in this book). Lazere provides rhetorical frameworks to students for analyzing ideologies in competing texts and media sources. The specific rhetorical techniques serve social critique here, insofar as the curriculum invites students to develop ideological sophistication in a society that mystifies politics, a society in fact where "politics" has become a repulsive "devil-word." Lazere uses problem posing at the level of topical and academic themes (social issues chosen by the teacher and subject matters taken from expert bodies of knowledge and then posed to students as questions) rather than generative themes (materials taken from student experience and language). (See Shor 1992b, 2–5, 46–48, 73–84.) My Deweyan and Freirean preference is to situate critical literacy in student discourse and perceptions as the starting points, but the "teach the conflicts" method of Graff and Lazere is indeed a critical approach worthy of study, especially because it teaches us a way to pose academic subject matters as complex problems, questions, and exercises rather than to merely lecture them to students.

Merging the study of formal technique with social critique is not simple, as the following chapters show, but this project is no more and no less "political" than any other kind of literacy program. The claim of critical literacy is that no pedagogy is neutral, no learning process is value-free, no curriculum avoids ideology and power relations. To teach is to encourage human beings to develop in one direction or another. In fostering student development, every teacher chooses some subject matters, some ways of knowing, and some ways of speaking and relating instead of others. These choices orient students to map the world and their proper place in society. Burke (1966) put it like this: "I take it for granted that any selection of terms used for explanatory purposes is, in effect, a 'point of view'" (vii).

Every educator, then, orients students toward certain values, actions, and language with implications for the kind of society and people these behaviors will produce. This inevitable involvement of education with values was called "stance" by Jerome Bruner (1986):

> the medium of exchange in which education is conducted—language—can never be neutral. . . . [I]t imposes a point of view not only about the world to which it refers but toward the use of mind in respect of this world. Language necessarily imposes a perspective in which things are viewed and a stance toward what we view. . . . I do not for a minute believe that one can teach even mathematics or physics without transmitting a sense of stance toward nature and toward the use of the mind. . . . The idea that any *humanistic* subject can be taught without revealing one's stance toward matters of human pith and substance is, of course, nonsense. . . . [T]he language of education, if it is to be an invitation to reflection and culture creating, cannot be the so-called uncontaminated language of fact and "objectivity." (121, 128, 129)

Also denying the neutrality of language and learning, poet Adrienne Rich (1979) said of her work in the Open Admissions experiment at the City University of New York that "My daily life as a teacher confronts me with young men and women who had language and literature used against them, to keep them in their place, to mystify, to bully, to make them feel powerless" (61). Rich ended her tribute to the cultural democracy of Open Admissions by connecting the writing of words to the changing of worlds:

> [L]anguage is power and . . . those who suffer from injustice most are the least able to articulate their suffering. . . . [T]he silent majority, if released into language, would not be content with a perpetuation of the conditions which have betrayed them. But this notion hangs on a special conception of what it means to be released into language: not simply learning the jargon of an elite, fitting unexceptionably into the status quo, but learning that language can be used as a means for changing reality. (67–68)

Thus, to be for critical literacy is to take a moral stand on what kind of humane society and democratic education we want. This is the ethical center of teaching proposed many years ago by the patron saint of American education, John Dewey, who insisted that school and society must be based in cooperation, democratic relations, and egalitarian distribution of resources and authority. Progressive educators since Dewey, such as George Counts, Maxine Greene, and George Wood, have continued this ethical emphasis. Freire openly acknowledged his debt to Dewey and declared his search "for an education that stands for liberty and against the exploitation of the popular classes, the perversity of the social structures, the silence imposed on the poor—always aided by an authoritarian education" (Freire 1990, 94).

The papers in this volume show some teachers' efforts to avoid fitting students quietly into the status quo. We can see in these reports attempts to invent what Dick Ohmann (1987) referred to as a "literacy-from-below" that questions the way things are and imagines alternatives, so that the word and the world may yet install a dream of social justice, bringing to life what Paulo Freire called the power not yet in power.

Works Cited

Anderson, Gary L., and Patricia Irvine. 1993. "Informing Critical Literacy with Ethnography." In *Critical Literacy: Politics, Praxis, and the Postmodern,* edited by Colin Lankshear and Peter L. McLaren, 81–104. Albany, NY: SUNY Press.

Anzaldua, Gloria. 1990. *Borderlands/La Frontera: The New Mestiza.* San Francisco: Spinsters/Aunt Lute.

Anyon, Jean. 1998. *Ghetto Schooling: A Political Economy of Urban Educational Reform.* New York: Teachers College Press.

Applebome, Peter. 1997. "Schools See Re-emergence of 'Separate but Equal.'" *New York Times,* 8 April, A10.

Aronowitz, Stanley, and Henry Giroux. 1985. *Education Under Siege.* South Hadley, MA: Bergin-Garvey.

Berlin, James A. 1987. *Rhetoric and Reality: Writing Instruction in American Colleges, 1900–1985.* Carbondale, IL: Southern Illinois University Press.

———. 1988. "Rhetoric and Ideology in the Writing Class." *College English* 50 (5): 477–94.

———. 1996. *Rhetorics, Poetics, and Cultures.* Urbana, IL: NCTE.

Berliner, David, and Steven Biddle. 1995. *The Manufactured Crisis.* New York: Addison-Wesley/Longman.

Bernstein, Aaron. 1996. "Is America Becoming More of a Class Society? New Data Show That, Increasingly, Workers at the Bottom Are Staying There." *Business Week,* 26 February, 86–91.

Berthoff, Ann. 1981. *The Making of Meaning.* Upper Montclair, NJ: Boynton/Cook.

Bizzell, Patricia. 1992. *Academic Discourse and Critical Consciousness.* Pittsburgh: University of Pittsburgh Press.

———. 1999. "Rhetorics of 'Color': The Example of *Bootstraps.*" In *Race, Rhetoric, and Composition,* edited by Keith Gilyard. Portsmouth, NH: Boynton/Cook.

Bizzell, Patricia, and Bruce Herzberg. 1996. *Negotiating Difference.* Boston: Bedford.

Blumenthal, Ralph. 1998. "Discord Mounts After Play Is Canceled." *New York Times,* 27 May, E1, E3.

Boutwell, Clinton E. 1997. *Shell Game: Corporate America's Agenda for the Schools.* Bloomington, IN: Phi Delta Kappa.

Bowles, Samuel, and Herbert Gintis. 1976. *Schooling in Capitalist America.* New York: Basic.

Bracey, Gerard. 1995. "The Right's Data-proof Ideologues." *Education Week,* 25 January, 48.

Brandt, Deborah. 1998. "Sponsors of Literacy." *College Composition and Communication* 49 (2): 165–85.

Brodkey, Linda. 1996. *Writing Permitted in Designated Areas Only.* Minneapolis: University of Minnesota Press.

Brooke, Robert. 1987. "Underlife and Writing Instruction." *College Composition and Communication* 38 (2): 141–53.

Brookfield, Stephen. 1987. *Developing Critical Thinkers.* San Francisco: Jossey-Bass.

———. 1995. *Becoming a Critically Reflective Teacher.* San Francisco: Jossey-Bass.

Bruner, Jerome. 1986. *Actual Minds, Possible Worlds.* Cambridge, MA: Harvard University Press.

Burke, Kenneth. 1966. *Language as Symbolic Action.* Berkeley: University of California Press.

———. 1984. *Attitudes Toward History.* Berkeley: University of California Press.

Coniff, Ruth. 1998. "Welfare Miracle, or Mirage?" *New York Times,* 7 March, A29.

Cooper, Marilyn, and Michael Holtzman. 1989. *Writing as Social Action.* Portsmouth, NH: Boynton/Cook.

Counts, George. 1932. *Dare the Schools Build a New Social Order?* New York: John Day.

Crowley, Sharon. 1996. "Around 1971: Current-Traditional Rhetoric and Process Models of Composing." In *Composition in the Twenty-first Century: Crisis and Change,* edited by Lynn Z. Bloom, Donald A. Daiker, and Edward M. White, 64–74. Carbondale, IL: Southern Illinois University Press.

Daniels, Harvey, Steven Zemelman, and Marilyn Bikar. 1998. "Teacher Alert! Phonics Fads Sweep Nation's Schools." *Rethinking Schools* 12 (4): 3, 13.

Delpit, Lisa. 1995. *Other People's Children: Cultural Conflict in the Classroom.* New York: The New Press.

Delpit, Lisa, and Theresa Perry. 1998. *The Real Ebonics Debate.* Boston: Beacon Press.

Dewey, John. [1938] 1963. *Experience and Education.* Reprint, New York: Collier.

———. [1916] 1966. *Democracy and Education.* Reprint, New York: Free Press.

———. [1933] 1971a. *How We Think: A Restatement of the Relation of Reflective Thinking to the Educative Process.* Reprint, Chicago: Regnery.

———. [1900] 1971b. *The Child and the Curriculum.* Reprint, Chicago: University of Chicago Press.

———. [1900] 1971c. *The School and Society.* Reprint, Chicago: University of Chicago Press.

———. [1909] 1975. *Moral Principles in Education.* Reprint, Carbondale, IL: Southern Illinois University Press.

Dougherty, Kevin J. 1994. *The Contradictory College: The Conflicts, Origins, Impacts, and Futures of the Community Colleges.* Albany, NY: SUNY Press.

Dowst, Kenneth. 1980. "The Epistemic Approach: Writing, Knowing and Learning." In *Eight Approaches to Teaching Composition*, edited by Timothy R. Donovan and Ben W. McClelland, 65–85. Urbana, IL: NCTE.

Elbow, Peter. 1991. "Reflections on Academic Discourse: How It Relates to Freshmen and Colleagues." *College English* 53 (1): 135–55.

Faigley, Lester. 1997. "Literacy After the Revolution." *College Composition and Communication* 48 (1): 30–43.

Faludi, Susan. 1991. *Backlash: The Undeclared War Against American Women*. New York: Anchor.

Fine, Michelle. 1987. "Silencing in Public Schools." *Language Arts* 64 (February): 157–64.

———. 1993. *Framing Dropouts*. Albany, NY: SUNY Press.

Flower, Linda. 1998. *Problem-solving Strategies for Writing in College and Community*. Fort Worth, TX: Harcourt Brace.

Foucault, Michel. 1980. *Power/Knowledge*, edited by C. Gordon. New York: Pantheon.

Fox, Tom. 1993. "Standards and Access." *Journal of Basic Writing* 12 (1): 37–45.

Freire, Paulo. 1970. *Pedagogy of the Oppressed*. New York: Seabury.

———. 1973. *Education for Critical Consciousness*. New York: Seabury.

———. 1978. *Pedagogy-in-Process*. New York: Continuum.

———. 1985a. *The Politics of Education*. Westport, CT: Greenwood.

———. 1985b. "Reading the World and Reading the Word: An Interview with Paulo Freire." By David Dillon. *Language Arts* 62 (January): 15–21.

———. 1990. Interview by Murray Cox. *Omni* 12 (April): 74–94.

———. 1993. *Pedagogy of the City*. New York: Continuum.

———. 1996. *Letters to Cristina*. New York: Routledge.

Freire, Paulo, and Antonio Faundez. 1989. *Learning to Question*. New York: Continuum.

Galbraith, John K. 1967. *The New Industrial State*. Boston: Houghton Mifflin.

Goodlad, John. 1984. *A Place Called School*. New York: McGraw-Hill.

Gordon, Linda. 1994. "How 'Welfare' Became a Dirty Word." *Chronicle of Higher Education*, 20 July, B1–B2.

Gose, Ben. 1998. "Minority Enrollment Rose by 3.2% in 1996." *Chronicle of Higher Education*, 5 June, A32–A41.

Gould, Stephen Jay. 1995. "Ghosts of Bell Curves Past." *Natural History*, February, 12–19.

Graff, Gerald. 1992. *Beyond the Culture Wars: How Teaching the Conflicts Can Revitalize American Education*. New York: Norton.

Graff, Harvey J. 1987. *The Labyrinths of Literacy*. London: Falmer.

Greene, Maxine. 1988. *The Dialectic of Freedom*. New York: Teachers College Press.

Hairston, Maxine. 1992a. "Diversity, Ideology, and Teaching Writing." *College Composition and Communication* 43 (2): 179–193. *See also* "Counterstatement"

(1993) by John Trimbur, Robert G. Wood, Ron Strickland, William H. Thelin, William J. Rouster, Toni Mester, and Hairston's "Reply" in *CCC* 44 (2): 248–56.

———. 1992b. *Successful Writing.* 3d edition. New York: Norton.

Heath, Shirley Brice. 1983. *Ways with Words.* Cambridge, England: Cambridge University Press.

Henwood, Doug. 1997. "Trashonomics." In *White Trash: Race and Class in America,* edited by Matt Wray and Annalee Newitz, 177–97. New York: Routledge.

Herrnstein, Richard, and Charles Murray. 1994. *The Bell Curve.* New York: Free Press.

Hershey, Robert D. Jr. 1996. "In Turnabout for Workers, Wages Grow More Slowly." *New York Times,* 30 October, D1.

Hill, Heather C. 1997. "The Importance of a Minority Perspective in the Classroom." *Chronicle of Higher Education,* 7 November, A60.

Hirsch, E. D. 1987. *Cultural Literacy: What Every American Needs to Know.* Boston: Houghton Mifflin.

———. 1989. *A First Dictionary of Cultural Literacy: What Our Children Need to Know.* Boston: Houghton Mifflin.

Hirsch, E. D., Joseph F. Kett, and James Trefil. 1988. *The Dictionary of Cultural Literacy: What Every American Needs to Know.* Boston: Houghton Mifflin.

Holmes, Steven A. 1996. "Income Disparity Between Poorest and Richest Rises." *New York Times,* 20 June, A1.

Horton, Myles, and Paulo Freire. 1990. *We Make the Road by Walking.* Philadelphia: Temple University Press.

Horton, Myles, with Judith Kohl and Herb Kohl. 1990. *The Long Haul.* New York: Doubleday.

Ingalls, Zoe. 1998. "'The Eye of the Storm' at New Paltz." *Chronicle of Higher Education,* 8 May, A10.

Jencks, Christopher, Marshall Smith, Henry Acland, Mary Jo Bane, David Cohen, Herbert Gintis, Barbara Heyns, and Stephen Michelson. 1972. *Inequality: A Reassessment of the Effects of Family and Schooling in America.* New York: Basic.

Karabel, Jerome, and Steven Brint. 1989. *The Diverted Dream: Community Colleges and the Promise of Educational Opportunity in America, 1900–1985.* New York: Oxford University Press.

Karp, Stan. 1997/1998. "Banned in Jersey, Welcomed on Broadway." *Rethinking Schools* 12 (2): 14–15.

Knoblauch, C. H., and Lil Brannon. 1984. *Rhetorical Traditions and the Teaching of Writing.* Upper Montclair, NJ: Boynton/Cook.

Kozol, Jonathan. 1991. *Savage Inequalities: Children in America's Schools.* New York: Crown.

Kretovics, Joseph R. 1985. "Critical Literacy: Challenging the Assumptions of Mainstream Educational Theory." *Journal of Education* 167 (2): 50–62.

Lazere, Donald. 1992. "Teaching the Rhetorical Conflicts." *College Composition and Communication* 43 (2): 194–213.

Lieberman, Trudy. 1998. "Hunger in America." *The Nation,* 30 March, 11–16.

Lindemann, Erika. 1995. *A Rhetoric for Writing Teachers.* New York: Oxford University Press.

Mayher, John. 1990. *Uncommon Sense: Theoretical Practice in Language Education.* Portsmouth, NH: Boynton/Cook.

Mayo, Peter. 1994. "Synthesizing Gramsci and Freire: Possibilities for a Theory of Radical Adult Education." *International Journal of Lifelong Education* 13 (2): 125–48.

Mickelson, Roslyn Arlyn, and Stephen Samuel Smith. 1998. "Can Education Eliminate Race, Class, and Gender Inequality?" In *Race, Class and Gender,* 3d edition, edited by Margaret L. Andersen and Patricia Hill Collins, 328–40. New York: Wadsworth.

Moody, Kim. 1998. "On the Line in Flint." *The Nation,* 13 July, 6.

Morris, Bonnie J. 1998. "Women's Studies: Prejudice and Vilification Persist." *Chronicle of Higher Education,* 19 June, A56.

Mortenson, Thomas G. 1995. "Post-secondary Education Opportunity: The Mortenson Report on Public Policy Analysis of Opportunity for Post-secondary Education." Mortenson Research Letter, November, Iowa City.

Nieves, Evelyn. 1997. "Pupils' Script on Workers Is Ruled Out." *New York Times,* 26 June, B1.

Ohmann, Richard. [1976] 1996. *English in America.* Middletown, CT: Wesleyan University Press.

———. 1987. *Politics of Letters.* Middletown, CT: Wesleyan University Press.

Orfield, Gary. 1993. "The Growth of Segregation in American Schools: Changing Patterns of Separation and Poverty Since 1968." Report of the Harvard Project on School Desegregation to the National School Boards Association, Washington, DC.

Orfield, Gary, and Susan Easton. 1996. *Dismantling Desegregation: The Quiet Reversal of Brown v. Board of Education.* New York: The New Press.

Orfield, Gary, et al. 1997. "Deepening Segregation in American Public Schools." Civil Rights Project, Harvard Graduate School of Education, Cambridge, MA.

Peck, Wayne Campbell, Linda Flower, and Lorraine Higgins. 1995. "Community Literacy." *College Composition and Communication* 46 (2): 199–222.

Perez-Pena, Richard. 1997. "Study Shows New York Has the Greatest Income Gap." *New York Times,* 12 December, A1.

Phelps, Louise Wetherbee. 1988. *Composition as a Human Science.* New York: Oxford University Press.

Pratt, Mary Louise. 1991. "Arts of the Contact Zone." In *Profession 1991,* 33–40. New York: MLA.

"Quality Counts—1998: The Urban Challenge—Public Education in the 40 States." 1998. *Education Week,* 8 January.

Ravitch, Diane. 1974. *The Great School Wars: New York City, 1805–1973.* New York: Basic.

————. 1983. *The Troubled Crusade: American Education, 1945–1980.* New York: Basic.

Rich, Adrienne. 1979. *On Lies, Secrets, and Silences.* New York: Norton.

Rose, Mike. 1990. *Lives on the Boundary.* New York: Penguin.

Rouse, John. 1979. "The Politics of Composition." *College English* 41 (1): 1–12.

Russell, David R. 1995. "Activity Theory and Writing Instruction." In *Reconceiving Writing, Rethinking Writing Instruction,* edited by Joseph Petraglia, 51–77. Mahwah, NJ: Lawrence Erlbaum.

Sandman, Jessica L. 1998. "California Colleges Going All Out to Woo Minority Students." *Education Week,* 29 April, 6.

Sarasohn, David. 1997. "Hunger on Main St." *The Nation,* 8 December, 13–18.

Schneider, Alison. 1998a. "Bad Blood in the English Department: The Rift Between Composition and Literature." *Chronicle of Higher Education,* 13 February, 14–15.

————. 1998b. "More Professors Are Working Part-time, and More Teach at Two-year Colleges." *Chronicle of Higher Education,* 13 March, A14–A15.

Scott, James. 1990. *Domination and the Arts of Resistance.* New Haven: Yale University Press.

Shaughnessy, Mina. 1977. *Errors and Expectations.* New York: Oxford University Press.

Shepard, Scott. 1998. "In Civil Rights Shift, EEOC Helps White People Most." *Atlanta Journal-Constitution,* 4 March, A13.

Shor, Ira. 1992a. *Culture Wars: School and Society in the Conservative Restoration, 1969–1991.* Chicago: University of Chicago Press.

————. 1992b. *Empowering Education: Critical Teaching for Social Change.* Chicago: University of Chicago Press.

————. 1996. *When Students Have Power: Negotiating Authority in a Critical Pedagogy.* Chicago: University of Chicago Press.

————. 1997. "Our Apartheid: Writing Instruction and Inequality." *Journal of Basic Writing* 16 (1): 91–104.

Shor, Ira, and Paulo Freire. 1987. *A Pedagogy for Liberation.* Westport, CT: Greenwood.

Sklar, Holly, and Chuck Collins. 1997. "Forbes 400 World Series." *The Nation,* 20 October, 5–6.

Smart, Tim. 1998. "GE '97 Profit Hits a Record $8.2 Billion." *Washington Post,* 23 January, G3.

Strauss, Neil. 1998. "Girl Power Is Squelched." *New York Times,* 27 May, E3.

Street, Brian. 1984. *Literacy in Theory and Practice.* New York: Cambridge University Press.

Stunkel, Kenneth R. 1998. "The Lecture: A Powerful Tool for Intellectual Liberation." *Chronicle of Higher Education,* 26 June, A52.

"Technology Counts." 1997. *Education Week,* 10 November, 8, 10.

"The Educational Progress of Black Students." 1995. Washington, DC: National Center for Education Statistics.

"The Educational Progress of Women." 1996. Washington, DC: National Center for Education Statistics.

Tyack, David, and Larry Cuban. 1995. *Tinkering Toward Utopia: A Century of Public School Reform.* Cambridge, MA: Harvard University Press.

U. S. Bureau of the Census. 1997. Statistical Abstract of the United States. Washington, DC.

U. S. Department of Education. 1997. Digest of Education Statistics. Washington, DC: Office of Educational Research and Improvement.

Viadero, Debra. 1998. "ETS Study Tracks Worrisome Trend in Rate of College Completion." *Education Week,* 25 February, 12.

Vygotsky, Lev. 1962. *Thought and Language.* Cambridge, MA: MIT Press.

———. 1978. *Mind in Society.* Cambridge, MA: Harvard University Press.

"Wealthiest Americans Getting an Even Larger Slice of the Pie." 1997. *New York Times,* 30 September, A26.

Weissglass, Julian. 1998. "The SAT: Public Spirited or Preserving Privilege?" *Education Week,* 15 April, 60.

Williams, E. I. F. 1937. *Horace Mann: Educational Statesman.* New York: Macmillan.

Williams, Raymond. 1977. *Marxism and Literature.* New York: Oxford University Press.

Williams, Wendy M., and Stephen J. Ceci. 1997. "Are Americans Becoming More or Less Alike? Trends in Race, Class, and Ability Differences in Intelligence." *American Psychologist* 52 (11): 1226–35.

Zehr, Mary Anne. 1998. "Black Students Found Less Likely to Access the Internet." *Education Week,* 29 April, 9.

2

"Teacher, Tell Me What to Do"

Elsa Auerbach

Editors' Note: We begin this volume with an excerpt from Elsa Auerbach's 1996 book *From the Community to the Community,* an extraordinary teacher's guide to participatory education for ESL students, from which we think all educators can learn. Auerbach, a longtime leader in critical pedagogy, reports on new teachers learning to use participatory approaches. The group of mostly Latina/o interns discuss their process of moving from traditional to participatory teaching in various Adult Basic Education sites, providing user-friendly models for teachers at all levels who want "hands-on" methods. They honestly describe how they handled resistance to their methods from their predominantly Central and South American students. This piece is valuable for its clear application of Freirean education to ESL instruction: Students' lives are at the center of the classroom, and teachers use problem posing to uncover generative themes, to design codes, and to elicit keywords and topics for discussion and writing. Auerbach allows us to see critical literacy in action and gives us a useful overview on adapting participatory approaches.

One of the central aspects of a participatory approach to adult literacy instruction is that teaching is context specific: curriculum content arises from the needs and interests of each group of participating learners as much as possible. Because the language of instruction, learner populations, and community contexts differed at each of our project sites, what happened in the classes varied as well. Thus, although there were some common underlying principles that guided the teaching, the ways that these principles were applied varied from class to class, teacher to teacher, and site to site. The guiding principles for participatory literacy instruction include the following:

- Start with learners' needs and interests.
- Involve learners in determining the content of instruction.

31

- Focus on meaning, not mechanics.
- Contextualize work on form (connect form to function and meaning).
- Center instruction around themes drawn from learners' social reality.
- Encourage dialogue and critical analysis of social realities.
- Use a variety of participatory tools to explore themes.
- Move toward action outside the classroom.
- Involve students in evaluation.

Because the essence of a participatory approach to literacy/ESL education is allowing the issues and concerns that preoccupy students to become the motor force of instruction, the starting point for curriculum development has to be an understanding of students' lives—their backgrounds, personal histories, strengths, and current situations. In many adult ESL programs, students are interviewed during in-take and composite profiles of the student populations are constructed for assessment and placement purposes. However, once students enter the classroom, these profiles, which include general information about years of schooling, occupational status, reasons for immigration, and so on, may be ignored in the push to work on competencies or survival skills for the new life in the U.S. Our experience is that each of these aspects of students' lives has real consequences for what happens in the classroom, and, further, that these general profiles only tell the beginning of the story. Behind every student profile there are powerful stories that affect learning and participation, stories which can only be uncovered through classroom interaction. Thus, the starting point for participatory curriculum development must be learning about the students, and understanding the contextual factors that shape their literacy acquisition.

The very power of these contextual factors in students' lives means that they have to be taken into account in teaching. Traditionally problems caused by unemployment, immigration, or family concerns might be dealt with primarily through structures external to the instructional process (by counseling, attendance regulations, legal assistance, etc.); in a participatory approach, issues that preoccupy students are central to the content of instruction itself (although, of course, support services are also important). Because students' real issues and concerns vary from group to group, teachers cannot rely on traditional textbooks, with a pre-determined, form-focused sequence of lessons, as the mainstay of the curriculum (although certainly there is a place for using published materials).

The first step towards developing a participatory classroom is learning about students. Often, however, students only share their concerns, needs, and preoccupations once a basis of trust has been built. As such, part of the art of teaching is creating an atmosphere where students feel comfortable about sharing their stories. Paradoxically, many students feel most comfortable at first in a traditional classroom where teaching is rote and decontextualized (focusing on vocabulary lists, grammar, textbook exercises, etc.). Although some of the Interns initially thought that the way to find students' needs was just to ask them what they wanted to do, whenever they asked this question, the response was, "You're the teacher, you're supposed to tell us what to do." They quickly discovered that finding compelling issues in students' lives entails more than just asking students for their input: it entails moving gradually from the traditional model that learners may expect to a more participatory one, consciously listening for opportunities to build on issues of importance to students, as well as creating a structured framework for eliciting these issues. The following excerpt from the minutes of a staff meeting describes how Felipe addressed this dilemma with a beginning Spanish literacy class:

> The transition to a participatory approach has not been easy because the students are used to a "ma-me-mi-mo-mu" approach and don't feel that they can learn unless they are using a book. This week, Felipe brought a paper with drawings of family members for the beginning class. At first they didn't want to work on it, saying, "What are we going to do with these pictures?" Felipe said, "Let's try it and then we'll see if you learned from it." They first read the words under the pictures and then Felipe used them to introduce new letters and showed them how to make words. Next, he then gave them some pictures with blanks under them and asked them to write the words for family members. They then wrote the names of their own brothers and sisters, etc. They were excited when they saw their family members' names in writing. Next, they plan to write stories about their families.

One way that teachers and Interns were able to find students' issues was through **conscious listening**. This process entails being tuned in to classroom dynamics and off-the-record spontaneous conversations that occur before, during, or after class. Teachers would often walk in on heated discussions of events in the news, in students' personal lives, or in the community as class was starting; alternatively, a debate might erupt unexpectedly during the course of a lesson. In some cases, teachers would follow up on these issues immediately (by incorporating the discussion into the lesson, pulling out key words, or developing a language experience story); in other cases, the teacher would think about the issue, discuss how to handle it, and develop a lesson related to it for a subsequent class.

> In one class, a student who had been absent came in talking excitedly because he had seen his ex-wife with another man; he had hit the man's car; they had argued and fought. This prompted a class discussion in which others talked about quarrels they had had and their experiences with the court system. They discussed ways of resolving conflicts that didn't involve violence and would not end up in court.

However, it is not enough to rely on conscious listening as the main way to find student issues. First, it is hard to predict when issues will arise spontaneously; especially at the beginning of a cycle, before students are comfortable bringing their experiences and concerns into class, the times that issues emerge in this way may be few and far between. Further, learning how to "hear" these issues and then utilize them is a skill which develops over time. Even when students' concerns have surfaced, students may not feel that discussing them is "real" school work: no matter how compelling a discussion may be, students may see it as a diversion from what they are "supposed" to be doing (worksheets, dictations, etc.).

Thus, a central way to legitimate an issue-centered approach involves introducing structured activities (or **tools**) that draw out dialogue while at the same time developing literacy and language. Deborah Barndt (1986), a Canadian popular educator, has suggested the notion of a **tool kit** of resources that teachers can draw from to elicit or develop themes. For her, tools are concrete ways of representing an issue (photos, drawings, socio-drama, etc.), designed to generate active responses, dialogue, and language or literacy work. We extended the term to refer to any artifact or activity that triggers student participation through a structured process with an open format. These structured activities serve two important functions: they provide a format for uncovering issues, and they serve to legitimize discussions that might otherwise seem to be diversions. By linking loaded thematically based content with structured literacy work, they provide a concrete format to focus dialogue so that it counts as "real work" in students' eyes. The following list includes tools that were utilized at various points:

- Charts
- Pictures and photos
- Key words
- Language experience stories (LEA)
- Published materials
- Codes (pictorial representations of problem themes)
- Role plays
- Student-generated writing
- Photostories

In practice, a combination of different tools was usually used to explore any given theme. Thus, for example, a class may have started with a discussion prompted by conscious listening on the teacher's part; they may have then pulled out key words, developed a language experience story, read a related published text, and written about the topic in journals. In addition, participatory tools were often integrated with traditional activities like grammar exercises in the ESL classes, handwriting or spelling work in the literacy classes. Further, many of the students requested math work and this was incorporated on a regular weekly basis in many of the classes. Finally, in the L1 (first language) literacy classes, as students became more confident with their first-language reading and writing, they also requested some ESL instruction.

Charts

Charts are useful because they provide a structure into which students can insert content from their own lives and experiences. They were used in a variety of ways in our project: to gather information about students' life histories, to compare cultural practices among different groups, to identify places where students used English or L1 literacy, and to elicit students' goals. The basic process in using charts is this:

- choose categories or questions as the focus (students can participate in this)
- elicit information from each other regarding the questions (through peer or teacher questioning in pairs, small groups, or whole group work)
- write the information for each individual on the chart
- follow up with both form- and content-focused work

Follow-up work focusing on form might utilize the information in the chart to develop sentences, practice grammar, or do reading/writing exercises. Content work might compare students' information, look for patterns, discuss their causes, and plan future work based on the information. The following excerpts from workshop minutes describe how several Interns used charts with their classes:

- In one of the ESL classes, an Intern divided the class into three groups (each of which had one fluent English writer in the group) and gave them a set of questions about their life histories. The groups discussed the questions and then interviewed each other in pairs within the groups. They then shared the information they had discussed and the fluent English writer wrote it on a chart. For follow up, the class worked on the past tense (*used to* forms). They discussed similarities and differences between their jobs in the U.S. and at home. The Intern then wrote a story using information from the chart and gave students copies of the stories with follow-up exercises.

- In one of the Spanish literacy classes, the Intern made a chart asking students their name, country, arrival date, important family members, persons affected by students' learning, and what you miss most from your country, jobs, and home. He had students write their answers on small pieces of paper; then students stuck their pieces of paper onto a large piece of cardboard with the blank chart on it. They then took turns reading each others' answers off the chart. For follow-up, they made games from the charts, and discussed jobs in each country.

• One Intern developed a chart about Valentine's Day with questions like: Do you have a holiday like Valentine's Day in your country? How do you celebrate it? Who is your valentine?

Pictures and Photos

Unlike traditional visual aids, the function of pictures or photos in a participatory classroom is to uncover themes or to evoke powerful responses. As such, the pictures themselves should represent a loaded, easily recognizable issue or dilemma from students' lives. Use of the picture should start with very concrete questions about what students see in the picture and move on to experiences and issues evoked by the picture. Once again, this tool can trigger dialogue which, in turn, may lead to a range of literacy activities: language experience stories, student writing and reading, as well as vocabulary and conversation development in ESL classes. The following excerpts from workshop minutes describe several variations on the use of pictures in our project:

• *Teacher-drawn pictures:* Felipe drew a picture of a farm/country scene because most of the students in his beginning class are from the countryside and he wanted to get ideas about their pasts and interests. He gave the picture to students face down and then asked them to talk about what they first noticed when they turned the page over. They liked the picture; some said it reminded them of their homes. After they discussed the picture, they wrote about it. They wrote their stories on the board, made some revisions, and did some corrections. They asked Felipe to type their stories. These students often say that they can't write, but they wrote a lot in this activity. The most beginning student wrote the most.

• *Student-drawn pictures:* Ana gave students newsprint and asked them to sit in pairs and draw a picture together without talking. Afterwards, they sat in small groups and discussed questions: How did you feel while doing this? How did you come up with the picture and how did you agree on what to draw without using words? Everyone was involved and talked about how it felt to have to communicate without words, mentioning issues like the confusion that you feel when you're on a train and have to ask directions. This activity led to the identification of places where students need English.

• *Photos:* One Mentor brought in a picture of a shovel (representing the key word *pala* in Spanish). Though he thought he might get a response, he didn't imagine it would be so strong: students talked for at least 45 minutes about the uses of shovels in their lives, telling stories about being forced by the police to bury people in their villages in El Salvador. They went on to discuss using shovels in the fields, crops, the various agricultural methods they used in their countries, and so on. As they spoke, he wrote down what they were saying, including other key words which became the focus of subsequent lessons.

Key Words

Key words provide a bridge between dialogue and decoding activities for literacy and ESL classes. They are chosen for their powerful meaning in students' lives (representing some important concept or issue for them) as well as for their structural features. Once the significance of the words and issues they represent has been explored, the words themselves become a way to link the discussion to further literacy activities. They can be broken into syllables, used to generate new words, or used as vocabulary for follow-up language experience stories, dialogue journal writing, and so on. Teachers can elicit key words in the students' first language as a bridge to English. The following excerpts from workshop minutes describe some of the ways key words were used in our project:

- *teacher-selected key words:* In this case the teacher introduces a key word based on his or her own knowledge of what may be important to students. A concept which has been introduced by a key word can be elaborated by a clustering exercise in which students free-associate the word with other words/ideas it brings to mind (the teacher may ask "What does this word make you think of? How have you experienced this?"); they may go on to explore the commonalities among people's experiences, their social causes, etc. Interns introduced the word *food* in a beginning ESL class, discussing food in different countries, cheap and expensive food, and why there is so much food in the U.S. but so little in other countries.

- *key words emerging from student dialogue:* In this case, the teacher pulls key words out of a discussion that has been triggered through some other means (a picture, a news story, etc.) or asks students to select them. For example, after viewing a video about the inauguration of Aristide in Haiti, a beginning ESL class discussed the video, first in terms of what they had seen and then in terms of how it related to their lives. The teacher wrote what the students were saying as they spoke. The teacher then asked them to find five words that they "liked best" in the story. They chose: *president, money, freedom, Tonton Macoute,* and *peace.* They proceeded to write stories based on the words.

- *as follow-up on a reading:* Key words can be selected from a reading to generate further dialogue and writing. After identifying problems with employers as an issue, the Mentor introduced a reading about workplace rights. Once the group had read the text together, he put the key word *discriminación* on the board as a way to facilitate discussion of the text and elicit students' own experiences. The group then did a clustering exercise to elaborate the concept and went on to write about particular problems at work and strategies for addressing them.

Language Experience Stories (LEA)

One of the most effective tools for connecting dialogue and literacy work is the Language Experience Approach (LEA), in which the teacher acts as a scribe while students dictate whatever they want to have written. When Interns were first introduced to the participatory approach, they often were quite successful in engaging the class in dialogue of current events or critical issues in their lives. However, there was sometimes a gap between discussions and literacy activities (which focused on decoding and mechanical skills work). The LEA provided a concrete bridge from discussions to reading and writing activities. The following are some of the ways LEA was used in our project:

- *to follow-up a class discussion of a heated topic:* Thus, for example, if students were talking about the Gulf War, the teacher might ask, "What would you like to write about the war?" The students would then dictate a story which the teacher wrote on the board. This, in turn, might be followed by a range of literacy activities (selecting key words, working on corrections or a particular grammar point, generating student writing about the topic, etc.). Alternatively, the teacher might take notes while discussion was in progress and type the story for further work and reflection in later classes.

- *to tell the story of a picture:* Teachers often started by introducing a picture and asking some concrete questions about it. They then facilitated dialogue about issues that were implicit in students' responses. The challenge at this point is to get beyond a physical description of the picture. One class used a Polaroid camera to take their own pictures. The task was to take a picture of "something important in the lives of Haitians in Boston." Thus, their photos became a way of both identifying important themes for the students and generating LEA stories. Questions used to start the process included: *What does this picture make you think of? What does it mean to you? Why is it important for Haitians in Boston?* As students talked, the teacher wrote key words on the board. Then students responded to the question, *What do you want to write about this picture?* Each student contributed one sentence to the story. The teacher read the story to the group; the group read it together; individuals read sentences with others' support. The story was typed with follow-up questions and key word exercises (grouping key words into patterns, etc.) and followed by more group and individual reading.

An important debate in the LEA process centers around the issue of corrections: should teachers write exactly what students say (even if it is not grammatical) or correct it? Many Interns felt uncomfortable writing anything that was not correct. This question (and the way we handled it) is discussed later in the section on Teaching Issues.

Published Materials

Students want books; books make them feel that their learning is real. They provide a sense of security and continuity. In addition, teachers often don't have the time or the experience to continuously generate their own materials; they want the structure that a textbook provides (even if they don't rely on it exclusively).

However, there are a number of problems relating to materials. The first, of course, for native language literacy classes, is that few textbooks are available, and those that do exist are often not suitable for literacy acquisition in the U.S., for adults, and/or for a participatory approach to literacy instruction. Most adult literacy texts for Haitian Creole or Spanish were developed for literacy campaigns in Haiti or Mexico, and, as such, use key words and concepts that relate to realities that are not always relevant for immigrants or refugees in the U.S. Other L1 literacy books may be written for children and have content or pictures that are patronizing and irrelevant for adult learners. Many of those written in North America are based on Puerto Rican or Mexican culture and on vocabulary which is unfamiliar to Central American students. Many focus on mechanical approaches to literacy. Even texts that aim to promote a participatory approach may have such an explicitly political agenda that students are put off by them.

For beginning ESL, where there is an abundance of commercial texts, finding a single, appropriate text was also problematic, again because the texts may be patronizing, mechanical, and not geared toward a participatory, learner-centered approach. Of course, many experienced teachers reject the notion of relying on a single text anyway: they say that, by definition, no text can meet the evolving needs of students and texts should be seen as resources rather than backbones of the curriculum. In our project, published materials were generally used to support the development of a theme (rather than as lessons in themselves). Issues relating to materials were addressed in several ways:

- *using published literacy texts:* Texts that had been developed for other contexts were used with adaptations for the U.S.; dialogue was framed in terms of how an issue related to students' lives here (with questions like, "How do you experience this problem in Boston?"). Interns and Mentors frequently asked family members in their home countries to bring back materials which could be used in L1 literacy classes.

- *using authentic materials:* Newspaper articles, cartoons, and leaflets were used as texts. Ana regularly asked students to bring in news articles that they wanted to read and discuss.

- *using published student writing:* Among the most powerful published materials that interns used were texts written by literacy and ESL students. Some of these had been published elsewhere (e.g., *Voices,* a magazine of student writings from Invergarry, British Columbia, and *I Told Myself I am Going to Learn,* by Elizabeth Ndaba, a photostory about a South African woman's struggles with her husband as she decides to go back to school). These materials are glossy and beautiful (satisfying students' desire for "real" texts) as well as powerful and relevant in terms of content. In addition, classes used locally published magazines, such as *Need I Say More,* a journal of Boston-area literacy students' writings, and magazines published at their own sites.

- *adapting ESL materials for L1 use:* Native language literacy teachers often used ESL texts to get graphics and ideas for exercises. For example, ESL materials on body parts were used in the Spanish literacy units on health.

- *generating L1 materials for the U.S. context:* The Mentor and Interns used some of their teacher-sharing time to develop Creole literacy materials for the U.S. context. Most of these were readings with thematic content, followed by questions about the text as well as opinion questions.

- *using children's literature:* Unlike literacy texts (basals) written for children, real literature often has beautiful illustrations and compelling stories which may have relevance for adults. Participants used some of these books with the Spanish literacy classes.

- *using culturally familiar genres (proverbs, riddles, songs):* Because of their own familiarity with the cultures of the learners, teachers and interns were able to integrate into instruction both forms and processes that were culturally congruent for learners. For example, Mentors and Interns developed a Creole proverb book based on one that had been started by a group of teachers at another Creole literacy program several years earlier. Ana often used slogans to elicit discussion. For example, she introduced the Spanish slogan, "*El pueblo unido jamas sera vendico*" and invited the Spanish-speaking students to explain its significance to the others; then she asked people from other language groups if they had slogans in their countries and, if so, to share them with the class.

Codes

Another tool used to explore themes from students' social reality is a *code;* this term comes from Freire's concept of codification by Nina Wallerstein (1983). In this case, the teacher selects or creates materials that represent a problem or dilemma facing students. Rather than suggesting solutions to the problem for students or referring them to an outside support service/expert, the teacher poses the problem back to the group in the form of a picture or a short dialogue.

This re-presentation of the problem depersonalizes it (framing it in a somewhat abstract way so that it doesn't refer to the specific dilemma, but captures its various aspects); in this way, learners can get some distance on the issue and generalize about a specific problem.

Once reactions have been triggered by the code, the teacher guides students through a structured five-step dialogue process in which they

- **describe what they see in the code:** Who is talking? What is happening?

- **identify the problem represented by the code:** What is the problem here?

- **relate the problem to their own experience:** Do you know anyone who has been in a similar situation? How have you experienced this problem?

- **discuss the root causes of the problem:** How has this problem come to be? What is happening in the broader society that causes this problem?

- **share strategies for addressing the problem:** What have you done in a similar situation? What can we do about this problem? In this final stage, collective action is stressed over individual action because this is often more effective and reinforces collaboration.

Teachers in our project used problem-posing codes to address a wide range of themes they had identified as significant for students, including the following:

- **issues of classroom dynamics:** how to deal with a student who talked too much; how much ESL the literacy classes should do each week; whether students should use their first language in ESL classes; what to do with hot topics like religion or politics when they come up in class

- **family issues:** men expecting women to stay home and watch the children while they go to school or socialize; kids acting as interpreters for parents; health issues like cancer, birth control, and AIDS

- **workplace issues:** discrimination at work, finding work

- **community issues:** dealing with the legal system, immigration, day care

Role Plays and Theater Techniques

Some Interns used role play and theater techniques to explore themes while at the same time providing contexts for language development.

- An Intern planned a week of classes around the theme of work; however, after the first class, the lesson for the rest of the week developed from what had happened on Monday. The Intern started by bringing in a reading about a case involving discrimination in the workplace. The class worked on vocabulary from the case (*prejudice, benefits,* etc.). The Intern used a picture of a store with a "Help Wanted" sign where a woman was telling someone, "No jobs." The class divided into three groups, discussed the picture, and then developed role plays about similar situations that they had been in. The Intern had been worried that the lesson would be too difficult for beginning students, but they had all experienced similar situations and were eager to talk about them. She said, *"I gave them the vocabulary and they went from that."*

› After a theater workshop, one Intern used theater techniques to motivate her students. She came to class one night and noticed that students seemed to be tired and without energy. She decided to do a warm-up activity to get them motivated. She started by explaining that the first activity would get them energized for work and asked them to stand in a circle and clap their hands with each other. After they had done this, she explained the purpose of the next activity, saying it is easier to have a dialogue by acting out the idea first. She then asked them to form two groups and choose a word which was meaningful to them. Each group acted out the word; the other group described each act afterwards and then guessed what the word was. One group chose the word *malad* (sick) and the other group chose the word *pov* (poor). After the acting, the students dictated a story about each word. She then typed up the stories and formulated some questions as a follow-up activity.

Student-Generated Writing

Despite the fact that many of the students in the literacy classes knew only a few letters and were not comfortable with the physical aspects of writing (holding a pencil, letter formation) when they began classes, most were able to do some independent, meaningful writing after about 6 months. Several factors seemed to support the development of their writing. The first was the **modeling** that took place in class through the group LEA process: students collectively went through a composing process, linking their ideas to written form with the support of the teacher and peers; they moved through various stages from this supported group writing to individual writing which, in turn, progressed from words to sentences to longer pieces. Second was the stress on **meaning over form:** students were encouraged to take risks, and teachers responded to their writing in terms of its content more than its surface features. Third, students were encouraged to write for real **communicative purposes,** for real audiences and about topics that were important to them. Fourth, they were immersed in contexts where **student writing was valued:** they read published pieces by other students, and saw peers working on writing and having it published in site magazines; they were included in this community of writers as their own writing sometimes was published. Several formats or genres were utilized by different classes in the project to promote the development of writing:

• **dialogue journals:** Dialogue journals are a place where teachers and students can have a written conversation on a private, one-to-one basis. In theory, students write about whatever they want to (although, in our experience, they may need to go through some guided steps before they are comfortable initiating topics of their own); teachers write back to students just as they would to a peer, responding communicatively in terms of the meaning or content, rather than attending to form. Their responses model correct usage, but don't explicitly correct students' mistakes.

- **letters:** One of the main goals expressed by many students when they started classes was to be able to write letters to family and friends by themselves, without having to depend on others. At the HCC, this process started with students writing letters to another Spanish literacy class in NYC. Although the exchange itself was sustained only for a few months, it gave students the confidence to begin writing letters to their families and friends.

- **articles for publication in site magazines:** All three sites in the project published their own magazines of student writings. Being invited to write for the magazine turned out to be a strong motivation for literacy students. As they became more proficient, they moved from submitting LEA stories written by the whole class to individual pieces of increasingly greater length.

Photostories

A photostory is a story which is about a key issue or set of issues identified by learners, accompanied by photographs. Interns were introduced to the idea of photostories through a workshop by an outside presenter. One Intern decided to follow up on the idea with her own class. They made a photostory about the life of a Haitian family in Boston using the following process:

1. **Picture plus analysis:** The Intern started by showing students a picture of a Haitian man looking pensive. She asked students to give their reactions to the picture: what did they see? They responded by saying they saw a man who is thinking and looking sad. Using a clustering format, she then asked why he might be sad and what he might be thinking. One student said he doesn't like the country where he lives. Others said he may have social problems: problems with the educational system or prejudice, no money, no food, no family; he may have sentimental problems like a wife who cheats or whom he doesn't trust. They then discussed the results of these problems, mentioning things like frustration, loss of confidence, humiliation, alcoholism, and drug problems. They went on to discuss possible solutions: go to school, be open about his problems, seek advice, and so on.

2. **Key words:** The Intern then pulled out some key words for syllable work and told the students that they would continue to discuss and write about the problems students had identified.

3. **Further exploration and writing about themes generated:** In subsequent classes (for about an hour each day), students discussed and wrote about various themes that had been identified in response to the picture: problems with their children's education, lack of respect and confidence, family problems, work, and so on.

4. **Writing their own photostory:** Students then gave the man a name and connected his various problems into a story. As the Intern said, "The sad man came alive."

5. **Looking at a model of a photostory:** The Intern brought in a South African photostory (*I Told Myself I am Going to Learn* by Elizabeth Ndaba) as an example of something that they could do with the story they had written.

6. **Taking pictures:** The students then assigned roles for the various characters and took pictures to go with each part of the story.

7. **Lay-out and copying:** The pictures were laid out with the story and copied.

8. **Revision:** There was some debate about the ending of the story; the students discussed the ending and revised it somewhat.

What Themes Did Classes Explore?

As Interns became more skilled in conscious listening and drawing out student themes, and students became more comfortable with the notion of centering learning around their concerns, a rich tapestry of themes and topics emerged. The following list gives a sense of the kinds of issues from the context of students' lives around which curriculum was developed in the programs:

educational issues
- why L1 literacy is important
- students' prior educational experiences
- issues of classroom dynamics: use of the L1 in ESL classes, students who talk too much, child care (for learners' children)
- funding for classes

personal histories
- reasons for immigrating
- family situations
- jobs in the home country vs. jobs in the U.S.

culture
- cultural phenomena (e.g. mythical animals from Central American folklore)
- cultural comparisons (food in various countries, medicines)
- men's roles, women's roles
- the significance of holidays in learners' lives/cultures (Mother's Day, Valentine's Day, Martin Luther King Day)

history and politics	• important events in Haitian, Salvadoran history
	• current events: the Gulf War, Aristide's election, the coup against him, children from Haiti being forced to work in the Dominican Republican, the political situation in Central America
	• English Only laws
community issues	• violence and safety: a Haitian cab driver being shot, a mugging
	• the court system; handling disputes without involving the legal system
housing	• homelessness; finding housing
employment	• workplace discrimination and other workplace problems
	• reasons for unemployment
	• strategies for finding jobs
health	• AIDS, nutrition, cancer, the reproductive system
family issues	• men's and women's roles; participation in schooling
	• domestic violence
	• family literacy: children as interpreters for parents

Teaching Issues

Many of the issues that Mentors and Interns encountered in working with students in the classroom were strikingly similar to the issues that arose in the training workshops: just as Interns had started by expecting a methods-oriented training, students started by expecting a mechanical approach to literacy and a grammar-based approach to ESL. Just as we had to work with different needs and starting points among Interns, they had to work with a range of levels and needs among students. Just as we had to balance planning with responsiveness, Interns had to find a similar balance in the classroom, and so on. This section summarizes the teaching issues touched on above and examines how they were addressed in our project.

"What are we going to do with these pictures?" Many of the initial issues centered around students' expectations of schooling and the transition to a participatory approach. Even if they hadn't been to school before, students often had an internalized notion of education that was quite traditional: school means sitting in rows, having a textbook, doing exercises from worksheets, speaking only when called on, listening and copying, taking tests, and so on. Some Interns, as well, felt that until beginning literacy students had "mastered" the basics of decoding (through a rote learning approach), they could not do meaningful work. Mentors addressed this by slowly demonstrating what could be

learned by integrating mechanical and participatory approaches. For example, Felipe brought drawings of family members to class; students who were used to the "ma-me-mi-mo-mu" approach questioned what they could learn by using pictures, but as he showed them how to generate and write their own words, they became excited.

"Why don't I have an American teacher?"   Some students (especially ESL students) are disconcerted at first when they find that their teacher isn't a White North American native speaker of English. They may feel that they can learn better from someone whose grammar and pronunciation are "perfect"; or, as Julio said, they may have internalized the view that a Black person's English isn't good enough. Interns and Mentors responded to this in a variety of ways: by inviting students to try the class with the option of changing if they didn't think they were learning, by inviting native speakers to class on a regular basis, by explicitly discussing variations in dialect and pronunciation, and by discussing when "correct" pronunciation is and isn't important. When one student complained about not having an American teacher, his Intern sent him to the class of an American teacher (who was a volunteer). He came back the next day, saying "All that teacher knows is how to speak English." In another case, a Guatemalan Spanish literacy student didn't want Felipe as a teacher because he is Salvadoran. Felipe responded by saying, "Well, let's see if I can teach you"; they ended up being good friends. In virtually every case, students were comfortable with non-native speakers as teachers after only a short time.

"Where's the book?"   As mentioned earlier, a key issue was the desire of both Interns and students for textbooks. However, most of those available, especially for L1 literacy, were not appropriate in terms of content or level: they were often geared toward a non-U.S. context, were too overtly political or too mechanical, too elementary or too advanced. Some L1 Interns tried to address this by using basals for children. Mentors and Interns developed a variety of other strategies to address the need for materials: in one setting, they met together to develop their own materials. As a whole group, we had two workshops focused on appropriate materials for adults; as they became more comfortable with the participatory approach and methods like LEA and dialogue journals, increasingly, Interns used learner-generated materials. Even so, both the Spanish and Creole literacy teachers continued to feel the need for good L1 texts.

"You're the teacher. . . . You're supposed to tell us what to do."   Students often initially viewed the teacher as the authority who is supposed to transmit information, ask questions, correct students' errors, enforce discipline and have the answer to any question. This posed a challenge in terms of developing a student-centered curriculum. For example, students were initially uncomfortable with the idea of helping to select topics. They felt that a good teacher should know what to do without having to ask. As Interns developed more

structured ways of eliciting themes and issues, students became more comfortable about contributing their ideas and experiences.

"What's the right answer?"   A related issue concerns students' notions of what counts as "real" knowledge. Often students didn't see their own knowledge or opinions as valid; they thought the teacher was the only one with the "right" answers. This meant that initially many were uncomfortable with dialogue or helping each other. At times, tensions arose when students answered each other's questions or corrected one another: some felt that others were trying to show their superiority. In one class, when asked their views in a discussion, students went through a period when each one would repeat exactly what the first one had said. Some students were uncomfortable with the idea of disagreeing, or debating ideas; many had come from cultures and/or political contexts where they hadn't had experience with dialogue or where it may even be dangerous to disagree with an authority figure, to state one's true beliefs. One way that teachers addressed this was by stating explicitly that they didn't know all the answers and by talking about the participatory approach to teaching. Another way was to try to turn students' questions back to them or to the group as a whole, eliciting their own answers to each other's questions.

"Homeless people are lazy."   Once Interns felt comfortable facilitating dialogues, they began to wonder whether they should give their own opinions or keep silent. For example, if students made statements that they strongly disagreed with (e.g., that homeless people are lazy or that women who are abused deserve it), should they intervene? Some Mentors felt that our responsibility as teachers is NOT to express our views because it will silence students. Others said that sometimes you have to participate as a person, not a teacher, and this means saying what you think. Ana said that the trick is to express your views without imposing them: you can be a facilitator and a person at the same time. One way of doing this is by asking questions that prompt people to think about their own statements or views.

"Let's stop talking and do our work."   Another issue that arose once Interns became more comfortable eliciting discussion and integrating it into class time was that students didn't always see this as legitimate learning. In ESL classes, dialogue was seen as conversation practice, but in L1 literacy classes students sometimes felt that open-ended discussion was not "real work." It was seen as a diversion from the lesson, rather than part of the lesson. Interns, too, sometimes saw it as outside the curriculum and didn't always know how to link it to literacy acquisition (as was the case with the Intern who elicited a heated discussion by introducing a picture of a jail, but then abruptly stopped the discussion, saying it was time to get back to work). As Interns learned to connect discussion with more structured learning activities, students began to see it as legitimate.

"Let's get back to the lesson plan."   A related dilemma was whether to stick to lesson plans or go with the flow when something interesting came up. The two extremes of this tension were having no plan (waiting for a lesson to emerge spontaneously) and sticking to a plan rigidly without allowing for the lesson to take its own direction. In order to insure coherence, some Interns decided to set a schedule for a whole week in advance; however, often whatever happened the first day caused them to revise the plan for subsequent days. Once Interns were familiar with a set of tools that could be drawn on in response to spontaneous dialogue, they were able to modify plans as needed.

"This class is too easy."   The differences in levels, needs, and wants within a given class may create tensions between students. In one of Ana's classes, the more advanced students wanted her to give a test to screen out lower level students; in Julio's advanced Creole literacy class, some students wanted transitional ESL every day while others wanted it once a week. Sometimes, the more advanced students did all the talking, leaving the others silenced. Strategies for addressing differing needs included preparing separate activities for different groups, developing peer teaching activities, getting tutors, and doing whole group activities which incorporated a range of student strengths (some students speaking, others writing, etc.).

"I can't concentrate. I'm too distracted."   Often students come to class preoccupied with worries that blocked their participation. Some Interns initially tried to get students to leave their problems outside the classroom door (telling them to stop talking about things unrelated to the lesson). Later, they became increasingly skilled at integrating these concerns into the lessons, asking questions like: *What makes it hard for you to come to class? What makes it hard for you to concentrate?* From these questions, they developed LEA stories, journals, and so on. At times, the students' problems seemed so great that the Interns felt overwhelmed by them.

"We don't have Indians."   When learning is centered on participants' experiences and social issues, tensions taking a variety of forms inevitably arise: there may be tensions based on historic differences between ethnic or nationality groups, differences in belief systems or even religious differences. This kind of tension arose in one of the Spanish literacy classes: in Guatemala, there is a great deal of pride in Indian culture (with traditions and customs having been preserved); this is not the case in El Salvador where Indians have been more assimilated. So when the teacher began to talk about Indian word origins, some of these students were offended and tried to dissociate themselves, saying, "We don't have Indians in El Salvador." There were sometimes tensions between students from different religious groups. These tensions were addressed in various ways: sometimes teachers tried to avoid them in class; sometimes, the class explored them from a historical perspective; sometimes, they were addressed through cultural sharing. Other tensions relate to classroom dynamics (e.g.,

students bringing their children to class or students who talk too much). Students initially expected the teachers to intervene to fix these problems, but teachers moved toward a problem-posing stance, presenting the issues back to the class so they could collectively generate solutions.

"It's embarrassing to talk about breasts." In some cases, the issues themselves were difficult to talk about because of cultural taboos. For example, as students began to talk about health care, the reproductive system, and breast cancer, the Interns found themselves having to explain vocabulary and concepts that were embarrassing in mixed gender classes. In many cases, they dealt with this by laughing and using humor to dispel tensions.

"If we wanted to learn about war, we would have stayed in El Salvador." An additional dilemma concerned how to connect literacy work with the social or political context of students' lives. Students often explicitly resisted political discussions when they were initiated by teachers; however, over and over, our experience was that they became very engaged when discussion of the same issues emerged spontaneously or in the context of language work. As Julio said, *"It's important not to impose your views because students think they have to agree with you because you're the teacher."* Further, once Interns came to understand how politics manifests itself in everyday life (rather than just through wars, elections, etc.), it was easier to integrate analysis into teaching.

How Did We Address Teaching Issues?

Just as the teaching issues themselves mirrored training issues, ways of addressing them paralleled ways of addressing training issues. Interns used many of the same processes with each other and with students to address teaching issues that we had used to resolve training issues. Through the following processes, Interns generally came to rely on their collective resources (rather than "university experts") to address classroom issues, adopting a stance of inquiry, posing problems back to students, and negotiating solutions with them.

- *Combining traditional and innovative approaches:* The primary strategy for dealing with students' expectations for traditional activities, materials, and student-teacher roles, was to integrate the more traditional and mechanical format (grammar, workbook, dictation) with more participatory activities. Likewise, a key way of legitimating dialogue, learners' knowledge, and critical thinking was to link discussion with structured literacy/ESL activities.

- *Teacher-sharing and problem-posing with each other:* The primary strategy Interns used when dealing with issues of classroom dynamics was to bring the issue back to their site-based group or to the workshop, drawing on each other's ideas and expertise to address problems. For example, when some Interns were having trouble figuring out how to follow up on a student's heated account of a personal problem, the group generated the following suggestions:

Listen a while and then ask if other students can relate similar experiences.

Write the story, or key words from it, on the board.

Ask for support/ideas from others about the problem.

Change the lesson and come back to it the next day.

Make a list of vocabulary from the discussion and use it the next day.

Ask students to speak slowly and watch to see who is participating; shift the focus to the dynamics of the discussion.

Change the subject but make sentences related to the topic the next day.

Avoid giving your own opinion as a teacher; set rules for dialogue so students learn to respect others.

Use the Language Experience Approach to record the discussion.

When the issue of whether or not to correct students in writing Language Experience stories arise, the group generated the following possible strategies:

Write exactly what they say first and correct it at a later stage.

Compliment students' language and then say, "In English (or in Boston), they say it this way . . . ," or "That's good but it's better to say. . . ."

Repeat their exact words and then say, "Is that what you want to say?"

Note errors silently, but don't correct them; then use that point in the next day's lesson.

Invite students to help each other, come to the board together to make changes.

- *Reflecting on ways of learning (metacognition):* Often when teachers tried a new activity, they would integrate discussion about why they were doing it and invite students to compare their own responses to more traditional versus innovative activities. For example, when students asked to have their dialogue journals corrected, one Intern explained why she would not focus on errors and then told them she would note language areas that needed work for future lessons. This kind of ongoing evaluation and metatalk about learning strategies helped to legitimate the new approaches.

- *Problem-posing with learners:* Interns often chose to address problems of classroom dynamics by creating a problem-posing code about the issue as a framework for language/literacy work and as a way of involving learners in the resolution of the problem. For example, Interns developed a code about use of the native language in the ESL classroom. This approach of involving students in addressing classroom problems moved classes toward sharing responsibility for learning. Further, it reinforced the underlying principle of the project, drawing on the resources of the community to address community needs.

What Was Our Approach to Evaluation?

Although more has been written about the evaluation of adult literacy *instruction* than about the evaluation of adult literacy *teacher training*, we felt that many of the same principles apply. One of the guiding principles in literacy evaluation theory is that *evaluation processes and tools should be congruent with the instructional approach* (Lytle, 1991). Because our approach to both instruction and training was a participatory one, emphasizing participant involvement, meaning-centered learning, and the relationships between learning and the social context, an evaluation model focusing only on the acquisition of discrete, decontextualized skills (measured through tests or formal assessments) would be inappropriate.

When instruction itself is responsive to participants' needs, evaluation must look at how they use what they've learned in their everyday lives. Likewise, the evaluation of Interns and Mentors must look at how they use what they've learned in their practice. We wanted the participants themselves to be involved in assessing their own learning; in addition, we wanted to see how they developed over time and integrated what they learned in their daily interactions. We felt that measuring outcomes of the project only in quantitative terms would be misleading and intimidating for participants. For these reasons, this report stresses qualitative evaluation in order to capture the varied ways that the impact of the project manifested itself. It was guided by the following principles that were originally formulated for assessing learner progress, but that apply equally to assessing teachers-in-training.

Participatory Evaluation Is*

* *contextualized, variable* . . . It doesn't try to measure isolated decontextualized skills, but rather examines actual usages and practices. Assessment tasks have a purpose. The particular forms that assessment takes can vary accordingly.

* *qualitative* . . . It involves reflective description, attempting to capture the richness of learning, rather than reducing it to numbers. It looks at metacognitive and affective factors.

* *process oriented* . . . It is concerned with how and why participants develop.

* *ongoing, formative* . . . It aims to inform curriculum development and training, or to explore a particular problem.

*adapted from Auerbach (1992, p. 114)

- *supportive* . . . It focuses on participants' strengths, what they *can* do rather than what they *can't* do. It starts with what they know and reflects their successes.
- *collaborative* . . . It is done *with* participants, not *to* them. Self-evaluation is an important part of developing metacognitive awareness and involvement in learning. Participants are subjects, not objects, of the evaluation process.
- *multi-faceted* . . . It invites various participants to evaluate each other. Not only do teachers evaluate students, but students evaluate teachers and program dynamics. Interns evaluate training as well as their development being evaluated.
- *open-ended* . . . It leaves room for and values the unexpected; non-predictable and one-time manifestations of change count.

In accordance with these principles, project evaluation emphasized self-evaluation, group dialogue, peer observation, interviews, and ongoing documentation of project work (through minutes of meetings and workshops, anecdotes, and samples of participants' work). In addition, evaluation was integrated as much as possible with training and instructional activities so that it did not impose additional time demands on participants.

Works Cited

Barndt, D. 1986. *English at Work: A Tool Kit for Teachers.* North York, Ontario: Core Foundations.

Auerbach, E. 1992. *Making Meaning, Making Change.* Washington, D.C.: Center for Applied Linguistics.

Lytle, S. 1991. *Living Literacy: Rethinking Development in Adults.* Unpublished ms, Philadelphia: University of Pennsylvania, Graduate School of Education.

Wallerstein, N. 1983. *Language and Culture in Conflict: Problem-Posing in the ESL Classroom.* Reading, MA: Addison-Wesley.

3

Teaching White Students About Racism

The Search for White Allies and the Restoration of Hope

Beverly Daniel Tatum

Editors' Note: Beverly Daniel Tatum draws in this essay on her experience as a workshop facilitator and professor of the psychology of racism. She proposes using Janet Helms' model of white identity development as a framework to understand student journal responses to learning about racism. She suggests the need for both white students and students of color to be exposed to empowered people of color and to white allies committed to dismantling racism in order to avoid their being limited to victim/oppressor roles as well as to clarify the role of the white ally.

Think of a nationally known white person whom you would describe as a racist. If you are like most of the students in my Psychology of Racism classes and the hundreds of workshop participants I address each year, at least one name comes to mind fairly quickly. The names of past and present Klan leaders and conservative southern politicians are usually the first to be mentioned.

Think now of a nationally known white person you would consider to be an antiracist activist, a white man or woman who is clearly identifiable as an ally to people of color in the struggle against racism. Do you find yourself drawing a blank? Perhaps you thought of Viola Liuzzo, James Reeb, or Michael Schwerner, white civil rights workers who were slain during the years of the civil rights movement. If we add the qualifier "still living," who comes to mind? If you have managed to think of someone who fits this description, notice that it probably took significantly longer to come up with an answer to this question than it did to the first.

The fact is there are white people who can be named in this category. You might have remembered Morris Dees, the executive director of the Southern Poverty Law Center and a vigorous anti-Klan litigator. The name of Anne Braden, a long-time civil rights activist, might have come to mind. Perhaps you knew the name of Virginia Foster Durr, a southern white woman who was actively involved in the struggle for civil rights in the South and who is featured in the first episode of the documentary series *Eyes on the Prize*. Maybe you have heard Bill Bradley, a senator from New Jersey, speak eloquently about issues of racism in our society and thought of him.

Other people might be named, but the point is that the names are typically retrieved very slowly, if at all. I have had the experience of addressing roomfuls of classroom teachers who have been unable to generate a single name without some prompting from me. If well-educated adults interested in teaching about race and racism in their classrooms have trouble identifying contemporary white men and women who have taken a public stand against racism, it is a reasonable assumption that our students will not be able to identify those names either.

Why is this lack of information of concern? As I have discussed elsewhere, one consequence of addressing the issue of racism (and other forms of oppression) in the classroom is the generation of powerful emotional responses in both white students and students of color.[1] White students, in particular, often struggle with strong feelings of guilt when they become aware of the pervasiveness of racism in our society. Even when they feel their own behavior has been nondiscriminatory, they often experience "guilt by association." These feelings are uncomfortable and can lead white students to resist learning about race and racism. And who can blame them? If learning about racism means seeing oneself as an "oppressor," one of the "bad guys," then of course there will be resistance. Few people would actively embrace such a self-definition.

But what alternatives do we offer to white students? This article is intended to explore this question and its implications for teaching about racism, using Helms's model of white racial identity development as a framework for understanding white students' responses.[2] The perspective I bring to this discussion is that of an African-American female college professor who has been teaching and/or leading workshops on racism in predominantly white settings since 1980. The student voices represented in this article come from journal entries written by students enrolled in my course on the psychology of racism.

Understanding White Identity Development

As Janet Helms explains in her model of white racial identity development, "racial identity development theory concerns the psychological implications of racial group membership, that is belief systems that evolve in reaction to perceived differential racial-group membership."[3] In U.S. society, where racial-group membership is emphasized, it is assumed that the development of a racial identity will occur in some form in everyone. However, the process will unfold in different ways for whites and people of color because of the different social positions they occupy in this society. For whites, there are two major developmental tasks in this process, the abandonment of individual racism and the recognition of and opposition to institutional and cultural racism. Helms writes: "Concurrently, the person must become aware of her or his Whiteness, learn to accept Whiteness as an important part of herself or himself, and to internalize a realistically positive view of what it means to be White."[4] Helms's six-stage model can then be divided into two major phases, the first being the abandonment of racism (a process that begins with the Contact stage and ends with the Reintegration stage). The second phase, defining a positive white identity, begins with the Pseudo-Independent stage and reaches fruition at the Autonomy stage.

Contact Stage

The first stage of racial identity for whites (the Contact stage) is a stage at which there is little attention paid to the significance of one's racial group membership. Individuals at this stage of development rarely describe themselves as white. If they have lived, worked, or gone to school in predominantly white settings, they may simply think of themselves as like the majority of those around them. This view is exemplified by the comment one of my white students made when asked to describe herself in terms of her class and ethnic background. She summed up her middle-class, white European background by saying, "I'm just normal." This sense of being part of the racial norm is taken for granted without conscious consideration of the systematically conferred advantages given to whites simply because of their racial group membership.[5]

While they have been influenced by the prevailing societal stereotypes of people of color, there is typically limited awareness of this socialization process. Often individuals at the Contact stage perceive themselves as completely free of prejudice, unaware of their own assumptions about other racial groups. I would describe the majority of the white men and women I have had in my course over the last twelve years as being in this stage of development at the start of the semester.

Disintegration Stage

However, participating in a classroom where the social consequences of racial group membership are explicitly discussed as part of the course content typically propels white students from the first stage to the next, referred to by Helms as the Disintegration stage.[6] At this stage, white students begin to see how much their lives and the lives of people of color have been affected by racism in our society. The societal inequities they now notice are in direct contradiction to the idea of an American meritocracy, a concept that has typically been an integral part of their earlier socialization. The cognitive dissonance that results is part of the discomfort experienced at this stage. One response to this discomfort is to deny the validity of the information that is being presented to them, or to withdraw from the class psychologically, if not physically.[7] However, if they remain engaged, white students at the disintegration stage typically want to deal with the guilt and other uncomfortable feelings by doing something, by taking action of some sort to interrupt the racism they now see around them. If students have learned (as I hope they have) that racism can take both active forms (e.g., verbal harassment, physical violence, intentional acts of discrimination) and passive forms (e.g., silence in the presence of another's racist remarks, unexamined policies and practices that disproportionately impact people of color, the failure to acknowledge the contributions of people of color), then they recognize that an active response to racism is required to interrupt its perpetuation in our society.

"But what action can I take?" is a common question at this point in their development. Jerri, a white woman from an upper-middle-class family, expressed this sentiment clearly in her journal.

> Another thing I realized when I got to college was the privileges attached to being white. My family had brought me up trying to make me aware of other people and their differences—but they never explained the power I had. I do not take advantage of my power—at least I try not to, but it seems inevitable. I feel helpless. There is so much I want to do—to help. What can I do? I do not want to help perpetuate racism, sexism and stereotypes.

Helping students think this question through for themselves is part of our responsibility as educators who have accepted the challenge of teaching about racism. Heightening student awareness about racism without also providing some hope for social change is a prescription for despair. We all have a sphere of influence, some domain in which we exercise some level of power and control. For students, the task may be to identify what their own sphere of influence is (however large or small) and to consider how it might be used to interrupt the cycle of racism.[8]

However, once again, students find that they can think of many more examples of racist behavior than they can think of examples of antiracist behavior. Many white students have experienced their most influential adult role models, their parents, as having been the source of overtly expressed racial prejudices. The following excerpts from the journals of two students illustrate this point:

> Today was the first class on racism. . . . Before today I didn't think I was exposed to any form of racism. Well, except for my father. He is about as prejudiced as they come. [Sally, a white female]

It really bothers me that stereotypes exist because it is from them that I originally became uninformed. My grandmother makes all kinds of decisions based on stereotypes—who to hire, who to help out. When I was growing up, the only black people that I knew were adults [household help], but I admired them just as much as any other adult. When I expressed these feelings to my parents, I was always told that the black people that I knew were the exceptions and that the rest of the race were different. I, too, was taught to be afraid. [Barbara, a white woman]

Others experienced their parents as passively silent on the subject of racism, simply accepting the status quo. As one young man from a very privileged background wrote:

It is easy to simply fade into the woodwork, run with the rest of society, and never have to deal directly with these problems. So many people I know from home . . . have simply accepted what society has taught them with little if any question. My father is a prime example of this. His overriding preaching throughout my childhood dealt with simply accepting reality. [Carl, a white male]

Those white students whose parents actively espoused antiracist values still felt unprepared for addressing racism outside of the family circle, a point highlighted by the following journal entry, written by Annette, a white female college senior:

Talking with other class members, I realized how exceptional my parents were. Not only were they not overtly racist but they also tried to keep society's subtle racism from reaching me. Basically I grew up believing that racism was no longer an issue and all people should be treated as equals. Unfortunately, my parents were not being very realistic as society's racism did begin to reach me. They did not teach me how to support and defend their views once I was interacting in a society without them as a buffer.

How do they learn how to interrupt someone else's racist (or sexist/anti-Semitic/homophobic) joke or challenge someone's stereotype if they have never seen anyone else do it? Despite the lack of examples, many students will begin to speak up about racism to their friends and family members. They often find that their efforts to share their new knowledge and heightened awareness with others are perceived negatively. Alice, a white woman, wrote:

I never realized how much sexism and racism there still is on TV. I don't know if I'll ever be able to watch TV in the same way again. I used to just watch TV shows, laugh at the funny jokes, and not think about sexism or racism. . . . I know my friends and family probably don't think I'm as much fun as I used to be because I can't watch TV without making an issue of how racist and sexist most shows are.

The fear of being alienated from these friends and family members is real, and is part of the social pressure experienced by those at the Disintegration stage of development to back away from this new awareness of racism. The dilemma of noticing racism and yet feeling the societal pressure not to notice, or at least not to speak up, is resolved for some at the Reintegration stage.

Reintegration Stage

At the Reintegration stage, whites may turn to explanations for racism that put the burden of change on those who are the targets of racism.

> Race-related negative conditions are assumed to result from Black people's inferior social, moral, and intellectual qualities, and thus it is not unusual to find persons in the Reintegration stage selectively attending to and/or reinterpreting information to conform to societal stereotypes of Black people.[9]

As Wellman clearly illustrates, such thinking allows the white individual to relieve himself or herself of guilt as well as responsibility for working toward social change.[10]

Because the pressure to ignore racism and to accept the socially sanctioned stereotypes is so great, unless we talk about the interpersonal challenges that often confront students at this point in the understanding, we place them at risk of getting stuck in the Reintegration stage. Identifying these challenges for students does not solve the problem for them, but it does help them to recognize the source of some of the discomfort they may experience. It is hoped that this recognition allows them to respond in ways that will allow for continued growth in their own racial identity development.

Pseudo-Independent Stage

Continued, ongoing dialogue about race-related issues is one way to promote such growth. As the students' understanding of the complexity of institutional racism in our society deepens, the likelihood of resorting to "blame-the-victim" explanations lessens. Such deepening awareness is associated with the commitment to unlearn one's own racism, and marks the movement into the next stage of development in Helms's model, the Pseudo-independent stage. This stage marks the beginning of the second phase of this developmental process, creating a positive definition of whiteness.

At the Pseudo-independent stage, the individual may try to deal with some of the social pressures experienced at earlier stages by actively seeking friendships with those who share an antiracist perspective. In particular, some white students may want to distance themselves psychologically from their own racial group by seeking out relationships with people of color. An example of this can be seen in the following journal entry:

One of the major and probably most difficult steps in identity development is obtaining or finding the consciousness of what it means to be white. I definitely remember many a time that I wished I was not white, ashamed of what I and others have done to the other racial groups in the world. . . . I wanted to pretend I was black, live with them, celebrate their culture, and deny my whiteness completely. Basically, I wanted to escape the responsibility that came with identifying myself as "white." [Lisa, a white female]

How successful these efforts to escape whiteness via people of color are will depend in part on the racial-identity development of the people of color involved.[11] However, even if these efforts to build interracial relationships are successful, the individual must eventually confront the reality of his or her own whiteness.

We all must be able to embrace who we are in terms of our racial cultural heritage, not in terms of assumed superiority or inferiority, but as an integral part of our daily experience in which we can take pride. But for many white students who have come to understand the reality of racism in all of our lives, whiteness is still at this stage experienced as a source of shame rather than a source of pride. Efforts to define a positive white identity are still tentative. The confusion experienced at this stage is clearly expressed by Bob, a white male struggling with these issues. Five weeks into the semester, he wrote:

There have been many talk shows on in the past week that have focused on race. Along with the readings I'm finding that I'm looking at the people and topics in very different ways than I had in the past. I'm finding that this idea of white identity is more important than I thought. Yet white identity seems very hard to pin hole. I seem to have an idea and feel myself understanding what I need to do and why and then something presents itself that throws me into mass confusion. I feel that I need some resource that will help me through the process of finding white identity.

Immersion/Emersion

The next stage of white racial identity development, Immersion/Emersion, is a stage at which individuals intensify their efforts to create a positive self-definition as a white person. Helms writes, "The person in this stage is searching for the answers to the questions: 'Who am I racially?' and 'Who do I want to be?' and 'Who are you really?'"[12] Students at this stage actively seek white role models who might provide examples for nonoppressive ways of being white. Such examples might be found in the form of biographies or autobiographies of white individuals who have been engaged in a similar process. Unfortunately, these materials are not easily found because the lives of white antiracists or "allies" have not generally been subjects of study, a topic I will return to shortly.

Participation in white consciousness-raising groups organized specifically for the purpose of examining one's own racism is often helpful in this process. At Mount Holyoke College, where I currently teach, such a group was formed (White Women Against Racism) following the 1992 acquittal of the Los Angeles police officers involved in the beating of Rodney King. Support groups of this nature help to combat the social isolation antiracist whites often experience, and provide encouragement for continued development of a self-definition as a white ally.

It is at this stage that the feelings of guilt and shame are replaced with feelings of pride and excitement. Helms writes,

> The person may begin to feel a euphoria perhaps akin to a religious rebirth. These positive feelings not only help to buttress the newly developing White identity, but provide the fuel by which the person can truly begin to tackle racism and oppression in its various forms.[13]

Mary, a senior writing her last journal entry of the semester, reflected this excitement at the changes she was observing in herself:

> This past weekend I went to New York. . . . As always we drove through Harlem on our way downtown. For the first time in four years I didn't automatically feel nervous when we turned that corner. For the first time I took an active interest in what was going on in the neighborhood and in the neighborhood itself. When the bus driver pointed out some points of interest like the Apollo, I actually recognized the names and was truly appreciative that the driver had pointed them out. I know this doesn't sound like much to get excited about, and in all honesty it doesn't really excite me either. In a way though, I guess this serves as an object lesson of sorts for me; I CAN unlearn the racism that I've been taught. It required some thought beforehand, but it certainly wasn't difficult by any means. Clearly, the next step is to identify something new to focus on and unlearn THAT as well. I can't help feeling like this is how a toddler must feel—each step is a challenge and although sometimes you fall, you don't usually hurt yourself. But overwhelmingly, each step is exciting and an accomplishment. This metaphor has at least one flaw, however. I really can't believe that this ever becomes as unconscious and unthinking as walking is for us all. Maybe it will become as effortless, but I think that if it becomes unthinking then an essential building block of unlearning racism will have been taken away.

Autonomy Stage

The last stage, the Autonomy stage, represents the culmination of the previous stages. The newly defined view of one's whiteness is internalized, and incorporated as part of one's own personal self-definition. This new sense of oneself must continue to be nurtured and supported, but as it is internalized, the individual may begin to expand his or her focus to awareness of other "isms."

> Thus one finds the Autonomous person actively seeking opportunities to learn from other cultural groups. One also finds him or her actively becoming increasingly aware of how other forms of oppression (e.g., sexism, ageism) are related to racism and acting to eliminate them as well.[14]

Though this is described as the "last stage," it is important to understand that this process is not a static or a linear one. In the process of moving through these stages, there may be back-and-forth-movement, revisiting earlier stages and then moving forward again. I find the image of a spiral staircase is a helpful one in explaining this concept to students. As a person ascends a spiral staircase, he may stop and look down at the pattern on the floor below. When he reaches the next level, he may look down again and see the same pattern, but the vantage point has changed.

Educational Implications

Each of these stages has implications for classroom interaction and student responsiveness to race-related content. The denial and resistance to the recognition of racism are characteristic of the first phase of white racial identity development. Strategies for responding to student resistance have been discussed in an earlier paper.[15] Here we will explore the particular challenges presented to the instructor and the student once the shift has been made to the second phase of development, the creation of a positive white identity.

Three Models of Whiteness

The process of developing a positive white identity, described in the later stages of Helms's model, is hindered by the fact that there are really only three major models of whiteness readily available with which students might identify. The first model, that of the actively racist white supremacist, is familiar to many students. They have seen Klan leaders on the news and on television talk shows. As was illustrated earlier, they may have grown up in homes with parents who, though not Klan supporters, actively embraced the notion of the superiority of whites and the inferiority of people of color. The "white supremacist" model, however, is one that is clearly rejected at this phase of development.

The second model of whiteness might be described as the "what whiteness?" view. As described in the Contact stage, many whites simply do not acknowledge their racial category as personally significant. This failure to acknowledge the salience of skin color in U.S. society is associated with the failure to acknowledge the reality of racism. However, once racism has been acknowledged as a system of advantage based on a race, the heightened awareness of white privilege eliminates this model as a personal option.[16] The individual can no longer ignore the fact that whiteness matters.

The third major model of whiteness might be described as the "guilty white" model. This style is characterized by the heightened awareness of racism and the accompanying shame and embarrassment about being white that so many of my students describe. Experiencing oneself as guilty is an uncomfortable state of being, and therefore is not a particularly appealing model for whites. In addition, the internal focus on one's own "guilt by association" can be immobilizing, and therefore interferes with one's ability to take effective action to interrupt expressions of racism. It is for this reason that people of color will often express impatience at what might be viewed as self-indulgent expressions of white guilt.

None of these three models of whiteness is attractive to the white individual struggling to define a positive sense of whiteness. Such an individual may feel that he or she is "re-inventing the wheel," and may retreat in frustration to an earlier stage of racial identity development. However, this frustration might be avoided if another, more positive model were readily available.

The Model of the White Ally

In fact, another model does exist. There is a history of white protest against racism, a history of whites who have resisted the role of oppressor and who have been allies to people of color. Unfortunately these whites are often invisible to students: their names are unknown.

Think back to the beginning of this article. How many names of white antiracists were on the tip of your tongue? If students have studied the civil rights era (many of my students are poorly informed about this period of history), they may know about Viola Liuzzo and Michael Schwerner and other whites killed for their antiracist efforts. But who wants to be a martyr? Do they know about white allies who spoke up, who worked for social change, who resisted racism and lived to tell about it? How did these white allies break free from the confines of the racist socialization they surely experienced to redefine themselves in this way? These are the voices that many white students are hungry to hear.

This information needs to be provided in order to help white students construct a pro-active white identity. In my class I try to provide concrete examples of such people. White professors teaching about racism who see themselves as allies may be able to share examples from their own lives and in this way might be role models for their white students. As an African-American professor, I am limited in this regard.[17] My strategy has been to invite a well-known white antiracist activist, Andrea Ayvazain, to my class to speak about her own personal journey toward an awareness of racism and her development as a white ally.[18] Students typically ask questions that reflect their fears about social isolation at this phase of development. "Did you lose friends when you started to speak up?" "My boyfriend makes a lot of racist comments. What can I do?" "What do you say to your father at Thanksgiving when he tells those jokes?"

White students, who often comment about how depressing it is to study about racism, typically say that the opportunity to talk with this ally gave them renewed hope.

> Today's class began with a visit from . . . a white woman who has made dismantling white privilege a way of life. . . . Her personal story gave me a feeling of hope in the struggle against racism. [Terri, a white woman]

> Now that we have learned about the severity of all of the horrible oppression in the world, it is comforting to know how I can become an ally. [Barbara, a white woman]

> What a POWERFUL speaker! Andrea was so upbeat and energetic. I think that her talk really boosted the spirits in our class. I personally have become quite disillusioned with some of our small group discussions of late, and having her talk brought some deep reflection and positive insight on the future—especially ideas and revelations concerning my role as perhaps a white ally. . . . Her presentation was overall very well received, and I enjoyed it *very* much. There *is* hope! [Robin, a white female]

One point that the speaker discussed at length was the idea that "allies need allies," others who will support their efforts to swim against the tide of cultural and institutional racism. This point was especially helpful for one young woman who had been struggling with the feelings of isolation often experienced by whites in the Disintegration stage. She wrote about being an ally, a positive role model:

> . . . it enhanced my positive feelings about the difference each individual (me!) can make. I don't need to feel helpless when there is so much I can do. I still can see how easily things can back-up and start getting depressing, but I can also see how it is possible to keep going strong and powerful. One of the most important points she made was the necessity of a support group/system; people to remind me of what I have done, why I should keep going, of why I'm making a difference, why I shouldn't feel helpless. I think our class started to help me with those issues, as soon as I started to let it, and now I've found similar supports in friends and family. They're out there, its just finding and establishing them—it really is a necessity. Without support, it would be too easy to give up, burn out, become helpless again. In any endeavor support is important, but when the forces against you are so prevalent and deep-rooted as racism is in this society, it is the only way to keep moving forward. [Joanne, a white woman]

In my view, the restoration of hope is an essential part of the learning process. Otherwise, students, both white and of color, become immobilized by their own despair.

Though the focus of this article is clearly on the process of white racial identity development, it should be pointed out that students of color also need to know that whites can be allies. For some students of color, the idea that there are white people who have moved beyond guilt to a position of claiming responsibility for the dismantling of institutional racism is a novel one. They too find hope in the possibility. Writing in response to the activist's visit, Sonia, a Latina, commented:

> I don't know when I have been more impressed by anyone. She filled me with hope for the future. She made me believe that there are good people in the world and that whites suffer too and want to change things.

In addition to inviting Andrea Ayvazian to my class, I try to provide written materials about white people who have been engaged in examining their own white identity and who have made a commitment to antiracist activity in their own lives. However, this information is not easily located. One of the consequences of racism in our society is that those who oppose it are often marginalized. As Colman McCarthy writes in the foreword to *The Universe Bends toward Justice,* "students know warmakers, not peacemakers."[19] As with other marginalized groups, the stories of peacemakers, of white allies, are not readily accessed. Yet having access to these stories makes a difference to students who are looking for ways to be agents of change. A resource list of materials I have been able to identify is included at the conclusion of this article.

Students, motivated by their own need for such information, can be quite resourceful in the generation of this knowledge. Recently, a white woman who had taken my Psychology of Racism course conducted an independent study project investigating the phenomenological experience of being a white ally on a college campus. Interviewing other white women, ranging in age from nineteen to forty-seven, she was able to generate valuable information about the daily implications of being an antiracist.[20] It was apparent that her research was more than an academic exercise—indeed a way to strengthen her own commitment to antiracist action. More of this kind of research needs to be done so that the fourth model of whiteness, that of the white ally, becomes a more visible option for white students.

Though the focus here has been on the provision of white role models for students trying to construct a positive white racial identity, it is important to acknowledge that there is a parallel need for both white students and students of color to see and read about clear examples of empowered people of color. Teaching about racism should not be only a litany of the ways people of color have been victimized by oppression. It must also include examples of the resistance of people of color to victimization. Just as white students are not eager to see themselves as oppressors, students of color do not want to be characterized as victims.[21] In addition, white students should not be led to believe that the role of the ally is to "help" victims of racism. The role of the ally is to speak up against systems of oppression, and to challenge other whites to do the same. Teaching about racism needs to shift from an exploration of the experiences of victims and victimizers to that of empowered people of color and their white allies, creating the possibility of working together as partners in the establishment of a more just society.

The Search for White Allies—Suggested Resources

The following resource list includes materials that examine the meaning of whiteness and/or provide biographical information about the lives of white allies. This list should not be considered an exhaustive one. It does represent the most useful materials I have been able to locate to date.

Barnard, H. F., ed. *Outside the Magic Circle: The Autobiography of Virginia Foster Durr.* Tuscaloosa: University of Alabama Press, 1985.

Barndt, J. *Dismantling Racism: The Continuing Challenge to White America.* Minneapolis: Augsburg Press, 1991.

Barndt, J., and C. Ruehle. "Rediscovering a Heritage Lost: A European-American Anti-Racist Identity." In *America's Original Sin,* 73–77. Washington, D.C.: Sojourner, 1992.

Berry, W. *The Hidden Wound.* Boston: Houghton Mifflin, 1970.

Blauner, B. *Black Lives, White Lives: Three Decades of Race Relations in America.* Berkeley: University of California Press, 1990.

Boyle, S. P. *The Desegregated Heart.* New York: William Morrow, 1962.

Braden, A. "An Unfinished Revolution: The Vision of a Common Destiny." In *America's Original Sin.* Washington, D.C.: Sojourner, 1992.

Colby, A., and W. Damon, *Some Do Care: Contemporary Lives of Moral Commitment.* New York: Free Press, 1992.

Dees, M., with S. Fiffer, *A Season of Justice: A Lawyer's Own Story of Victory over America's Hate Groups.* New York: Touchstone Books, 1991.

Dennis, R. M. "Socialization and Racism: The White Experience." In *Impacts of Racism on White Americans,* edited by B. Bowser and R. G. Hunt, 71–85. Beverly Hills: Sage, 1981.

Derman-Sparks, L., C. L. Higa, and B. Sparks. "Suggestions for developing positive racial attitudes." *Interracial Books for Children Bulletin 11,* no. 3–4 (1980): 10–15.

Hampton, H., and S. Fayer, *Voices of Freedom: An Oral History of the Civil Rights Movement from the 1950s–1980s.* New York: Bantam Books, 1990.

Helms, J. E. *A Race Is a Nice Thing to Have: A Guide to Being a White Person or Understanding the White Persons in Your Life.* Topeka: Content Communications, 1992.

Johnson, R. E. "Making a Stand for Change: A Strategy for Empowering Individuals." In *Opening Doors: Perspectives on Race Relations in Contemporary America,* edited by H. J. Knopke, R. J. Norrell, and R. W. Roger, 151–164. Tuscaloosa: University of Alabama Press, 1991.

Katz, J. *White Awareness: Handbook for Anti-Racism Training.* Norman: University of Oklahoma Press, 1978.

King, L. *Confessions of a White Racist.* New York: Viking, 1971.

Lester, J., "What Happens to the Mythmakers when the Myths Are Found to be Untrue?" Unpublished paper available from Equity Institute, Emeryville, Calif., 1987.

Levy, D. S. "The Cantor and the Klansman (an interview with Michael Weisser and Larry Trapp)." *Time,* February 17, 1992, pp. 14–16.

Mizell, L., S. Benett, B. Bowman, and L. Morin. "Different Ways of Seeing: Teaching in an Anti-racist School." In *Freedom's Plow: Teaching in the Multicultural Classroom,* edited by T. Perry and J. W. Fraser. New York: Routledge, 1993.

Nieto, S. "Vanessa Mattison: A Case Study." In her *Affirming Diversity: The Sociopolitical Context of Multicultural Education,* 60–68. New York: Longman, 1992.

Pratt, M. B. "Identity: Skin, Blood, Heart." In *Yours in Struggle: Three Feminist Perspectives on Anti-Semitism and Racism,* edited by E. Bulkin, M. B. Pratt, and B. Smith, 11–63. Ithaca, N.Y.: Firebrand, 1984.

Smith, L. *Killers of the Dream* (rev. and enl.; originally published 1949). New York: Norton, 1978.

Stalvey, L. M. *Education of a WASP* (originally published 1970). Madison: University of Wisconsin Press, 1989.

Terkel, S. "Beyond Hatred: The Education of C. P. Ellis." *Quest,* 1980, pp. 23–26, 100–101.

Terkel, S. *Race: How Blacks and Whites Think about the American Obsession.* New York: Anchor Books, 1992.

Terry, R. W. *For Whites Only.* Grand Rapids, Mich.: William B. Eerdmans Publishing, 1970.

Wallis, J. "By Accident of Birth: Growing Up White in Detroit." In *America's Original Sin,* 64–68. Washington, D.C.: Sojourner, 1992.

Ware, V. *Beyond the Pale: White Women, Racism and History.* London: Verso, 1992.

I would like to gratefully acknowledge the assistance of Stacy Chandler in the compilation of this resource list.

Notes

1. See Beverly Daniel Tatum, "Talking about Race, Learning about Racism: An Application of Racial Identity Development Theory in the Classroom," *Harvard Educational Review* 62 (February 1992): 1–24.

2. Janet E. Helms, *Black and White Racial Identity: Theory, Research and Practice* (Westport, Conn.: Greenwood Press, 1990).

3. Ibid., p. 3.

4. Ibid., p. 55.

5. For further discussion of the concept of white privilege and the advantages systematically conferred on whites, see Peggy McIntosh's working paper, *White Privilege and Male Privilege: A Personal Account of Coming to See Correspondences through Work in Women's Studies* (Wellesley, Mass.: Wellesley College Center for Research on Women).

6. Helms, *Black and White Racial Identity,* chap. 4, p. 58.

7. Tatum, "Talking about Race, Learning about Racism."

8. For a discussion of the use of action-planning projects in a course on racism, see ibid.

9. Helms, *Black and White Racial Identity,* p. 60.

10. David Wellman, *Portraits of White Racism* (New York: Cambridge University Press, 1977).

11. For further discussion of the interaction effect of stages of racial-identity development for people of color and for whites, see Tatum, "Talking about Race, Learning about Racism."

12. Helms, *Black and White Racial Identity,* p. 62.

13. Ibid.

14. Ibid., p. 66.

15. Tatum, "Talking about Race, Learning about Racism."

16. Wellman, *Portraits of White Racism.*

17. Though I cannot speak from experience as a white ally, I do use examples of being an ally in those areas in which I am a member of the dominant group. For example, as a Christian, I can give examples of being an ally to Jews by interrupting anti-Semitism. Similarly, as a heterosexual, I can give examples of interrupting homophobic and heterosexist behavior.

18. I am fortunate that Andrea Ayzavian lives in my local community. For those interested in more information about her work, she can be contacted at Communitas, Inc., 245 Main St., Suite 207, Northampton, MA 01060.

19. Angie O'Gorman, *The Universe Bends towards Justice: A Reader on Christian Non-Violence in the U.S.* (Philadelphia: New Society Publishers, 1990).

20. Stacy K. Chandler, "White Allies in a College Community: An Exploratory Study of the Subjective Meaning of Being an Anti-Racist" (Paper presented at the 46th Annual Mount Holyoke Undergraduate Psychology Conference, May 1, 1993). Copies available from B. D. Tatum, Department of Psychology and Education, Mount Holyoke College, South Hadley, MA 01075.

21. See Beverly Daniel Tatum, "African-American Identity, Achievement Motivation, and Missing History," *Social Education* 56 (1992): 331–34.

4

Basic Writing as Cultural Conflict

Tom Fox

Editors' Note: In this overview, Tom Fox examines three predominant theories of basic writing—"Deficit," "Initiation," and "Clash of Cultural Styles"—and finds each failing to account for racial differences in power and authority carried into classrooms. Fox proposes a fourth theory, "Oppositional Culture," based upon the work of anthropologist John Ogbu, whose research on African Americans' history of slavery, or involuntary immigration, helps explain their resistance to assimilation into Standard English. Fox believes that critical reflection on the role education plays in cultural conflicts can "(1) legitimate the cultural discourses students bring with them, and (2) challenge the notions . . . that those discourses are somehow inadequate to do academic work."

Basic writing programs have been limited by narrow definitions that misrepresent the languages and communities of their students. Virtually all the labels for basic writers are inaccurate in one way or another. "Remedial," as Mike Rose (1985) has shown, implies metaphorically that the writer has a "disease" or a "mental defect" (p. 349). "Developmental" suggests that the writer is young or immature. And "basic," the term I will reluctantly use, implies that these writers are simple or stuck on some rudimentary level. All these terms reflect the reluctance of basic writing researchers, until very recently, to acknowledge cultural and political influences on writing. More recent explorations into discourse communities have seen basic writers as "initiates" into the foreign world of academic discourse. But, as I will show, even these social

I would like to thank the following people for their contributions to this article (including their thoughtful disagreements with it): Herman Leon Frazier, Jr., Pamela Spoto, David Bartholomae, Patricia Bizzell, Mike Rose, Lois Bueler, Hertha Wong, and Susan Pereira.

theories underestimate and misrepresent the discourse communities of basic writers. Drawing from John Ogbu's (1974, 1987) work on African Americans' education, I propose redefining basic writing as cultural conflict, a definition that more richly conceives of basic writing, basic writers, and their communities. First, however, I will turn to a series of pedagogical ideologies—deficit theories, skills instruction, and service courses—that continue to shape how teachers, administrators, and students conceive of basic writers.

Deficit Theory, Skills, and Service

The first of these, deficit theory, was the topic of a session at the 1988 National Council of Teachers of English annual meeting. The session was entitled "The Reemergence of Deficit Theories." The panelists, Geneva Smitherman, Jacqueline Jones Royster, and Barbara M. Flores, all noted that these theories tend to go underground, then resurface in new forms (see Flores, 1988; Royster, 1988; Smitherman, 1988). The point of the panel was that while deficit theories—those theories of language learning that presume ignorance and inability in students and children—may change terms, the ideas are the same, and they continue to harm the same kind of students: speakers of non-standard dialect, almost always African American students. Deficit theories have been around a long time—before Martin Deutsch (1968) and Bereiter and Englemann (1966) codified them—and no doubt they'll be around as long as racism and sexism and classism affect education. Certainly deficit theories have influenced the shape of basic writing programs. Consider, for instance, the documents that officially shape college-level basic writing programs in California, including the program at California State University, Chico where I work. *The Master Plan Renewed* (1987), a state publication that shapes policy for all segments of higher education in California, defines the students in my program this way: "Students who are nearly college ready, but exhibit *serious multiple skill deficiencies* that require instruction at two levels below the Freshman level in English" (p. A–5; my emphasis). Deficit theory, at least in California higher education, seems never to have gone underground at all. It remains the official policy.

In addition to defining students by their deficiencies, deficit theories—especially in their application to basic writers—tend to reduce writing to a set of discrete skills to be learned, especially the countable ones such as punctuation and spelling. Workbooks and grammar modules populate basic writing workshops and computer work stations from the mistaken idea that students need to develop "basic skills," skills that, in fact, they already possess. (Any approach that separates language features from intention and meaning for the purpose of "practice" is a skills approach.) Richard Ohmann (1987) has explored the ideological consequences of teaching style as a skill in "Use Definite, Specific, Concrete Language." Ohmann's essay shows how the stylistic advice of textbooks, by transforming style to a set of skills (use definite, specific, concrete language), separates style from questions of meaning, intention, and especially action. Instead, the textbooks "push the student writer always toward the language that most nearly reproduces the immediate experience and away from language that might be used to understand it, transform it, and relate it to everything else" (p. 250). The consequence for students is that when we teach "a skill like this we may inadvertently suggest to students that they be less inquiring and less intelligent than they are capable of being" (p. 242). The consequence for teachers is that they begin to see student writing as a set of techniques, not a product of culture. Several authors, from the less overtly political Frank Smith (1986) to the overtly political Stanley Aronowitz and Henry Giroux (1985), have demonstrated how teaching basic skills underestimates and undermines both teachers and students.

Mike Rose's "The Language of Exclusion" (1985) explores how writing as "skill" works in the university, showing how the focus on skills has reduced the teaching of writing and the discipline of writing to a "second-class intellectual status." The skills view of writing instruction grew from a particular historical context—the early 20th century's stress on efficiency and utilitarianism—and led teachers to concentrate mostly on "mechanical/grammatical" features at the expense of "rhetorical/conceptual" dimensions. Rose makes clear that this history is still with us, as we have "writing skills hierarchies, writing skills assessments, and writing skills centers" (p. 346). He is also clear about the problems with this approach:

> Such work is built on a set of highly questionable assumptions: that a writer has a relatively fixed repository of linguistic blunders that can be pinpointed and then corrected through drill, that repetitive drill on specific linguistic features represented in isolated sentences will result in mastery of linguistic (or stylistic or rhetorical) principles, that bits of discourse bereft of rhetoric or conceptual context can form the basis of curriculum and assessment, that good writing is correct writing, and that correctness has to do with pronoun choice, verb forms, and the like. (p. 345)

The definition of writing as skill leads to a diminished and specialized role for writing in the university curriculum. Writing courses are the best known and purest example of service course. While other general education courses, math, critical thinking, and occasionally speech courses are designed as courses that "serve" the university as a whole, most of these courses also introduce students to disciplines. Because writing courses are housed either in English departments usually dominated by literature faculty or in no department at all (many writing courses are part of a "program"), they often lose the connection with a discipline and field of inquiry and the professional authority that comes with that connection. This is especially true of basic writing programs, which are sometimes housed outside the English department even when the rest of the writing courses are taught within the department. The university conceives of these courses as devoid of content, teaching only a set of neutral tools. The role of such courses is "service" and the obligation of the curriculum is to benefit all the other content areas. Such a role often leaves curricular decisions in the hands of those who are not especially knowledgeable about writing instruction and removes curricular responsibility from the teacher. Service course ideology, like the skills approach with which it is connected, prevents basic writing from becoming an area of inquiry, a discipline. In the absence of this connection with content, basic writing "content" becomes a matter of bureaucratic concern. If basic writing programs primarily concern themselves with serving the university, then political questions—in fact, *any* questions that challenge existing definitions of basic writing—become irrelevant to the bureaucratic task of reproducing the program.

This bundle of interconnected ideologies—deficit theory, skills instruction, and service—has dislocated the authority of both the teacher of basic writing and the student. Teachers of basic writing, as Rose points out, are frequently non-tenure-track staff and are institutionally less secure. What to teach is usually decided by a program coordinator who may or may not be educated in the teaching of writing. Set syllabi and required textbooks leave little choice for the teacher and little inspiration for the students. Students, more often than not, are not given baccalaureate credit for the course and consequently the course feels like a punitive experience. With important exceptions, the curriculum in basic writing has lagged behind the enormous changes in writing instruction. All too often it remains focused on the learning of grammatical conventions.

The influence of these ideologies on writing instruction, added to the fact that basic writing programs typically enroll a high percentage of students of color and working-class students, give basic writing programs enormous potential to work oppressively. The students who have historically been excluded from university education are taught an outmoded, limiting curriculum based on wrong-headed assumptions. These assumptions prevent students from seeing writing as an opportunity to reflect critically on the cultural conflicts and continuities they have experienced coming to the university, reflections that may help basic writers find their place in the university. Basic writing teachers, like their students, are denied the intellectual support to enliven their jobs. They have little control over their curriculum and teach in institutional settings that prevent thoughtful consideration of their course and their students.

Initiation Theory

While the ideologies of deficit theories, skills instruction, and service course refuse to be dislodged easily from the academy, what many have seen as a "social revolution" in composition studies has influenced basic writing, too. Particularly in the work of David Bartholomae and Patricia Bizzell, we find definitions of basic writing that focus on social group membership and the exploration of discourse communities. This work, influenced by anthropologists' understanding of culture and community, defines the basic writer as an "initiate" into the academic community. While initiation theories have been enormously helpful in shaping curriculum and in defining basic writers, early formulations of it simplified both the academic community and the students' communities, representing both as homogeneous and mutually exclusive. Pedagogies based on these early formulations shared common purposes with service courses; they taught the students what they did not know so that they would fit into the university. Critics of the initiation theory, including Bizzell herself (1988), have argued that communities are far more heterogeneous than the initiation model suggests.

Despite this simplification of community, two articles, David Bartholomae's (1985) "Inventing the University" and Patricia Bizzell's (1986) "What Happens When Basic Writers Come to College" are helpful in many respects. They ask basic writing teachers and researchers to reconceive their work in the social and political terms that give dignity to their own and their students' efforts. Bartholomae, for instance, challenges writing researchers (and that includes all teachers) to "conceive of a writer as at work within a text and simultaneously, then, within a society, a history, and a culture" (p. 162). I would like to explore these two articles, in part because they continue to influence our definitions of basic writing, and in part because they best represent "initiation theory." I should reiterate that both Bartholomae and Bizzell have reconsidered their arguments. Bizzell has been particularly forceful, showing both how unified understandings of academic discourse are oppressive, and how pedagogies based simply on initiation may not work in the interests of oppressed students.

The central argument in "Inventing the University" is that basic writers' unfamiliarity with academic discourse causes them to "approximate" the language of the academy without really knowing its discourse conventions, and that this "approximate discourse" is a necessary step in the initiation process:

> What our beginning students need to learn is to extend themselves, by successive approximations, into the commonplaces, set phrases, rituals and gestures, habits of mind, tricks of persuasion, obligatory conclusions and necessary connections that determine the "what might be said" and constitute knowledge within the various branches of our academic community. (p. 146)

This process is necessary only because of assumptions Bartholomae makes about the relationship between the students' discourse community and the academy's. First, Bartholomae presents the two communities as distinct and separate, focusing on how the academy's discourse is very different from the students'. Throughout "Inventing the University" Bartholomae describes the academy as having "peculiar" ways of knowing, "specialized" discourse, giving the impression of a large distance between what students know and all they need to know. Second, Bartholomae assumes that the academic discourse community is basically stable while the students' discourse is dynamic. Students are initiated into, but do not change, the academic community.

Bizzell, too, in "What Happens," shares these assumptions. She describes the discourse gap in terms of "world view":

> Basic writers, upon entering the academic community, are being asked to learn a new dialect and new discourse conventions, but the outcome of such learning is acquisition of a whole new world view. Their difficulties, then, are best understood as stemming from the initial distance between their world-views and the academic world view. (p. 297)

The gap is signified by the "whole new world view" that basic writers must acquire. Both Bizzell and Bartholomae are sensitive to the costs of this change, the sense of loss that many students might feel abandoning their world view. Bizzell, for instance, states that basic writers learn the conflict of world views "immediately and forcefully when they come to college . . . , when they experience the distance between their home dialects and Standard English and the debilitating unfamiliarity they feel with academic ways of shaping thought in discourse" (p. 300). Like Bartholomae, Bizzell presents the academy as essentially stable; students will change for it, but not the other way around. Both articles suggest that because of the power and value of the academic world view, the change, and its attendant losses, will be worth it.

Let me consider the central assumptions of the initiation argument, starting with the distance between students' discourse and academic discourse. Bartholomae bases his argument in "Inventing the University" on his examination of freshman placement tests. In these kinds of timed tests students believe that they must do something called "college-level" writing, perhaps for the first time. Students who are most *socially* uncomfortable with the university tend to exaggerate the newness and difference of "college-level." These exams test both writing ability in a timed-test context and the degree of comfort and authority that students feel in such circumstances. This second fact may be the reason for the higher representation of socially marginalized students in basic writing programs. Bartholomae, however, privileges textual evidence, assuming that the timed tests can reveal, among other things, basic writers' "native arguments." But the discomfort that he so eloquently writes about may stem less from basic writers' ignorance of the academy's discourse conventions than from a fear that their own resources of discourse may be irrelevant or damaging to their success in college.

Certainly, Bartholomae's analysis fits with the experiences basic writing teachers have with their students, especially in the first weeks of class. Students are sincerely uncertain, frequently guessing and mis-guessing what the academic game will be like. What makes me uncomfortable about Bartholomae's argument is that he turns this situation into a pedagogy. Basic writings students, because of their social insecurities, may in fact be exaggerating their "outlandishness," and underestimating the relevance and validity of their own discourse community to work in the academy. To *teach* the distinctiveness of academic discourse, its separation from student literacy, perpetuates the cultural divisions and conflicts that cause the discomfort of many of our students. By overstating the differences between academic discourse and students' discourse, especially by attributing the differences to linguistic habits or cognitive conventions, we send a message to those who are most uncomfortable, most anxious, about the status of their language in the university (African Americans, Chicanos, non-native speakers). The message is: We write a different "English" here, forget what you know. Students in this situation must feel as if they are facing a linguistic abyss. The language with which they are familiar is an interference; they must abandon it. This is a rough initiation.

In addition to underestimating the students' own discourse community and its relevance to academic work, the initiation argument also exaggerates the stability and coherence of the discourse of the academy. Both Bartholomae and Bizzell have articulated concerns about the initiation model in the last several years. Bizzell has been particularly frank and insightful about her earlier work. For instance, in "Arguing About Literacy" (1988), she states that understanding academic literacy as "monolithic" is "misleading, and itself politically oppressive" (p. 141). In many ways, she has led explorations that go beyond initiation theory. Joseph Harris (1989), in "The Idea of Community in the Study of Writing," supports Bizzell's later speculations on community by arguing that all discourse communities are varied:

> There has been much debate in recent years over whether we need, above all, to respect our students' "right to their own language," or to teach them the ways and forms of "academic discourse." Both sides of this argument, in the end, rest their cases on the same suspect generalization: that we and our students belong to different and fairly distinct communities of discourse, that we have "our" "academic" discourse and they have "their own" "common" (?!) ones. The choice is one between opposing fictions. The "languages" that our students bring to us cannot but have been shaped, at least in part, by their experiences in school, and thus must, in some ways, already be "academic." Similarly, our teaching will and should always be affected by a host of beliefs and values that we hold regardless of our roles as academics. What we see in the classroom, then, are not two coherent and competing discourses but many overlapping and conflicting ones. (pp. 18–19)

Once academic discourse is understood as "overlapping and conflicting," its dominance is less total. The requirement to join it thus requires students to give up much less; total deracination isn't necessary. Henry Giroux (1983) argues for a definition of educational institutions that supports Harris's sense of the polyvocal nature of the academic discourse community. Giroux critiques reproductive theories of education, arguing that they have misconceived of schools as only institutions of domination and reproduction, as uniform "factories of oppression" reproducing dominant culture. Giroux objects to this analysis of schools, mainly because it omits the possibility of *agency* for working-class students, the possibility and existence of resistance. This resistance is documented by ethnographic studies of education such as Paul Willis's (1977) *Learning to Labor* and Paul Cusick's (1983) *The Egalitarian Ideal and the American School.* And what this resistance shows is that schools are "contested," reproducing "the larger society while containing spaces to resist its dominating logic" (1988, p. xxxiii). As such, the academic discourse community isn't a complete or unified community to be initiated into. It already contains portions of the discourses (plural) that students, even basic writers, bring with them.

Basic writing teachers' experiences with two groups of students, nonnative speakers and speakers of Black Vernacular English, would seem to argue against the claim that students' language is not significantly different from academic discourse. The claim, of course, rests on the word "significantly." No doubt, the language of basic writers differs from academic discourse (no matter how we define it). But the pedagogy of initiation makes it *more* difficult for basic writers to succeed. They not only have to master "skills" (as in the service course), but they have to acquire a new way of understanding, knowing, arguing, reflecting.

The "Clash of Cultural Styles"

The distinctiveness of discourse communities, as an explanation for basic writing, has a parallel in the work of educational theorists trying to explain why education has failed to reach African American students. This body of work, which I will call "The Clash of Cultural Styles," focuses on how cultural difference interferes with communication, especially classroom talk. While this work brings cultural conflicts into focus, these conflicts are presented without a strong sense of the historical forces that have shaped them. A magnificent analysis of this "clash of cultural styles" is Shirley Brice Heath's (1983) *Ways With Words.* Heath spent 10 years living with and studying two communities in the Piedmont area of the Carolinas, one white, which she called "Roadville," and one black, which she called "Trackton." In fascinating detail, Heath shows how the language learning styles of these communities differ, yet how neither community's style of language use fits well with the "mainstream" culture of school. With regard to African American students, Heath shows how Trackton children see language as "performance": playful, inventive, designed to entertain. Although rich and complex, this view of language isn't understood well or appreciated by mainstream teachers. Consequently, students from Trackton don't do well in school.

A similar, more specific example of the "clash of cultural styles" explanation comes from Sarah Michaels's (1986) chapter in *The Social Construction of Literacy* (edited by Jenny Cook-Gumperz) examining the response of a teacher to an African American student's narrative. Deena, the black student, narrates in what Michaels calls a "topic associating" style, which Michaels calls typical of African American speakers. In a topic associating style, narratives consist "of a series of segments or episodes which are implicitly linked in highlighting some person or theme" (p. 103). This style clashes with a "topic-centered" style, preferred by the teacher and by white students. So when Deena takes her turn in "sharing time," the teacher believes that Deena has difficulty planning in advance and sticking to one idea. Consequently, she interrupts Deena's story with what Deena considers inappropriate and irrelevant questions, confusing and angering Deena and compounding the teacher's sense that Deena can't focus.

Solutions to the "clash of cultural styles" explanation usually involve new consciousness on the part of the teacher, rather than attending to larger social and political changes. In Deena's case, the researcher spoke with the teacher about topic associating style as a legitimate way of constructing narratives. The teacher, Michaels reports, subsequently dealt with the perceived lack of coherence in the narratives in a very different way. Instead of assuming incoherence, she asked the children to explain the connections, which she now knows are there. Similarly, in Heath's study, the teachers learned about different language styles and gained consciousness of their own ethnocentricity (p. 270). Both studies assume well-meaning people on both sides of the cultural clash who can step easily out of their historical roles. They pay little attention to the *meaning* of the stylistic difference and pay more attention to the *fact* of the difference. "Misunderstandings" among well-meaning teachers and students cause poor performances in school.

These explanations, however, underestimate the historical and social facts of marginalization and oppression, just as Bartholomae's and Bizzell's conceptions of students' discourse communities too tightly circumscribe basic writers' worlds. Bartholomae and Bizzell carefully consider issues of power and authority, although I believe their early explorations of discourse communities underestimate the students' power to resist. Michaels and Heath, while more specific about the facts of cultural difference, leave unexamined the difference in the power and authority on the two sides of the clash, and thus their studies do not stress enough the historical nature of this difference. Even though the research for *Ways With Words* was motivated by court-mandated desegregation, and even though it compares a black community with a white community, Heath's book ignores issues of rac*ism* and even warns readers away from considering such issues. While Heath is right to defend against simplistic generalizations on the basis of race, the enormous influence of the history of enslavement in the U.S. must profoundly influence the performance of black students in mainstream schools.

A More Promising Theory: "Oppositional Culture"

The influence of racism on education is at the core of another, more satisfying, explanation of our schools' failure to educate African American students: John Ogbu's theory of "oppositional culture," a theory that will lead us to a more comprehensive understanding of basic writing. In a series of works over the last decade, Ogbu has attempted to account for the varying degrees of success among many minority groups. If, as Heath, Michaels, and others claim, clashes in cultural style account for minority students failure, why is it that some groups, with cultural styles that differ widely from the mainstream, don't fail? For example, Ogbu (1974) shows that although the Chinese community in Stockton, California has conversational styles that differ greatly from mainstream styles, their children do not suffer in school performance. Such facts lead Ogbu to conclude that success in school rests on these central contingencies:

> first, whether or not the children come from a segment of society where people have traditionally experienced unequal opportunity to use their literacy skills in a socially and economically meaningful and rewarding manner; and, second, whether or not the relationship between the minorities and the dominant-group members who control the education system has encouraged the minorities to perceive and define acquisition of literacy as an instrument of deculturation without true assimilation. (p. 151)

Ogbu emphasizes the issues of historically based discrimination and the association of literacy as an instrument of domination. For African American students these issues result in the following skeptical questions about education: "If I learn to do school reading and writing will I then be economically and socially rewarded?" Note how really different this focus is from both the clash of cultural styles and initiation theory. Instead of wondering how or if African Americans *can* fit into mainstream school culture, Ogbu's explanation assumes that African American students *can* fit in, but focuses on the economic, social, and cultural consequences of doing so.

African American students are skeptical of schools' ability to provide them with the means to "get a good job" because they see that neither their skills nor their education is the main problem; it's racism. Ogbu argues that because of a history of economic and political oppression, African American cultural identity has developed in *opposition* to white majority culture; African Americans define themselves, in part, by opposing white culture. And since the white majority dominates schools, to succeed in school is not just irrelevant to economic and social success, it also threatens the social and cultural identity of the successful student.

This oppositional identity, growing from the specific history of slavery, Jim Crow, segregation, and institutional racism, is what differentiates African Americans from other minorities. Success in school means joining the opposition, threatening their identity as black Americans; to do well in school is understood by some as "acting white." Though the strength of this attitude varies from student to student, most African American students feel it to some degree.

The "oppositional culture" explanation of schools' inability to educate African American students explains, in part, why "initiation," let alone "skills," doesn't work as a curricular strategy. The need is not so much to initiate students into the discourse community, to teach them the particular forms of language in the academy. Instead we need to convince students that this community is *theirs,* that it will not work against their identity and their interests. The following paper illustrates how the conflicting senses of communities shape writing. It was written by a student, Herman Leon Frazier, Jr., in the Basic Writing Program at California State University, Chico. In it, Leon demonstrates the effects of "oppositional identity" in both social and psychological terms. He builds it into the structure of his discourse. Although the paper is lengthy, I believe that it shows more dramatically than most the degree to which cultural conflicts and continuities can affect, and even define, basic writing students.

The Boy Who Saw the Light

This pertckler experience in my life started in 1978 and ended in the summer of 1982. This is a story about a boy who finally seen the light before it was to late. This is a story about a boy who was catch between to different world's trying to adjust to them both at the same time not knowing that it would take year's for him to realize that he didn't fit in the one everybody thought he was going to fit in.
This is his experience.
    We live in Hawthorne CA, Harwthorne is a quite city it has know gang's volince if it did it was some crazy white boy punk rock group.
When we moved to Hawthorne from Compton it was only about three percent black and latino. That didn't stop me from becoming a member of one the most violent gang's in east L.A. even though I lived miles and miles away from anykind of gang war fare.
    The year was 1978 and I was just a young confused little kid at the same time nedding attention if I couldn't get it at home I looked else were. . . .
    I have always been one for causing conflict and trying to be different but I didn't know that the stuburnness was going to help get the ghetto out of my system.
When I went to school with all the white kid's it was a total trip I didn't know how to handle it because 98 percent of the staff and student's were white I couldn't deal.
From a person like me at the time it was a strain on the brain I wasn't use to being the black sheep in the crowd so I conplained to my parent's all the time that the white student's gave me a hard time so I could go to school with my cousin's in the getto. . . .
    When I got back to regular classes at school I did better on my work for a while I spoke up more in class and pertisapated in all event's but in all good there's bounded to be some bad somewere in there and it came up.
People were calling me the little rich kid just because I didn't live in the getto know more and even though we weren't rich we were not poor either. That braught me a lot's of problem's I had to prove to them that I was just as wild as they were, back then it was a big then to go to jail luck (uh lee) I never went so I would be tested all the time.

By me living in Hawthorne and going to school in Compton I had to work twice as hard to be tuff at school even though I loved to fight I didn't like beating up people for nothing like many of them did. Haven't you heard that saying "only the strong will survive" believe me in Compton it's true.

As time progress like most people at my school we all were in a gang it wasn't the same as if someone was asking you to be in there frat, know it was the opposet, either you were down with the gang and help beat people up or not down and get beat up.

It wasn't as bad as it sound's believe me, we played sport's and stuff together it just was some of the stuff I didn't like.

As fight's in the gang arose it affected me in a much more deeper way than just my fist" you see when the day was over I had to get on the bus and go home the rest of them stayed there I didn't. I found it hard for me to deal with both world's, so I went to the stronger of the two. . . .

I came home with a black eye one day my mother didn't say anything but I could tell she was worried but in my cousin's neighborhood people thought that it was just a sign of war scar's preparing you for man hood I gues that's one of the reason's why the name of the gang was nieghborhood ganster C'rip. As day's passed I found it harder and harder to deal with both world's to me Hawthorne and Compton was two different world's not just two different city's far a part. When I was at home meaning my parent's house I could never set still I was alway's jumppy.

I had white friend's and they use to ask me all the time why do you go to school with those hood's and I would say because I'm a hood, a neighborhood ganster C'rip. When people at my school would ask me if I had white friend's I would say know because they would take it the wrong way, they would take it as a sign of weakness or trying to be white as they say.

This same process went on for a long time intill oneday I meet this old white lady that lived down the street from me she toll me that knew of me and that I wasn't what she exsteced as a gangster.

I looked her died in thee eye and smiled then she turned away from me for a minute and then turned right back around and started right back talking. She ended by saying that my face makes people preserve that I'm mean and crazy but just by talking to me and looking into my heart she knew I was a teddy bear. I just laughed and said thank you I have to go. . . .

One morning I woke up extra early so I could talk to my mother. . . . I walked into her room and said (mama) she turned around with a mean look on her face and started to cry I walked toward's her and all of a sudden she slap me in the face my eye's opened up wide because my mother had never hit me before, she didn't scream she just talked and talked for along time I guess that's why it stuck so deep in my head like it did because she never did raise her voice that day. That night my home boy brandon called me and said everybody is looking for you somebody shot babydee (what) I screamed out over the phone, yo home's brandon said we are going to get throw's fool's back for fucking with our home boy like that.

The next day at school everybody was hyped we all wanted to get them back for shooting baby dee.

The fight toke place sometime after school everybody was going to be there I wasn't scared but something inside me toll me that it wasn't right for me anymore even though baby dee was my friend I just didn't want to fight. I was hard to say it even to myself but it was even harder to do. . .

The hour's went by slow every ten minutes I had to use the restroom that was the first time I ever had to shit that much before a gang fight that got me worried because that was a sign of weakness. Something was wrong I knew it, my brain knew it but my (heart) was it down with my gang no more.

It's an old saying in gang's DO-OR-DIE everybody and every gang lived by that saying it meant that do what you have to do or die like a scared women. It was almost time to go to the fight and what the old white lady and my mother toll me stuck in my head.

It was time to leave to go to the fight and for the first time in my life I wasn't ready, everybody was over my cousin's house ready to walk out the door but I wasn't. I turned to my cousin who was one of the leader's at the time and said lucky, lucky I anit down know more I'm out of here (what he screamed out) he grabed me and said punk you anit shit.

This had been the person that I had admired all this time and he was fronting me in front of everybody when I finally got a grip on everything I hit him and we started fighting he toll all the home boy's what I said and they all started beating me up when they finally got threw beating me up my arm was broke my hand's and mouth were bleeding and my resept was going, in that neighborhood that was you most pride presetion.

I knew that after all of that I could go back to that school anymore so I went back to school were I should have gone in the first place the one right down the street from my house it was hard adjusting but after a while I finally did. I'm glad that I didn't fight that day because I found out that after the gang fight was over 12 of my home boy's died fighting in that little war. If I would have stayed I could have been one out of those 12 gangsters shot god was looking out for me he most have meant for me to be doing some else besides gang banging.

Leon's paper demonstrates the insufficiency of deficit theory or skills approaches in defining basic writing. To see Leon's paper as evidence of "serious multiple skill deficiencies" misrepresents the complexity of his writing. It ignores the very tricky rhetorical situation that Leon successfully negotiates, that of an urban African American male writing about gangs to a basic writing class in a residential, mostly white university located in a rural area. A skills approach that focuses only on Leon's errors would miss the fact that Leon successfully argues for a particular interpretation of his experience, developing it, supporting it with evidence. It would focus on minor, easily changed features of Leon's text (such as spelling and punctuation), and suggest to him that his writing is not academic.

I would like to focus on how Ogbu's understanding of literacy can help basic writing teachers understand their students more generously by examining Leon's text in terms of oppositional culture. This paper is interesting for a number of reasons, not least of which is the story of the person that wrote it. Although there is something of a genre of "gang papers," this one argues for an explanation; it goes beyond telling a story about the time he almost died. Leon constantly explains his story in the "oppositional" terms that inform Ogbu's explanation of educational failure. First, let's look at the oppositions themselves. Hawthorne and Compton stand out as the most obvious; they are the "two different worlds." Leon takes pains to show that Hawthorne is white (it's only "three percent black and latino," no gang violence, except perhaps by "some crazy white boy punk rock group," and "98 percent of the staff and student's were white"). Note that he doesn't say that Compton is black; black is the "unmarked" case, the characteristic that is assumed. He writes from this "unmarked" point of view; he points out the white people.

Neither community allows Leon to move easily from one to the other; these oppositions are socially enforced. We know that Leon feels the tensions because he shows us his discomfort in the white school in Hawthorne: "I couldn't deal" and "it was a strain on the brain" and he mentions feeling "jumppy." And he shows us why he feels that way: "I had white friend's and they use to ask me all the time why do you go to school with those hood's and I would say because I'm a hood, a neighborhood ganster C'rip." But the move outward to Hawthorne makes Compton even more socially dangerous: "People were calling me little rich kid just because I didn't live in the getto know more and even though we weren't rich we were not poor either." The threat is so great that Leon denies even that he has white friends: "When people at my school would ask me if I had white friend's I would say know because they would take it the wrong way, they would take it as a sign of weakness or trying to be white as they say."

"Weakness" recurs as a threat in Leon's essay and it is associated with whites and with women. Two women figure prominently in shaping Leon's refusal to fight, which he initially characterizes as a weakness. In one sense then, Hawthorne—the location of his mother, the white woman who called him a "teddy bear," and his white friends—is "weakness," and Compton is "strong," the place where "only the strong will survive." That's why Leon says "I found it hard for me to deal with both world's, so I went to the stronger of the two," meaning, at first, Compton. The effect of this opposition on Leon's school performance is only suggested in the paragraph that follows his statement that returning to Compton improved his school attitude "for a while." He then discusses the pressure to "prove" his belongingness to Compton by working "twice as hard to be tuff at school," and that after refusing to fight he writes that he "could[n't] go back to school anymore." We can infer that success in school in

Compton has more to do with toughness, with strength. Success in school in Hawthorne, on the other hand, involves losing respect and strength in Compton.

This strength/weakness opposition is undercut by the end of the essay. The "Do or Die" command is completely reversed; the women, denigrated by him as "scared," have saved his life; the "strong" have died, and the "weak" are alive to write.

There is another opposition working in Leon's paper that parallels the Compton/Hawthorne one and is more relevant to how "oppositional culture" works. That is the opposition between the university classroom and Compton. This opposition is obvious in phrases like this: "As time progress like most people at my school we all were in a gang it wasn't the same as if someone was asking you to be in there frat, know it was the opposet, either you were down with the gang and help beat people up or not down and get beat up." When Leon writes that "it wasn't the same as if someone was asking you to be in there frat," he's setting up an opposition for the students in the class who were unfamiliar with Compton. He's also aware of the potential ostracism that might occur by disclosing his gang history (he's experienced it already in Hawthorne) and he compensates for that by stating, "It wasn't as bad as it sound's believe me, we played sports and stuff together."

Less obviously, there are opposing languages in Leon's paper that signify this opposition. One strikes me as particularly important: the journalistic exposé that chronicles the escape from the ghetto's gangs and the playful, yet violent voice of Compton. In fact, what makes this paper different from the ordinary gang paper is the continuing presence of the journalistic voice. It is not just present at the beginning and at the end; instead Leon alternates these voices masterfully. He begins by highlighting *story*. "This is a story," he says twice. The percentages and the phrase, "That didn't stop me from becoming a member of one of the most vilent gang's in east L.A.," both present his experiences in the language of an outside observer (such as his real teacher and many of his classmates who belong to fraternities). He continues with this perspective when he describes himself as a "confused little kid . . . nedding attention" and when he describes his experience as a "process." This voice has a counterpoint in the voice from Compton, which is playful, sometimes violent, and no less analytical. This is voice that says, "From a person like me at the time it was a strain on the brain I wasn't use to being the black sheep in the crowd" and, after telling about his black eye, "I gues that's why the name of the gang was the nieghborhood ganster C'rip." The Compton voice, at times, attempts to capture even the phonology of the streets. That's why Leon puts the apostrophe in "C'rip," so it sounds like how he says it, *Kerrrip*. That's also why he spells luckily *luck (uh lee)*. Sometimes the two voices coexist in one sentence, as in "every ten minutes I had to use the restroom that was the first time I ever had to shit that much before a gang fight." Again, I have to stress that these oppositions are something that Leon himself calls attention to, as in the passage I cited earlier comparing gangs and fraternities.

Although Leon's paper shows us how oppositional cultures work and their effect on education, it isn't itself an example of the negative consequences. "The boy who saw the light" is more of an example of successful academic work, where the author articulates cultural oppositions without becoming a victim of them. The essay doesn't pretend to "solve" these conflicts. The competing languages in Leon's essay must also reveal competing cultural ideologies. They are certainly not going to be solved by an essay. Just how conscious Leon is about these conflicts is revealed by the following anecdote. Leon's teacher asked him to revise "The boy who saw the light" for an English department publication. In reply, Leon leaned over and said, "You mean 'whiten' it up a little?" Leon's ability to call explicit attention to the competing and conflicting voices allows him to participate better in Hawthorne and the university by not having to abandon Compton completely (he retains its language, and he calls upon his experience "there" to help his success "here").

I have called Leon's essay a successful piece of academic work, but I would like to be specific about that claim. I don't mean the misspellings (particularly the ones that are not related to Compton speech) or idiosyncratic punctuation. No doubt and no argument, Leon needs to work on his spelling and punctuation. I don't doubt that he can do this with a minimum of effort. While it is true that Leon does not know how to spell "particular," he *does* know how to use literacy to explore and discover the connections and conflicts of two vastly different social scenes. He knows how to use literacy to reflect on and gain wisdom from complex experiences. And he knows how to use literacy to help others share these experiences. These "fundamentals" characterize academic literacy at its best: a focused exploration of a complex topic. Joseph Harris (1989) argues that writing courses need not "initiate our students into the values and practices of some new community, but to offer them the chance to reflect critically on those discourses—of home, school, work, the media, and the like—to which they already belong" (p. 19). This seems to be what Leon is up to in "The boy who saw the light," putting together several familiar discourses to try to see where, between Compton and the university, he now wants to live.

As teachers of basic writing, we need to understand both what is specific about Leon's experience and what generalizations we can make. Ogbu's work shows the importance of understanding the specific history of African Americans and its effects on education. So in some senses, Leon's paper has little to do with, say, the Hmong immigrant who may be in the same class. But Leon's paper can operate as a heuristic device for understanding a great many students whose social and cultural backgrounds conflict with their idea of the university—and that includes many non-native speakers, Native Americans, Chicanos, Asians, working-class students, gay and lesbian students, and others. The terms of the conflict vary greatly, but the fact of it does not. After all, the placement tests which classify some students as basic writers test—as much as anything else—uneasiness with the value of one's own discourses for the university. Thus, perceived (and often real) cultural conflicts best define basic writers. A basic writing pedagogy ought to help students explore the cultural conflicts and continuities that attend their entrance into university.

Defining basic writers as negotiators of cultural conflicts obviously complicates any theory of initiation and makes irrelevant the deficit-theory-driven skills and service approaches. The exclusion many basic writers feel does not originate in significant differences in discourse forms. It derives instead from many other factors. Among them are educational practices which foster the belief that large gaps exist between what students know and what students need to know; these practices, in turn, stem from mistaken ideas about the value and characteristics of both students' discourse and academic discourse. The exclusion also reflects racism, classism, and sexism—conscious or unconscious beliefs that working-class students, students of color, and women students really do not belong in the university because they are different. The goal of a basic writing program ought to be to help students focus on these factors, explore them, and make conscious choices about what to do about them. We are obligated to help our students "succeed" in the university so that by virtue of their participation they redefine it more democratically.

Primarily, the task facing basic writing teachers is an interpretive one: seeking to understand the cultural forces that shape their students and understanding how their students are accommodating, resisting, or reproducing these forces, the same tasks facing the student. Unfortunately, interpretation is not usually the central activity of the basic writing classroom for either students or teachers; evaluation is. Perhaps the most difficult and most important change that has to occur in basic writing programs (and all parts of the curriculum) is to remove evaluation as the main focus of the classroom. Evaluation dominates basic writing classrooms as students and teachers constantly work to judge the quality of the students' texts to determine "entrance" to the university. The emphasis on evaluation is the most powerful means of keeping the "skills" ideology in place, since the evaluative necessity of finding concrete (hopefully countable) features of language on which to grade focuses the curriculum on those features. If one were asked to evaluate "meaning" or "consciousness of cultural conflict" then the grading system would be understood as political as it really is. Though the prospect of changing the grading system is a daunting one, for a basic writing program to really work progressively, evaluation as the central activity must go. If teachers were "interpreters" and not "graders," they would be one step closer to what Giroux (1988) calls "transformative intellectuals," engaged in the academic task of the interpretation of text and context so that they can work to change the inequities they see. Basic writing teachers, themselves underestimated by university structures, understand from the inside how schools unequally distribute authority. This complex understanding of the part that educational institutions play in the creation of the cultural conflicts can be useful. It can frame the teachers' interpretation of basic writers, showing students how their home communities and the academic community overlap in some places and conflict in others. This reflection can serve two aims: 1) legitimate the cultural discourses students bring with them, and 2) challenge the notions (held by both the students and parts of the university) that those discourses are somehow inadequate to do academic work.

Finally, since the classroom discourse conflicts are local manifestations of social and political ones, teachers of basic writers need to carry this pedagogical work outside their classrooms to the university as a whole. The Writing Across the Disciplines movement is a natural forum for such activity and many such programs seem increasingly concerned with issues of equity and political change. The success of a basic writing program dedicated to transformation of the university and society minimizes the distinction between work inside the classroom and political activism outside the classroom. While such aims may seem overly ambitious, we ought to keep in mind that in places like University of Massachusetts—Amherst, University of Pittsburgh, California State University, Chico, this work has already begun.

Works Cited

Aronowitz, S., & Giroux, H. A. (1985). *Education under siege.* South Hadley, MA: Bergin & Garvey.

Bartholomae, D. (1985). Inventing the university. In M. Rose (Ed.), *When a writer can't write* (pp. 134–165). New York: Guilford Press.

Bereiter, C., & Englemann, S. (1966). *Teaching disadvantaged children in the preschool.* Englewood Cliffs, NJ: Prentice-Hall.

Bizzell, P. (1986). What happens when basic writers come to college. *College Composition and Communication, 7,* 294–301.

Bizzell, P. (1988). Arguing about literacy. *College English, 50,* 141–153.

Commission for the Review of the Master Plan for Higher Education. (1987). *The master plan renewed.* Sacramento: State of California.

Cook-Gumperz, J. (Ed.) (1986). *The social construction of literacy.* Cambridge: Cambridge University Press.

Cusick, P. (1983). *The egalitarian ideal and the American school.* New York: Longman.

Deutsch, M., & Associates. (1967). *The disadvantaged child.* New York: Basic Books.

Flores, B. M. (1988, November). *Resistance to non-deficit models.* Paper presented to the National Council of Teachers of English. St. Louis.

Giroux, H. A. (1983). Theories of reproduction and resistance in the new sociology of education. *Harvard Educational Review, 53,* 257–293.

Giroux, H. A. (1988). *Teachers as intellectuals.* South Hadley, MA: Bergin & Garvey.

Harris, J. (1989). The idea of community in the study of writing. *College Composition and Communication, 40,* 11–22.

Heath, S. B. (1983) *Ways with words.* Cambridge: Cambridge University Press.

Michaels, S. (1986). Narrative presentations: An oral preparation for literacy with first graders. In J. Cook-Gumperz (Ed.), *The social construction of literacy* (pp. 94–116). Cambridge: Cambridge University Press.

Ogbu, J. U. (1974). *The next generation: An ethnography of education in an urban neighborhood.* New York: Academic Press.

Ogbu, J. U. (1987). Opportunity structure, cultural boundaries, and literacy. In J. Langer (Ed.), *Language, literacy and culture* (pp. 149–177). Norwood, NJ: Ablex.

Ohmann, R. (1987). *The politics of letters.* Middletown, CT: Wesleyan University Press.

Rose, M. (1985). The language of exclusion. *College English, 47,* 341–359.

Royster, J. J. (1988, November). *Cultural literacy and the literary tradition.* Paper presented to the National Council of Teachers of English, St. Louis.

Smith, F. (1986). *Insult to intelligence.* New York: Arbor House.

Smitherman, G. (1988, November). *Language variation across disciplines.* Paper presented to the National Council of Teachers of English, St. Louis.

Willis, P. (1977). *Learning to labor.* New York: Columbia University Press.

5

Multicultural Classrooms, Monocultural Teachers

Terry Dean

Editors' Note: Terry Dean offers some working solutions to the conflict between home cultures and academic cultures, a subject also addressed by Tom Fox, Raymond Mazurek and Caroline Pari in this volume. Essentially, Dean argues that nonmainstream students fail or drop out of college because of cultural dissonance with academic life and language. Dean claims that bridging the gap between ethnic and academic culture requires a teacher's knowledge of students' backgrounds. He suggests several ways of doing this based on the models of Jim Cummins, Shirley Brice Heath, and Paulo Freire. But Dean also describes his own pedagogy that helps culturally diverse students master academic discourse without giving up their own languages and cultures. He includes very useful exercises that focus on students' races/ethnicities and discourses.

> Remember gentlemen, John Chrysostom's exquisite story about the day he entered the rhetorician Libanius' school in Antioch. Whenever a new pupil arrived at his school, Libanius would question him about his past, his parents, and his country.
>
> Renan, *La Réforme*
> *intellectuelle et morale*

Sometimes more than others, I sense the cultural thin ice I walk on in my classrooms, and I reach out for more knowledge than I could ever hope to acquire, just to hang on. With increasing cultural diversity in classrooms, teachers need to structure learning experiences that both help students write their way into the university and help teachers learn their way into student cultures. Now this is admittedly a large task, especially if your students (like mine) are Thai,

Cambodian, Vietnamese, Korean, Chinese, Hmong, Laotian (midland Lao, low-land Lao), Salvadoran, Afro-American, Mexican, French, Chicano, Nicaraguan, Guatemalan, Native American (Patwin, Yurok, Hoopa, Wintu), Indian (Gujarati, Bengali, Punjabi), Mexican-American, Jamaican, Filipino (Tagalog, Visayan, Ilocano), Guamanian, Samoan, and so on. It may take a while for the underpaid, overworked freshman composition instructor to acquire dense cultural knowledge of these groups. But I have a hunch that how students handle the cultural transitions that occur in the acquisition of academic discourse affects how successfully they acquire that discourse. The very least we can do, it seems to me, is to educate ourselves so that when dealing with our students, in the words of Michael Holzman, "We should stop doing harm if we can help it" (31).

Some would question how much harm is being done. If enough students pass exit exams and the class evaluations are good, then everything is OK. Since we want our students to enter the mainstream, all we need worry about is providing them the tools. Like opponents of bilingual education, some would argue that we need to concern ourselves more with providing student access to academic culture, not spending time on student culture. But retention rates indicate that not all students are making the transition into academic culture equally well. While the causes of dropout are admittedly complex, cultural dissonance seems at the very least to play an important role. If indeed we are going to encounter "loss, violence, and compromise" (142) as David Bartholomae describes the experience of Richard Rodriguez, should we not be directing students to the counseling center? And if the attainment of biculturalism in many cases is painful and difficult, can we be assured, as Patricia Bizzell suggests, that those who do achieve power in the world of academic discourse will use it to argue persuasively for preservation of the language and the culture of the home world view? (299) This was not exactly Richard Rodriguez's response to academic success, but what if, after acquiring the power, our students feel more has been lost than gained? I think as teachers we have an obligation to raise these issues. Entering freshmen are often unaware of the erosion of their culture until they become seniors or even later. Like Richard Rodriguez, many students do not fully realize what they have lost until it is too late to regain it. Let me briefly outline the problem as I see it and offer some possible solutions.

The Problem

A lot is being asked of students. David Bartholomae describes the process: "What our beginning students need to learn is to extend themselves, by successive approximations, into the commonplaces, set phrases, rituals and gestures, habits of mind, tricks of persuasion, obligatory conclusions, and necessary connections that determine 'what might be said' and constitute knowledge within the various branches of our academic community" (146). "Rituals and gestures, tricks of persuasion" mean taking on much more than the surface features of a culture. Carried to an extreme, students would have to learn when it is appropriate to laugh at someone slipping on a banana peel. When we teach composition, we are teaching culture. Depending on students' backgrounds, we are teaching at least academic culture, what is acceptable evidence, what persuasive strategies work best, what is taken to be a demonstration of "truth" in different disciplines. For students whose home culture is distant from mainstream culture, we are also teaching how, as a people, "mainstream" Americans view the world. Consciously or unconsciously, we do this, and the responsibility is frightening.

In many situations, the transitions are not effective. Several anthropological and social science studies show how cultural dissonance can affect learning. Shirley Brice Heath examines the ways in which the natural language environments of working-class Black and white children can interfere with their success in schools designed primarily for children from middle-class mainstream culture. The further a child's culture is from the culture of the school, the less chance for success. Classroom environments that do not value the home culture of the students lead to decreased motivation and poor academic performance (270–72). In a study of Chicano and Black children in Stockton, California schools, John Ogbu arrives at a similar conclusion. Susan Urmston Philips analyzes the experiences of Warm Springs Native American children in a school system in Oregon where the administrators, teachers, and even some parents thought that little was left of traditional culture. But Philips shows that "children who speak English and who live in a material environment that is overwhelmingly Western in form can still grow up in a world where by far the majority of their enculturation experience comes from their interaction with other Indians. Thus school is still the main source of their contact with mainstream Anglo culture" (11). Philips describes the shock that Warm Springs Native American children experience upon entering a school system designed for the Anglo middle-class child. Because of differences in the early socialization process of Native American children (especially in face-to-face interaction), they feel alienated in the classroom and withdraw from class activities (128).

Pierre Bourdieu and Jean-Claude Passeron examine how the cultural differences of social origin relate directly to school performance (8–21). Educational rewards are given to those who feel most at home in the system, who, assured of their vocations and abilities, can pursue fashionable and exotic themes that pique the interest of their teachers, with little concern for the vocational imperatives of working-class and farm children. Working-class and farm children must struggle to acquire the academic culture that has been passed on by osmosis to the middle and upper classes. The very fact that working-class and farm children must laboriously acquire what others come by naturally is taken as another sign of inferiority. They work hard because they have no talent. They are remedial. The further the distance from the mainstream culture, the more the antipathy of mainstream culture, the more difficulty students from outside

that culture will have in acquiring it through the educational system (which for
many is the only way):

> Those who believe that everyone would be given equal access to the highest
> level of education and the highest culture, once the same economic means
> were provided for all those who have the requisite "gifts," have stopped halfway
> in their analysis of the obstacles; they ignore the fact that the abilities mea-
> sured by the scholastic criteria stem not so much from natural "gifts" (which
> must remain hypothetical so long as the educational inequalities can be traced
> to other causes), but from the greater or lesser affinity between class cultural
> habits and the demands of the educational system or the criteria which define
> success within it. [Working-class children] must assimilate a whole set of
> knowledge and techniques which are never completely separable from social
> values often contrary to those of their class origin. For the children of peas-
> ants, manual workers, clerks, or small shopkeepers, the acquisition of culture
> is acculturation. (Bourdieu and Passeron 22)

Social and cultural conditions in the United States are not the same as in France,
but the analyses of Bourdieu, Passeron, Heath, Ogbu, and others suggest interesting lines of inquiry when we look at the performance of students from different cultures and classes in U.S. schools. Performance seems not so much
determined by cultural values (proudly cited by successful groups), but by class
origins, socio-economic mobility, age at time of immigration, the degree of
trauma experienced by immigrants or refugees, and the acceptance of student
culture by the mainstream schools. Stephen Steinberg argues in *The Ethnic
Myth* that class mobility precedes educational achievement in almost all immigrant groups (131–32). I really do not believe that Black, Native American, and
Chicano cultures place less emphasis on the importance of education than Chinese, Jewish, Vietnamese, or Greek cultures do. We do not have over one hundred Black colleges in the United States because Blacks don't care about education. I have never been to a Native American Studies Conference or visited a
rancheria or reservation that did not have newsletters, workshops, and fund-
raisers in support of education. Bourdieu and Passeron's analysis suggests that
educational success depends to a large extent on cultural match, and if an exact match is not possible, there must at least be respect and value of the culture
children bring with them. Acculturation (assimilation) is possible for some, but
it is not viable for all.

Acculturation itself poses problems. Jacquelyn Mitchell shows how cultural conflict affects the preschool child, the university undergraduate, the graduate student, and the faculty member as well. Success brings with it, for some
people, alienation from the values and relationships of the home culture. "In
fulfilling our academic roles, we interact increasingly more with the white
power structure and significantly less with members of our ethnic community.
This is not without risk or consequence; some minority scholars feel in jeop-

ardy of losing their distinctive qualities" (38). The question Mitchell poses is, "How can blacks prepare themselves to move efficiently in mainstream society and still maintain their own culture?" (33) Jacqueline Fleming, in a cross-sectional study of Black students in Black colleges and predominantly white colleges, found Black colleges more effective despite the lack of funding because Black colleges are more "supportive" of students (194). Long before the recent media coverage of racial incidents on college campuses, Fleming noted that "all is not well with Black students in predominantly white colleges" (162). And in California, the dropout rate of "Hispanics" (a term that obscures cultural diversity much as the term "Asian" does) is greater than that of any other group except possibly Native Americans. But despite gloomy statistics, there is hope.

Theoretical Models for Multicultural Classrooms

Several theoretical models exist to help students mediate between cultures. In "Empowering Minority Students: A Framework for Intervention," James Cummins provides one:

> The central tenet of the framework is that students from "dominated" societal groups are "empowered" or "disabled" as a direct result of their interactions with educators in the schools. These interactions are mediated by the implicit or explicit role definitions that educators assume in relation to four institutional characteristics of schools. These characteristics reflect the extent to which (1) minority students' language and culture are incorporated into the school program; (2) minority community participation is encouraged as an integral component of children's education; (3) the pedagogy promotes intrinsic motivation on the part of students to use language actively in order to generate their own knowledge; and (4) professionals involved in assessment become advocates for minority students rather than legitimizing the location of the "problem" in the students. For each of these dimensions of school organization the role definitions of educators can be described in terms of a continuum, with one end promoting the empowerment of students and the other contributing to the disabling of students. (21)

Like Bourdieu, Cummins sees bicultural ambivalence as a negative factor in student performance. Students who have ambivalence about their cultural identity tend to do poorly whereas "widespread school failure does not occur in minority groups that are positively oriented towards both their own and the dominant culture, [that] do not perceive themselves as inferior to the dominant group, and [that] are not alienated from their own cultural values" (22). Cummins argues that vehement resistance to bilingual education comes in part because "the incorporation of minority languages and cultures into the school program confers status and power (jobs for example) on the minority group"

(25). But for Cummins, it is precisely this valuing of culture within the school that leads to academic success because it reverses the role of domination of students by the school.

Shirley Brice Heath's model is similar to Cummins'. The main difference is that she focuses on ethnography as a way for both reachers and students to mediate between home and school cultures. A consideration of home culture is the only way students can succeed in mainstream schools, increase scores on standardized tests, and be motivated to continue school: "Unless the boundaries between classrooms and communities can be broken, and the flow of cultural patterns between them encouraged, the schools will continue to legitimate and reproduce communities of townspeople who control and limit the potential progress of other communities who themselves remain untouched by other values and ways of life" (369). Like Cummins, Heath aims for cultural mediation. As one student stated: "Why should my 'at home' way of talking be 'wrong' and your standard version be 'right?' . . . Show me that by adding a fluency in standard dialect, you are adding something to my language and not taking something away from me. Help retain my identity and self-respect while learning to talk 'your' way" (271). Paulo Freire, on the other hand, wants those from the outside to totally transform mainstream culture, not become part of it: "This, then, is the great humanistic and historical task of the oppressed: to liberate themselves and their oppressors as well" (*Pedagogy* 28). Yet in almost all other respects, Freire's model, like Cummins' and Heath's, is grounded in a thorough knowledge of the home culture by teachers, and actively learned, genuine knowledge by the student. Each of these models has different agendas. Teachers should take from them whatever suits their teaching style, values, and classroom situations. I would simply encourage an inclusion of the study of the wide diversity within student cultures.

Teaching Strategies for Multicultural Classes

Cultural Topics

Culturally oriented topics are particularly useful in raising issues of cultural diversity, of different value systems, different ways of problem solving. Several successful bridge programs have used comparison of different cultural rituals (weddings, funerals, New Year's) as a basis for introducing students to analytic academic discourse. Loretta Petrie from Chaminade University in Hawaii has a six-week summer-school curriculum based on this. Students can use their own experience, interview relatives, and read scholarly articles. Reading these papers to peer response groups gives students additional insights into rituals in their own culture as well as making them aware of similarities and differences with other groups. I have used variations of Ken Macrorie's I-Search paper (Olson 111–22) to allow students to explore part of their cultural heritage that they are not fully aware of. One Vietnamese student, who was three years old when she came to America, did a paper on Vietnam in which she not only interviewed relatives to find out about life there but sought out books on geography and politics; she literally did not know where Vietnam was on the map and was embarrassed when other students would ask her about life there. Several students whose parents were from the Philippines did research that was stimulated by the desire to further understand family customs and to explain to themselves how the way they thought of themselves as "American" had a unique quality to it. One student wrote:

> For over eighteen years I have been living in the United States. Since birth I have been and still am a citizen of this country. I consider myself a somewhat typical American who grew up with just about every American thing you can thing of; yet, at home I am constantly reminded of my Filipino background. Even at school I was reminded of my Filipino culture. At my previous school, the two other Filipinos in my class and I tried to get our friends to learn a little about our culture.

But classmates were not always open to cultural diversity, and their rejection raised the central question of just how much you have to give up of your culture to succeed in the mainstream society:

> During the Philippine presidential election, there were comments at my school that we Filipinos were against fair democracy and were as corrupt as our ex-President Marcos. Also it was said that Filipinos are excessively violent barbaric savages. This is partly due to our history of fighting among ourselves, mostly one group that speaks one dialect against another group of a different language within the islands. Also maybe we are thought savages because of the food we eat such as "chocolate meat" and "balut," which is sort of a salted egg, some of which may contain a partially developed chicken. So, to be accepted into society you must give up your old culture.

"You must give up your old culture" is misleading. The student had to be careful about sharing home culture with peers, but he isn't giving up his culture; he is gaining a greater understanding of it. His essay ended with:

> I now have a better understanding of why I was doing a lot of those things I didn't understand. For example, whenever we visited some family friends, I had to bow and touch the older person's hand to my forehead. My mother didn't really explain why I had to do this, except it was a sign of respect. Also my mother says my brother should, as a sign of respect, call me "manong" even though he is only two years younger than I. At first I thought all this was strange, but after doing research I found out that this practice goes back a long way, and it is a very important part of my Filipino culture.

Richard Rodriguez's widely anthologized "Aria" (from *Hunger of Memory*) allows students to analyze his assertion that loss of language and culture is essential to attain a "public voice." Although the student above seems to agree in part with Rodriguez, most students find Rodriguez's assertions to be a betrayal of family and culture:

> I understand Rodriguez's assertion that if he learned English, he would lose his family closeness, but I think that he let paranoia overcome his senses. I feel that the lack of conversation could have been avoided if Rodriguez had attempted to speak to his parents instead of not saying anything just because they didn't. I am sure that one has to practice something in order to be good at it and it was helpful when his parents spoke in English to them while carrying on small conversation. To me, this would have brought the family closer because they would be helping each other trying to learn and grow to function in society. Instead of feeling left out at home and in his society, Rodriguez could've been included in both.

I have used this topic or variations on it for a half dozen years or so, and most of my freshmen (roughly 85% of them) believe they do not have to give up cultural and home values to succeed in the university. I find quite different attitudes among these students when they become juniors and seniors. More and more students graduate who feel that they have lost more than they gained. Raising this issue early provides students more choices. In some cases it may mean deciding to play down what seem to be unacceptable parts of one's culture (no balut at the potluck); in other cases it may lead to the assertion of positive values of the home culture such as family cohesiveness and respect for parents and older siblings. Courageous students will bring the balut to the potluck anyway and let mainstream students figure it out. I often suspect that some of the students who drop out of the university do so because they feel too much is being given up and not enough is being received. Dropping out may be a form of protecting cultural identity.

Cultural topics are equally important, if not more so, for students from the mainstream culture. Many mainstream students on predominantly white campuses feel inundated by Third World students. Their sense of cultural shock can be as profound as that of the ESL basic writer. One student began a quarter-long comparison/contrast essay on the immigration experiences of his Italian grandparents with the experiences of Mexicans and Vietnamese in California. As the quarter went on, the paper shifted focus as the student became aware that California was quickly becoming non-white. It scared him. The essay was eventually titled "Shutting the Doors?" and ended with:

> I have had some bad experiences with foreigners. On a lonely night in Davis, three other friends and I decided to go to a Vietnamese dance. When we got there, I couldn't believe how we were treated. Their snobbishness and arrogance filled the air. I was upset. But that was only one incident and possibly I am over reacting. I often reflect on my high school teacher's farewell address. He called for our acceptance of the cultural and religious background of each

other. But after long days thinking, I, like many others, am unable to answer. My only hope is that someone has a solution.

The student had grown up in Richmond, California, a culturally diverse East Bay community, and was friendly with students from many cultures (it was his idea to go to the dance). The very recognition on the part of the student of what it feels like to be surrounded by difference at the dance is a beginning step for him to understand what it means to try to be who he is in the midst of another culture. I see this student quite often. He is not racist. Or if he is, he at least has the courage to begin asking questions. The solution for which the student yearned was not immediately forthcoming: his yearning for one is worth writing about.

Language Topics

It is not unusual for ESL errors to persist in the writing or the pronunciation of highly educated people (doctors, lawyers, engineers, professors) because, consciously or unconsciously, those speech patterns are part of the person's identity and culture. The same can be true of basic writers. Language-oriented topics are one way to allow students to explore this kind of writing block. Assignments that require students to analyze their attitudes toward writing, their writing processes, and the role that writing plays in their lives can make these conflicts explicit. For example, one student wrote:

> Moreover, being a Chinese, I find myself in a cultural conflict. I don't want to be a cultural betrayer. In fact, I want to conserve my culture and tradition. I would be enjoyable if I wrote my mother language. For example I like to write letter in Chinese to my friends because I can find warmth in the letter. The lack of interest in writing and the cultural conflict has somehow blocked my road of learning English.

Overcoming this block may, however, cause problems in the home community. In response to Rodriguez, one student wrote:

> I can relate when Rodriguez say that his family closeness was broken. Even though I speak the language that is understood and is comfortable at home, when I speak proper English around my friends at home, they accuse me of trying to be something I'm not. But what they don't realize is that I have to talk proper in order to make it in the real world.

Jacquelyn Mitchell writes of returning to her community after college:

> My professional attire identified me in this community as a "middle-class," "siddity," "uppity," "insensitive" school teacher who had made her way out of the ghetto, who had returned to "help and save," and who would leave before dark to return to the suburbs. My speech set me up as a prime candidate for

suspicion and distrust. Speaking standard English added to the badges that my
role had already pinned on me. (31)

In some way problems like this affect us all. In the small town that I grew up
in, simply going to college was enough to alienate you from your peers. Although my parents encouraged me to get an education, they and their peers saw
college as producing primarily big egos—people who thought they knew
everything. No easy choices here. It took my uncle, who made the mistake of
becoming a Franciscan priest, forty years to be accepted back into the family
by my mother.

Another way to help students with cultural transitions is to make the home
language the subject of study along with the different kinds of academic discourse they will be required to learn. Suzy Groden, Eleanor Kutz, and Vivian
Zamel from the University of Massachusetts have developed an extensive curriculum in which students become ethnographers and analyze their language
patterns at home, at school, and in different social situations, using techniques
developed by Shirley Brice Heath. This approach takes time (several quarters
of intensive reading and writing), but such a curriculum has great potential for
helping students acquire academic discourse while retaining pride and a sense
of power in the discourse they bring with them.

Peer Response Groups

Peer response groups encourage active learning and help students link home
and university cultures. The Puente Project, in affiliation with the Bay Area
Writing Project, combines aggressive counseling, community mentors, and
English courses that emphasize active peer response groups. The Puente
Project has turned what used to be a 50–60% first-year dropout rate into a
70–80% retention rate in fifteen California community colleges. All of the students are academically high risk (meaning they graduated from high school
with a D average), they are Chicanos or Latinos, and all have a past history of
avoidance of English classes and very low self-confidence when it comes to
writing. Writing response groups give the students a sense of belonging on
campus. As students make the transition from home to school, the groups become, in the students' own words, "una familia":

> Now after two quarters of Puente, it's totally different. My writing ability
> has changed to about 110%. I might not be the best speller in the world, but I
> can think of different subjects faster and crank out papers like never before
> . . . having Latinos in a class by themselves is like a sun to a rose. This is the
> only class where I know the names of every student and with their help I de-
> cide what to write. (*Puente* 20)

Joan Wauters illustrates how structured non-confrontational editing can
make peer response more than a support group. Students work in pairs on stu-

dent essays with specific training and instructions on what to look for, but the author of the essay is not present. The author can later clarify any point she wishes with the response group, but Wauters finds that the non-confrontational approach allows students to be more frank about a paper's strengths and weaknesses and that it is "especially valuable for instructors who work with students from cultures where direct verbal criticism implies 'loss of face'" (159). Wauters developed these techniques with Native American students, but they apply equally well to other cultures.

Response groups do not have to be homogeneous. Any small group encourages participation by students who may not feel comfortable speaking up in class for whatever reason. They provide a supportive environment for exploring culturally sensitive issues that students might hesitate to bring up in class or discuss with the teacher. The following paragraph was read by a Black student to a group consisting of a Filipino, a Chinese, and two Chicano students:

> I am black, tall, big, yet shy and handsome. "I won't hurt you!" Get to know who I am first before you judge me. Don't be scared to speak; I won't bite you. My size intimidates most people I meet. I walk down my dormitory hallway and I can feel the tension between me and the person who's headed in my direction. A quick "Hi!" and my response is "Hello, how are you doing?" in a nice friendly way. It seems that most of the guys and girls are unsure if they should speak to me. I walk through the campus and eyes are fixed on me like an eagle watching its prey. A quick nod sometimes or a half grin. Do I look like the devil? No, I don't. Maybe if I shrink in size and lightened in color they wouldn't be intimidated. Hey, I'm a Wild and Crazy Guy too!

This small group discussion of what it felt like to be an outsider spilled over into the class as a whole, and students that normally would not have participated in class discussion found themselves involved in a debate about dorm life at Davis. I know that peer response groups have limitations, need structure, and can be abused by students and teachers alike. But I have never heard complaints from teachers using peer groups about how difficult it is to get ESL students to participate. In some cases the problem is to shut them up.

Class Newsletters

Class newsletters encourage students to write for an audience different from the teacher, and they generate knowledge about multicultural experiences. I use brief 20-minute in-class writing assignments on differences between the university and home, or how high school is different from the university, or ways in which the university is or is not sensitive to cultural differences on campus. Sometimes I simply have students finish the statement, "The university is like. . . ." These short paragraphs serve as introductions to issues of cultural transition, and when published, generate class discussions and give ideas for students who are ready to pursue the topic in more detail. Newsletters can be done in a variety of formats from ditto masters to desktop publishing. Students who feel comfortable discussing ethnic or cultural tensions establish a forum for those students whose initial response would be one of denial. For example, the story of a Guamanian and a Black student who thought they were not invited to a white fraternity party led to an extended class discussion of whether this kind of experience was typical and whether they had not been invited for ethnic reasons. The next time I had students write, a Chicana student articulated her awakening sense of cultural conflict between the university and her family:

> I was so upset about leaving home and coming to Davis. I was leaving all my friends, my boyfriend, and my family just to come to this dumb school. I was angry because I wanted to be like all my other friends and just have small goals. I was resentful that I had to go away just to accomplish something good for me. I felt left out and angry because it seemed that my family really wanted me to go away and I thought it was because they did not love me. I was not studying like I should because I wanted to punish them. My anger grew when I realized I was a minority at Davis. My whole town is Mexican and I never thought of prejudice until I came to Davis.

Family is central to Chicano/Latino/Mexican-American students. The pull toward home can create ambivalence for students about their school commitments. In this case, the family was aware of this pull, and encouraged the student to give college the priority. The daughter interpreted this as a loss of love. The student's ambivalence about home and school put her on probation for the first two quarters at Davis. She is now a junior, doing well as a pre-med student, and her chances for a career in medicine look good. I don't think just writing about these issues made the difference. The class discussion generated by her article helped her realize that her situation was shared by others who were experiencing the same thing but had not quite articulated it. She was not alone.

Bringing Campus Events into the Classroom

I recently assigned a paper topic for a quarter-long essay that made reading of the campus newspapers mandatory. I was surprised to find that many students did not read the campus newspapers on a daily basis and in many cases were quite unaware of campus issues that directly concerned them, for example, the withdrawal of funding from the Third World Forum (a campus newspaper that deals with Third World issues), compulsory English examinations for international graduate teaching assistants in science and math classes, and increasing incidents of hostility toward Asians (as reflected in bathroom graffiti, "Lower the curve: kill a chink"). Admission policies at UC Berkeley, particularly as reported in the press, have pitted Blacks and Chicanos against Asians, and quite often students find themselves in dorm discussions without having enough specific knowledge to respond. The more articulate students can be about these issues, the greater the chance the students will feel integrated in the university.

Assignments can make mandatory or strongly encourage students to attend campus events where cultural issues will be discussed within the context of campus life—issues such as the self-images of women of color or how Vietnamese students feel they are perceived on campus. A panel entitled "Model Minority Tells the Truth" called for Vietnamese students to become more involved in campus life partly in order to overcome misperceptions of some students:

> Vietnamese students feel inferior to Americans because Americans do not understand why we are here. We are refugees, not illegal immigrants. There are a lot of unspoken differences between Vietnamese and Americans because the memory of the Vietnam war is so fresh, and it is difficult for Americans to be comfortable with us because we are the conflict. Vietnamese students also suffer an identity crisis because the Vietnamese community has not established itself yet in America as other Asian groups have.

Anecdotes

Anecdotes about oneself and former class experiences are another way to generate discussion and raise issues of cultural transition and identity. The teacher's own curiosity and experience of cultural diversity will often give students ideas for other topics. Cultural identity does not depend on a Spanish surname alone nor does it reside in skin color. Richard Rodriguez, for example, does not consider himself a Chicano and was insulted when he was so identified at Berkeley during the sixties. I mentioned this in class and described the experiences of several former students whose parents were from different cultures (so-called "rainbow children"). Several weeks later, a student whose mother was Mexican and whose father was Anglo wrote:

> Someone once told me that I'd have to fight everyday to prove to everyone that I wasn't "another stupid Mexican." He was convinced that the whole American population was watching his every move, just waiting for him to slip and make a mistake. Having it emphasized that he is a minority certainly won't help his attitude any. It will just remind him that he is different. All of my life I never considered myself a minority. I didn't speak Spanish, I didn't follow Mexican customs, and I hung around with "American" kids. It is real hard for me to understand why minorities get so much special treatment.

This student found the existence of different student cultural groups on campus to be disturbing:

> When I came to Davis, instead of seeing a melting pot like the one I expected, I saw distinct cultural groups. When I first heard about CHE (Chicanos in

Health Education) I was furious. I could not see any need for a special club
just for Hispanic students interested in health careers. It seemed that the students in CHE were segregating themselves from the real world. They should
actually be interacting with everyone else proving that they weren't different.

After interviewing members of CHE and VSA (Vietnamese Student Association), this student was able to see how some people benefited from these clubs:

> I didn't think I could find some positive aspects about these clubs, but I found
> some. Some clubs help immigrants assimilate into the Western culture. They
> provide the member with a sense of pride about who they are and they
> strengthen cultural bonds. If students attend classes and become discouraged
> by lower grades than they expected, they can go to a CHE meeting and see
> "one of their own" explain how they made it through the bad times and how
> they came back to beat the odds. I asked Trinh why she joined the VSA. She
> said she joined to learn more about her culture and to improve her language.
> But others join to help themselves assimilate into Western culture. I was won-
> dering what was so important about her culture that Trinh couldn't retain
> unless she went to these meetings. She said, "I can't explain it." But there is
> an atmosphere there that she can't get anywhere else. And if this gives her a
> good feeling, then more power to her.

This student still has reservations about cultural differences on campus (primarily because she does not want to see herself as "different"), but the movement from "I was furious about CHE" to "more power to her" is a step toward
recognizing her own cultural diversity. Cultural identity is not always simple. I
have seen second-generation Vietnamese, Indian, Korean, and Chinese students
who saw themselves primarily as "American" (no hyphens), and in some cases
as white. One Chinese student, from a Black neighborhood in Oakland, grew
up wanting to be Black. It was the cool thing to be.

For some students, examining home culture and the culture of the university can cause anxiety. Teenagers often do not relish the idea of being "different." They have enough difficulty keeping their grades up, forming peer
relationships, adjusting to being in a new environment. My sixteen-year-old
stepson argues constantly that he is just like his peers. He certainly tries to be.
But all you have to do is walk on the school grounds, look around a few minutes, and it is impossible to miss the six-foot-tall, dark-skinned, handsome boy
bobbing up and down amongst a sea of white faces: definitely Indian (other
Indians can identify him on sight as Telegu). It is becoming increasingly difficult on predominantly white campuses for students to deny differences in culture. What is important to learn is that while differences between home and
school can lead to conflict, differences in themselves do not inherently cause
conflict. The home culture can be a source of strength which can enable the student to negotiate with the mainstream culture. One of the major factors of success of students coming from cultures least valued by society is the ability of

the family to help the student maintain a positive self-image that allows her to withstand rejection and insensitivity of mainstream peers. Occasionally, I have discovered some parents who did not want their children in school at all and did everything in their power to deter the education of their children. But most often, it is not the home culture that causes problems, but a fear on the part of students that elements of that culture will not be accepted in the university environment.

Implications for Teacher Training and Classroom Research

These topics and assignments not only help students mediate between school and home cultures, they provide windows for the teacher into the diversity within each of the cultures that students bring with them. They can serve as a base for ongoing teacher research into the ways in which home and university cultures interact. There simply is no training program for teachers, and can be no definitive research study that will ever account for the realities our students bring with them. Change is constant. Each generation is different. Given the lack of homogeneity in our classes, given the incredible diversity of cultures we are being exposed to, who better to learn from than our students? The culture and language topics I have described here comprise roughly 30–50% of the assignments I give in a ten-week course that meets for two hours twice a week. Some quarters I find myself using more cultural topics than others; it depends on the students. The course is English A, a four-unit course (two units counting toward graduation) with English Department administered, holistically-graded diagnostic, midterm, and final exams. The point is that if one can begin to integrate cultures under these constraints, one should be able to do it anywhere.

The cultural transitions we ask of our students are by no means easy. Cultural transition is ultimately defined by the student, whether she decides to assimilate and leave her culture behind, or attempts to integrate her world view with the academic world view. As composition teachers we are offered a unique opportunity to make these transitions easier for students, and at the same time increase our skills in moving between cultures. Clifford Geertz puts it this way: "The primary question, for any cultural institution anywhere, now that nobody is leaving anybody else alone and isn't ever again going to, is not whether everything is going to come seamlessly together or whether, contrariwise, we are all going to exist sequestered in our separate prejudices. It is whether human beings are going to be able, in Java or Connecticut, through law, anthropology, or anything else, to imagine principled lives they can predictably lead" (234). But we may find, and this has been my experience, that in helping students make cultural transitions, we learn from them how to make transitions ourselves.

Works Cited

Bartholomae, David. "Inventing the University." *When a Writer Can't Write.* Ed. Mike Rose. New York: Guilford, 1985. 134–65.

Bizzell, Patricia. "What Happens When Basic Writers Come to College?" *College Composition and Communication* 37 (October 1986): 294–301.

Bourdieu, Pierre, and Jean-Claude Passeron. *The Inheritors: French Students and Their Relation to Culture.* Chicago: U of Chicago P, 1979.

Cummins, James. "Empowering Minority Students: A Framework for Intervention." *Harvard Educational Review* 56 (February 1986): 18–36.

Fleming, Jacqueline. *Blacks in College: A Comparative Study of Students' Success in Black and in White Institutions.* San Francisco: Jossey-Bass, 1985.

Freire, Paulo. *Pedagogy of the Oppressed.* New York: Continuum, 1982.

———. *The Politics of Education: Culture, Power, and Liberation.* South Hadley, MA: Bergin & Garvey, 1985.

Geertz, Clifford. *Local Knowledge.* New York: Basic Books, 1983.

Groden, Suzy, Eleanor Kutz, and Vivian Zamel. "Students as Ethnographers: Investigating Language Use as a Way to Learn Language." *The Writing Instructor* 6 (Spring-Summer 1987): 132–40.

Heath, Shirley Brice. *Ways with Words: Language, Life, and Work in Communities and Classrooms.* New York: Cambridge UP, 1983.

Holzman, Michael. "The Social Context of Literacy Education." *College English* 48 (January 1986): 27–33.

Mitchell, Jacquelyn. "Reflections of a Black Social Scientist: Some Struggles, Some Doubts, Some Hopes." *Harvard Educational Review* 52 (February 1982): 27–44.

Ogbu, John. *The Next Generation: An Ethnography of Education in an Urban Neighborhood.* New York: Academic Press, 1974.

Olson, Carol Booth, ed. *Practical Ideas for Teaching Writing as a Process.* Sacramento: California State Department of Education, 1986.

Petrie, Loretta. "Pulling Together the Multicultural Composition Class." CCCC Convention, New York, March 1986.

Philips, Susan Urmston. *The Invisible Culture: Communication in the Classroom and Community on the Warm Springs Indian Reservation.* New York: Longman, 1983.

The Puente Project: Building Bridges. Berkeley: Bay Area Writing Project, 1985.

Rodriguez, Richard. *Hunger of Memory.* Boston: Bantam Books, 1982.

Steinberg, Stephen. *The Ethnic Myth: Race, Ethnicity, and Class in America.* New York: Atheneum, 1981.

Wauters, Joan. "Non-Confrontational Critiquing Pairs: An Alternative to Verbal Peer Response Groups." *The Writing Instructor* 7 (Spring/Summer 1988): 156–66.

6

Resisting Assimilation[1]
Academic Discourse in the Writing Classroom

Caroline Pari

Editors' Note: In this chapter, Caroline Pari begins with a personal examination of her assimilation in the academy that nearly erased her working-class, Italian American identity. In the second part of this essay she shows how this examination led to experiments with a critical pedagogy that encourages students to examine and to resist their assimilation processes. She details her experience teaching at both four-year and two-year campuses at the City University of New York, where she developed writing projects centered on the students' assimilation experiences. Like Houston Baker's teaching (see Chapter 7), her pedagogy was unexpectedly transformed by her students (at a community college) who asserted their own perceptions of race and class against the ones she presented.

From "Italian American" to "American"

In the 1920s, my grandparents came to New York City from two regions in Southern Italy, Calabria and Sicily, along with thousands of others like them, searching for a better life. Settling in America, they started forgetting their dialects because their parents emphasized speaking English more than anything. Arriving here as a child, my maternal grandmother was able to master the new language and took great pride in her flawless, accentless English, the way she had erased clues to her Sicilian origin. But my paternal grandmother, who arrived as an adult, never quite attained "perfect" English; she spoke broken English, which I often laughed at as a child. I was embarrassed to hear her half-finished words and extra vowels, like when she asked for the "newsapape" every morning when she came from her apartment next door. Did these half-

English/half-Calabrian words reflect her unspoken ambivalence toward her assimilation process? Later on, when my grandparents had their own kids, which
included my own mom and dad, they did not teach their dialects to them. The
dialects managed to survive between the two sets of grandparents as a secret
language when they wanted to talk past the kids. These dialects also survived
in the predominantly working-class, Italian American community in which my
family lived. Though I sometimes laughed at my grandma's speech, eventually
I loved to hear these words, being proud of my cultural heritage, and tied to
these streets. So, as I grew up, I desperately wanted to know my grandparents'
Italian, but I heard too little of it to pick up more than a few Sicilian phrases
and expressions, like calling my aunt who lived with us *beda maggia* (*bella
madre:* "beautiful mother"). I wanted more.

As a teenager in the 1980s, when I entered John Adams High School in
Ozone Park, Queens, I decided to study Italian for my language requirement. I
eagerly anticipated learning the language of my ancestors, to see what the words
I heard looked like. But when I entered room 109, I didn't find the Sicilian or
Calabrian dialects there. Instead, the teacher, Mr. Ippolito, began instructing us
in the official dialect, Standard Italian, the "proper" form.

Mr. Ippolito, one of the few gems at Adams, was a kind and gentle man in
his fifties whose gray hair glistened under the fluorescent lights and whose
warm smile welcomed students. He was fiercely devoted to transmitting Italian
language and culture to his mostly Italian American students who all adored
him. In three years with Mr. Ippolito, I completed some of my most meaningful schoolwork. I believed him when he said that Italy desperately needed to
unify its dialects into a standard language because people could not communicate with each other. For example, he claimed that Italians from Rome do not
understand Sicilians, so Standard Italian was needed for wider communication.
But he didn't tell us how poorly Sicilians were treated by Northern Italians who
stereotyped them as ignorant and impoverished. I remember how confused I
was, learning that all those Sicilian expressions and words from home were
"wrong." I started to think of my home dialect as a low-status, regional speech
needing translation into "correct" Italian, a language that was clearly more
prestigious and apparently more useful. So, I changed the Sicilian *b*s into the
Standard Italian *p*s, the *g*s into *c*s, and the *r*s into *d*s: *Gabeesch?* was really
Capisce? (Do you understand?); *Geesta ga?* was really *Questa che?* (What's
that?); the expletive *Marrone mia* was *Madonna mia,* and so on. What I really
learned then, was that of the many dialects of a language, one is prestigiously
elevated to the elite standard, while other forms are targets of correction. Proper
speech was learned at school and could be written or spoken, whereas the "dialects" were used at home and could not even be represented orthographically. I
also learned that in order to do well in school, I literally had to erase a dialect
with which I was familiar and now ashamed of.

Years later, I encountered a similar conflict between standard usage and
nonstandard dialect in graduate school, where I first felt really out of place in
the academy. While an undergraduate at Queens College (CUNY), I was in a

familiar environment, speaking the same way as my classmates, some of whom
were also from John Adams, but in the doctoral program at the CUNY Grad
School, I encountered class differences. I felt the distinctive shame of being
marked "working-class" in an upper-class world because of my urban ethnic
accent and speech. In the late eighties, the CUNY Ph.D. program in English
was anachronistically stuffy, not something you'd expect from CUNY, given its
working-class constituency. The program was in national competition for top
billing among graduate schools. Today, the program's growing diversity has
helped tone down its exclusive club atmosphere. But, when I first went to the
Grad Center, I felt like I was entering, rather trespassing, a foreign world. I
heard the sounds of a new language, strange words, unheard-of theories, and
eagerly wanted to understand and speak them, so that I could join the club. The
way I spoke English was considered non-Standard, much like Sicilian was non-
Standard Italian. Fellow students frequently asked me, "What?" when I spoke
because my non-elite dialect left *r*s off the end of words like *huh* (her). And,
although I spoke quite loudly, I also spoke too fast, so that my words slurred. I
mispronounced words often. I felt much more comfortable using words like
asshole or *fuck* than I did speaking this sterile, unflavored language. But, in
being comfortable, I *sounded* dumb. It did not help either that I was a recent
college grad attending classes with recent M.A.s and published authors. Over-
night I became a "basic writer," even though I had earned As for my writing in
college. Feeling out of place with my non-elite habits, speech, and writing, I
soon realized that I was not prepared for graduate work, but I was determined
to succeed.

　Since I wanted to earn a Ph.D. and teach in a college, I had to learn elite
usage and manners in graduate school, a shift that dramatically marks my assimilation process. Like the nineteenth-century naturalist Emile Zola, who
shocked his contemporaries by using working-class language in his novels, I
seemed to offend my professors with usage errors, such as contractions, split
infinitives, made-up words, and unclear referents. In addition, I had many
rhetorical errors, such as weak thesis statements (I didn't like arguing only one
point—and still don't), heavy reliance on plot summary (I didn't really know
how to make my point), and unsophisticated theory (actually, I made few references to scholars); I had a preference for narrative, personal experience, and
subjectivity. The words of literary critics would be sprinkled throughout my
essays only for flavor. I consciously imitated literary "academic discourse" as
I struggled to find my own language. Because I wanted to be a good student, I
was complicit in assimilating the language of the academy, doing what many
upwardly mobile working-class people do. According to Pat Belanoff (1990),
studies show that "working-class speakers are likely to adjust their language toward the formal more radically than other language users" (67). But there is a
price to pay for this adjustment.

　In my hunger to master a prestigious academic language, one that I did
not have to be ashamed of and that erased markers of my ethnicity and class, I
eventually let go of both my Italian and my "New Yawk" English in favor of

academic English. Further forgetting took place when I chose to fulfill a requirement with German, the language of "high" academics; I had even lived in Germany during an intensive summer program. I discovered there was little place for Standard Italian in British literature, except for the Romantic poets' patronizing fascination with Italian culture and the pre-Raphaelite devotion to it, just as there was no place for a working-class idiom. Italian, like my "New Yawk tawk," was devalued in this part of the academy and of little use to my study of nineteenth-century British literature. As I studied German, and as my Italian disappeared along with my colorful, urban English, I was in a long-term process of academic assimilation, leaving my class and ethnicity behind to become a full-blooded American scholar. But now I think it's sad that I was able to speak German fluently and Italian only in bits and pieces, and that I visited Germany twice in my life, for as long as six weeks one time, but have never been to Sicily. By studying for a Ph.D., I was furthering the assimilation process that began with my Italian grandparents who insisted their children speak only English. But, before I lost it all, I set off on a backward journey to reclaim my class and ethnic language. One path of recovery involved testing a writing pedagogy that critically challenges deculturation and assimilation, which I experimented with and will discuss shortly. Another landmark in this road to recovery was my encounter with Richard Gambino's *Blood of My Blood: The Dilemma of the Italian-Americans* (1974), one of the texts responsible for halting my rapidly progressing assimilation in its tracks.

From "American" to "Italian American"

I came across Gambino's book while doing a research project on ethnicity and race for a cultural studies course. In a conference about the project with my professor, he had the audacity to suggest I study Italian Americans. I must have looked puzzled because he then told me I had the map of Italy on my face. Shocked and embarrassed, I thought, "He can tell?" I mean, no one had ever said such a thing to me. You see, while assimilating in graduate school I had become so distant from my Italian roots that they seemed invisible to me. But my professor suddenly reminded me that I could not erase some visible signs of my Mediterranean identity: thick, wavy, brown-black hair and eyebrows; olive skin; large, dark brown eyes; and the dark hairs above my lip that I bleach. I was now being implored not only to reveal my identity, but to study it. I thought I had become what one English professor, Linda Brodkey (1994), believed she could be: the "classless, genderless, raceless scholar" (543), something we are dangerously encouraged to become in the academy. In fact, I was close to becoming what Gambino (1974) warns against: the "transparent" American who has rejected her ethnic identity. I was experiencing what he terms "shame-born-of-confusion." In this condition, Italian American youngsters "resist being identified as Italian American because [they are] only vaguely aware of [their] roots and ashamed of them in [their] confusion." They insist they are "just Americans" (363).[2] At this crucial discovery, through Gambino's book, of how Southern Italian customs, rituals, and values shaped me, I began the process of reclaiming my Italian American and mixed-class identities. Gambino gracefully weaves his personal experience as a son of Italian immigrants with a sociological analysis of the conflicts of assimilation among second- and third-generation Italian Americans. He documents how Italian Americans are affected by their negotiation between *la via vecchia* (the old world) and *la via nuova* (the new world). I needed to read only as far as the first chapter, "The Family System," to realize that I experienced a conflict common to third-generation Italian Americans, for whom Gambino tells us "it is impossible to be untouched, if not determined, by *la via vecchia*" (5). Old world customs place the family at the center of one's identity. I began to understand typical immigrant conflicts I had with my parents' traditional, Sicilian ways, between their restricted gender roles and my American desires for female independence and intellectual fulfillment.

According to Gambino, this "tortured" compromise between the old and the new leaves many Italian Americans "permanently in lower middle-class America." Indeed, one of the many conflicts second- and third-generation Italians face is between Italian and American work ethics. For Italian Americans, Gambino tells us, "One labors for the positive well-being of those one loves on earth, one's family. To succeed in this is a source of great pride. And the closer the relation between the work and the family, the more assured of its success" (38). Due to their family-based, rather than self-centered work ethic, Italians move out of the working class slowly, as Gambino documents.

In my family, this non-elite, family-centered work ethic may help explain why no one has entered the corporate world, despite the B.A.s in Business both my father and older brother earned. It may explain why my father didn't make much money selling insurance and kept his office in our apartment. He struggled all his life with the stress of being the sole provider for a large, Italian American family while not feeling successful by American standards. In addition, the family-based work ethic may explain why no one in my family seems to understand my self-absorbed academic "work," because they don't see what I produce or its connection and value to the family; yet they somehow acknowledge that I have increased my family's status with my Ph.D. To confess, the reasons I chose to be a college professor are connected to this Italian, family-based work ethic and to being a woman—I wanted to do meaningful work that could give me a flexible schedule so that I could eventually devote myself to raising my own family. Academic women of other ethnicities may find this reason familiar, but I think it's predominant for me. Obviously other privileges of this profession attracted me to it—gaining a public voice, intellectual activity and writing, feminism, teaching, helping others, and becoming middle class—but I am still drawn into family-centered decision making typical of my Italian roots. In short, my Italian family made me uncomfortable with the solitude of intellectual life reported by Linda Brodkey (1994) who said that she exchanged the company of her family in the kitchen for the company of her books in her office.

What Class Am I?

Class is always complicated by ethnicity, gender, and other identities. Although I see my roots as working class, my parents have always said we were middle class. Because her father was a lawyer, dabbled in real estate, and owned land, and her three sisters graduated college, my mother tells me that her family is middle class. But her two brothers entered the trades of plumbing and tailoring. My mother's learning disabilities prevented her from finishing college, although she is impressively self-educated, even "expert" in business and investment ideas, medical diagnoses, and nutrition, knowledge she has gained from life experience and from reading, watching TV, and listening to the radio. Two of her sisters worked as high school teachers, while a third one earned a Ph.D. and became a school psychologist. They attracted and married professional men. My uncles also married well. Education, marriage, and hard work were the ways my mother's side of the family assimilated into American culture and into a middle-class identity.

My father's family, however, is lower down the class ladder, closer to working class. His parents were not formally educated. His father was a shoe-maker with his own shop on 125th Street in Harlem from 1920 until the late 1950s. His sister worked as a secretary, married at twenty-three, and worked later in life as a bank teller. My father, encouraged by his mother to get "educated" (read: "assimilated") got a higher degree from Baruch College, CUNY, and worked in retail for some time before becoming a self-employed insurance agent with a marginal income similar to his self-employed cobbler father.

I have thus inherited an uncertainty about my class position. I wonder if we have denied our modest roots in our determination to be middle-class. There are so many class contradictions in my mother's family and in our own that make us part of several classes. While my parents always rented an apartment, they bought property later in life; while my father was self-employed, with an income near the poverty level that qualified us for free school lunches, my parents were able to save up quite a nest egg and invest in stocks; while his commission-based salary was low and erratic, he didn't have to punch a clock or deal with a boss; while we don't speak proper English all the time, we are educated. Our low income also put middle-class consumerism out of our reach, like new cars, fancy restaurants, elite education, European vacations, and a large suburban home.

However, my family's social position becomes much clearer to me when I look at it in terms of ethnic assimilation and Italian American values. According to Gambino (1974), Italians are one ethnic group that lives below its means, which would explain our shabby apartment and clothes, and hidden wealth. My parents' two families came to America to better themselves, and they did. As a result of this class-crossing union during a time of heightened pro-American assimilation values, we lost not only our mother tongue, but also a distinct class identity in one generation. My Italian immigrant families, like all immigrants, were supposed to escape their peasant class in their quest for economic stability, yet I feel a sense of regret and loss when Italian is no longer spoken, Italian customs are no longer followed, and Italian foods are no longer served. While I can attribute many of my beliefs, much of my behavior, and my speech to my class position, I learned from Gambino that much of what makes me tick can be explained by my ethnicity, by *la via vecchia*. As my experience shows, class is informed by ethnicity, gender, family, occupation, region, and even neighborhood. By graduate school, I was losing a complex identity I'm only now understanding. The price of academic assimilation made me ask how to pay less and save more.

A Critical Pedagogy Challenging Assimilation

This piecing together of my life, reuniting with my Italian heritage, and disrupting an assimilation process that threatened to dilute my very sense of being, has profoundly influenced my pedagogy. I know that I would not have been so anxious to assimilate by dismissing my Italian American identity if I had been asked to write about it earlier in school or college. My students at CUNY, who are predominantly immigrant and working class, perhaps have these same special needs to hold on to their ethnic identities in the face of assimilation.

While finishing my Ph.D., I taught basic writing, ESL, freshman comp, and literature for seven years as a part-timer at Baruch College, a four-year CUNY school. Now, I teach writing as a full-time assistant professor at Borough of Manhattan Community College (BMCC), a two-year CUNY unit where approximately 45 percent of the students are African American, 30 percent are Hispanic, 15 percent are from other ethnic groups, 10 percent are Asian, and about 90 percent report having an income of less than fifteen thousand dollars, which is below the federal poverty line.[3] Over these years I have been experimenting with a critical pedagogy that centers on students' cultural and class identities in terms of assimilation.

With some understanding of CUNY's student population, I set out to design a writing course that would reflect their lives, languages, interests, and conflicts, a connection that John Dewey ([1916] 1966), and more recently Paulo Freire ([1970] 1990), argued as key to reflective learning. Dewey insisted that a student's school experience must be connected to his or her outside world experience. Doing so would avoid limiting a student's knowledge to a "teacher's requirements" or to a prepackaged body of information that reduces knowledge to facts and makes learning mechanistic. Instead, Dewey defined education as a *process* of meaning making. Similarly, Freire's problem-posing pedagogy uses "generative themes" to integrate learners' languages and worldviews.

Further, my own disturbing experience, reflecting some of the assimilation conflicts reported by Keith Gilyard (1991), Mike Rose (1990), Min-zhan Lu (1987), Victor Villanueva (1993), and Pat Belanoff (1990), also influenced my pedagogy. The difficulty minority students have in mastering Standard English persuades me that the acquisition of dominant literacy must coincide with a recognition of our students' other languages. We must open the space of the classroom to include "home" dialects and should avoid devaluing students' ethnic or racial heritages by "correcting" them, if we want students to master the standard form.

As a pedagogical practice, I ask my working-class and my immigrant students to reflect critically on their cultural conflicts and to examine their class and ethnic identities. My classroom is a place where students use multiple discourses to ensure their active participation, where they need not silence the languages they bring to class by adopting a discourse that erases their class and ethnicity. I invite my students to use the languages and knowledge they already have and value, because a fundamental assumption of sociolinguistics is that one's primary language is an essential part of one's identity. I do not believe the sole aim of basic writing and freshman composition courses should be to "initiate" students into academic discourse, though Standard English should still be taught.[4] But, as Peter Elbow (1991) puts it, we should teach "something else" in addition to academic discourse in our composition courses.[5] We need "something else" because there is not just one academic discourse, but many versions of it, and it is a language form that masks power relations, Elbow reminds us. Further, we can accomplish the general goals of academic discourse—giving reasons and evidence while acknowledging one's interest and identity—with nonacademic discourse. In fact, Elbow claims, "Students can do academic work even in street language" (149). He powerfully argues that there is room in our classrooms for our students' languages. But I am also aware that many of my students want to learn Standard English while it's still considered the high-status language of power and upward mobility. However, I do want them to examine their "choices," American cultural values, and the effects of assimilation.

Outside college, many of my students are currently engaged in even higher-profile assimilation, both that of "Americanization" and becoming "middle class." Immigrants are literally "uprooted" from a familiar place, planting themselves in a new land. While attending college they are temporarily dislocated from their class positions, languages, belief systems, and communities, as are many native working-class students. Assimilation takes many different forms such as adopting new dress, food, gestures, manners, religion, attitudes toward work and money, consumerism, and the acquisition of Standard English. This is hardly a uniform process. Students assimilate to varying degrees and at varying speeds. Some are so caught up with becoming American that they disassociate abruptly from their home cultures and languages. Others reject American culture and refuse to speak English outside of class. African Americans and other ethnic groups without the option of "becoming white," on the other hand, experience "oppositional conflict," a cultural theory developed by John Ogbu (1974, 1987), and adapted to basic writing by Tom Fox, which helps explain these students' linguistic difficulties with standard usage (see

Chapter 4). I agree with their notion that assimilation conflicts are key to understanding my students' linguistic, social, and classroom experiences.

Because I oppose cultural erasure, I want to open up a path of critical assimilation that includes resistance. One way to do this is to confront our own assumptions about our students' desires to assimilate at any cost. For example, Jane Nagle, a twelfth-grade English teacher (see Chapter 9), cautions against assuming that all working-class students want to join the middle class: "If the price for school literacy, for most working-class students, is to deny or at least not express working-class values, then it would seem that educators need to examine closely their attitudes about social class. . . . I have always believed that the working class was something everyone needed and wanted to leave. My students . . . have awakened me to the fact that the working class is exactly where most of them want to be. My assumption that education was a way out of working-class status was elitist." In her courageous self-analysis of how her lectures and responses to students' journals were biased against their working-class values, Nagle claims that much of what goes on in our classrooms is shaped by our class identity.

In an effort to make assimilation visible, as Nagle does, I encourage students in my writing classes to describe how they were complicit with, confused by, or resistant to assimilation into American culture. The theme of assimilation also enables students to examine the interactions between different ethnic and racial groups in America. I ask students to look at their lives as I am looking at my own, to discover what values, beliefs, or traditions that shaped them are now under collegiate pressure to retreat.

Writing Back to Our Roots

In my early teaching years at Baruch, my freshman composition students would complete a semester-long research project containing four sections: (1) autobiography and self-identity; (2) research on one's family history; (3) cultural history; (4) American identity, being an American, assimilation. This writing project was multigeneric, combining autobiography with expository writing and research. Each month students would submit five- to ten-page drafts of one of the four sections for feedback from classmates and me. At the end of the semester, each would submit the entire collection as a four-part essay for a final grade. The excerpts below come from these final versions. While drafting these papers throughout the semester, students read essays and stories relevant to each section of the project: about ethnic groups, about what it means to be American (early "melting pot" theories), about diverse American families, and about the scope of American culture. At first I compiled my own collection of articles, but then found several readers that worked remarkably well for this focus on assimilation in America: Gary Colombo's *Rereading America* (Colombo, Cullen, and Lisle 1989), Sandra Mano and Barbara Rico's *American Mosaic* (1991), and Diana George and John Trimbur's *Reading Culture* (1992).

While the project seemed to favor the large portion of immigrant students, native-born students could also complete the research with some adaptation. I came to realize during this project that New York's diversity meant we had students who were here on temporary visas, or were resident aliens, or were not immigrants at all, groups I had not accounted for at first. What follows is a report of what I discovered during my experiment with the assimilation theme for writing assignments. In this study of assimilation, you will hear mostly from my students. I conclude with an evaluation of these early experiments before turning to more recent coursework.

Just American?

During these early experiments, I discovered that student difficulty in writing about their ethnic or racial groups related to the degree of assimilation they had undergone. The more assimilated a student seemed to be, the more difficult it was to trace back to his or her ethnic/racial identity(ies). Surprisingly, some claimed to be already "just American," a denial of their background that perplexed me because I was busily trying to recover my own roots and trying to teach a critical connection to theirs. For these students, their families may have been living in America for as many as five generations and had lost touch with their roots; or they were black students who may have had roots that extended more deeply into American history. But, even some children of recent immigrants claimed this status of being "just American," announcing their rapidly completed assimilation as behind them. I could see it was not going to be easy to sort out identities and origins.

To my surprise, some students who seemed so certain about their American identity, eventually revealed a profound quest for ethnic or racial identity, having lost theirs in the process of Americanization. My four-part project revealed in them a sense of emptiness from their parents' failure to transmit their ethnicity. But some were able to identify with other cultures, as the complex case of Sarah showed.[6] Growing up with free-spirited, artist parents greatly influenced by the sixties, Sarah, a freshman defiantly majoring in business, discovered that she had been left out of touch with her parents' various ethnicities. As a result, she reported that

> To this day I have difficulty with my specific cultural identity, I am an American, I love to visit the France of my father's birth, I want to be Jewish. The stress on our relationship with my maternal grandparents was on celebrating Hanukkah and Passover, but only in terms of Jewish food. We had Passover Seders with their friends, but many of the symbols were forgotten. . . . I remember visiting my maternal grandparents in Florida one Hanukkah. We played with the dreydahl and tried to win the little chocolate candies symbolic of the holiday. When we went to bed, however, I hung a stocking by my window for Santa Claus and his Christmas offerings. . . . I want to be more reli-

gious than my parents were and I want to bring up my children with a greater sense of cultural identity and roots.

Although Sarah was distinctly aware that she could participate in different cultures by choice, enjoying their symbols, she didn't see this as empowering, but rather as a loss of identity, what Gambino might call the emptiness created by assimilation.

Some students who claimed they were "just American" identified themselves as overassimilated. Note how Dermot, a quiet Irish sophomore, personalized this process:

> Since the British had practically wiped out Gaelic before the Irish came to America and there is no Irish cuisine, I often wonder what it means to be Irish. Although I consider myself Catholic, I do not attend mass and disagree with several teachings of the Church. I keep abreast of the situation in Northern Ireland but I follow all world news closely. I've read Joyce and Yeats, but then I've read Tolstoy and Dostoyevsky too. I enjoy listening to traditional Irish music by the Chieftains and the Clancy Brothers, but I enjoy other ethnic music as well. I am proud of my Irish heritage but perhaps Andrew Greeley is right and we Irish are over-acculturated.

While Dermot still identified himself as Irish, other students claimed to have *no* cultural roots to write about, something we might only expect with homogenous groups of Americanized students outside a multiethnic mecca like New York City. I suspected this ethnic denial was a form of resistance to the actual project. Was I being too nosy, even though I revealed my own roots in class? However, I also considered this resistance to indicate the extent to which students felt assimilated enough to have disassociated from a specific heritage, like I had. These students seemed to be denying their ethnic ties, much the same as working-class students might deny their class roots, because of the lower prestige of such identities. In fact, as I discuss later, my working-class students tended to avoid identifying themselves as working class for this same reason.

For other students not in denial of their roots, feeling torn by diverging cultural experiences, assimilation meant a loss of ethnic identity. Tina, a self-identified "Nuyorican," for example, explained that she felt

> like a Puerto Rican in America because, among other things, I can read, write, and speak some Spanish and because my family eats Spanish food. But I don't feel like a Puerto Rican in Puerto Rico because again, among other things, I can't speak Spanish fluently. I don't know much about the country itself and I don't recognize half the foods they serve. So you see, I don't consider myself a true Puerto Rican but I don't consider myself a true "American" either. To my surprise, however, according to [the U. S. Bureau of the Census], I am a Puerto Rican.

According to her research, the Census defines a Puerto Rican as an individual whose birthplace is in Puerto Rico, a territory of the United States, or who has one parent who was born there, and includes even grandchildren of migrants. Of course, Puerto Ricans are not typical immigrants since they are U. S. citizens, but they do possess a distinct ethnic identity.

Tina's confusion about her ethnic identity shows she was not exactly home in either half of her hyphenated identity, and not exactly sure about fitting into assimilation models. She surrounded the word "American" with quotation marks as if to distance herself from this identity, but then she was surprised by her research efforts to be defined as a Puerto Rican. Although she did not explicitly contest the Census Bureau, she questioned whether the term applied to herself. As she sorted out the markers for her separate American and Puerto Rican identities, she revealed the ways in which she saw herself and how others saw her, creating what Mary Louise Pratt (1991) calls an "autoethnographic text," which is a self-description that engages dominant representations of subordinate groups.

Assimilation into mainstream America represents a desire for the privileges and power that is accorded affluent whites. The "whiteness" of Irish Americans is an interesting case in point, as Roediger (1991) tells us. Irish Americans, once viewed as close to blacks because of their unskilled, manual labor and low-status national origins (a colonized people), gradually distanced themselves from blacks as they moved toward a white identity when dominant groups sought to increase the "white" vote in the mid 1800s. Racism was the vehicle by which the Irish could eliminate job competition from blacks and gain for themselves social prestige as well as some political power. Because race in America is enormously complex and frequently emerging in my New York City classroom, it's important to examine assimilation among my apparently white as well as my apparently black students.

"Just (Black) American"

During my early experiments with the assimilation theme in the four-part, semester-long writing and research project, I discovered that my black students, like white ethnics in class, also identified themselves as "just American," but for different reasons. Obviously, the native-born black students could not identify with an "Ellis Island" immigrant model in their past because their ancestry leads back to slavery, or involuntary immigration. Some defined themselves as "American," using the term "Black American"; others emphasized their racial identity with the term "black." Others took a different approach by using the term "African American." The difference in the usage of the terms of identity corresponded to the students' conception of their cultural history. For example, the students who identified themselves as "African Americans" focused their research on Africa, whereas those who called themselves "blacks" traced their progress as a race from slavery until the present, writing mostly about the Civil

Rights Movement. As one student wrote: "As a black, my cultural history can be traced by the crisis of race relations."

The majority of my black students who were recent immigrants from Nigeria, Kenya, Jamaica, Haiti, Guyana, Cuba, Barbados, Trinidad, and Antigua discussed their cultural identity in terms of their ongoing assimilation in America. John, the son of immigrants, described the complexities of his black identity in America:

> Even though I am American, my parents always told me that I am not a "Yankee Boy." This has always stayed in my head. I guess they don't want me to get Americanized. . . . Both of my parents immigrated from the Caribbean and speak English with a distinct accent. . . . My mother is from Grenada and my father was born in Grenada but moved to Trinidad at the age of ten. . . . My culture will stay with me because of the way I was raised and the way I live. The little things like the food I eat, the people I live with and the music I listen to will keep my culture going.

John was oriented by his parents to cling to his Caribbean culture. He seemed to resist assimilation, although he was born in America. I learned from John and others like him that race introduces special complexities to the assimilation scheme. For example, my black immigrant students will tell my black American students that they are "black," not "African American," because they are not from Africa. However, my black students feel that "black" does not represent the color of their skin, which is brown, or beige, and so on. These students are suggesting the social construction of race, without using this academic concept. I've come to understand that race is very real in my students' lives, that racial tension dominates their lives.

The writings of students of color at Baruch also taught me that their experiences in America and the ways they describe those experiences are heterogenous. While some reflected the immigrant life, or enacted resistance to dominant cultural values, others attached themselves to a high-status American identity. But what stands out in all the student writings of this earlier teaching period are conflicting claims by students who were supposedly "already assimilated" Americans, claims that echoed eerily in my ears as a self-identified *Italian* American. I would be reminded of these claims several years later at BMCC when I began asking working-class students about their social class identity only to be told that they were "just middle class."

These students' assimilation stories also indicated to me that an archaic model such as the "melting pot" was problematic because it assumes that immigrants must exchange their cultural identities, especially their languages, traditions, and foods, for American ones. Such a model does not question assimilation. It also obscures complex variations in degrees of, attitudes toward, and resistance to assimilation, which my students' writings disclose. Students usually do not feel they have a new identity in America, nor do they feel they need to give up their culture. My students' writings and conversations revealed a need to redefine how we describe assimilation and to question whether we should expect assimilation at all.

At the time I was teaching freshman composition and basic writing courses in the early 1990s at Baruch, the outdated model seemed to be the only one available to me. Since then, scholars in our field have taken the lead in teaching and composing "literacy narratives" that uncover the complexities of assimilation. Keith Gilyard (1991), for example, describes the profound psychological and sociolinguistic conflicts of a working-class, African American who succeeded academically but nearly split at the seams under the enormous pressure of fitting in with white middle-class mainstream culture. Pat Belanoff (1990) and Linda Brodkey (1994), among others, reveal the particular problems working-class women face in the academy adjusting to a patriarchal, middle-class language style. Their reported struggles raise the question of whether assimilation entails erasure of one's roots, as Richard Rodriguez (1982) poignantly insisted. These critical reflections on academic assimilation are more useful than the bland, faceless sociological models of assimilation I had been using during my early teaching years at Baruch College such as Milton Gordon's (1964) *Assimilation in American Life.*

Updating the Experiment: Resisting Assimilation

My introduction of the assimilation theme encountered problems that helped me to adjust the projects. Recently, while teaching full time at BMCC, and taking on basic writing courses that do not require "the research paper," I adapted the four-part, semester-long personal history project with some surprising results. In my basic writing courses, students write essays on their cultural identity guided by a handout like the following:

Cultural Identity

For this essay, you will describe your cultural identity. Include details about your cultural background such as language, religion, history, geography, music, art literature, sports, beliefs and values, traditions, holidays, rituals, clothing and style, and so on. Here are some questions to guide you. You do *not* have to answer all of them.

(1) What term would you use to describe America: mosaic, melting pot, tossed salad, or something else? Explain what the term or symbol means to you and why you would use it.

(2) Explain how you feel about being born, raised, or an immigrant in America. Are you able to retain much of your cultural identity or have you given something up?

(3) Do you have a split identity? Do you feel confused about your identity?

(4) How does your cultural group fit in with the larger American society? How is it excluded from it?

(5) What is the most important part of your culture?

(6) How important is cultural identity in America?

In these BMCC essays, students showed an increased resistance to assimilation not evident in the earlier project at the more elite Baruch. This resistance is most obvious with Maria, who wrote parts of her cultural identity essay in Spanish and then translated for me. In response to the questions on the handout (above), she describes *dos diferente mundos* (two different worlds) that she comes from as a child of Dominican and Cuban parents. And she expresses resistance to being Americanized: "Pero la conciencia no me permitirá hacer gringa. (But my conscience wouldn't let me be an American)." Not only does this student reveal the delicate complexities of cultural identity, but she demonstrates how central language became to her identity, as it did to mine:

> The first language I learned was *español* (Spanish). While I was growing up my *español* started to fade away. After I got to High School, I made a decision that *español* was what I needed to relearn. Now I speak both *español* and English, but when I'm with my friends, I try to even eliminate English totally.

As she illustrates, and as Richard Rodriguez (1982) confirms, assimilation can mean the loss of one's native language but, more important, this loss can be consciously halted, as Maria's was, and as mine was while in graduate school. Further, Maria reported that she carefully chose when and where to speak English. Some critics of bilingual education see Spanish-speakers as resistant to, or worse, incapable of, learning English, yet although this student spoke English beautifully, there were times when she did not want to speak it, a response possibly explained by Ogbu's (1974, 1987) theory of oppositional conflict. Similarly, recalling Jane Nagle's discovery that her students were content with their working-class life, such resistance as Maria's could be found in working-class students who refuse to speak "proper" English or to adapt to white middle-class customs. My lower-income community college students apparently had more pride of the subordinate than did the more upwardly mobile students I taught at Baruch, a four-year school.

Moreover, in their essays on their cultural identity, the BMCC basic writing students tended to critique the established assimilation models, often rejecting them in favor of others, just as my previous students had. Students generally preferred their own metaphors, symbols, or images for assimilation in American society. Urania Muniz wrote:

> "Melting Pot" the way I understood it doesn't make sense anymore. "Mosaic" and "Tossed Salad," to me, are just other phrases for separation and segregation. I don't agree with the terminology because of its unifying conclusion. Although America has become multi-cultural it does not . . . impose the American culture on its residents. As a result adverse segregation among people has taken place. . . . This unique separation is self imposed and has created what I call clusters. Clusters being people who only acknowledge their own

personal realms and exclude our great countries one significant strength of unity. . . . To be an American, to me, means sharing the American dream. To do what is best for one's own family no matter what culture or heritage is followed, as well as, considering America our own country and give back what we have taken from her, instead of using her as an umbilical cord.

In such complex theorizing, Urania distinguishes herself, not only by her sophisticated writing talent, inventing a unique metaphor of America as birth mother, but by her criticism of cultural diversity's legacy of nationalism, individualism, and segregation. Of Puerto Rican descent, Urania once told her predominantly African American and Hispanic classmates that the identity of "American" could establish some sort of unity to dismantle the separation of ethnic and racial groups. Though she acknowledges her place in American society as a woman of Spanish descent, she confidently claims that she is American, "born, bred till buried." But was she just American? She was a beautiful, bilingual, dark-skinned Puerto Rican, and everyone recognized her as such. She dramatically challenged the class to reconsider what an "American" was, expanding its meaning to include herself. She was at home with both halves of her hyphenated identity, proclaiming allegiance to both America and Puerto Rico. The critical question, though, remains: Can class, race, and gender inequities be wished away so easily? If so, BMCC would be less populated by low-income female students of color and Harvard would be less white.

More Experiments: Class Identity and Race

Assimilation in America implies that one becomes middle class, and as Lynn Bloom (1996) argues, freshman composition has a long history of serving this aim. Yet, like the field of composition itself, assimilation studies usually pay little attention to class identity. It is often assumed that certain ethnic and racial groups want to adopt white, middle-class values, lifestyles, and language, and that this process will be rewarded. To question class identity in my own ethnic American life and in the lives of my students, I began emphasizing social class in my basic writing courses along with race and gender, with some peculiar results.

Midway through my first semester at BMCC (in the fall of 1996), after students had written about their cultural identity, I turned their attention to social class in America, hoping to emphasize its virtual invisibility in popular discourse and to raise critical consciousness. I also wanted to show how we cannot separate race, class, and gender. Though each is emphasized separately (and artificially), students are asked to consider how the three issues interact through the writing assignment below. I will discuss what happened in two different sections of basic writing during the Fall 1996 semester at BMCC when "class" was an explicit part of my writing curriculum, and then what happened in Spring 1997 when it was not.

To elicit writing on the tough issue of class that first semester, I chose the following prompt:

> For this essay, you will revise one of your previous essays by adding a discussion of class identity. Depending upon your choices, your entire essay may change or you may just have to add a paragraph or two.
>
> Review all your essays. Decide upon one that is appropriate for a discussion of class. You may include a discussion of your class identity. Or you may want to just discuss class differences that you've encountered in school, work, or in your community.

Just before giving the prompt, I introduced the topic of social class by inviting and recording students' ideas about our class system, which I examine shortly below. I wanted this exercise grounded in their conceptions of class differences, their myths and realities. I also asked my students to answer a questionnaire, borrowed from *Radical Teacher* (Smulyan 1995), about their parents' occupations and values, the socioeconomic nature of their family and larger community, and feelings about their class background. This questionnaire referred to familiar terms we defined together: working class, lower/middle/upper middle class, lower/middle/upper upper class, and ruling class. At the students' request, I put these terms on the blackboard, after which they described the jobs, incomes, educations, material goods, values, and lifestyles associated with each class group.

To begin, one student did suggest that the minimum wage, which he calculated to be a full-time salary of ten thousand dollars, was a defining characteristic of the working class. Another student said that such people live from check to check, having no savings or money for anything but necessities. Their spontaneous ideas, though on target, ended there, so I intervened with some exercises.

Because the students were having difficulty elaborating their definitions of the working class, I suggested we list some occupations we associate with working-class people and the minimum wage. My wonderfully neat approach introduced only more complex problems because students created apparent contradictions. For example, some of the working-class jobs they listed earned high salaries, not minimum wage, like union and construction jobs. However, I continued to record their responses on the blackboard, so we could analyze their ideas.

At this point, I asked them about the questionnaire. I hoped that their definitions of class would aid their analyses of social class in upcoming readings and essays. But some students seemed equally confused about their class identity. Nicole actually asked about herself, "What am I?" Because she wrote that her parents had only high school diplomas and worked in low-paying manual labor jobs, I explained that this probably indicated she was "working class." She looked disappointed and said, "Oh, I thought I was middle class." She rejected the working-class identity, which seemed to mean a lower status. I knew how she felt, though, having grown up thinking I was middle class. During this awkward discussion, I sensed my students' shame and confusion as they discovered their disfavored working-class identities for the first time and confronted the American myth that everyone is middle class. I felt I was demoralizing them, which was not exactly what I had in mind.

Differentiating people by class seemed unfair or discriminatory to these students, whereas class denial seemed to promote equality and to promise upward mobility through college. Some students thought that *everyone* who worked was working class, not distinguishing between kinds of work, or examining power relations. In their eyes, doctors, secretaries, and meat packers were one homogenous group of "workers." For example, one student, Delia, would later write, "In my community [the Bronx] you have the working class, lower middle class and middle class. But I believe that no class in my community is superior than the other. Most of the people in the working class have just as much as the people in the middle class in terms of material possessions. . . . [I]t really does not matter which class is higher because we all must work to purchase the things we need to survive in life." Delia insisted that class mattered less than the fact that all her neighbors had to work.

Not surprisingly, students were more comfortable with describing the middle class with which they identified: suburban homes, cars, college degrees, professions, savings accounts, material possessions, and nice incomes. Though most of them were the first in their family to attend college and still lived "hand-to-mouth" in the inner city, they used the term *middle class* most frequently in their essays to describe their class status. They seemed to be denying class differences as a means to imagine themselves already middle class or assuredly on their way up.

In contrast to Jane Nagle's white students (see Chapter 9), who clung to their working-class identities in the face of an assimilationist curriculum, the few minority students of mine who identified themselves as working class expressed a desire to escape, to better themselves. They saw education and work as the ways to do this. Gene, one of the handful of students who used the term "working class" explained that "Everyone in the neighborhood belongs to the same class. We all are in the working class. Most of us live from check to check. I call it a working class because we as a whole strive for a better job, a better neighborhood. We want to own our own homes."

While these students paid little attention to class distinctions, students in another of my basic writing sections that semester strongly denied the importance of class identity and stuck to the issue of race. One black male student even blurted out that "there are no classes, there's just black and white." With his encouragement, the students in this section insisted on breaking down social class categories by race, arguing that the middle class is white, and the poorer classes are made up of blacks and minorities. While I agreed that this seemed to be the case in some parts of the country, and certainly how the media represented class differences in its attack on welfare, I said that many of the poor in our country were white. I didn't have the exact figures then, but they would have helped: There are four times more white households than black with incomes under fifteen thousand dollars, the poverty level.[7]

I hoped these basic writing students would identify a working class, a middle class, and a ruling elite or wealthy, as my morning section had, using the same terms on the *Radical Teacher* questionnaire. But, they wanted to start with "the poor." One student insisted there were some who were poorer than the poor, which he called "dirt poor." Because these college students had roofs over their heads, they insisted on a special category for the homeless. Eagerly waiting for the term "working class" to be called out, I asked for other terms, but got "welfare recipients" instead, yet another group they felt should be represented. I obviously never got to focus on the traditional class categories I had in mind. Such are the potentials of student-based pedagogy.

At first I thought these students were simply resisting my introduction to class identity every step of the way, but instead they were actually developing their own "class" discourse. As Paulo Freire would tell us, they were "reading the world" in the words they brought to this problem. When we look closely, we see that they resisted the tripartite conception of class I preferred in favor of a much more experiential scheme that included underrepresented groups like the homeless and welfare recipients, which was also complicated by race and worklessness. Given BMCC's student population, it should not have surprised me that class would be racialized, that white supremacy would supersede corporate supremacy. And given my student-based teaching, I should not have been surprised that my students would take the opportunity to discuss class in their own terms. By frontloading my students' knowledge in this dialogic inquiry, I discovered the way they read "class." Because my view of class was posed as one way to interpret class, I did not "deposit" it into their minds. These students' reevaluations of social class lead me to question the pedagogical usefulness of my own class discourse and to explore further the ways in which my students are constructed by race and ethnicity.

This relationship between racial identity and class proved to be the basis of many students' essay revisions that included discussions of class identity. A majority of the students in both classes chose to revise their essays on their cultural identity to include a discussion of class. Since I gave little direction, allowing them to make their own choices, they found their own ways to link cultural assimilation and class identity. My immigrant students, approximately 38 percent of the class, seemed more aware of class differences because they have been more directly exposed to them in their move to America. For example, Janine's move from a farm in Jamaica to America changed her class status. She identified her family as "poor working class" while in Jamaica and describes her family's leap into the middle class when they immigrated: "Now living in America, my family has progressed a great deal. They went to college and have graduated with many degrees, which has given them an opportunity to make a decent living. Many members of my family can now afford some of the luxury they once wished they had. They have bought many homes and cars, and have traveled all over the world. They are now considered to be living a middle-class lifestyle." Janine's family income was obviously higher than the norm at BMCC. Immigrant students often raise their standard of living by coming here, and with higher incomes, they increase their purchasing power, which brings them closer to the middle class.

Immigrants and children of immigrants were also more aware of the role class plays in assimilation through language. For example, Julio, born in Puerto Rico, recognized that

> The dynamic mix between culture and class results in moral codes and behavioral codes which create interesting interactions within the family. For example, when I speak to my parents, I speak in English or Spanish, depending on the mood I am in. Everyone in my family is bilingual. Being fluid in two or more languages can be one factor used to determine one's class and class assignments bestow privileges which are deeply respected within the family or in society. When I am at school or at work, I usually speak English. . . . But I am aware that the ability to speak two or more languages will ultimately help me in attaining a class status "superior" to most other Latinos.

Julio (yes, a basic writer!) had a sophisticated sense of class and how it functioned in American society. He began his definition with income and education levels, but moved toward larger cultural symbols of prestige like gender and beauty. Moreover, like the students in my second basic writing class, Julio racialized class identity. But most interesting was his belief not only that knowing Standard English contributed to his class status, but that his knowledge of Spanish also had economic value on the job market, in a society where recent immigrants have limited access to English and to good jobs.

Students also linked their class identity to their ethnic or racial identity, even when I did not explicitly raise class issues as in the Spring 1997 semester. When students decided to write letters of protest against New York Governor Pataki's proposed financial aid cutback and tuition hike, immigrant students declared how their assimilation was related to their economic success in America. Liya wrote:

> The reason I came to the United States is to achieve my goal and have a better opportunity for my future. Because of the difficulty in learning a new language, my father who I live with, had to work for a minimum wage in Chinatown where only Chinese is spoken. Not only does he have to support me, but also my mother who is still in China. Therefore, I am attending BMCC, a CUNY school where I can get Financial Aid. That is the only way for me to get the education I want, and when I graduate from college, I can get a good salary job to better our lives. But in the meanwhile, I have a part-time minimum wage job which I have to work twenty-five hours a week, just to help my father out.
>
> Life is not easy for my father and I from the first day that we stepped on this land. Because of our language and culture barriers, we have to struggle to

survive. If you, Governor Pataki, keep on proposing tuition hikes and the cut backs on financial aid, [i]t is not going to be any easier for us. . . . Please take some consideration of us, the minority—new immigrants, do not let us become the losers in this society.

Liya connected her identity as a member an economically deprived group living on minimum wage and depending on financial aid to her status as a new immigrant. Typically, she saw education as a path toward economic success. As this letter and the revised essays showed, these students primarily embraced a language of mobility. They linked their class identity to their aspirations as well as to assimilation and their race/ethnicity. Hence, I am persuaded that issues of class identity are undoubtedly part of questioning assimilation in and out of the academy, because of the mobility goals dominating student attention, reminding me of the fierce assimilation desires my own grandparents brought from Italy. Several generations later, I can question what they didn't.

Working with mostly immigrant students, I found assimilation a topic on which students could produce provocative essays and at the same time express their confusion, frustration, or delight in becoming "Americanized." Because CUNY was founded as a public institution to provide higher education to the city's immigrant and working-class population, its students remain largely of those groups. Cultural, linguistic, or class assimilation, however, are issues that can provoke fruitful discussion and writing at many other institutions and with different student populations. Critiques of assimilation are appropriate for working-class students at elite institutions who struggle with feelings of class displacement. And a pedagogy that places students' languages, cultures, and knowledge at the center of the writing classroom is especially appropriate for blacks, Latinos, and other marginalized groups.

With the growing number of minority and ESL students entering our colleges nationwide, populations already predominant in CUNY, it is our responsibility as faculty to help them succeed. But the question remains, At what cost? Terry Dean asked this same question ten years ago in *College English* (see Chapter 5). Recognizing the difficulties marginalized students felt in college, Dean centered his composition courses on "culturally oriented topics" in order to bridge students' home culture with mainstream school culture and "make these transitions easier for students." As a result of these changes in teaching strategies, Dean hoped we'd learn to transform ourselves, recognizing that as English instructors, we are positioned at the forefront of the political battles over literacy. I join Dean and many other composition scholars who are committed to questioning assimilation and to uncovering its hidden costs.

Though my students may want or *need* to excel at academic discourse, just as I did, I want them to do so while examining their choices and desires, what they gain or lose. My pedagogy, then, can be placed in a recent tradition in composition studies that privileges our students' discourse and encourages them to develop their own language when faced with the struggle with academic discourse. I do not believe that academic success should depend on breaking our students' ties with their communities, nor do I encourage the denial of working-class roots as the price to pay for upward mobility. My complicity in silencing my own working-class, Sicilian culture makes me redouble my efforts to allow my students the right to use and reinvent their own language, to rethink their places in society. I believe, like Richard Gambino, that without a strong sense of our ethnic, racial or class identities, we will feel an inexplicable, inner emptiness.

Notes

1. An earlier version of this essay appears in *Teaching Working Class,* edited by Sherry Linkon. 1999. Amherst: University of Massachusetts Press.

2. In comparison, David Roediger (1994) discusses such groups as "not-yet-white ethnics" who have to win their uneasy assimilation into the white middle-class mainstream.

3. Figures are from Office of Institutional Research and Academic Affairs, *Fact Book: 1995–1996* (Borough of Manhattan Community College, The City University of New York) and one of BMCC's NSF grant applications.

4. The "initiation" theories expressed in David Bartholomae's "Inventing the University" (1985) and Patricia Bizzell's "What Happens When Basic Writers Come to College" (1986), for example, have been challenged in recent years by these very scholars themselves, although forced assimilation continues to dominate curriculum in higher education, as my own experience shows.

5. See Raymond Mazurek's introduction to his chapter in this volume. He refers to Patricia Bizzell's later argument, like Elbow's, that "we should be trying to do something more than teach academic discourse, namely to help students acquire the language using abilities that will be of most use to them as citizens" from her article "Argument, Community, and Knowledge" in *Diversity: A Journal of Multicultural Issues* 1 (1992): 9–23.

6. The names I use are not my students' real names, with the exception of Urania Muniz, who gave her permission to be identified.

7. Sixteen million white, 4 million black, and 2.5 million Hispanic households live at poverty level (U. S. Bureau of the Census 1997, Table 719). For a deeper study of why myths of minorities on welfare are perpetuated in our culture, see Michael Zweig's forthcoming book, *The Working-Class Majority.*

Works Cited

Bartholomae, David. 1985. "Inventing the University." In *When a Writer Can't Write,* edited by Mike Rose, 134–65. New York: Guilford Press.

Belanoff, Pat. 1990. "The Generalized Other and Me: Working Women's Language and the Academy." *Pretext* 11 (1–2): 60–74.

Bizzell, Patricia. 1992. "Argument, Community, and Knowledge." *Diversity: A Journal of Multicultural Issues* 1: 9–23.

————. 1986. "What Happens When Basic Writers Come to College." *College Composition and Communication* 7: 294–301.

Bloom, Lynn Z. 1996. "Freshmen Composition as a Middle-Class Enterprise." *College English* 58 (6): 654–74.

Brodkey, Linda. 1994. "Writing on the Bias." *College English* 5 (5): 527–47.

Colombo, Gary, Robert Cullen, and Bonnie Lisle. 1989. *Rereading America*. 1st ed. New York: Bedford Books.

Dewey, John. [1916] 1966. *Democracy and Education*. Reprint, New York: Free Press.

Elbow, Peter. 1991. "Reflections on Academic Discourse." *College English* 53 (2): 135–55.

Freire, Paulo. [1970] 1990. *Pedagogy of the Oppressed*. Reprint, New York: Continuum.

Gambino, Richard. 1974. *Blood of My Blood: The Dilemma of the Italian-Americans*. Garden City, NY: Anchor Press/Doubleday.

George, Diana, and John Trimbur. 1992. *Reading Culture*. New York: HarperCollins.

Gilyard, Keith. 1991. *Voices of the Self: A Study of Language Competence*. Detroit: Wayne State University Press.

Gordon, Milton. 1964. *Assimilation in American Life*. New York: Oxford University Press.

Lu, Min-zhan. 1987. "From Silence to Words: Writing as Struggle." *College English* 49 (4): 437–48.

Ogbu, John. 1987. "Opportunity Structure, Cultural Boundaries, and Literacy." In *Language, Literacy and Culture,* edited by J. Langer, 149–77. Norwood, NJ: Ablex.

————. 1974. *The New Generation: An Ethnography of Education in an Urban Neighborhood*. New York: Academic Press.

Pratt, Mary Louise. 1991. "Arts of the Contact Zone." In *Profession 1991,* 33–40. New York: MLA.

Rico, Barbara, and Sandra Mano. 1991. *American Mosaic*. New York: Houghton Mifflin.

Rodriguez, Richard. 1982. *Hunger of Memory: The Education of Richard Rodriguez*. Boston: David R. Godine.

Roediger, David. 1994. *Toward the Abolition of Whiteness: Essays on Race, Politics, and Working-Class History*. New York: Verso.

————. 1991. *The Wages of Whiteness: Race and the Making of an American Working Class*. New York: Verso.

Rose, Mike. 1990. *Lives on the Boundary*. New York: Penguin.

Smulyan, Susan. 1995. "Social Class Questionnaire." *Radical Teacher* 49: 19.

U. S. Bureau of the Census. 1997. Statistical Abstract of the United States. Washington, D.C.

Villanueva, Victor. 1993. *Bootstraps: From an American Academic of Color*. Urbana, IL: NCTE.

Zweig, Michael. In press. *The Working-Class Majority*. New York: Oxford University Press.

7

Local Pedagogy; or, How I Redeemed My Spring Semester

Houston Baker

Editors' Note: This chapter was Houston Baker's 1992 Presidential Address to the Modern Language Association in which he poignantly describes the value of critical pedagogy and Freire's work. Baker's enchanting personal narrative takes us from his early teaching years, during which he bored students with brilliant "spirit-of-the-age" lectures, to his later movement away from teaching because of professional commitments. In spring 1992, he rediscovered critical teaching in terms of what he calls "local or situated pedagogy." At that time, he failed to connect his black women's literature seminar to black experience in Philadelphia, the site of his institution. Baker confesses denying one student's demand for his course's "relevance" to campus racism. In his self-analysis of his failed semester, Baker argues favorably for a pedagogy that considers the world beyond the classroom, confronts race, recognizes power structures, and is "designed to transform the world we all locally inhabit."

Long ago, during a time when the East Coast had bitter-cold winters, I made my first journey to a Modern Language Association convention. It was December of 1968. The moment stands out because I am by temperament a southern boy who feels green leaves should be on display twelve months a year and Thanksgiving family football games should be played in short sleeves. But New Haven, the city to which my wife and I moved for a first teaching job, distinguished itself in October of 1968 by turning to ice. Two months later I stood at our apartment window in Branford College and watched December snow cover our pale-blue Valiant desolately parked at 74 High Street. Hence, I chose my warmest and most stylish clothes—which is to say my only winter clothes—

as I prepared to drive to New York for the 1968 convention. (Yes, in those days one could still drive to New York.)

My thrill on arriving at the old Americana Hotel on a Manhattan winter afternoon is as vivid today as it was a quarter century ago. "I've done it," I thought as I pinned on my staid convention badge. Indeed, I had completed a PhD in British Victorian literature, and I had succeeded in securing a respectable academic job—one that would at least pay the heating bills. I felt like a young man righteously inducted into the academic profession. My first four months at Yale had constituted a bone-wearying regimen of three courses per term, arduous normal schools devoted to pedagogy of the Western classics, endless hours in the library preparing for classes, inescapable committee obligations, and formidably long office hours.

I had learned in graduate school how to write critical prose and how to carry myself with professional decorum and collegial good taste. I had not actively prepared myself to teach, however, for I assumed that teaching was merely a technical delivery system for critical knowledge. I thought of the activity as the last relay in an academic olympiad—the final transfer of the fire of the gods by the newly minted PhD. I envisioned the process as one entailing quiet student reverence. I believe I felt that teaching was a calling in the old, pastoral sense—a salvific role into which one slipped as if making a graceful fifty-meter dive. I did not then realize that a calling is, in fact, a profoundly personal and rigorous commitment to a life of integrity and service. With my easygoing and folk-religious notion of a calling, I naturally expected student reverence.

What stunning surprises were in store! During those early months, reverence was in short supply. And most of the classroom illumination came not from me but from students. There was the day, for example, when one of my better students knocked on the office door about an hour before class. He was visibly embarrassed, saying, "Sir, I'm sorry. I mean, I really shouldn't be here."

"Oh, come in, Hugh," I intoned. "Don't worry about my class-preparation time. I'm always happy to see students."

"No, sir, you don't understand," he continued. "I shouldn't be here because the rest of the class is meeting to figure out how to get your course ejected from Branford College. Those spirit-of-the-age lectures are driving us crazy, sir!"

I thanked Hugh for his disloyalty to his classmates and vowed to become, at least, an *interesting* teacher.

With the demanding rhythms of my pedagogical life somewhat out of sync, I longed in December of 1968 for a larger view of the profession—a perspective that could be acquired, I had been told, only by attending the annual Modern Language Association convention. During my two and a half days at the Americana, I saw only one other person of color. He looked in my direction and then seated himself a *long* way away across a half-empty ballroom in which four white men read, seriatim, their thoughts on British Victorian literature.

The other colored man obviously did not want blacks to "segregate themselves." We needed to "mingle."

The most unsettling moment came when I stepped off the hotel elevator on the second morning. I felt a hand on my shoulder and turned to encounter a ruddy-faced giant who drawled, "Excuse me. Do you know where I can find any good Negro boys to teach at my school?" I balked, sputtered, and felt goose bumps rising but managed to respond that he might have more luck if he tried looking for black *men*. His companion guffawed, and I hastened to escape.

After strolling the corridors of the Americana and visiting the neighboring Hilton in 1968, I knew quite well what the profession at large looked like. It was very, very white; very, very male; and distinctively middlebrow in its ceremonial forms. But unbeknownst to me, even as I was seeking a response to a request for Negro boys, Louis Kampf and others, who had placed insurrectionary posters on the walls of the Americana, were calling for revolutionary professional action.

I learned only later of this "alternative convention" and its radically disruptive effect on the normal practice of Modern Language Association business. And, in truth, the full and distressing import of that early MLA experience did not come to me from the profession at large or from a Left-based insurgency within it. No, the excessive whiteness, smug complacency, racial insensitivity, and black mutual avoidance evident at the 1968 convention were elucidated for me not by my colleagues but by my students.

Students laid myriad challenges before me in those beginning days of the late sixties, dramatically altering my life and my life's work. My Victorian literature PhD, the putative privilege of being in the company of "1,000 male leaders" (as the college designated the undergraduates), the invitations to contribute to the *Yale Review*—all these paled before the amazing student interactions that engaged my energies in the late sixties.

For it was an extraordinary community of black graduate and professional students who first suggested to me, during the spring semester of 1969, that as an African American teacher, I had a uniquely important role to play in an institutional setting such as Yale's. And it was a cadre of perspicacious white undergraduates who constantly challenged my New Critical readings of literary and cultural texts and questioned my rationalist, black bourgeois assumptions about the ways of the American world. These students were clearly in touch with dramatic, world-altering forces beyond my life and academic ken and were intent on carrying me, the academy, their parents, and, if permitted, all America into a future that looked nothing like either Branford College or the Americana Hotel in the winter of 1968.

I thus came to regard the classroom—as did many of us who entered the academy during the late sixties—as a locale not for spirit-of-the-age lectures but for critically reading one's self and the world with the goal of changing both. I came, suddenly and with great joy, to think of teaching as a calling in a profoundly political and socially engaged sense. During class deliberations, my students and I almost always expected the world of New Haven, of America, and of an embattled global order to be too much with us—whether in the form of Black Panther rallies on the New Haven green, antiwar demonstrations in the nation's capital, or committed feminist organizing begun in earnest by the brilliant women who belonged to Yale's entering class of 1969.

It is simple truth to say that students taught me to stop defining my black skin as an accident of birth or as a discomforting magnet for affirmative action offers. They taught me that skin is, in fact, what the West Indian novelist George Lamming metaphorically claims it is—a castle of one's own. To learn to inhabit the castle of my skin was to educate myself in the repertoire and resources of African life in America. To be inside this castle, I had to make myself adept in the economics, aesthetics, history, and, yes, the often bizarre politics of essential difference and semiotic *différance* in the New World.

Through pedagogy, then—through the life of everyday teaching—I personally departed the old world of my British Victorian literary studies and began to educate myself as a black student and teacher of the Americas comprehensively defined. I did not so much abandon the Victorian world, I think, as *endorse*—out of passion and a felt sense of the scarcity of black personnel in my new field—the world of Afro-American literary and cultural studies. One goal of my energetic self-redefinition was to become a more engaged and engaging teacher. But, paradoxically, it seemed that each intellectual stride toward this goal carried me farther from the classroom.

I am certain from talking with colleagues and from reading their often fascinating autobiographical accounts that most professors sometimes feel there is an inverse correlation between their intellectual achievements—their academic accomplishments—and the amount of time, energy, and patience they devote to teaching and to students.

The leaves of the academic calendar blew turbulently away between the late 1960s and the early 1990s. And by December of 1991, I was, remarkably in the estimation of some, the first black president of the Modern Language Association of America. My schedule of obligations had filled both home and office with myriad strategically piled books and papers, hundreds of fax receipts, jottings of more telephone numbers than AT&T and Sprint combined have, and a sea of pink slips flowing from room to room. People were always complaining on encountering me, "You a *hard* man to catch up with, Brother Baker!"

Assuming the castle of my skin through teaching had unexpectedly brought me to a plane where I heroically proclaimed to fellow professionals, "Oh, yes, I still teach. I always try to make room for students . . . even if it kills me." In fact, my pedagogy did progress from those early spirit-of-the-age lectures at Yale. And my classroom commitment and performance undoubtedly inspired the University of Pennsylvania to award me a Christian R. and Mary F. Lind-back Foundation prize for distinguished teaching in 1984. But the extent to which I had unwittingly moved away from my pedagogical calling came home to me only during a notable spring-term instance, which I would like to share with you.

One of my friends, a secondary school teacher in Philadelphia, has labeled this anecdote "a story of cowardice." I believe that my friend is partially correct. But I also believe that the following story is one of re-call, redemption, and revisionary possibility—specifically, the possibility of overcoming cowardice, of balancing innumerable professional obligations, and of engaging a rigorous local pedagogy designed for the twenty-first century. The story concerns my 1992 course Black Women's Writing.

The course began on a sunny January day as students filed into a somewhat cramped seminar room furnished with a weary array of movable chairs and a table large enough to accommodate the passengers and crew of the *Queen Elizabeth II*. It was impossible to arrange a democratic semicircle of participants. The enrollment consisted of black and white graduates and undergraduates who ranged in age from the late teens to the mid-twenties. Their dress ran from Neiman Marcus heights to Gap informality. There was a lone white man, acutely conscious of his singularity and his Wharton School shirt and tie.

Our introductory session proceeded without a hitch as I learned names, discussed my syllabus, and assigned Phillis Wheatley's poetry for our next meeting. That second session is painfully etched in my mind. A number of students—most of them graduate returnees from my fall course Black Autobiography—were energetically holding forth on neoclassical literary conventions in Wheatley's poetry. Quietly, a black female undergraduate spoke from a back corner of the room: "You know, we have been going on and on about conventions and how Wheatley subverted them and everything. But I'm not so much interested in conventions as in what Phillis means to the black community per se. I'd like to see us talk about Wheatley in more direct ways."

I was taken aback. Here were echoes of a critical debate in which I had become embroiled a number of years earlier. The principal question in that debate was, Is the author or critic of black literature obligated to write and speak in a register easily accessible to nonspecialists? Surely there were echoes of this question of "access" in the student's comment. Her observation thus seemed a visitation by the critical uncanny, appearing suddenly to complicate a perfectly amiable discussion. But the comment also had the ring of a digression, summoning memories for me of an earlier semester, in which a fiercely angry nationalist student terrorized a class of mine for three sessions and then withdrew, leaving a shambles of hurt feelings and restless silences. Finally, the comment seemed historically belated, an avatar of a 1960s field of interrogation in which the word *relevant* was always only a heartbeat away.

These thoughts raced through my mind in the nanosecond before I spoke. "Well," I retorted, "in this class we are going to deal with conventions. You and

I can discuss the black community during office hours. In this course, we are going to learn to be sophisticated readers of black expressive-cultural texts. I mean there are a lot of things we can do, but in this course we are going to concentrate on reading skills."

"Reading skills"? I was not even sure what I meant by the phrase. I believe I had last heard it from a Philadelphia politician describing the city's adult literacy program. A moment of silence elapsed, and then our discussion of neoclassical conventions and Phillis Wheatley resumed.

The semester turned out miserably. Most of the undergraduates earned low grades, and my conscience was troubled by unshakable feelings of failure. Somehow I knew that the downward spiral of the course had begun with the student's comment. Why had that moment proved so unsettling to me? Who or what, precisely, was I addressing in my quick and peevish invocation of "reading skills"?

As I compulsively recounted the incident to colleagues and friends, I insisted that my response was intended to prevent "racial" polarization and to facilitate polite, professional classroom discourse. I also insisted that the reply was meant to forestall the privileging of a single subject position. Such privileging would, after all, be anathema in the American academy, which is currently advertised as diverse, multicultural, and full of distinctive new stories waiting to be heard. I have sometimes concluded this narrative of tolerance with the following coda: "Why should I allow one truculent black woman undergraduate to disrupt an entire learning process? Why should she be permitted to deal with her personal interests at the expense of the multiple interests of the class as a whole?" The story sounds convincing. It has brought solace and commendation from listeners who intuited its intended effects—and my middle-aged need for psychological support.

After all, a new multiculturalism manqué suggests the necessity of reining in particulars in order to steer the fragile craft of pedagogy with authoritative, nationalist vigilance. As recent best-sellers have phrased it, to prevent the "disuniting of America" we must keep the "American mind" open to absorb what "every American needs to know." Perhaps there is an admirable impulse to inclusiveness in such diatribes, but they seem hopelessly xenophobic and abstract to me. For I believe that our eagerness to be nationalistically multicultural all the time in every place and on every occasion can place amazing constraints on classroom proceedings. It can even lead, at our most frustrating moments, to justifiable charges that our resolute inclusiveness amounts to no more than a thoughtless pandering to high-flown, abstract ideals. "PC" might then signify a "pandering calculus"—a rhetoric of limits designed to standardize variations of "race, class, gender" for normal multicultural classroom settings.

Certainly, I was guilty of such pandering and its consequences when I compulsively narrativized that moment of the course. I now realize that what motivated

my first response—a response quickly rationalized in the name of multicultural inclusiveness—was not pluralistic idealism at all. Rather, my response
was motivated by cowardice, a quick terror of the particular and unknown
places that the undergraduate black woman's narrative might have taken us had
it been granted pedagogical entrée.

I babbled of reading skills, gesturing transcendently toward a utopian multicultural professionalism. In retrospect, I know that the *reading* most appropriate for a course devoted to black women's writing was a cultural-political
one emphasizing local geographies. What was needed was a reading designed
to highlight the particular "hereness" or "situatedness" of, say, black women on
the campus of the University of Pennsylvania. Such a reading would have
recognized the undergraduate voice from the corner not as a multicultural ab-
straction of "race and gender" but as an actual black woman's voice rife with
narrative potential. The first step toward the local pedagogy I have in mind
would have carried me out of Bennett Hall—the building that houses the Penn
English department and the seminar room in which the undergraduate uttered
her comment—across Thirty-Fourth Street and onto Locust Walk, the main
thoroughfare joining the east and west ends of this urban campus.

The sign "locust" in the name Locust Walk is intended to signify nature, drawing the campus walkway into the lexical field of "chestnut," "walnut," "pine,"
"spruce," "osage"—the quaint tree names adorning other streets that traverse
the University of Pennsylvania's West Philadelphia setting. And at certain moments in the very late afternoon, when the surrounding traffic has abated, it is
possible, if you are on the tree-lined walk, to slip into Oxonian reveries of
dreaming spires and pastoral punting. In the light of average day, however, it is
impossible to conceive of the walk as anything but the social and institutional
result of power. For what is now called a walk was once a bustling urban
thoroughfare for public passage. Locust *Street* was on a busy trolley line and
was the site of not only student residences but also private row homes of West
Philadelphia citizens. At the beginning of the 1950s, the street was an open
road into and through a predominantly black American, urban neighborhood.
A paragraph from a recent university report provides details on the emergence
of the walk:

> Locust Walk in its current form evolved as the central core of the campus of
> the University of Pennsylvania expanded westward. Locust Street with its fra-
> ternity, sorority and private row houses was closed as a city street, properties
> were condemned by the Redevelopment Authority to make way for the build-
> ing now known as Steinberg-Dietrich Hall.

This excerpt is taken from the report of the Committee to Diversify Locust
Walk, established in the fall of 1990, and the passage captures in vaguely imperialistic tones ("expanded westward") the historical matrix of power that
transformed a public Philadelphia roadway into a private campus walk. The

"building now known as Steinberg-Dietrich Hall" is, in fact, headquarters for the renowned Wharton School, for business. By the late 1960s, Locust Walk had become what the 1990 committee designates as "the primary east-west artery of campus," which "functions as both a heavily used corridor and as a campus outdoor living room" (7).

The problem with this idealized description of urban imperialism is that thirteen exclusively white fraternities—boasting a combined membership of three hundred—occupy the center and heart of this "outdoor living room." And these exclusive inhabitants have made life miserable, violent, and dangerous for women and members of minorities for decades. To traverse the campus on this route, therefore, is to journey through the heart of fraternal darkness, where three hundred uncivil and privileged white occupants hold a community of twenty-two thousand hostage.

The fraternities of Locust Walk that surround the imposing Wharton School can surely be seen as a metonymy for certain general arrangements of power. For Locust Walk, I would submit, is merely a local example of writings of power that exist on all our campuses, on all our American thoroughfares, and even, sometimes to our own great astonishment, in our personal living rooms. The Locust Walk fraternities, therefore, have not only been an enduring source of violence and insult against black, women, Hispanic, gay, and lesbian students in West Philadelphia. They have also been a metonymic inscription, at the center of everyday campus life, of American—indeed, global—maps of white male power and privilege.

Locust Walk, that is to say, is not only a local hazard to the health of any nonfraternal cross-campus walker from west to east after dark but also a devastating emblem of general cartographies of white, man-centered legitimacy and control. All attempts to remove the fraternities from Locust Walk have, to date, proved unsuccessful.

Now, if we return to the English department seminar room where the undergraduate woman spoke, we do so with an array of locally inflected and pedagogically useful questions for a course devoted to black women's writing. How does it feel for a black woman to negotiate the physical and symbolic geographies of Locust Walk? How safe does she feel in this public zone of white men who deem it their right to comment openly and rudely on her anatomy? What effect does her walk from home to English department culture have on her notions of multiculturalism? Do campus realities (i.e., the economic and cultural capital of Locust Walk) work to convince her that she should suppress her individual black "womanist" voice in the office of normative pluralism?

I do not think that these questions are either substitutes for or mere supplements to the professional discourse of literary study. Rather, they are inextricably coextensive interrogatives. By mapping the local, we immediately half create and half invoke an inescapably shared situation. And this shared situation in turn produces an inescapable sense of immediate responsibility. An

earnest white female student may, for example, justifiably and resolutely refuse
to assume any responsibility whatsoever for her great-great-great-grandfather's
relation to American slavery. The same student, however, would be hard-
pressed to abjure all responsibility for the cultural politics that empower white
fraternity dominance on the central campus walk, which she traverses every
day and night. Similarly, a professor of postmodern literary studies may forward with great panache the claim that contemporary modes of analysis no
longer require an identitarian concern for "race," assuring students that "race"
has been thoroughly discredited as a scientific category and semiotically de-
mystified as a representational construct. The same hypothetical professor,
however, would have the devil's own time providing a "race-free" analysis of
the dominant ideology signified by Locust Walk. Finally, students and instructors who insisted on curtailing reference in class to "narrowly personal" or "re-
strictively individualistic" experiences in favor of universal modes of appre-
hension and analysis would be brought up short, I think, by an open discursive
mapping of the different emotional and psychological costs paid by white men
and black women in their crossings of Locust Walk.

Thinking of the intemperate black undergraduate who abandoned my class
after three terrorizing sessions, I dug out a 1989 report entitled *State of Black
Undergraduate Affairs with Regards to the University Administration* that she
and one of her black male classmates compiled. The report, which is randomly
assembled, lists on its "fact sheet of routine racial harassment and discrimination against black students" the following items:

> Black students are not safe walking the campus; there have been various
> cases of physical and verbal assault.

> Black students feel "invisible" in the classroom and in the University com-
> munity. They feel little or no power to control their own fate, but that it is
> in the hands of people who do not care about their futures.

> Black people routinely verbally and physically harassed by white fraterni-
> ties on Locust Walk.

> Fraternity parties held with racial epithets as party themes.

> Black student assaulted by two white fraternity members.

The list goes on and on and on. It claims are nowhere supported by documentation or appendixes. Yet the report itself signals a perceptual formation that was
endorsed by the Black Student League, the Caribbean American Student Association, and undergraduate members of the Pan-African Student Association.

Now, this common sense of discrimination and violence against blacks
does not excuse the student's terror tactics in the classroom, but it highlights
the significance of local geographies in determining conditions of possibility
for "civil" classroom discourse between black and white students. The report's
compilers undoubtedly believed that defensive classroom behavior was a necessary and legitimate mode of converse in a university that privileges a segre-

gated and violent Locust Walk as the institution's public, discursive norm—as the bizarre spatial statement that the university makes in the ambient air of a black, urban, West Philadelphia community.

When that undergraduate voice of spring 1992 came to the conversational floor, I am sure that, despite the reasonableness of its tone, it arose from the same perceptual field as *State of Black Undergraduate Affairs*. For the voice belonged to an enterprising young woman, Juanita Irving, who had singlehandedly organized Black Unity Week during the fall 1991 semester. The inaugural event of Black Unity Week was a Sunday performance by the rap artist Sister Souljah. The black community of Philadelphia composed a significant portion of the audience that evening.

I believe that Black Unity Week and especially its opening rap event were deemed necessary answers or responses to perceived conditions of *lack* on the University of Pennsylvania campus. As such, the week and the performance stood in an interestingly symbolic relation to the white excess on Locust Walk.

The dimensions of a local or situated pedagogy are marked by the mapping of local territories and by the overlapping black women's narratives (the story of the "terrorist," the spring undergraduate's tale, the expressivity of Sister Souljah, the dialectical lack signified by, or signifying on, Locust Walk excess) that converge in a reconsideration of spring 1992. Such a pedagogy draws on cultural studies propositions about "inside" and "outside" textualities; it assumes that local mapping cannot be separated from the development of anything approaching useful and practical reading skills for the twenty-first century.

Had I been invested in such a pedagogy, I would certainly have recognized—even if dimly—the young black woman's question as commensurate with the reception history of both Phillis Wheatley herself and her poetry. After all, was it not precisely Wheatley's relation to an African community in America that concerned Thomas Jefferson when he pronounced the eighteenth-century black woman writer's work "below the dignity of criticism" (140)? Yes, it was the putatively debilitating effects of blackness on higher enterprises such as rational and creative thought that prompted Jefferson's judgment. And it was a similarly communal consideration of blackness that motivated Amiri Baraka—nearly two centuries after Jefferson—to declare that Wheatley was not a "black" poet, because her poetry failed to address the enslaved condition of the masses of Afro-America (Jones 106). Historically, Wheatley's reception, by whatever man has occupied the Locust Walk of criticism at the moment, has been largely determined by precisely what the spring-term student brought to the fore—namely, Wheatley's relation to "the black community per se."

At the moment the student made her comment, however, I was not tuned to cultural studies frequencies, reception aesthetics, or the richly imbricated black women's narratives striving for a hearing. I was not invested in a local pedagogy.

If I had been, I might have stepped down from authoritative heights and said, "Could you be more specific? Could you please say more?" This simple call might have produced a personal response from the undergraduate that helped us to understand the connections among Phillis Wheatley, the seminar room, male critical power, the white university geographies of Locust Walk, and the surrounding world of black West Philadelphians. We might have received insight on the dynamics of Sister Souljah's popular-cultural expressivity in relation to a professional, academic discourse on black women's writing overseen by a black male professional.

Needless to say, none of this happened.

I maintained a narrowly professional and safe line of discourse because I was, in fact, an overproud professional. I knew the content of the course with the scholarly intimacy of one who had written a book on the subject. Moreover, I had mastered the techniques for teaching black women's writing during nearly a decade of giving courses on the subject. Most important, I was grossly overcommitted during the spring of 1992 to an encyclopedic array of outside professional projects.

As I traveled the country in my capacity as president of the Modern Language Association of America, I boasted about the association's progress during the past quarter century. With more than thirty-two thousand members, whose colors, languages, ethnicities, sexual orientations, and intellectual proclivities are light-years removed from the white convention corridors of 1968, the Modern Language Association of 1992, I insisted, is well positioned for the decades ahead. Its dedication to innovative strategies and resources for teaching is apparent in the MLA's general publications program as well as in the work of its Association of Departments of English and its Association of Departments of Foreign Languages.

It was strenuous and demanding work to carry this good professional news to waiting academic enclaves. So, anything I said in the brief time of a seminar I considered almost a charitable contribution, carrying the special auric force of my other professional engagements. I was like a middle-aged actor with a remembered script, hoping to gain credibility, authority, and applause for having made it into somebody's *Who's Who in the Dramatic Arts*. What precisely I was not was a patient and committed teacher with an active sense of local geographies and of their effective mapping within a pedagogy intended for critical participation and for transformative social action.

Professionalism can become a job. Critical and transformative pedagogy is a calling. Too narrow professionalism minimizes risks in the office of efficiency. Local pedagogy often risks serious career discomfort in critically demystifying shared situations. Professionalism sometimes plays a strictly careerist politics, while critical pedagogy works to define the teacher as politician. A blind professionalism is the penultimate refuge of the career scholar-intellectual as teacher (the final one is voluntary early retirement).

If the recollections of time, space, and occupational incumbencies that I have set forth so far have a purpose, therefore, it is one of *re-call*—a summons to a renewed life of teaching in all the activity's acutely political dimensions. It is Paulo Freire who reminds us of what he terms the "great discovery":

> This is a great discovery, education is politics! . . . [All teachers must ask] in favor of whom am I being a teacher? By asking in favor of whom am I educating, the teacher must also ask against whom am I educating. Of course, the teacher who asks in favor of whom I am educating and against who[m], must also be teaching in favor of something and against something. This "something" is just the political project, the political profile of society, the political "dream." After that moment, the educator has to make his or her choice, to go farther into opposition politics and pedagogy. (Shor and Freire 46)

Freire describes his personal relation to this great discovery with the following observation: "There was a time in my life as an educator when I did not speak about politics and education. It was my most naive moment" (61).

It seems to me that what is in danger of being lost to professionalism, theory, multicultural pietism, and plain cowardice in the present era is the great discovery admirably stated and lived by Freire. For the pedagogical project elaborated in his classic work *Pedagogy of the Oppressed* and extended in recent years by such scholars as Ira Shor, Henry Giroux, Gerald Graff, and Stanley Aronowitz bears no resemblance to the valorizing academicism that often marks everyday life in the university.

I have no wish, however, to be misinterpreted as a fierce-eyed prophet decrying the betrayal of teaching in a godless age. Nor do I wish to be seen as a misty-eyed guru summoning the spirit of John Dewey along with that of Third World liberators to a tony consciousness-raising séance that would make the 1960s look like a mere rehearsal for activist teaching. Indeed, there is no need whatsoever for me even to dream of such a signal and prophetic role.

For thousands on thousands of teachers—at all levels of the American educational process and especially in elementary and secondary schools—work assiduously every hour of the night and day to foster change. Some of them map geographies in places we would not even drive through on our way to the college or university. And most of them are far in advance of me with respect to the dynamics of pedagogy and politics.

Yet, in the lifeworld of the university that I inhabit, I do not find a general, commonsensical, or theoretical agreement among colleagues that Freire's great discovery should be a welcomed signpost in our everyday pedagogical lives. Is it fear that drives us continuously away from his insight?

In *A Pedagogy for Liberation,* Freire continues his reflections on politics and pedagogy:

> To the extent that I become more and more clear concerning my choices, my dreams, which are substantively political and adjunctively pedagogical, to the extent to which I recognize that as an educator I am a politician, I also understand better the reasons for me to be afraid, because I begin to foresee the consequences of such teaching. Putting into practice a kind of education that

critically challenges the consciousness of the students necessarily works *against* some myths which *deform* us. (Shor and Freire 55)

An "education that critically challenges the consciousness of the students" begins for Freire and others with dialogue. And if I were to give a single description of the entire project that I am calling local pedagogy, it would be Freire's stunningly poetical and compelling definition of dialogue: "Dialogue is a moment where humans meet to reflect on their reality as they make and remake it" (98).

What was missed in my course Black Women's Writing was the dialogic occasion that might have instituted a useful local pedagogy. For what our group efforts might have yielded was a lesson in how to read a shared local situation in the light of its multiple textualities and symbolic writings of power. We might, in fact, have profitably queried whether the course itself would more accurately have been called Some Books by Women Who Happen to Be Black and Who Have Written according to Protocols Deemed to Be Literary and Professional. We might have abjured the title Black Women's Writing as merely a content for multiculturalism and taken the phrase up as the inaugural sign for an engaged reading designed to transform the world we all locally inhabited.

How to read black women's writing in the world and how collectively to enter into dialogue with their texts in order to map the symbolic politics and configurations of this era are only two of the tasks that might have begun with my student's comment. The resulting readings would have been preludes to a local, dialogic pedagogy of liberation. And such a pedagogy would ultimately begin to change the Locust Walks of the world forever and to make credible this claim by a dynamic black woman:

> I'm coming up from the bottom and I'm damn sure rising.
> You tried to stop me so I guess I'm surprising.
> I'll never keep quiet, so don't even try it.
> Sit in the back row, I won't buy it.

These lines from Sister Souljah's "360 Degrees of Power" read like an uncanny "dissing" (dismissing) commentary on my poor spring semester performance of 1992. I summon them in closing, however, as sounds of re-call, as admonitions from a black voice that is definitely from the back row, out of the corner, and demanding a new, local pedagogy for a new day of freedom. The Locust Walks of the world must be changed. They must be changed. They must be replaced by open, democratic public spheres in which black women and black West Philadelphia residents, white women and gay and lesbian students can meet as "subjects" (yes, with white men as well) to critically and dialogically *name* the world anew. And Lord knows it will almost certainly be— as it was in the times of the indomitable Rosa Parks, the inimitable Harriet Tubman, and the still-to-be-expertly-comprehended Phillis Wheatley—the very soul of a sister who shall lead them.

Works Cited

Black Student League, Caribbean American Student Association, and Pan-African Student Association. *State of Black Undergraduate Affairs with Regards to the University Administration.* Philadelphia: Black Student League, 1989. N. pag.

Freire, Paulo. *Pedagogy of the Oppressed.* New York: Continuum, 1990.

Jefferson, Thomas. *Notes on the State of Virginia.* Ed. William Peden. Chapel Hill: U of North Carolina P, 1955.

Jones, LeRoi. "The Myth of a 'Negro Literature.'" *Home: Social Essays.* New York: Morrow, 1966, 105–15.

Shor, Ira, and Paulo Freire. *A Pedagogy for Liberation: Dialogues on Transforming Education.* New York: Bergin, 1987.

Sister Souljah. "360 Degrees of Power." *360 Degrees of Power.* Sony, DIDP077232, 1992.

University of Pennsylvania. Committee to Diversify Locust Walk. "Report from Committee to Diversify Locust Walk." *Almanac* 17 Sept. 1991: 4–12.

8

Education for Humanization
Applying Paulo Freire's Pedagogy to Learning a Second Language

Tomas Graman

Editors' Note: Early in his career while teaching rural farm and factory workers in Colorado, Tomas Graman applied Freirean concepts to his ESL classes after traditional methods proved too detached from his students' lives. He shows how he used problem-posing and dialogic methods to focus on student experience and elicit generative themes. Freire's method, which Graman sketches in this chapter, enabled him to teach language as a tool, a way to "name the world, to change it." However, Graman finds much institutional resistance to these methods in the ESL classroom because there is more concern for administrative efficiency (keeping programs "uniform and orderly") and for literature, and too little for language acquisition, as the course of study. Graman wants education to go beyond teaching language, to engage students and teachers in a "humanizing" purpose: "to think and act as critically conscious beings."

Twelve years ago I began teaching English as a Second Language (ESL) to adults in a rural area of Colorado. My students were farm workers, shepherds, and canning and turkey-processing workers from several Latin American countries and Spain. Since I had had little previous teaching experience, I began without preference for any particular methodology. After thinking it over, I decided to teach the class by talking with the students, discussing pictures and photographs, and reading articles and stories to find topics for discussion. The students were just beginning to learn English, so we had to negotiate meaning through drawings on a blackboard, gestures, pantomime, and the use of loan words that English and Spanish have in common (for example, from Greek) or cognate words—in this case, English words related in form to Spanish ones "by systematic sound correspondences." [1]

We spent two weeks trying to learn about each other in English and were successful in most cases. By the third week I received books and other materials for teaching ESL from the college sponsoring the class. These materials offered translation exercises, as well as repetition, substitution, and other drills that focused primarily on grammatical aspects of English. Also included was a drillbook on English pronunciation that contrasted minimal pairs—that is, words differing by one sound only; its purpose was to get students to focus on the sounds of English.

Being an inexperienced teacher, I decided to rely on some of the language teaching textbooks prepared by professionals, and I began using the materials the college had given me. As a result, unfortunately, the class degenerated into sessions in which I, like a trainer, would get the students, like parrots, to make sounds and repeat sentences and phrases that in no way reflected the immediate reality of the challenges of their lives: working in canning and turkey-processing factories under dangerous conditions, bending over all day picking cucumbers, or worrying about where the money would come from to pay the rent. I found that focusing on language per se destroyed language's function as a tool,[2] since it was difficult to make the transition from mechanistic language drills to what the students and I wanted to do—namely, to converse and write about the vital themes and issues relevant to their daily lives. And since no one enjoyed or was motivated by the new method, I returned to the initial one.

A few months later, I read Paulo Freire's book *Pedagogy of the Oppressed*,[3] and it confirmed many of the ideas I had acquired about learning. For instance, I found the notion that learning is self-generated rather than merely receptive especially important.[4] In my experience as a student, teachers had focused on transferring accepted information and getting us to endorse, remember, and reproduce it in class and on tests. Freire refers to this approach as the "banking concept of education."[5] "Banking education" is an attempt to intercede "on students' behalf" by presenting them with a humanitarian aid package that includes this unstated proviso: Instead of using the reality of your existence and your innate capacity to construct knowledge and language, we (the knowing teachers) will invent "reality" in the classroom and *give* "knowledge and language" to you as deposits of information; you simply must reproduce what we have planned for you. As Freire explains it:

> The banking notion of consciousness [is] that the educator's role is to regulate the way the world "enters into" the students. His task is to organize a process which already occurs spontaneously, to "fill" the students by making deposits of information which he considers to constitute true knowledge— deposits which are detached from reality, disconnected from the totality that

engendered them and could give them significance. Words are emptied of their concreteness and become a hollow, alienated, and alienating verbosity.[6]

According to Freire, the teacher using the banking method will ask "such vital questions as whether Roger gave green grass to the goat, and insist upon the importance of learning that, on the contrary, *Roger* gave green grass to the *rabbit*."[7]

As I narrated the empty words from the ESL materials to the farm workers, the class became less and less engaged in the naturally human act of talking about things which pertained to their lives. The words and structures of the English language became meaningless because they were no longer part of the students' world (or of mine). The students' non-native grammar and pronunciation came about through their active work of building language necessary for discussing topics pertinent to their lives.[8] The mechanically well-formed though contextually meaningless sentences that the students repeated in order to *practice* sounds—such as "Miss Meek lives on Fifth Street" or "Did he vote for Victor Vogel?"[9]—signified very little to them. These sentences were both artificial and alienating for many of the workers who lived in migrant camps where there were no streets; further, none of them were members of the voting segment of the population. Not surprisingly, the farm workers experienced similar alienation from drills on vocabulary items and syntactical structures.

The farm worker ESL class illustrated to me the motivational importance of tying students' experiences to the process of learning language. Students are more likely to develop intellectually and linguistically when they analyze their own experiences and build their own words to describe and better understand these experiences. Access to this constructive process must come through dialogue, as Freire defines it: "an encounter among men who name the world, it must not be a situation where some men name on behalf of others."[10] Through authentic dialogue, learners and teachers, with different experiences and knowledge, critically reflect on beliefs and information; in such dialogue, both have the opportunity to build knowledge. Freire and Donaldo Macedo cite the Italian social theorist Antonio Gramsci, who expresses this concept in the following way:

> One is persuaded that a truth is fertile only when an effort has been made to conquer it. That it does not exist in itself and for itself, but results from a conquest of the spirit. Similarly, in each individual it is necessary to reproduce that state of anxiety that the studious person has crossed before reaching [a truth]. This representation is much more educational than the schematic exposition of this same knowledge to the hearer of efforts, errors, and gradual dexterity through which men have passed to reach actual knowledge. Teaching, developed in this way, becomes an act of liberation.[11]

The act of liberation can occur when teachers and learners both recognize that learners have the ability to pose their own problems and to struggle to achieve their own solutions. The state of anxiety Gramsci describes is gained through critical, reflective dialogue among learners and teachers; its importance to cognitive development is confirmed by Piagetian research. Like Gramsci, Jean Piaget emphasized the importance of experiencing states of cognitive disequilibrium and of reequilibration in order to advance intellectual development; for such anxiety, disequilibrium, or conflict is part of the struggle for knowledge that all learners must experience in order to understand or make that knowledge their own.[12] In my ESL class, the farm workers had been experiencing such cognitive and linguistic conflict in their active attempts to understand and make themselves understood in their own words. The following conversation between two ESL students illustrates linguistic conflict; in this case, in understanding the meaning Juan intends to convey to Christos. The choice of words is the focal point.

Juan: But what about the people of the government?

Christos: Of the?

Juan: Of the government, who belongs . . .

Christos: Oh.

Juan: . . . to the government.

Christos: Oh, [*in a very low voice*] government.

Juan: The people wh— Ah! [*pause*] Of course, they don't live like the rest.

Christos: What about the people? [*pause*] In other words, uh, the *members* of the government?

Juan: The *members* of the government.[13]

Through their successive, constructive attempts to understand and make themselves understood, the learners discover within their own knowledge a better way to express an idea. The "reaching of actual knowledge" and the "learners' own words" of which Freire and Gramsci write are part of the tacit component necessary to the attainment of a deep and personal knowledge.[14]

Students build critical knowledge and language to express it, as Gramsci indicates, through engaging in "problematizing" reality—that is, learners must identify problems and come to recognize and understand the significance of those problems in relation to their own lives and the lives of others. Such critical reflection and consciousness must then lead to attempts to overcome the problems and to improve the conditions that give rise to them. Authentic, dialogic problematizing of what Freire calls "generative themes" is the sort of activity in which learners must engage in order to construct knowledge and language both actively and critically. Such dialogue must be authentic because inauthentic language—what Freire calls "verbalism"—divides reality from language and learning, as in the sort of artificial practice described earlier. Freire argues that "human existence cannot be nourished by false words, but only true words with which men transform the world."[15] Further, as he explains, "to exist, humanly, is to name the world, to change it."[16]

Education as the posing of questions or problems expressed in "generative themes" is an attempt to connect student and teacher realities to learning. Freire defines a generative theme as a "concrete representation of many ideas, values, concepts, and hopes, as well as the obstacles which impede man's full humanization."[17] Such themes vary according to the context, the population, and the era. Freire has termed such themes "generative" because they contain the possibility of unfolding into again as many themes.[18]

In the class for migrant farm workers, themes that students brought up were coded in single words or phrases ("generative words").[19] "Bonus" and "short-hoe" were among these words. The farm workers had learned them in the context of their work, since they contained elements of farm worker reality related to the language of the boss. On the surface, "bonus" means extra money. However, in this case it means a system in which growers deduct money from the workers' paychecks and then offer it later as a "bonus" in an attempt to keep them at the same farm until all the fruit or vegetables have been picked. But since they work at a piece rate, the workers are at a disadvantage if they remain at a farm site where the harvest is thin. The short-hoe is about a foot long and is used to weed fields. Growers believe that workers will do a more thorough job of weeding with it, but its use causes pain and damage to the back. Nevertheless, growers often insist that it be used.

By engaging in critical dialogue about such generative themes, learners connect concrete ideas like those of the bonus and the short-hoe to more abstract ones, like exploitation or domination and their opposite, liberation. Freire argues that such themes concern "the frontier between being and being more human."[20] Further, he stresses acting to "negate and overcome, rather than passively accept the 'given.'" Through critically analyzing these types of boundaries, learners can come to recognize, as Freire puts it, "the existence of persons who are served by these situations, and of those who are negated and curbed by them."[21] For example, after discussing the terms *bonus* and *short-hoe,* the farm workers began thinking about and discussing the practices and conditions of their work. Their analyses, their construction of arguments, and the English (in this case) used to denounce these practices were genuine acts of overcoming what many people had considered to be their unfortunate lot in life.

Banking education, by contrast, prevents students from naming their world in order to understand it better and improve it. Indeed, it disqualifies the very language they speak. Macedo, coauthor with Freire of *Literacy: Reading the Word and the World,* describes this characteristic of the banking system of education, arguing that in such a system those with power "refuse to accept and legitimize the students' language."[22] A humanizing pedagogy, on the other hand, places a high value on the language of the learner. Moreover, as Freire points out, "the successful usage of the students' cultural universe requires respect and legitimation of students' discourses, that is, their own linguistic codes, which are different but never inferior."[23]

The students in ESL and foreign language classes in the United States suffer from an abuse of professional authority that denies the value of their ideas and interlanguage constructions.[24] Many teachers and administrators refer to much of these students' language as inferior, as gibberish, or as "mindless ungrammatical chatter."[25] In the Freirean sense, however, "mindless chatter" results not from the language's lack of standard or native-like grammar, or from any aspect of the form of language, but rather from the absence of meaningful content.

The most important thing is that words be genuine and that their aim be to understand and name some element of the world relevant to them. The criteria of grammaticality and pronunciation, on the other hand, ignore the importance of the transforming experience involved in constructing language. Teachers who focus on the form of language are emphasizing what Freire calls the "sonority of words" in a way that subordinates what students say to how they say it.[26] For Freire, the point is to focus on the meaning that learners construct. This is the essence of the transforming power of the learning experience. On the other hand, he notes, "an unauthentic word . . . is one which is unable to transform reality when dichotomy is imposed upon its constitutive elements, is deprived of its dimension of action, [and] reflection automatically suffers as well; and the word is [then] changed into idle chatter."[27]

Furthermore, ample research in second language learning indicates that people learn language best when the focus is on content, as in natural language acquisition,[28] rather than on the explicit instruction of grammar, vocabulary, and pronunciation.[29] Several studies demonstrate the efficacy of the focus on content. Joel Saegert, Margaret Sue Scott, John Perkins, and G. Richard Tucker, for example, discovered that while students "who had experienced learning academic subjects in English" became steadily more proficient in English, students "who studied English only in a formal language classroom situation did not improve as steadily."[30]

By ignoring this research in second language learning, teachers and beginning language textbooks focus on adults' non-native linguistic deviations rather than on the content of their utterances; and what's more, the content they concern themselves with does not acknowledge the political and socioeconomic nature of education. Many North Americans have come to believe that politics must be left out of education in the United States, claiming that education must be neutral. I believe, however, that politics is implicit in all education and that it is particularly important to expose this fact in relation to language education. Freire supports this point of view. He emphasizes the need to overcome the U.S. mentality in which "the political nature of pedagogy is negated ideologically."[31] He states that "it is necessary to negate the political nature of pedagogy to give the superficial appearance that education serves everyone, thus assuring that it continues to function in the interest of the dominant class."[32]

Indeed, foreign language instruction in the United States does serve the interest primarily of the "dominant class" to which Freire refers.[33] In a recent article, Sheila Slaughter draws our attention to U.S. government and Business–Higher Education reports such as *A Nation at Risk* and *America's Competitive Challenge: The Need for a National Response,*[34] noting that these reports "use the rubric of excellence and quality to call for a greatly tightened U.S. educational stratification system, one that revalues the college degree and re-empowers the middle class."[35] She also points out that "those who test well will learn to master literature as the language of upper discourse, to prepare for work in fields where a second language facilitates overseas assignments."[36]

While the upper socioeconomic strata are gaining access to foreign language education, the lower strata may be losing their right to education in the languages of their birth. English First (also known as English Only), the national lobbying organization based in Springfield, Virginia, is working to assure that government publications, ballots, and public signs are in English only and to see that decisions for retaining bilingual education for impoverished ethnic groups are left up to local governments, which typically do not represent the interests of these groups.[37] George Trifiadis, the organization's director for governmental affairs, claims that the motivation behind the movement is that "we want every immigrant to be able to learn English [so that] he will have a world of opportunity opened to him that he wouldn't have if he spoke no English whatsoever in this country."[38] But as the American Civil Liberties Union (ACLU) points out, "over 95 percent of the first generation native Mexican Americans [for example] are proficient in English,"[39] which suggests a profound contradiction. How can the English Only organization argue that the purpose for its existence is to "help immigrants to learn English"[40] when immigrants already succeed in doing so without English Only's help? In addition, as the ACLU further argues, "by the second generation, over 50 percent of Mexican Americans have completely lost their mother tongue, speaking no Spanish at all."[41]

Learning, or, as in the case of many ethnic groups, maintaining, another language in addition to English is part of the "stratification system" Slaughter identifies.[42] While the Business–Higher Education Forum is encouraging certain layers of society to develop bilingual abilities, the bilingual heritage of others is beginning to be threatened.[43]

Quoting from the Forum's publication, *America's Competitive Challenge,* Slaughter suggests the motivation behind the "stratification" of foreign language instruction. She reports that "the Forum begins by clearly stating that the function of the educational system, as well as of all other social systems, is service to the economy."[44] The Business–Higher Education Forum, she states, expects universities "to develop a curriculum for multinational executives, one that would teach foreign management practices, foreign language and culture as well as offer an international studies program designed to strengthen programs and data bases in the areas of industrial, commercial, legal and financial practices and institutions."[45] Of course, to gain access to such foreign language and international business opportunities, students must be able to afford the cost of expensive institutions, as well as study abroad. So those without the financial resources to pay for these options—that is, the lower socioeconomic classes—find themselves either without the opportunity for formal language education or in foreign language programs geared merely toward satisfying a foreign language requirement, rather than providing vigorous foreign language education.

A study I completed in 1986 further illustrates the failure to successfully foster foreign language education, in this case in the Utah Spanish program.[46] I discovered, for instance, that at Utah, 94 percent of the students in upper-division Spanish courses did not come up through the ranks to reach those levels—in other words, most upper-division students had not taken lower-division courses. Those students enrolled in the upper-division course were either native Spanish speakers from abroad or students who had lived for a considerable period of time in a Spanish-speaking environment.[47] In addition, the only sorts of courses beyond the first two years of study are in literary analysis, or in some cases linguistics or business—but not in other areas of human experience or interest. My experience as a teacher and student suggests that this tendency may be limited neither to Spanish, nor to a single university. In fact, John B. Carroll has reported findings similar to those at Utah for university foreign language programs throughout the United States, in French, German, Russian, and Spanish.[48]

The pedagogy outlined by Freire contrasts with the ones most widely used in U.S. foreign language programs (that is, communicative and form-oriented approaches), precisely because they omit the most important aspect of education: the humanization of mankind.[49] What is needed in the field of second language pedagogy is an approach that addresses the existential, political, and axiological questions touching the lives of both students and teachers. If the teachers and students want to encourage critically conscious second-language learning, they should take action to put Freire's pedagogy into practice in the classroom.

In order for people to develop the critical consciousness and linguistic ability needed to function not as servants but as active decisionmakers, people must strive to foster authentic dialogue about reality so that the immediate need to confront real problems and resolve them can be met. The need for such confrontations does not imply that the classroom should prepare students *for* the real world; rather, the classroom must *be* the real world in which students and teachers critically analyze real problems and take action to solve them.

This focus on the immediate reality implies that language classes should not emphasize so-called practical things for tourists, like ordering a cup of coffee or asking directions, shopping, engaging in travel or business,[50] or, as

Dorothy James stresses, satisfying "most survival needs and limited social demands."[51] In short, only if foreign language classes are held in shopping centers, restaurants, or foreign countries might there be an immediate need to focus on such topics.[52] Moreover, if and when students do find themselves in such contexts, requiring authentic "survival needs," they can easily learn the language to accomplish these tasks.

Learning through posing and resolving existential problems entails what Henry Giroux calls "critical literacy." This means "developing the theoretical and practical conditions through which human beings can locate themselves in their own histories and in doing so make themselves present as agents in the struggle to expand the possibilities of human life and freedom."[53] Critically learning another language enhances our ability to gain access both outwardly to the data of interrelated societies and inwardly to the society of birth or adoption, thereby giving us an opportunity to "locate ourselves" in a broader economic and sociopolitical context. It can be a first step in gaining a critical consciousness of the interconnection among the lives of all people. In addition, learning a language that reflects another culture allows people in the acquisition process to encounter and confront linguistic, cognitive, and axiological conflicts. These states of confusion are optimal moments for acquiring not only a new-language and higher levels of intellectual development but also other perspectives on human values. Unfortunately, most teaching methods and foreign language programs in the United States discourage such states by using English or by averting these natural, necessary conflicts in the classroom.[54] Nevertheless, in spite of the counterproductive methods used in many instructional settings, people become proficient in language, and more humanized, when they struggle with the problems of human existence.

Putting Freire's pedagogy of critically conscious struggle into practice in the United States is not always easy. Part of the difficulty is caused by the curricula, textbooks, and tests that language programs employ, which in turn dictate what the programs will be. To complicate matters further, funding for language programs depends on meeting the demands established by government agencies and the testing companies working with them. For example, "responsibility" as defined by programs such as Competency-Based Adult Education/English as a Second Language (CBAE/ESL) and the "proficiency" movement means accountability.[55] This implies, according to the banking perception, being able to reproduce the prescribed subunits of "knowledge," no matter how distorted these subunits are by their alienation from the reality out of which they were carved, and no matter how much they promote control rather than the creative building of language and knowledge. Elsa Auerbach notes how some apologists for CBAE/ESL stress the goal of accountability; C. A. Findley and L. A. Nathan, for example, "promote" competency-based instruction as a "successful model for the delivery of educational services that allows for responsible and accountable teaching."[56] In implementing the prescribed curriculum, Auerbach argues, teachers emphasize such tasks as "reading directions and following orders in a job," but not the ability "to change or question the nature of that job."[57] With CBAE/ESL, she claims, "students are taught to receive knowledge rather than to generate it." Further, such programs "transmit cultural values and reproduce class relationships."[58] Elsa Auerbach and Denise Burgess also demonstrate that materials (including textbooks) used in ESL seldom reflect authentic language and, further, are intended to prepare students for subservient roles in society.[59] Auerbach emphasizes that current CBAE/ESL programs, sanctioned by "national policy-makers" such as the Center for Applied Linguistics, "train students from lower socioeconomic strata in just those skills, values, and behaviors necessary for blue-collar jobs," while "in middle-class schools, the focus is on the cognitive processes involved in the tasks; upper-class schools emphasized creativity and self-management." At these lower levels, she argues, "mechanical, rote behavior," is emphasized, with "little decision-making."[60]

In a similar fashion, foreign language departments adopt first-year textbooks that establish the curricula. I have worked as coordinator of the beginning language programs at two major universities (1985–1988) and as a language teacher and student at these and five other universities (1969–1988); I have also held many discussions with university colleagues, students, and textbook salespeople. These experiences have suggested that the main objective of most university foreign language programs is not to foster second language acquisition, but rather to keep the program and teaching assistants uniform and orderly. In effect, the textbooks serve an administrative purpose in a context where the goal of the departments is to promote the study of literature, not language acquisition.[61] Foreign language courses past the first four semesters are strictly for majors in literature (and in some cases linguistics or business). Literary analysis is the only route available for most graduate and upper-division undergraduate students who want to continue foreign language study in the United States. Thus, first-year textbooks are the optimal solution for such lack of interest. They provide voguish, "teacher-proof" packages for teaching assistants in the foreign language programs and are almost always banking rather than dialogic in nature.[62]

Such foreign language programs do not change the fact that it is as vital for other students and teachers as it was for the ESL class of farm workers to determine their own themes within the context of their experiences. Freire has consistently supported this point; for example, when he states that "men *are* because they *are in* a situation [and] the content thus constantly expands and renews itself."[63] Finding, naming, and resolving real problems in people's "situations" are precisely the sorts of activities in which teachers and students must engage themselves in order to grow as critical users of language. Instead of becoming the receptacles of banking education or merely "communicating" without critically examining humankind's conditions and chances for improvement, all learners must come to be social and political scientists and must begin to democratize society by becoming critical agents of change in themselves and in their world.

As an alternative to the banking approaches to second language education, I propose a method in which teachers and adult and adolescent students, even at the earliest levels of linguistic proficiency, begin to find and elaborate their own generative themes and to connect their existential experience to the world of those whose language they are learning. This approach to learning a second language, which at early stages of linguistic development involves the negotiation and successive approximation of meaning, helps students not only to build critically their own ideas and views about vital issues, but also to build their own words in the new language and to act upon them.[64]

By focusing on their hopes, desires, problems, and confusions, students have a built-in reason for wanting to learn. In the following conversation, two ESL students jointly solve a problem with the first draft of one of their essays. Most important, they make use of their experience and curiosity cooperatively in developing a generative theme and a reason to want to learn.

Cecilia: So I would like to ask, to write something about this, but I don't know if to incorporate this in the beginning or at the end. [*pause*]

Hana: I think at the last.

Cecilia: At the last.

Hana: After you said, take although, when was, was where he decided to marry the other one, the, the city o— he feel that he's made a mistake, but he feel he missed something . . .

Cecilia: Sí.

Hana: . . . in his life.

Cecilia: And maybe wi— if will marry Megan . . .

Hana: [*laughs*]

Cecilia: . . . he was going to feel the same, no?

Hana: Of course, yes, I think that everyone think that maybe if he was marry, because we, we are marry, we miss something because we are in in the family and we are belong to our husband, something we miss or what's better. [*sigh*] Yeah, everybody feel it.

Cecilia: Yes, that's why I want to write something about it.

Hana: Ah.

Cecilia: Why is that every person feels that?

Hana: Because this is the nature of human being, I think. That, uh, every time you think that you want something more, you want something else. It's not good what you have; what's good if we were there, and there, you know.

When it's summer, you want winter, and when it's winter, you want summer. I thin— think that it's our nature, not to be satisfied.
Cecilia: Never.

When Hana says, "I think it's our nature not to be satisfied," she is introducing a generative theme that later becomes the focal point of further discussion and writing.

Other ways I have found of generating themes for discussion and writing are to examine pictures, photographs, and pieces of writing (unedited for second language students), such as newspaper and magazine articles, short stories, essays, and books that contain such themes. Students' own written work is also a good source of generative themes that pertain to their lives. At early linguistic levels, reading and discussing in the new language newspaper articles on topics with which students are already familiar is a good way to find themes and begin the guessing necessary for figuring out the readings.[65] Before too long, students will be able to use the same guessing strategy to read other works.

In the discussions that should precede and follow reading, students and teacher search for authentic questions and themes and tie them to personal and social concerns. Such authenticity implies that the class does not merely practice language by asking and answering questions to which students and teachers already know the answers. Students quickly realize that such activities are artificial and are meant to focus on language, the tool, rather than on the true goal of becoming more critically conscious and concerned human beings. Even those methods of teaching a second language that attempt to focus on content rather than on the language itself often fail to stress the importance of such authenticity. People learn best when they have the immediate need to use language to resolve real existential problems. After deliberating upon concrete and generalized aspects of generative themes, students begin the task of writing questions pertinent to the readings and discussions. They then analyze and revise these questions and use them as topics in writing first drafts of essays. In the first drafts, students confront existential problems, support their arguments with well-chosen examples and a logical connection of ideas, and construct the new language to express these ideas. After writing the first drafts, classmates (in pairs or small groups) read and critically discuss the content and form of their essays. (Teachers can often contribute to this endeavor a better understanding of how to read and listen critically to language, focus on authentic dialogue, and comment on the writings.) The students learn to become critical of the writings by carefully listening to and reading their own work, as well as that of their class companions.

The following conversation between two ESL students exemplifies this constructive, dialogic process and the type of sessions the students experienced. Shinobu and Hana are conferring with one another. Shinobu tries to make himself understood, and Hana conveys the fact that she does not understand.

Finally, Shinobu confronts a linguistic problem and gradually moves closer to the message he hopes to make known to Hana. The conflict, in this example, involves the use of the quantifier *any* instead of *some.*

Shinobu: For human being every day or every moment is struggle. We always work or study with any aim.

Hana: No aim? No aim? You said.

Shinobu: With something like, something aim.

Hana: With . . .

Shinobu: Some, any; not negative, positive.

After these sessions for editing and revising, the class reunites to exchange information on the conceptual and linguistic problems encountered and on the solutions they proposed. Later, students like Shinobu and Hana write revised drafts to present to the class for further analysis and critique. Through the procedures described, students and teachers gradually see such activities as sessions for personal growth in which the point is not reproducing information but developing critical perception with regard to language, logic, information, and values.

One factor that can interfere with such development is the teacher's position of authority, which can threaten or intimidate students. In order to prevent abuses of professional authority the teacher must understand that "right answers" are not the goal in a Freirean class. Rather, the objective is to examine beliefs and the basis for them analytically and critically and to arrive at supporting arguments that reflect sincere and intelligent work to resolve problems. The point is not to learn *what* to think and say, but rather *how* to think for yourself and express those thoughts in a new language.

Applying Freire's pedagogy to learning a second language is especially challenging with less critically conscious groups. The biggest problem in this case may have to do with a concept elaborated by Erich Fromm.[66] Fromm pointed out that the existence of freedom of speech can disguise the fact that people usually think or say what everyone else does—that is, within the paradigm endorsed by public opinion—instead of thinking or speaking in an original way—that is, for themselves. The concept Fromm describes is partially responsible for the great challenge involved in the Freirean pedagogy. In other words, the most difficult thing about applying the Freirean pedagogy is not disagreement or debate, which is highly desirable; rather, it is people's refusal to think for themselves. Thus, the most challenging task is to help people begin to search for and examine critically the bases for their views.

One feature that becomes evident early on is that students recognize that the problem-posing, dialogic teacher is not requiring them to memorize information and reproduce it on tests. Nevertheless, in most cases students do read the material and become engaged in discussions of the existential questions related to their lives and to the readings. Such engagement, regardless of the point of view, is the crucial starting point of dialogic, problem-posing education.

For example, a student in one of my Spanish classes spoke and wrote about the story "Bernardino"[67] (by the Spanish writer Ana María Matute), in which the larger boys of the community label a frail young boy as *mimado* (spoiled) and eventually whip him because he represents not a physical threat, but a greater one—an example of something different from the standard of the dominant group. The student related the story to her own experience when she had acted in a "cowardly" way, having feared as a child the wrath of a powerful group. She went on to discuss the frequency of such behavior and then tied it to the arms race and to the invasion of small, defenseless countries like Grenada.

After reading another work in Spanish, one student discussed and wrote about the importance of knowing the motives behind desires and of working to make decisions based on values that do not merely reflect public opinion. Another student wrote of how she had accepted a doctor's opinion regarding a serious operation because she thought she should always believe authorities; another spoke and wrote about the peer pressure that led him to use drugs such as "crack," which almost took his life.

These and other students used the class experiences to examine critically their behaviors (or those of others); in some cases, they even changed their own lives. One became ostracized from his religious group because of his new perspective on Nicaragua. He later began to ask himself profound questions that will probably have a lasting effect on his intellectual and ethical life. Another student spoke of the willpower she gained in the dialogic class which enabled her to seek a divorce she had wanted for years. Another told of becoming assertive in other classes to the point where she would not passively accept the "banking concept" of education that she felt was oppressing her. Yet another observed her child's elementary school Spanish class, told the teacher that it would be better for the third grade students to converse *in* Spanish, and then demonstrated to the class how this could be done.

One of the most distinctive features of this kind of foreign language class was that all elements—stories, "tests," debates, movies, documentaries, essays, discussions, and the new language itself—proved to be means of accomplishing larger life tasks, such as personal, social, and political growth. Most of the students gained good oral and written proficiency and great confidence in communicating in Spanish, and they learned how to continue building language. More important, in my opinion, these students have formed a collective force not only for learning language through dialogic problem posing, but also for rejecting an educational system that works to direct their lives *for* them, but not *with* them.[68] Likewise, by applying Freire's pedagogy to learning, students and teachers have the opportunity and the means to do more than learn language:

they can win the freedom to think and act as critically conscious beings. This is the humanizing purpose of education.

Notes

1. See Ronald W. Langacker, *Fundamentals of Linguistic Analysis* (New York: Harcourt Brace Jovanovich, 1972). Langacker states that "lexical items in different daughter languages are cognates if they are continuations of the same lexical items in the proto language. Thus [the words in the sister languages] Latin *pater*, Greek *patēr*, Sanskrit *pitā*, and English *father* are cognates, since they can all be traced back to a single root of the proto Indo-European." Suzette Haden Elgin, in *What Is Linguistics?* (Englewood Cliffs, NJ: Prentice-Hall, 1973) also stresses that cognates are not loan words and are not related by chance.

2. Michael Polanyi supports this position, arguing that "comprehension can be destroyed altogether by shifting attention from its focus to its subsidiary particulars; [that is, by] shifting attention from the meaning of a symbol to the symbol as an object viewed in itself, you destroy its meaning." See Polanyi, *The Study of Man* (Chicago: University of Chicago Press, 1962), pp. 30, 32.

3. Paulo Freire, *Pedagogy of the Oppressed* (New York: Seabury Press, 1970).

4. Piagetian research has found that people construct knowledge and understanding through assimilative and accommodative processes and through a process of cognitive reequilibration. See, for example, Hans G. Furth, *Piaget and Knowledge: Theoretical Foundations,* 2nd ed. (Chicago: University of Chicago Press, 1981). Annette Karmiloff-Smith and Bärbel Inhelder also point out in their article "If You Want to Get Ahead, Get a Theory," *Cognition, 3* (1974–1975), 195–212, that learning (and development) involves a combination of trial and error and theory building.

5. Freire, *Pedagogy,* p. 58.

6. Freire, *Pedagogy,* pp. 57, 62–63.

7. Freire, *Pedagogy,* p. 61.

8. See Tomas Graman, "Teaching and the Routes to Learning a Second Language," *Foreign Language Annals, 19* (1986), 381–389, on constructing a second language; and Talmy Givón, "From Discourse to Syntax: Grammar as a Processing Strategy," in *Syntax and Semantics, 12* (1979), 81–111, on the "pragmatic" basis for the construction of syntax.

9. Lois C. Schneider, *Teaching English Sounds to Spanish Speakers* (Galien, MI: Allied Education Council, 1971), pp. 17, 36.

10. Freire, *Pedagogy,* p. 77.

11. Paulo Freire and Donaldo Macedo, *Literacy: Reading the Word and the World* (South Hadley, MA: Bergin & Garvey, 1987), pp. 78–79. See also Antonio Gramsci, quoted by Angelo Broccoli, in *Antonio Gramsci y la Educación como Hegemonía* (Mexico: Editorial Nueva Imagen, 1979), p. 47.

12. Jean Piaget, *The Equilibration of Cognitive Structures* (Chicago: University of Chicago Press, 1985); Jean Piaget, *Experiments in Contradiction* (Chicago: University of Chicago Press, 1980); and Bärbel Inhelder, Hermine Sinclair, and Magali Bovet,

Learning and the Development of Cognition (Cambridge: Harvard University Press, 1974).

13. See Graman, "Teaching and the Routes to Learning a Second Language."

14. Michael Polanyi, *Personal Knowledge: Towards a Post-Critical Philosophy* (Chicago: University of Chicago Press, 1962).

15. Freire, *Pedagogy,* p. 76.

16. Freire, *Pedagogy,* p. 76.

17. Freire, *Pedagogy,* p. 91.

18. Freire, *Pedagogy,* p. 92.

19. Freire, *Pedagogy,* p. 101.

20. Freire, *Pedagogy,* p. 93.

21. Freire, *Pedagogy,* p. 92.

22. Freire and Macedo, *Literacy,* p. 124.

23. Freire and Macedo, *Literacy,* p. 127.

24. Larry Selinker, in his article "Interlanguage," *IRAL, 10*(3) (1972), p. 214, defines *interlanguage* as "a separate linguistic system based on the observable output which results from a learner's attempted production of a target language norm." For an insightful revision of the notion of "interlanguage," see Robert Bley-Vroman's article, "The Comparative Fallacy in Interlanguage Studies: The Case of Systematicity," *Language Learning, 33,* 1–17.

25. As Dorothy James calls it, "Toward Realistic Objectives in Foreign Language Teaching," *ADFL Bulletin, 16*(2) (1985), 11.

26. Freire, *Pedagogy,* p. 57.

27. Freire, *Pedagogy,* p. 75.

28. See, for example, Leonard Newmark and David Reibel, "Necessity and Sufficiency in Learning Language," *International Review of Applied Linguistics in Language Teaching, 6* (1968), 145–164; John Macnamara, "The Cognitive Basis of Language Learning in Infants," *Psychological Review, 79* (1972), 1–13; Stephen Krashen, *The Input Hypothesis: Issues and Implications* (New York: Longman, 1985); Arthur P. Sorenson, "Bilingualism in the Northwest Amazon," *American Anthropologist, 69* (1967), 670–683; and Dan I. Slobin, *Psycholinguistics* (Glenview, IL: Scott, Foresman, 1979).

29. See, for example, John Oller, Jr., and Patricia Richard-Amato, eds., *Methods That Work: A Smorgasbord of Ideas for Language Teachers* (Rowley, MA; Newbury House, 1983), pp. 50, 257, 259; Leonard Newmark, "How Not to Interfere with Language Learning," *IJAL, 32*(1 and 2) (1966); Tracy Terrell, "The Natural Approach to Language Teaching: An Update," in Oller and Richard-Amato, *Methods That Work,* p. 268; Macnamara, "The Cognitive Basis of Language Learning in Infants"; Newmark and Reibel, "Necessity and Efficiency in Language Learning"; Krashen, *The Input Hypothesis;* and Graman, "Teaching and the Routes to Learning a Second Language."

30. Joel Saegert, Margaret Sue Scott, John Perkins, and G. Richard Tucker, "A Note on the Relationship Between English Proficiency, Years of Language Study and Medium Instruction," *Language Learning, 24* (June 1974), 99–104; Marina K. Burt and

Heidi C. Dulay, "Optimal Language Learning Environments," in Oller and Richard-Amato, *Methods That Work,* p. 40.

31. Freire and Macedo, *Literacy,* p. 122.

32. Freire and Macedo, *Literacy,* p. 122.

33. See Ana Celia Zentella, "Language Minorities and the National Commitment to Foreign Language Competency: Resolving a Contradiction," *ADFL Bulletin, 17* (1986), 32–42.

34. National Commission on Excellence in Education, *A Nation at Risk: The Imperative for Educational Reform* (Washington, DC: U.S. Department of Education, 1983); Business–Higher Education Forum, *America's Competitive Challenge: The Need for a National Response* (Washington, DC: Business–Higher Education Forum, 1985).

35. Sheila Slaughter, "The Pedagogy of Profit," *Higher Education, 14* (1985), 217–222.

36. Slaughter, "The Pedagogy of Profit," p. 219.

37. This plan, which resembles that of government policy of the 1950s and 1960s for integration of the public schools, has already been passed into law in California and will soon be voted on in several other states.

38. George Trifiadis, debate with Tomas Graman on "Afternoon Edition," with Maggie St. Claire, KUER-FM 90, Salt Lake City, Utah, Spring, 1987.

39. *Civil Liberties,* a publication of the American Civil Liberties Union, Summer/Fall (1986), p. 8.

40. Trifiadis, "Afternoon Edition" debate.

41. *Civil Liberties,* p. 8.

42. Slaughter, "The Pedagogy of Profit," p. 217. For more information on the linguistic "stratification system" see also Jim Cummins, "Language Proficiency and Academic Achievement," in John W. Oller, ed., *Issues in Language Testing Research* (Rowley, MA: Newbury House, 1981).

43. According to Slaughter, the Forum, housed in the American Council on Education and partly funded by the Andrew W. Mellon and National Science Foundations, is made up of chief executive officers of great corporations and great universities. Among the signatories of the report, for example, are John F. Burlingame of General Electric, Philip Caldwell of Ford, Robert Anderson of Rockwell International, James E. Olson of AT&T, together with Derek Bok of Harvard, David Saxon of the University of California, Richard Cyert of Carnegie-Mellon, and Matina Horner of Radcliffe ("The Pedagogy of Profit," pp. 219–220).

44. Slaughter, "The Pedagogy of Profit," p. 220.

45. As quoted from *America's Competitive Challenge,* p. 14; in Slaughter, "The Pedagogy of Profit," p. 220.

46. Tomas Graman, "The Gap Between Lower- and Upper-Division Spanish Courses: A Barrier to Coming up through the Ranks," *Hispania, 70* (1987), 929–935.

47. Graman, "The Gap." See also Terrell, "The Natural Approach to Language Teaching: An Update," p. 268, on "massive failure of classroom language teaching."

48. John B. Carroll, "Foreign Language Proficiency Levels Attained by Language Majors Near Graduation from College," *Foreign Language Annals, 1* (1967), 131–151.

49. For a discussion of communicative and form-oriented approaches to second language teaching, see Jack C. Richards and Theodore S. Rodgers, *Approaches and Methods in Language Teaching: A Description and Analysis* (Cambridge: Cambridge University Press, 1986), p. 74.

50. Unfortunately, these are the sorts of things they usually do emphasize. See Richards and Rodgers, *Approaches and Methods in Language Learning,* p. 74.

51. Dorothy James, "Toward Realistic Objectives in Foreign Language Teaching," *ADFL Bulletin, 16*(2) (1985), 11.

52. The Freirean pedagogy, aiming toward critical consciousness through authentic dialogue, contrasts not only with a form-oriented approach but also with the communicative approaches to second language teaching outlined by Richards and Rodgers in *Approaches and Methods in Language Teaching,* pp. 64–86 and 113–168.

53. Henry Giroux, in the introduction to Freire and Macedo, *Literacy,* pp. 10–11.

54. See Graman, "Teaching and the Routes to Learning a Second Language."

55. See Renate A. Schulz, "Proficiency-Based Foreign Language Requirements: A Plan for Action," *ADFL Bulletin, 19*(2) (1988), 24–28.

56. Else Auerbach, "Competency-Based ESL: One Step Forward or Two Steps Back?" *TESOL Quarterly, 20* (1986), 411–412. See also C. A. Findley and L. A. Nathan, "Functional Language Objectives in a Competency-Based ESL Curriculum," *TESOL Quarterly, 14* (1981), 221–231.

57. Auerbach, "Competency-Based ESL," p. 416.

58. Auerbach, "Competency-Based ESL," p. 417.

59. Elsa Auerbach and Denise Burgess, "The Hidden Curriculum of Survival ESL," *TESOL Quarterly, 19* (1985), 475–495.

60. Auerbach, "Competency-Based ESL," pp. 418–419.

61. See Karen L. Smith, "Moving Spanish Language Programs into the 80's: Hypotheses and Questions," *Hispania, 69* (1986), 223–229.

62. Furthermore, beginning foreign language textbooks, like ESL textbooks, often distort the reality of the countries and people they describe. For further information on the this topic, see Tomas Graman, "The Politics of Foreign Language Instruction in the United States," a paper presented at the National Association of Chicano Studies Conference, Boulder, Colorado, April 1988.

63. Freire, *Pedagogy,* p. 100.

64. See Graman, "Teaching and the Routes to Second Language Learning."

65. See Kenneth S. Goodman, "Reading: A Psycholinguistic Guessing Game," paper read at the American Educational Research Association, New York, February 1967, and published in the *Journal of the Reading Specialist* (1967) reprint.

66. See Erich Fromm, *El miedo a la libertad,* 7th reprinting in Mexico, translated by Gino Germani (Mexico: Editorial Paidós Mexicana Publishers, 1987).

67. In John A. Crow and Edward Dudley, *El Cuento,* 2nd ed. (New York: Holt, Rinehart & Winston, 1984), pp. 62–69.

68. See Terri Cononelos (a student in one of the Freirean-based Spanish classes), "Expanding Chicano Studies Through Foreign Language Teaching: One Model and Its Implications," an unpublished paper chosen "the best undergraduate paper" at the National Association of Chicano Studies Conference in Boulder, Colorado, April 1988. Cononelos reports that 69 percent of the students who continued to upper-division Spanish courses came up through the Freirean courses, even though students in these courses composed only 17 percent of the total student population during the 1986–87 school year. Cononelos's research supports my argument that the Freirean pedagogy can help foreign language students to bridge the gap between lower- and upper-division courses (described by Graman, "The Gap," and Carroll, "Foreign Language Proficiency Levels Attained by Language Majors"), and ultimately come up through the ranks to reach those courses.

9

Social Class and School Literacy

Jane Nagle

Editors' Note: This chapter contains a critical self-portrait of a vocational high school teacher who learned how social class has shaped her and her students' different views of gender roles, religion, and work. From her self-analysis, Jane Nagle learned to understand and accept her working-class students' views rather than try to change them or impose her own middle-class values. This essay challenges our assumptions that working-class students want to join the middle class and continues the earlier focus on resistance to assimilation.

As part of my doctoral program at the University of Massachusetts at Amherst, I conducted ethnographic research as a pilot study. My original purpose was to examine a literacy classroom and to observe the students' interactions with the texts in a traditional American literature curriculum. Of particular interest at the start of the study were discussions of texts in peer groups and general class discussions with the teacher. I discovered by the end of the project that I had uncovered less about the students' interactions with the texts than about issues of class dynamics and the role of social class in education. Highlighted for me was the incongruence between the teacher's social background and the social backgrounds of the students.

I did the research in a twelfth-grade English classroom at a vocational high school in a New England town. The students had a biweekly schedule: one week they had academic classes, including two English periods, one math, one American history, one physical education, and three shop-related math and science periods. The other week they had an entire day of shop in their trade areas. During this week they had hands-on experiences applying the knowledge gained in their related classes. The school has a strong reputation for its vocational training. Students express a general feeling that their academic subjects are useless in preparing for the world of work.

The students in the class were all from working-class backgrounds. All of their parents worked in blue-collar jobs, paid an hourly wage for their time, not necessarily for their skill. Most students were the second or third generation in their families to select vocational education. They were tracked into the highest academic grouping and took pride in that accomplishment. As one girl said during an interview with the researcher:

> I worked hard to get into the top group, I deserve to enjoy being there. I know
> I wouldn't be in the top group in my old school. There were too many people
> smarter than me. Here we are all alike. Do you know what I mean?

In talking about being at a vocational school, one boy said:

> Guys at my old school thought voke schools were for losers. It used to bother
> me but it doesn't anymore because I am always going to have a job and be able
> to support my family.

The teacher has taught at the school for fifteen years. She has two masters degrees and is working on her doctorate in Education. She claims to see education as transformational. She feels that her students have been cheated out of early access to school literacy. She wants to make up for lost time and encourages them often to continue to grow through education. She talks about her desire to introduce them to as many of the major American authors as possible in the short time she has them in class.

The class is very structured. Three specific literacy events happen each day: personal journal writing (a ten-minute writing period spent responding to the texts; students have the option of sharing the journal with the teacher), teacher-directed class discussion, and small peer group discussions. Every Friday the class does essay writing in blue examination books. Students usually complete the tests at home and return them the following academic week. On these test days the teacher and students spent a great deal of time talking informally. Sometimes the talk was centered on the text. At other times it was about topics seemingly unrelated to the school work. During this time it seemed that a strong bond existed between teacher and students.

The study began with a broad overview of these literacy events. Through a close examination of the data a pattern of themes emerged. Those that occurred in all events were: work ethic, traditional religious references, and male/female roles. These themes revealed a contrast between the teacher's and the students' points of view, a tension between their two world views.

For the students, one's work ethic defined one's social status. If someone was a hard worker he/she was admirable. When the students referred to work, they usually meant physical labor. They respected people who put in a full day's work. They had little respect for "pencil pushers" and no respect for anyone who did not work. The teacher viewed physical labor as less important than what she called "intellectual work." She felt that working at a desk exploring ideas was the kind of work one should respect. She accepted the fact that some people could not work and she believed it was society's obligation to take care of those people.

The students had strong religious convictions. Their Christian faith was nurtured in a fundamentalist dogma. They were very comfortable bringing their religion into the classroom because they felt their religious beliefs were universal and were shared by most people. They saw God as the ultimate judge who rewarded good and punished evil. The teacher was very uncomfortable when religion became a part of class discussions. She believed passionately in the separation of church and state and always discouraged any classroom talk that was of a religious nature. She saw her students as being intolerant of religious differences and so avoided what she perceived as a volatile issue.

The roles of males and females in society were clearly drawn in the students' eyes. There was man's place as bread winner and then there was woman's place as homemaker (and maybe part-time worker if money was needed). They saw feminism as a dirty word and one that meant that those clearly defined boundaries between men and women were being threatened. The teacher saw herself as a struggling feminist. She was trying to find her own place as a female teacher in a male-dominated and at times sexist school environment. She wanted her female students to challenge the traditional roles for women in our society.

The researcher requested that the class and the teacher decide what they meant by each of the identified themes. On the work ethic, teacher and students seemed to be closest in terms of agreement:

Mike: You go to work every day.

Paul: Yes, so you can support your family.

Mike: That's why I came here. I knew I'd always have a job. I'll never be on welfare.

Teacher: What if you get sick? Remember welfare is set up to help the working man.

Mike: I'll never be on welfare. Period.

In talking about traditional religious values the students seemed to feel more at ease than the teacher.

Jenn: Everyone believes in God.

Dan: Or at least cares about being good.

Michelle: So the world needs standards. Do you know what I mean?

Teacher: Yes so we'll call it a moral code? Is that acceptable?

About the final theme, male/female roles, the class and the teacher were in obvious conflict:

Sam: Women shouldn't work but if they do, they are still responsible for the housework.

Teacher: God help your wife (teacher laughs/students moan).

Nancy: He's right. He shouldn't have to vacuum. I'll expect my husband to cut the grass but I'll do the rest.

Specific literary texts provoked interaction between the teacher and students around these themes. Two texts that inspired strong responses from the students and interesting reactions by the teacher were *A Streetcar Named Desire*, a play by Tennessee Williams, and "Bernice Bobs Her Hair," a short story by F. Scott Fitzgerald.

The journal writing for *A Streetcar Named Desire* generally reflected the students' identification with the story and characters. The three themes were evident in most of the eight journals students shared with the teacher. The following example shows one student's attempt to express her personal reactions to the story and the teacher's attempt to clear up any misconceptions.

Journal Entry

I can relate to Stanley in many ways because I can see parts of Stanley in a lot of guys I know especially my boyfriend. I have been in many arguments with guys like Stanley and I have been hit. I guess you just have to take it because they are in the driver's seat. Stella didn't have any place to go. I guess she thought she needed Stanley.

Teacher's Written Response

I hope you can understand that no one has the right to ever hit you. Stella (or any woman in this kind of relationship) must get out.

In the peer group discussion the students attempted to express their strong personal reactions to their peers. The following is an example of a single voice speaking out against the popular opinion:

Tim: What does she want us to talk about?

Brenda: We're supposed to talk about how we feel about the characters. So what did you think of Blanche?

Ted: She's crazy. She got what she deserved.

Brenda: No one deserves to be raped.

Ted: Oh, right.

Brenda: I suppose if it was your mom or girlfriend, it would be just fine?

Ted: My mother and my girl wouldn't do the things Blanche did.

Tim: Ted is right, Brenda, just accept it.

Brenda: Why don't you say something [she is talking to the other female in the group]? Ms. Miller wants all of us talking.

Grace: I agree with Ted and Tim. She was always flirting. She got what she deserved.

Brenda: Ms. Miller can we go back to general class discussion? You guys make me sick.

When the first girl attempted to question Stanley's action, she received no support from the other group members. When she realized that she was standing alone in questioning traditional male/female roles as perceived by her group, she called to the teacher for rescue.

The third literacy event, the formal writing for the teacher, reflected the teacher's lectures more than the students' own opinions as expressed in their journals or peer discussions. In the formal writing the students modified their opinions to meet the standards set by the teacher. One question that the teacher gave was: "Is Stanley a loser at the game of life? Explain." The teacher's total disrespect for Stanley was evident in her lectures and class discussion. In the journals and in peer group discussions it was evident that most in the class did not share her judgment. Yet in answering this question, three fourths of the class began their responses by saying, "Yes, Stanley is a loser at life."

The reaction to "Bernice Bobs Her Hair" was strong. The students expressed a dislike for the story and a lack of interest in the characters who in the eyes of the students lived useless lives and were not worth the time it took to read about them.

One student wrote in his journal:

Well, Miss. Miller, you really blew it this time. This story was a total waste of my time. Who wants to read about these lazy foolish people who don't work and only want to impress each other with stupid flirting.

The teacher's response to this journal was:

You seem to have had a stronger reaction to these characters than you realize. They seemed to have made you angry. What about their lives bothers you?

During the peer group discussion the lack of interest in the story and a disrespect for the lives of the characters became evident:

Michelle: Did you like the story?

Nancy: I hated it. Those girls were bimbos.

Dan: Does anyone have the math done? Can I copy it?

Nancy: Miller is going to have a stroke if she catches you.

Dan: I'll tell her it's her fault for picking such a stupid book about people I'm not interested in.

Nancy: She'll say [mimicking the teacher] you don't want to broaden your horizons.

Dan: And she'll be right. Now give me the math. I hope that stupid tape recorder isn't near me or I'm dead.

Ms. Miller overheard this conversation and immediately became directive. She instructed the class to take out their notebooks and she gave a formal lecture during which she stressed the importance of the author's work, especially if the students were planning to go on to college. She began her lecture by saying: "You seem to have missed the point of this story. Let's see what the experts say." On the essay test which was done the following day, the majority of the class fed back the teacher's words to her. Few risked expressing their own biases.

At first glance, the personal journals seem to provide the most nonjudgmental format for the student freely to express his/her opinions. Over the time span of the study students wrote 1,208 journal entries and shared only 54 with the teacher. In each of these 54 entries the student expressed strong personal reactions to the texts. The teacher's response also showed a strong bias either in favor of or in opposition to the student's comments. It is interesting to note that the student never responded in writing to the teacher's comment. The teacher wrote her comments as if she was trying to correct misconceptions. Her middle-class values became truths. The students' unwillingness to share their journals may reflect their inability to articulate their own beliefs in the face of the dominant discourse of the middle class as voiced by the teacher.

In the peer group discussions there usually was a consensus of opinions. The only time there was a conflict was on the issue of male/female roles and the challenging voice was always the same female student. There was never any support from either the males or the other females in the group. The lone dissenter always turned to the teacher for help and her request was always the same: "Can we go back to general class discussion?"—discussion where the teacher's voice would be the loudest.

In essay test writing the students adjusted their opinions to meet the standard of acceptability set by the teacher. Of the 273 essay tests completed, 261 had phrases taken directly from the teacher's lectures. The teacher was fed her own words. These students were taking no risks.

At this point I want to reveal that I was not only the researcher in this study, but also the teacher. Looking at my own presuppositions and biases was not easy. Listening to the tapes of my classes, I heard myself force-feeding my opinions to my students and this was painful. I knew in my heart and in my head that I was committed to my students and their access to school literacy. I knew that if I was honest with myself about what I saw, I would be able to make changes where they were needed and my teaching would improve. By writing and thinking about myself in the third person, I was able to distance myself from personalizing, and from needing to justify, my mistakes. On one tape I heard myself saying:

> Those of you who are going on to college next year need to take this term paper assignment very seriously. Those of you who are not going to college just need to hand something in to show your commitment to this class.

Could this message be any clearer?

One student approached me after class one day and quietly said:

> You know, we're all Stanleys [from A Streetcar Named Desire] in this class. If you taught at Willard [a local prep school], those kids would probably think about Stanley the way you do. You know that guy Holden [from The Catcher in the Rye] that we read about last year, well, we didn't understand him. We understand Stanley. That doesn't make us bad.

The fact that the student could articulate what he saw as the teacher's bias speaks highly of his courage. The fact that he would not say this in a formal classroom discussion says that he may have learned school rules late but he learned them well. School literacy was not an easy acquisition and so risk taking was not something most of my students were willing to do.

The last day of school one boy wrote about his future plans. He said that he was presently working as a machinist at Ore Industries and if God was willing he would be there for the next forty-five years. Before I did this study that statement would have depressed me and I would have felt that I had failed. Now I realize that his being able to tell me his life goals in a straightforward way shows that he feels comfortable incorporating his working-class values into his work in my classroom.

If the price for school literacy, for most working-class students, is to deny or at least not express working-class values, then it would seem that educators need to examine closely their attitudes about social class. As a vocational high school teacher I have worked with predominately working-class students for most of my career and I have always believed that the working class was something everyone needed and wanted to leave. My students in this study have awakened me to the fact that the working class is exactly where most of them want to be. My assumption that education was a way out of working-class status was elitist. This awareness has led me to a new respect for my students' world view and a realization that my classroom needs to be a place where school literacy enhances the life experiences of all students, not only those who share my middle-class biases.

10

Reading and Writing on Strike [1]

Kelly Belanger, Linda Strom, and John Russo

Editors' Note: These three Youngstown State University professors describe what happens when the working class goes to the university, or in their case, when the university goes to the working class. They tell us about their courses in a program in labor studies and business for local steelworkers. They offer the same classes in a union hall in both morning and evening hours so that workers on changing shifts can attend either. This flexible scheduling and the professors' teaching methods reflect their commitment to the "organizing model" of unionism and to what they call "*working-class* student centered" courses. Moreover, the writing course takes "work" as its subject matter and integrates community resources for historical research on local union activity.

Historians say that the past, present, and future are connected in ways not always predictable or well understood. Perhaps nowhere are these connections more evident than in Youngstown, Ohio, where attempts to prevent the closing of steel mills in the late '70s and early '80s led to landmark pro–labor legislation regarding plant closing, eminent domain, and pension reform that could not have been anticipated. Despite these progressive labor laws, the major steel mills in the area still closed, with reverberations felt today, especially for unionized steelworkers who carry memories of the past upheaval into their present jobs. Remembering the swift disappearance of the community's chief livelihood, the steelworkers of the 1990s have had little faith that their present jobs will be there in the future. In part to prepare for an uncertain tomorrow, members of the United Steelworkers of America negotiated in 1989 a career development program in their national contract. For the union and for the companies, such a program also holds the potential to develop workers' literate abilities to

166

participate in the world where they live and work, ideally resulting in more skilled employees and more involved union members.

As a result of the national contract, in September 1994 Steelworkers Local 1375 approached Youngstown State University for a program of on-site courses leading to an associate's degree in business or labor studies. Besides the obvious appeal of labor studies, the Steelworkers Union found a business curriculum attractive because such a degree would offer members opportunities in the event of another mill closing or if workers' jobs were phased out because technology made them "redundant." University administrators responded positively, viewing it as one strategy to combat dwindling enrollment and as a means to serve adult learners in the surrounding working-class communities. To allow students to satisfy requirements for the degree, the first courses offered were in labor history and in writing to meet general education requirements. The three of us were the first YSU faculty to teach at the off-campus site: John, who had taught labor studies courses at the union hall in the past; Linda, who became involved because of her interest in working-class studies; and Kelly, who brought to the program expertise in teaching writing to nontraditional and "at-risk" students. Because John's labor history students were also simultaneously enrolled in Linda's and Kelly's writing courses, this teaching experience gave us an exciting opportunity to collaborate across disciplines and link content area to language arts.

For the labor studies classes, course content and teaching methodologies reflected what is called the "organizing model" of unionism (see Figure 10–1), a model that emphasizes developing current union members' problem-solving skills, commitment to ongoing education, effective communication, and ability to work within a union environment where authority is decentralized. The goal of the organizing model is to create active members who feel personally responsible for the effectiveness of the union. As we collaborated on the courses, we realized that many of the values that underpin the organizing model reflect some basic tenets of Freirean critical pedagogy that have influenced current composition pedagogy. For example, in the broadest sense, a Freirean model of education, like the organizing model, contends that "education is politics." Both Freirean education and the organizing model of unionism share a common political goal: to decentralize authority and empower disenfranchised people within an organization or community to take transformative action that questions the status quo (Freire 1970, 34). However, in the union hall program, the pedagogical approaches used in the labor studies and writing courses, like most actual classroom practices, do not fit neatly into any single model. Thus, the labor studies and the writing courses embodied several models. In concert, however, the writing and labor studies courses employ three key elements of both the organizing model of unionism and Freire's approach to critical pedagogy: blurring boundaries between teacher and learner, honing critical and analytical skills in a social context, and empowering people to act upon their world.[2]

Figure 10–1.
Models of Unionism

Servicing Model	Organizing Model
1. Union leadership solves problems for members on basis of complaints or requests	1. Stimulates and involves members in problem-solving in group process or collective action
2. Total reliance on grievance and negotiations process	2. Not limited to the bargaining process
3. Passive membership or limited to leadership requests for co-operation	3. Commitment to education, communications, and participation in the union
4. Reliance on specialists, experts, and union staff	4. Development of and dependence on members' skills
5. Secretive and closed communication	5. Information sharing and open communication channels
6. Centralized and top-heavy organizational structure	6. Decentralized organizational structure
7. Dependent on management; reactive	7. Independent of management; proactive
8. Makes distinctions between internal and external organizing activities	8. Makes no destinction between internal and external organizing activities

These models are not mutually exclusive but reflect a difference in emphasis.

All the parties involved in this program—including the university administration and the union leaders—agreed to adapt the content and structure of the courses to students' needs and experiences. Perhaps the most significant structural adaptation was necessary because steelworkers work on a system of "21 turns" in which workers rotate weekly between day, afternoon, and night shifts. To accommodate their schedules, we offered the same course twice each day at the union hall so that students could attend a morning or afternoon class depending on their shift that week. In an interview, Alan, a learning steward for the union who helps recruit steelworkers for the classes explained that the "availability of the classes at the hall makes it easier. It's closer for me, it's a little more comfortable because you're with people your own age, not sitting where young students are." Denise, a single mother and full-time steelworker, agreed, and emphasized the importance of the classes being taught on shifts: "The fact that we could take [the classes] twice a day and we didn't miss [them] because we were on certain shifts [was important]. Having them here rather than traveling to the university made it much easier in fact. I don't know if I could've done it as well as I did had we not had them here." These adaptations, which all the students described as beneficial to them, represent one of the first steps in the university and the union's ongoing collaboration aimed at making the college courses accessible and friendly to working people.[3]

In addition to designing course schedules around work lives and locations familiar to students, faculty and union representatives agreed that the union hall courses should be consciously *"working-class* student–centered"; that is, in every decision from text selection to assignment design, working-class history and experience would be at the center of the curriculum. To create a curriculum that validated working-class culture and experience, John focused on labor history from workers' perspectives, while Kelly and Linda designed the first union hall writing course around the theme of "work" in their lives, which segued with John's labor studies.[4] In both courses, students were encouraged to construct working-class histories of their communities, becoming active constructors of knowledge rather than passive recipients of experts' versions of history.[5]

The Writing Courses

In the writing courses, Kelly and Linda sought a student-centered classroom where students could develop confidence in themselves as thinkers and writers. Many of these working-class students brought feelings of inadequacy, fear of failure and embarrassment, and negative memories of past school writing experiences. Therefore, Kelly and Linda believed their first priority was to help these students recognize that written language could be a source of power rather than a roadblock to reaching educational goals and taking civic action. Once gaining that confidence, students could undertake assignments that asked them to use writing to develop a critical perspective on issues that impacted their own lives and the broader culture.

Initially, Kelly and Linda focused on helping students explore their ideas about the purposes of writing and what they wanted or expected to learn in a college-writing course. This effort to build a syllabus beginning with the concerns of the students reflects the Freirean concept of the "generative theme." As Freire (1970) writes in *Pedagogy of the Oppressed,* any successful educational program must "respect the particular worldview held by the people" (86). In a Freirean spirit, each course began with individual conferences in which students set their own writing goals for the quarter. Typically, students' lists included improving spelling and punctuation as well as desires to take transformative actions: to write better grievances, help children with homework, and send convincing letters to the editor. Rather than simply imposing teacher-centered goals on students, Kelly and Linda sought to establish from the beginning that student concerns and ideas would be integral to the course. Periodically, students wrote self-evaluations to reflect upon their progress toward their initial goals and to record their developing ideas about effective reading and writing processes.

These self-evaluations built students' confidence in part because they celebrated successes, but also because they gave students a sense of control over their learning process. Further, these texts allowed follow-up discussions with students to be dialogic negotiations that balanced students' own perceptions of their progress with teachers' expectations for particular assignments. This process of negotiation and self-reflection established mutual trust between students and teachers, laying a foundation for collaborative peer response and small group discussion that made up the daily activities of the classes.

In small groups during class, the writing students often shared drafts and informal responses to readings to prepare for whole class discussions. A typical early assignment invited students to explore social and cultural factors that affected their identities and beliefs by answering the question "Who am I?" in ten different ways, then exploring which self-descriptions are most important to them and why.[6] Through discussing such an assignment in groups, students began to see how factors such as race, age, class, and gender shape how they see and are perceived by the world. One woman, who worked for an automobile parts manufacturer, described the impact of being raised in a primarily male environment (she'd "rather have a dirt bike than a diamond ring") where her mother was a "typical dependent housewife." Her list prompted her to analyze ways she consciously sought to emulate what she saw as the positive masculine role models and eschew the "negative" feminine one by seeking technical work, a managerial position, self-sufficiency, and independence. As she began developing her own research project later in the course, we encouraged her to explore possible connections between her upbringing, her identity, and the anti-union positions she took in a later writing assignment. While some students were able to make such connections better than others, the goal of the assignment was to help students identify where their opinions came from and how reading, writing, and thinking processes are affected by socially constructed beliefs and values. Asking students to identify the source of what they often accept as common knowledge or universal "truth" provides them with a foundation for developing critical literacy. As Catherine Walsh (1991) puts it, critical literacy "should relate to the contexts of learners' lives, be interesting, purposeful, engaging, incite dialogue and struggle around meanings, interpretations, and identities and promote among learners a critical understanding of their relationship to a broader society, and of their and its political nature, and transformative possibilities" (17). Like educational philosophers from Dewey to Freire, we see this kind of literacy as essential for thoughtful participation in the social and political processes of a democratic society.

The Union Goes on Strike

Although all three writing courses offered have focused on developing critical literacies, a writing course in the fall of 1995 when their union was on strike gave students a context for becoming active agents in a highly charged situation that not only affected them personally, but also impacted the community at large. At that time, the course's reading and writing assignments were developed around the "Little Steel" Strike of 1937 against Republic Steel plants in Chicago, Youngstown, and Warren, Ohio (where our students' union hall is located). Since many of our students' fathers and other family members worked at Republic Steel as both rank and file and as managers, they brought a collective memory of this earlier violent conflict to the class. For our students and for the Warren community, the strike of 1995 became a kind of palimpsest of the 1937 strike, with rhetoric, key players, and artifacts of the earlier conflict resurfacing to imbue the current situation with the spirit of the past.

In the weeks preceding the '95 strike, our students read accounts accompanied by original photographs of the '37 strike in *The Warren Steelworker*, the union's newsletter. In an issue featuring articles on the '37 strike, newsletter editor and union President Dennis Brubaker's (1995) editorial entreated current members to prepare for a possible lockout or strike if the upcoming negotiations broke down. Then, just two months before the '95 strike (and three months before our class began), the Ohio Historical Society hosted a colloquium that brought together members of the Steelworkers Organizing Committee (SWOC, the precursor of the United Steelworkers of America), a local journalist who covered the earlier action, and community members indirectly affected by the strike. The colloquium served to publicly create an oral history of the "climactic and often violent 'Little Steel' Strike of 1937" (*The Warren Steelworker* 1995, 1). Many of the organizers, including the strike captain and Communist leader Gus Hall (then eighty-five-years-old), returned to the Youngstown–Warren area, and, through their reminiscences, reawakened in community members and in many Local 1375 steelworkers the legacy of activism that galvanized the strikers in 1937. The public oral history they created was framed by an account of the strike presented by a labor history student and a labor historian. This event, by weaving "expert" academic opinion with "history from below," reinscribed the pedagogical approach students experienced in the writing and labor studies classes, where students conducted original research based on interviews, analyses of original documents in the archives of the labor museum and experts' conflicting representations of history.[7]

Just as the '95 strike went into full swing, the fall quarter writing courses began, centering on the strike of '37. Students sandwiched their course work between shifts on the picket line, and our classes were moved from room to room to make space for meetings, food distribution, and child care. The first assignment asked students to write what they knew and felt about the current or past strikes. One purpose of the assignment was to bring out what the few nonsteelworker students in the class knew and felt about labor issues. As one of these students, an eighteen-year-old woman, wrote, she felt "nervous about taking the class at the union hall with so many older students." She was also "worried that she didn't know enough about unions to take the class"—her only experience with them was walking past people holding picket signs outside a local nonunion grocery store. Another purpose of the assignment was to encourage all the students to express various prejudices, biases, assumptions, and emotional reactions. One steelworker-student vented his anger at the company for hiring replacement workers:

> When we were first locked out and I realized that there were replacement workers, hundreds of them, in the plant, I became very angry at the company . . . the goons were a symbol of the company's willingness to use brute force if necessary to ride out the first storm until they could get an injunction that would permit semicivilized disorder. . . . That first 48 hours many thoughts streaked in and out of my temporarily shell-shocked mind. As I joined my brothers and sisters on the picket line and at the union hall, it soon became apparent that there was hope from many individuals that this would be a work stoppage of short duration and things would return to normal. This false hope scared me. The company was successful at everything they attempted, and to think that they would be unsuccessful suggested diminished rationalization based on hopes for a favorable outcome to this confrontation.

Through this assignment, students began to see writing as a useful means of self-expression, laying the groundwork for future exercises in rhetorical analysis and critical thinking.

Tools for Critical Thought

To give students some tools for analysis, the class worked through a series of applications from Vincent Ryan Ruggiero's (1995) text *Beyond Feelings: A Guide to Critical Thinking,* a brief rhetoric that could be easily applied to our "case study" of the strike. *Beyond Feelings* acknowledges the important role intuitions and emotion play in critical thinking while also exploring their limitations, so it seemed especially appropriate as a guide to analyzing the highly charged past and present strikes. Though we do not equate Ruggiero's concept of "critical thinking" with Freirean critical consciousness (e.g., "desocialized thinking"), Ruggiero's exercises provide a useful starting point for developing "critical literacy," which Shor (1992) identifies as one of four qualities that make up Freirean critical consciousness (129–30). The text asks students to apply concepts of objectivity and subjectivity by exploring what constitutes truth, knowledge, and a "sound" opinion. As one student explained in his midterm self-evaluation, the applications led him to see that responses to issues are filtered through individuals' experiences and biases: "There are many factors that control the outcome of your response. Issues that may seem clear cut to you may be less black and white to others. Initial reaction to a topic may keep you from seeing both sides. You might only favor views that support yours, and discredit all others."

While this assignment gave students practice applying critical strategies to situations in their personal lives, the next assignment moved from examining personal experience to analyzing published discourse surrounding the '37 strike. First, the students read conflicting versions of the strike by David

Brody (1987), labor historian and author of *Forging a Union of Steel;* Gus Hall
(1987), the strike captain and author of *Working Class USA: The Power and the
Movement;* and Tom Girdler (1943), the company president of Republic Steel
and author of *Bootstraps.* For each reading assignment, we asked students to
use Ruggiero's critical thinking strategies to analyze the truth value of the
varying accounts. This posed problems for them. In journal entries on their first
readings of each text, students tended to summarize material rather than analyze, and stuck to their personal viewpoints, often shaped by the degree to
which they felt allegiances to the union. This excerpt from a student's response
to Gus Hall's book is one of the most problematically uncritical:

> In this article there were a lot of good points about Communism. Gus Hall was
> a very courageous person. I think in the beginning he could foresee what was
> going to happen. . . . I think the Communist Party cared about the workers. I
> think Gus Hall should be looked up to for the factory workers' rights of today.
> Where would we be without him?

After reading such initial responses, we then asked the class to reread the
three texts dialogically, imagining what Gus Hall might say in response to
Girdler's account of the strike, how Girdler might respond to Hall, and what
Brody might say about each of their accounts. We also asked that they review
Ruggiero on evaluating the truth value of an argument. Subsequent class
discussions pushed students' thinking—for example, they began to question
Girdler's assertion that his climb through the ranks of the steel industry made
him an "insider" who could understand the concerns of working people better
than "outside agitators" such as Hall. Numerous students also interrogated Hall's
self-representation as the hero of the strike:

> Gus Hall's tribute was very biased toward the greatness of Gus Hall. The au-
> thor was willing to downgrade anyone it could to make Gus Hall look supe-
> rior. Very strong unsubstantiated claims were made in this writing, especially
> saying in effect that Ronald Reagan appointed criminals to the White House.
> Gus Hall was wanted on warrants in six different states, yet the author never
> explains each warrant directly, you are only led to believe that each of them
> was false.

Similarly, students began to see how the Brody labor study could be read as in-
tervening in this debate by putting Girdler's and Hall's accounts of the strike in
a larger historical framework, one in which neither of the two men were even
mentioned by name.

Along with giving students a framework in which to reread Hall and
Girdler, the Brody piece challenged students to decipher its academic language
and to immerse themselves in a discourse community difficult for students
unfamiliar with the history of steelworkers' organizing efforts. In the morning
"shift" of the class, often attended by traditional YSU students and workers in
other industries, many of the students struggled to make even literal meaning

of the academic text. Together, the class identified unfamiliar terms and names, working collaboratively to piece together enough background to make a second reading easier. Whereas key terms and players in the historical events were unfamiliar to many of the morning students, steelworker-students in the afternoon shift of the class took over the teaching of that text, explaining ideas such as the difference between an open and closed shop and the significance of the Wagner Act. Through this experience, the steelworkers, teachers, and other class members collectively constructed a foundation of knowledge for rereading all three texts in order to prepare for the first major writing assignment.

Identifying Bias in Sources

The first multidraft essay assignment placed students in rhetorical situations, asking them to analyze the three sources we read as a class to evaluate the texts' arguments for a specific audience. In one option, students wrote to a friend interested in researching the "SWOC years"; for a second option, students prepared the text for a colloquium talk on the SWOC years much like the one recently held at the Youngstown Museum of Labor and Industry. Both options required that students draw upon the readings in Ruggiero's text as well as their own experiences in considering the kinds of evidence and arguments used by the authors. In addition, students reflected on how their own biases had led them to "read" this moment in history in a particular way. This complex assignment, which called upon students to generate criteria with which to evaluate their sources, apply the criteria, and then adapt their analysis for a specific audience, proved challenging for them.

In our experience, a layered assignment like this one often meets with some confusion and resistance in first-year students, both on campus and at the union hall site. We find students often struggle when asked to "read against the grain" as David Bartholomae and Anthony Petrosky (1996) describe it: to question a writer's arguments, examples, or vision; to engage in a dialogue with the text (10–12). In an interview, one student, Anna, laughingly reflected upon her earlier naive readings of the opposing accounts of the '37 strike by Hall and Girdler: "One text was management and one was the workers . . . first [we read] Gus Hall and we hated management, and after reading the CEO, my opinion changed completely and I hated Gus Hall." Another possible explanation for Anna's difficulties is that inexperienced college writers have not been exposed to a wide range of written discourse patterns required of academic writers, as Bizzell (1992), Shaughnessy (1977), and Rose (1983) have argued. The complex reading and writing assignments in this course gave students contact with various discourse options, which as Mike Rose notes, are "essential to the making and conveying of meaning in our culture" (116). Meanwhile, the applications in Ruggiero's *Beyond Feelings* provided a kind of balance: they validated students' abilities as sophisticated thinkers by helping them discover ways in which they already used these same interpretive and evaluative strategies to discover meanings in their everyday lives.

In midterm analyses of their work, many students commented on what they had learned from the SWOC assignment. Dan, for example, wrote that "researching different sources was good to do because I usually try to rush my process and sometimes do not find the time to read different sources. The way this class is structured forced me to take the time to read different sources and see the biases that occur in writing." While some students were never quite able successfully to organize and present their analyses, others—as Dan's comment suggests—attained through this assignment a richer understanding of how critical analysis can make them more self-reflective and better able to evaluate different points of view. We attribute students' varied levels of success with the assignment to factors including the level of their critical thinking and writing skills, degree of familiarity with the course theme, and the time they allowed for revision.

Constructive Conflict

Midway through the course, students' abilities to respond thoughtfully to opposing viewpoints were tested when one student, Cheryl—a nonsteelworker in a management training position—wrote an essay that critiqued the union's actions during the '37 strike. On the day Cheryl presented her draft to the class, she was nervous about her point of view not being well-received or respected. Fortunately, the discussion was lively but not hostile. Focusing on the effectiveness of her argument, many students concluded that they found her ideas persuasive and challenging, but disagreed with her conclusion. Significantly for Cheryl, this experience reinforced the idea that even potentially hostile audiences can be receptive to an opposing argument if the writer makes her case by fairly presenting opposing points of view and openly acknowledging her own biases. The draft she presented in class gave a balanced view, conceding, on the one hand, that "the 1930s was a time in history [memorable because of] the contributions of the CIO, SWOC and the dedicated men and women who fought to shape the future environment for the working-class people" while still asserting that "it is also important to take into account that the companies also had a valid position for their stand against the unions." In the end, though many of her classmates disagreed, they appreciated that this balanced approach effectively supported her main claim that union organizers of the 1930s used objectionable means to achieve their goals. For pro-union students, Cheryl presented a worthy rhetorical opponent against which they could bring to bear their own developing arguments. Cheryl's articulate essay put pressure on pro-strike students to meet her standard of discourse. In her midterm self-evaluation, "Writing Behind the Scenes," Cheryl wrote:

> Writing is more than having a pen and pencil in hand. It involves critical thinking, interpretation of the ideas of others, and being able to formulate a theory leaving some of our personal biases behind. Critical thinking is the topic that has hit me the hardest. Everyone is quick to say that they are a critical thinker.

The [steel company] employees feel the union is a necessary stronghold and are quick to defend it, right or wrong. Yet, I found myself in my initial draft taking the other stand and jumping down the union's throat. A day or two later when I read it again, the bias of my writing was alarming. I too had fallen victim of my environment and beliefs.

Cheryl's process of making an informed argument, presenting it to a knowledgeable audience, and then reevaluating her position in light of her own biases demonstrates some literate strategies that help empower students with the knowledge and critical tools to be effective members of their union, workplace, and community.

Labor in Crisis: The History Course

Because the writing classes—like the organizing model of unionism—emphasize active rather than passive learning, nonauthoritarian leadership, and the importance of students constructing contending knowledges rather than relying solely on experts, these courses complement the more direct focus on the organizing model that underpinned the labor studies courses taught by John. In those classes, John emphasized that this model of unionism sees the labor movement in a crisis it can survive only by adopting new methods for a culture of organizing and education. In introductory lectures, John explains that the organizing model differs from the servicing model because it is proactive, that is, structurally decentralized to stimulate and involve members/students in problem solving, group activities, and collective action. The model is based on a commitment to education, open communications, and participation; therefore, without ongoing development of union members' abilities the model cannot succeed. As students learn about the organizing model in John's union hall classes, both union and nonunion class members are asked to address the following questions: (1) How am I creating a culture of organizing and education within my local? (2) What elements in any situation can I use to mobilize membership support in order to achieve membership goals and gains? (3) Am I asking for membership participation or cooperation? (4) Do my words and/or actions mobilize or demobilize members? and (5) How have I gotten people to care and believe in their organization? John's questions pose the organizing model in practical terms to accomplish two goals: to give all class members a concrete understanding of the organizing model and to mobilize union members in class to take action.

In the history of labor course he taught several times at the union hall, John divided his two-day-a-week course into one session where he presented a critical lecture while the other session employed a more dialogic pedagogy. The use of both lecture (teacher-centered) and dialogic (student-centered) approaches was the result of tension between John's predisposition to Freirean pedagogy and what he perceived as these students' initial discomfort with the dialogic approach. That is, while there is some evidence that adult learners generally prefer dialogic approaches, he observed in his students considerable traditional expectations for a teacher-centered pedagogy. His once-a-week lecture met this expectation while modeling how to critically examine conventional labor history.

In the student-centered, dialogic part of his class, John required students to conduct their own historical research, an assignment that put into practice the organizing model's stress on active, participatory learning. As mentioned above, parallel with this student-centered learning, John's lectures presented critiques of mainstream labor history, which tried to model questioning. His lectures identified recent paradigm shifts in the discipline of labor history, in which scholars moved from an emphasis on major strikes and great labor leaders to charting the everyday history of working-class people and working-class agency. Through lectures, he argued for the importance of working people making and documenting their own histories, which introduced the research project that became the focus of the course.

John's commitment to students' and union members' constructing knowledge in addition to receiving it was best reflected in his practice of using the second day of class each week as a research workshop. In these workshops, students might, for example, formulate ideas for their projects, getting input from John and their classmates. At first, some students resisted the shift from lecture to project discussions, perhaps because they initially saw more value in hearing expert analysis of labor issues than in gathering and interpreting data themselves. John compares students' resistance to doing their own research with the unions' frequent requests that he conduct research for them. To both unions and students, he gives the same standard response: "I will teach you to do your own research." Because John began his course by critically lecturing, students' discomfort with the shift to a more participatory mode is understandable, especially considering John's charismatic speaking ability and his strong ethos as a labor expert. The degree of resistance that naturally comes with combining two such contradictory teaching methods is so far acceptable to him because he sees value in both.

The benefits of the more dialogic part of John's pedagogy are apparent in the story of how two labor history students' projects became connected. The idea for the first student's project emerged when Rex found at his grandfather's house a book of 1920s photographs of Truscon Steel Corporation, the forerunner of Republic Steel. The photographs' visual power opened up for Rex a moment in which the past and present coalesced, producing a sense of timelessness. He saw in the photographs evidence of both continuity and change: some machines looked the same as ones currently in use, while others had been replaced. When Rex brought the book to class, John encouraged him to consider the photographs as a critical primary source, one that might potentially help to fill in gaps in the written historical accounts of the steel industry. Yet, it was not until other students began examining the photos that some of their most significant contents came to light. Denise, who had sought to discover the earliest presence of women in the mills, had no sources of information revealing their employment in steel mills during the 1920s until she looked at the photographs. Her interviews with elderly nursing home residents had provided some information, but in the Truscon photographs, she noticed women dressed in crisp uniforms and working in the tin mill, a finding that gave her the same personal sense of continuity with the past that Rex had experienced.

This sense of a real historical connection became the starting point for many students' writing projects, which used research techniques from Jeremy Brecher's (1988) *History from Below* rather than traditional library methods and sources. Brecher's techniques include, for example, transcribing oral histories obtained through interviewing participants as well as analyzing videos or photographs documenting the building of local unions. His community-based research was particularly appropriate for the union hall classes because it allowed students who had mixed experiences with reading and writing in high school to engage in academic projects that legitimized familiar working-class culture. Such legitimization of students' working-class lives is valuable because it introduces them to new ways of reading, writing, and seeing the world without erasing their working-class identities.

Students Evaluate the Program

Almost unanimously, students' responses to the curricula in interviews and course evaluations indicate that they experienced significant individual growth. One student, who had been out of school for many years, used a visual image to describe the experience of taking classes: "I was like an old rusty gate, just couldn't open up, but now that the gate is opened, the knowledge has flowed through. . . . It was closed for 25 years" (Austin). For most students, the opening of the "gate" suggested an attitude of confidence they could imagine transferring to other endeavors: "even if you never use the things you learn in these classes professionally, it gives you a mind-set. You get a sense of accomplishment that makes you strive for more . . . it does make you see the possibilities that weren't there before" (Alan). Along with mentioning this shift in attitude, students also reported more confidence in expressing themselves and using language for practical goals such as writing strong grievances within the union, composing letters to the editor, and writing for hobby and sports magazines, goals that were originally set at the beginning of the course. As this next student quote suggests, there was also a sense that through taking these courses, they had gained increased respect in the workplace: "I think they [coworkers and management] seem to respect you a little more if you're trying to expand your knowledge, wanting to learn instead of staying on a plateau and saying you're satisfied with yourself" (Denise). For her, however, this respect came at a price. She described "a little bit of antagonism" toward her from male coworkers who were not taking classes. She had to listen to comments such as "Oh, you're takin' college—what're gonna be, the next Union President?"

The personal and academic development students experienced was complemented for some by a growth in commitment to union activity. Such growth was, for John and for union President Denny Brubaker, a goal of the education program in general. For them, education provides steelworkers the opportunity to gain the critical tools to understand better their role in building and rebuilding their union. They see the education programs as key to getting union people to care about each other and believe in their organization. Their most hopeful vision for the program is illustrated in the words of the "rusty gate" steelworker: When asked how the classes affected the way that he perceives or does his job, he responded, "I think we've tried to put our efforts into finding more ways of making our union strong." In response to another question about how the courses affected his perception of the union, he answered, "We studied unions and how they were formed, way in the 1800s and early 1900s, right up to the present—and we've seen how unions have been strong and have carried on. And I think our unions will always be there. There's no question about it. We have to continue." Through his enthusiastic participation in the classes, this student became part of a community already existing among many union members, but to which he had related only tangentially. While his transformation was by no means typical of most students, it does suggest that classroom practices emphasizing cooperative learning, mutual support, and students' buried histories can carry over to other aspects of students' lives, in this case providing this steelworker with a new impetus to work in solidarity with other union members committed to a common cause.

Other students, though benefiting from the classes, saw fewer connections between their classroom experiences and possibilities for increased union activity. Their reactions to the organizing model, with its emphasis on union members' active participation, were negative or mixed. In one case, a student who belongs to a United Auto Workers' local but took courses with the steelworkers saw the organizing model as basically a ploy to get all the union members doing the work their representatives are getting paid to do. She interpreted the organizing model—or the "new theory"—as suggesting that "the union reps are too overworked." This interpretation led her to laughingly but emphatically offer a series of questions and statements: "What am I paying my dues for? Get up there and *deal with it!* If I don't have to pay dues, I'll do my own work." Her objections to the organizing model demonstrate her ability to think critically and offer legitimate reasons for her point of view.

This student's experience—although positive in terms of her growth as a critical thinker and writer—obviously did not draw her closer to her union. Other students also had mixed reactions to the new model of unionism. One student described how the classes made him feel more a part of the union, but at the same time he admitted to "selfish motivations" to learn for his own self-improvement and career growth, which he saw as separate from growth as a union member. For another student, the classes didn't significantly impact his ambivalence toward both the company and union. He explains, "I've always seen myself as an individual, and the union serves a purpose and the company serves a purpose. The union keeps the company at bay—back and forth—and I just try to eke out a living in between." The fact that this ambivalent attitude was expressed by one of the most academically successful students points to the limitations of an educational program that enrolls students by self-selection, not by prior commitment to labor politics. Unlike students who had less knowledge of why and how unions were formed and the impact they've had on the steelmaking industry, this "in-between" student brought to the courses an informed opinion about unions and an awareness of their history. *His* lack of enthusiasm for the benefits of unionism may reflect the general dissatisfaction or disinterest that many U. S. workers today have regarding organized labor.

In the end, what we see as most important about this union hall program is not how it affects students' thinking about unions, but the extent to which the classes help create among the workers a culture that values empowering education and Freirean critical literacy. Included in this culture is a heightened sense of how the events of history, which are constructed differently by the many voices who write it, echo and resound into the present and future. Through the union hall classes, many students began to see themselves not just as passive inheritors of history, but as active agents who can reinterpret the events of the past and help shape the course of the future. In the words of a student who collaborated on a book the class wrote and dedicated to the Steel Museum in Youngstown, "we really have something to contribute to future generations."

Notes

1. Portions of this essay have appeared in *Radical Teacher* and *Writing Instructor*. We gratefully acknowledge the editorial assistance provided by the editors of those journals, as well as the many helpful suggestions offered by Ira Shor and Caroline Pari.

2. For a detailed discussion of an "agenda of values" that inform Freirean models of literacy education, see Ira Shor (1992, 17–30).

3. Interviews ranging from twenty to forty-five minutes were conducted and transcribed over a period of a year (September 1995 to June 1996) by two research assistants, who also observed several class sessions. All interviews were tape-recorded and most took place at the union hall, sometimes with two or three students meeting to be interviewed as a group. Additional insights about the course and students come from our own teaching logs, observations of each other's classes, photocopies of students' work (we copied all the work produced by the classes), and our extensive, ongoing discussions about the courses with each other and with the union hall learning coordinator.

4. For a detailed description of this course, see Belanger and Strom (1996).

5. Students could write one eight- to ten-page research project that would count for both the labor studies and the writing classes. One student researched the impact a family-owned aluminum plant had on his community's development, investigating why the company remained a nonunion shop, how it maintained a reputation for fairness to its employees, and why it survived the demise of the local steel industry In "The Valley That Time Forgot," a steelworker-student who lost his job to a mill closing analyzes the social, psychological, emotional, and economic effects of job loss on individual workers and their communities. We discuss other examples in more detail later in this essay.

6. This exercise comes from Vincent Ryan Ruggiero (1995, 12).

7. Of course, we remind students that participants' testimony in oral histories can be just as conflicting (or even as inaccurate) as traditional approaches to labor history and business unionism. Nevertheless, Brecher's *History from Below* (1988) provides a methodological framework that promotes the development of basic and historical research skills and the strengthening of participatory and community unionism.

Works Cited

Bartholomae, David, and Anthony Petrosky, eds. 1996. *Ways of Reading: An Anthology for Writers.* Boston: Bedford.

Belanger, Kelly, and Linda Strom. 1996. "Teaching on 'Turns': Taking Composition Courses to a Union Hall." *Writing Instructor* 15 (2): 71–82.

Bizzell, Patricia. 1992. *Academic Discourse and Critical Consciousness.* Pittsburgh: University of Pittsburgh Press.

Brecher, Jeremy. 1988. *History from Below: How to Uncover and Tell the Story of Your Community, Association, or Union.* New Haven, CT: Advocate.

Brody, David. 1987. "The Origins of Modern Steel Unionism." In *Forging a Union of Steel: Philip Murray, SWOC, and the United Steelworkers,* edited by Paul F. Clark, Peter Gottlieb, and Donald Kennedy. Ithaca, NY: ILR Press.

Brubaker, Dennis. 1995. "From the President's Desk." *The Warren Steelworker* 2 (1): 2.

Freire, Paulo. [1970] 1990. *Pedagogy of the Oppressed.* Reprint, New York: Continuum.

Girdler, Tom. 1943. *Bootstraps.* New York: Scribners.

Hall, Gus. 1987. *Working Class USA: The Power and the Movement.* New York: International Publishers.

Rose, Mike. 1983. "Remedial Writing Courses: A Critique and a Proposal." *College English* 45 (2): 109–28.

Ruggiero, Vincent Ryan. 1995. *Beyond Feelings: A Guide to Critical Thinking.* Mountain View, CA: Mayfield.

Russo, John, and Andy Banks. 1996. "Teaching the Organizing Model of Unionism and Campaign-Based Education: National and International Trends." AFL-CIO/Cornell University Research Conference on Organizing in Washington, D.C., April 1.

Shaughnessy, Mina. 1977. *Errors and Expectations: A Guide for the Teacher of Basic Writing.* New York: Oxford University Press.

Shor, Ira. 1992. *Empowering Education: Critical Teaching for Social Change.* Chicago: University of Chicago Press.

"Steel Museum to Host SWOC Years 1937–42." 1995. *The Warren Steelworker* 2 (1): 1.

Walsh, Catherine, ed. 1991. *Literacy as Praxis: Culture, Language, and Pedagogy.* Norwood, NJ: Ablex.

11

Participatory Literacy Education Behind Bars
AIDS Opens the Door

Kathy Boudin

Editors' Note: In this chapter, Kathy Boudin, an inmate and literacy educator, describes critical literacy education with incarcerated women. Guided by a Freirean approach, Boudin helped transform ABE students into an active, literate group with a curriculum based on AIDS, their "generative theme" that brought them together as a community. Their knowledge and authority on AIDS gave them special roles as other inmates sought them out for help. Some of these women became even more active in the prison, helping form an AIDS group. Like Tomas Graman, Boudin demonstrates how to implement Freire's problem-posing method and dialogic approach. Still, the institutional limits on her critical pedagogy remind us of the constraints faced by any single teacher or class in a restrictive structure.

I started hanging out and not taking school seriously when I was a teenager. At seventeen I met my first baby's father, and he had a lot of control over me. After he went to jail, I started using drugs. I had a job for one or two years on and off in a grocery store, running a cash register. But I left that job to sell drugs, because I could earn more money that way. I always wanted to be a bookkeeper, but you have to know how to read, filing, math. Now I think about a porter job in a hospital. Nothing I have to use reading for. I would like to think of nice things: nice clothes, an investigator, a secretary, nice jobs. I see ladies all dressed up, legs crossed. I like things like that,

bubble baths, but I can't be thinking too many dreams cause I got
five kids. I hope I can make it when I go home.

—Anna, Adult Basic Education
student, Bedford Hills
Correctional Facility[1]

Prison lies at the end of a road taken. Although women arrive for many reasons,
we have one thing in common: we share a deep desire to leave prison and not
return. Many of us are looking for alternatives to the actions that brought us
here. We are working to imagine new choices, to widen options, and to figure
out how to make these real.

When Anna spoke, she was in an Adult Basic Education (ABE) literacy
class, hoping it would open doors for her. She was not alone with her literacy
problem. In Bedford Hills Correctional Facility, New York State's maximum
security prison for 750 women, 63 percent of the incoming women do not have
a high school diploma and almost 20 percent do not read at a fifth-grade level
(Nuttall, 1988).

Although having limited literacy proficiency is a serious problem, it is
only one of many that women in Bedford Hills face.[2] Prior to their imprisonment, most were confronting more pressing problems: poverty, drugs, domestic abuse, neighborhood violence, single-mother parenting, and immigration issues. Many, feeling permanently locked out of the economic mainstream, were
trying to make fast money illegally, usually through involvement with drugs.
Basic literacy education meant a time commitment, a slow, long-term investment in a life moving fast, so fast that it got out of control, and ended up with
imprisonment. In prison, life slows down enough for these women to take time
for such things as a literacy class, yet the women know that when they leave
here, most will return to the same broad problems, problems that loom as per-
manent and intractable. Improved literacy will not be the miracle that will
change their lives, especially since the average stay in prison is less than three
years (Division of Program Services, 1992) and literacy growth is a slow process. It is rare for a woman to leave Bedford with a goal of changing social conditions, even if she believes those very conditions contributed to her ending up
in prison. "You can't change the world" is a commonly held attitude. Trying to
deal with immediate issues such as housing, jobs, and child raising are fore-
most in most women's minds when they leave. The urgent need many of us
from a diversity of backgrounds feel is to change the things inside ourselves
that landed us here, to be more able to negotiate the system and to cope with
the problems we will face when we leave. Improved literacy is part of something bigger, part of their whole struggle to grow. As one woman said, "The
only way out . . . is in."

What kind of literacy education would best meet the needs of the women in prison who face these issues? This is the question I grappled with some years ago, when I came to prison, as I became involved in studying and teaching adult literacy. I am an insider, a prisoner myself, a woman and a mother, serving a twenty-to-life sentence. I am also something of an outsider—White, from a middle-class background, college educated, and a participant in the social movements of the 1960s. I had not shared some of the most common realities of the women in the ABE class, realities including racism, drugs, family violence, immigration, or poverty. Nevertheless, twelve years of prison life has broken down barriers: living through the daily experiences such as lock-ins or cell searches, cooking or gossiping; deep friendships; working on AIDS, foster care, and literacy; and sharing the life events such as mothering, deaths, and graduations. All of this has created for me windows into the lives, past and present, of women from different backgrounds and has also led to a new commonality among us.

Early in my master's degree work in adult education (which I undertook when I first entered prison), I learned about Paulo Freire's problem-solving approach to literacy education, an approach that places literacy acquisition in the context of learners' daily concerns and social reality (Freire, 1970, 1974). I hypothesized that it would be effective at Bedford because it could offer an education in which women could think and act around urgently felt needs while developing their literacy ability.

I, like many other prisoners, wanted to be productive and to do something meaningful with my time in prison, and I looked to teaching literacy as one way to do this. Yet prison administrators usually limit the amount of responsibility and independence a prisoner can have, and teachers who have inmate teacher aides usually use them only in very limited roles. Would I, a prisoner, as a teacher's aide to a civilian teacher, be able to create the space to do meaningful work?

Would it be possible in a prison classroom to create conditions for self-awareness, a space where people felt safe to identify and address their own problems and then struggle toward solutions, to imagine the world as it could be otherwise? Prisons are founded on assumptions of control, obedience, and security. Thus, independent thinking and individual and collective initiative create sharp tensions around these assumptions.

Prison is a metaphor for failure, the failure of those who end up there, while a sense of self-worth is a foundation for active learning, for being willing to take risks. Would it be possible, in the prison atmosphere, to break through the prevailing ideology about prisoners as failures, an ideology that had been internalized to varying degrees by the women themselves, and to release their psychological energy for creative learning? These were among the questions I faced as I began to think about becoming a literacy educator in prison.

In this article, I tell the story of what happened between 1986 and 1990 at Bedford Hills Correctional Facility as I struggled to develop a literacy program that was meaning-based, problem-posing, and relevant to learners' lives. Written from my perspective and observations as both a teacher and a prisoner, with quotes drawn from my detailed journal entries over a five-year period, I start by examining the prison environment, and then relate my experience of teaching while evaluating which educational approach best met the needs of incarcerated women at Bedford. Finally, I discuss the possibilities and constraints that the prison context creates for establishing participatory education.

The Prison Context

The primary missions of prison—control, punishment, and deterrence through social isolation (Sullivan, 1990)—serve to intensify the powerlessness and dependency that many women prisoners have already experienced outside of prison. The loss of the ability to make decisions permeates every aspect of prison life cumulatively in the way it increases powerlessness. The authorities move women freely among the nine female prisons in New York State; thus, within a moment, a woman's entire world may shift. Lack of control over where one lives means lack of control over all the pieces of a life—friends, work, education, routine, possessions, environment, and, of central importance to women, contact with children and family. If a woman is in prison near her children, she can maintain an active relationship with them; when she is moved, the ties are ruptured.

Prison policies dictate what clothing to wear and what colors are permitted. When the telephone rings, a prisoner cannot pick it up. Only guards can open doors. Intimate relationships are illegal and must be hidden. This lack of control extends to life outside prison as well. For example, a woman may learn that her child is in the hospital, but cannot be present to comfort her or him. When a child runs away from home, the mother is helpless to work on the problem. We as prisoners must rely on people outside to help with the details of daily living—from buying clothes, food, and presents for children, to phoning lawyers who don't accept collect calls.

While women's prisons can be brutalizing, they are often infantilizing.[3] The social conditioning in a women's prison encourages a childlike dependency (Burkhart, 1976). For example, at Bedford Hills we constantly have to ask permission to do some of the most basic things: when at work or at school we must ask an officer for toilet paper, and she or he will then tear off a few pieces and hand them to us; we must wait for an officer to turn the lights off or on in our cells, since cell lights are controlled by a key that the officer has; we may stand by a gate or a door for five minutes or more until an officer feels we are quiet enough, and only then will she or he open it. Women operate within the confines of power and control, reward and punishment; women typically express their overall sense of having no control when they refer to authorities and say, "This is *Their* jail."

Although prison intensifies powerlessness, for many women it paradoxically also offers a space for growth. There is a release from the pressures of everyday survival, abusive relationships, family responsibilities, and drug addiction; some women have their first drug-free pregnancy while in prison. Incarceration can be a time for women to reevaluate and reflect on their lives, to get an education and acquire skills they never had a chance or didn't want to get, and to think about issues they may never have thought about.

There are numerous educational and social programs that women can make use of in prison.[4] These programs are shaped by the conflicting goals of security, control, and punishment on the one hand, and rehabilitation or self-development on the other (Bellorado, 1986; Sullivan, 1990). The various basic education programs at Bedford Hills—ABE, pre-GED, GED, ESL, Bilingual Literacy—can serve either as a means of control (primarily used to keep prisoners occupied and having limited educational goals) or as a fruitful context for deep growth. It was in this environment of constraints and possibilities that I set out to teach.

Entering the Classroom: Education for Control

I started to work as a teacher's aide in the ABE class in February 1986. I requested to work in this class because the teacher had expressed support for my teaching ideas and, from my observation, seemed to have a strong rapport with the students. By this time, I had spent a year-and-a-half in both graduate study and individual tutoring of ABE, GED, ESL, and college students. This range of experience led me to define three goals for my work in the ABE classroom: first, to teach reading and writing; second, to foster participants' intellectual and emotional strengths (e.g., analytical ability, imagination, and self-esteem); and third, to create a context for exploring and possibly acting on personal and social issues faced by women in the prison. When I entered the classroom, I was in for a rude awakening.

On an average day, the women in the ABE class ranged in age from seventeen to seventy, with the vast majority in their mid-twenties. They were primarily African-American or Hispanic, coming from a variety of cultures and places: New York City, the South, Puerto Rico, Jamaica, Colombia, and the Dominican Republic. A few were working-class White women from upstate New York, and some came from other countries (Hong Kong, Yugoslavia, and Israel).

Typically, women arrived in class and took their individual folders and workbooks from a shelf. Their work consisted of reading paragraphs or short passages on various unrelated themes (e.g., popcorn, insects, and newspapers), and then answering multiple-choice questions that focused on skills (e.g., finding the main idea, understanding a particular word, or locating a detail). When a student finished a designated amount of work, the teacher or aide checked the answers against the answer key. The student then tried to correct her wrong responses.

The class was silent, except when the teacher spoke to individual students or when friends exchanged a few words. There was no instruction to the whole class by the teacher. What mattered most was whether the students answered workbook questions correctly. The answer key and the teacher were the only sources of knowledge. The learning process was entirely defined by the teacher, and it was narrowly confined to a limited body of information.

Occasionally, group discussion followed a movie; the teacher might encourage writing a few times a year, for example, during Black History month. Once in a while there was a lesson on a life skill relating to the state-mandated functional competency program or computer work, but these activities were not the norm. Day after day, year after year, women came to class and silently read workbooks in which they repeated discrete skills in preparation for periodic tests.

My first reaction to the classroom was physical. My eyes strained from trying to match up answer sheets with hundreds of tiny boxes, and my mind went dull. I found myself de-skilled and transformed into a clerk. I was neither expected nor able to use any intellectual or emotional aspects of myself. I found no room for choice, judgment, or authentic interaction. The experience of almost two years in this role contributed to passivity, conformity, and a feeling of uselessness, which, as a prisoner, I was constantly struggling against anyway.

For the women in the literacy class, reading paragraphs day after day and taking tests with similar paragraphs resulted in incremental improvement on test scores over time, and, therefore, in some sense of progress and satisfaction. Yet communication and meaning, the essential core of reading, were not the point of the classroom experience. There was no writing, no explicit development of strategies to enhance construction of meaning from texts, no exposure to various literacy genres such as poetry, stories, or drama, and no building on interaction between the different language processes of reading, writing, listening, and speaking.

I asked myself what we were telling women about the importance of literacy, when there was no link between literacy and self, no development of literacy as a powerful means to construct a world. What message were we giving the women about themselves and their lives in this classroom, where their thinking and all their experience were irrelevant? The women I taught brought into the classroom a rich tapestry of knowledge, experience, and cultures. They knew firsthand about the social problems of crack, homelessness, the crisis of being mothers behind bars, the immigrant experience; they shared basic human conditions of love and friendship, betrayal, death, community, work. If learning materials did not portray a life that was familiar, did not reflect their reality, did not contain their voices or their languages, what did that tell them about their cultures? If the teacher and the workbooks were the only sources of knowledge and authority, what did that say about their capacity to know and to create?

I believe that this approach, with its excessive emphasis on obedience and limited possibility for initiative or constructive learning, with its lack of attention to self and its undervaluing of affect in learning, was detrimental to basic mental health. This kind of instruction could not foster self-esteem or self-confidence. And, in denying the possibility of making choices, solving problems, looking at different options, or figuring out one's own opinion, it thwarted the possibility of helping women to change their lives.

Educational policy and curriculum for all New York State prisons is set by the Department of Education of the New York State Department of Correctional Services (Nuttall, 1988). The approach used in the prison literacy classes, like that used in many adult literacy programs throughout the country (Fingeret, 1984; Hunter & Harman, 1979), is a decontextualized, subskill model of reading in which content, real life issues, creativity, and imagination are all irrelevant. It is individualized and programmed, precluding interaction or social action (Nuttall, 1983). The reading process is conceptualized as a bottom-up process in which comprehension of the message of the text is slowly built up by accumulating small pieces, sound by sound, word by word, moving from lower to higher levels of complexity (LaBerge & Samuels, 1985). An adult who has failed to learn to read adequately is presumed to be lacking in particular subskills. Initial testing identifies those particular weaknesses, remediates for them and then retests in this diagnostic prescriptive model (Nuttall, 1983). The concept of literacy that guides the curriculum in the ABE class is based on grade level: a literate inmate is defined as one who scores at or above the 5.0 reading level on the standardized achievement tests used throughout the system (Nuttall, 1983).[5]

As in any other teaching context, the rationale for the choice of approach to prison literacy education is informed, in part, by assumptions about learners. A report from the Education Department of the New York State Department of Correctional Services states:

> The most serious obstacle to a successful program and "habilitation" or "rehabilitation" is the make-up of the population itself. For the most part, commitments to the Department represent individuals who have little education, who have no viable occupational skill, who have a history of substance abuse, and who often have a long history of criminal activity (Nuttall, 1988, p. 2)

This policy statement characterizes prisoners themselves as the main obstacle to their own rehabilitation. Although it identifies objective problems, it fails to recognize strengths that prisoners bring to the learning process. From my observation, viewing prisoners primarily as a problem meant that correctional services' education personnel were unlikely to involve prisoners in their own education, let alone to think they might make a contribution to society. I knew from my years in prison that this perception of women exclusively as "problems" was inaccurate, and that this prevailing view would never lead to a process of meaningful educational growth.

Women who have committed serious crimes may well have survived serious pressures. Many women have not just survived, but have actively refused to accept a passive or victimized role. While women may have acted in a destructive and/or self-destructive way, assertiveness can be a lever that opens options for new action. The ability to survive and fight back may be a strength on which to build. It is crucial to discover and work with this and other strengths because, however deeply hidden, they are, in the end, women's greatest allies. And so a question began to form and to follow me: Could I create a process whereby the potential and strengths of the women could be expressed and developed, becoming part of the literacy process and fueling it with energy?

An Alternative Vision

I developed an alternative vision through a combination of my past history as a community organizer, my experience in the individual tutoring and ABE class, and the theory and methods that I learned through my graduate studies. In the 1960s, I had been involved in teaching about welfare rights, housing, and health issues. I had worked with women who had little formal education and who were regarded by society as inadequate, or as "victims" to be helped by those who were more educated by formal academic standards. Yet these women and people like them throughout the United States were learning together, acting on their own problems, and, at the same time, providing social insights that affected the entire society. I brought to my classes a certain optimism from my experience as an educator outside the classroom. I believed that, even in the controlled prison environment and in a different historical period, it might be possible to create a participatory learning process in which people felt a relative sense of empowerment.

My studies confirmed that, when literacy was taught as a collection of skills outside of any meaningful context and divorced from any importance in the learners' lives, the work would not fully tap their intellectual capacity. Neither would it draw on their prior knowledge, which, as schema theory had taught me, is so critical in the development of reading proficiency (Anderson, 1985; Bransford, 1985). Taken together, my community organizing experiences, my graduate studies, and my observations of prison classrooms led me to hypothesize that a meaning-driven, whole-language orientation might be more effective in the prison context (Altwerger, Edelsky, & Flores, 1987; Goodman, 1973, 1985; Smith, 1973).

I believed that such an approach would be stronger not only cognitively, but affectively as well. The women whom I taught were once the children who had failed in school or, more accurately for many of them, whose schools had failed them. From my interaction with the women in and out of class, I learned that they brought with them negative feelings about education and about themselves as learners. Attitudes about race, class, and gender undermined their confidence to learn academically, compounding the insecurities about school. I knew from conversations that many were only in the ABE class because it would look good for the parole board or because they had been assigned to be there. It was critical to use an approach that built on the women's intelligence, experience, and culture in order to counter these forces.

The existing classroom process, depending as it did on passivity and the rote learning of isolated skills, did not link literacy learning with the daily needs of the women, nor did it equip them to take an active role in their own education. As such, it ran counter to what we know about adult learning in general: a) the complexity of adult social roles and related responsibilities (spouse, worker, parent, community member) means that adults want learning to be applicable to their needs; b) the broad knowledge and life experience that adults have acquired mean that they have a great deal of prior knowledge that can be used as a strength in developing literacy ability; and c) the independence and self-direction that characterize adults mean that learning—both in content and in process—should be participatory (Ellowitch, 1983; Knowles, 1984).

For the women with whom I worked, the general needs of all adult learners were magnified by the multitude of urgent issues they faced; thus, the need to overcome powerlessness and to create new choices was essential. Freire's approach to literacy education was particularly relevant, as it is rooted in work with marginalized and oppressed groups. His ideas influenced my work in several ways. First, his approach begins with students developing the ability to analyze their experiences and their social reality, as they explore the meanings of this reality in the words and the sentences they are learning to read and write. The literacy class can, at times, become a place where students may even act on issues, using and further developing their literacy ability. Second, his work raises issues about teachers, their methods, and their relationships with their students. I had been frustrated with the one-way street of teaching that left the ABE students in a passive situation. Freire argues that this passivity comes, in part, from the tendency of many middle-class teachers to feel superior to their students from poorer backgrounds. He proposes a "dialogic" method, in which students and teachers together explore a shared set of issues. This dialogue, while not removing the teacher's responsibility to teach a body of knowledge, can unleash an active role for the learners, enhancing not only their present learning, but also their lives beyond the classroom (Freire, 1970, 1974).

These views resonated with my community work with African-American and poor White women, largely from Appalachia, prior to my incarceration. As I had come to know these women and their life stories, I became acutely aware that my formal education represented only one kind of knowledge; in fact, my own background, while having given me certain advantages, also had left me with certain blinders. My work with these women had been a two-way street— we learned from and taught one another. I wanted now to build on both the reality we shared as women prisoners and the differences in our backgrounds and experiences.

The Struggle for Change

For almost two years as a teacher's aide, I struggled to implement this alternative vision. Sometimes I worked with small groups of women, reading a particular text of interest, striving always to keep meaning in front of us. We read plays, did interviews, and read stories. Although each project engaged women and taught them a wider range of literacy skills, nothing altered the overall routine. The women frequently did not want to work with other women, feeling either embarrassed and ashamed of themselves or contemputuous of the others.

In many cases, they did not want to attempt any writing, which was rarely required by the teacher. The classroom context was still set by the teacher and the sub-skill approach; the approach I was using was simply not considered "real work." Moreover, I found myself experiencing the same frustration as other teachers with the "call-out" system (in which students could be pulled from class at any time for appointments). This system, along with transfers to other prisons, pushed the curriculum toward individualized work and away from a content focus, since it was difficult to develop a cohesive unit of study with a constantly changing group of people.

Slowly, the sub-skill model began to seduce me. Although I never lost my aversion to this limited sense of education, I began to become preoccupied with how women were doing in their workbooks and on the tests, measuring my worth as a teacher in these terms. I lost a strong sense of initiative. The structure and machinery of school were undermining my vision of education. I was turning into the teacher I did not want to be. I understood what had happened to other teachers, many of whom encouraged me and seemed to identify with my vision, but didn't have the energy to implement it.

The existing curriculum materials, testing apparatus, and overall conception of literacy set terms for success and failure that brought all of us—teachers and students alike—into its orbit. From my observations in class, and from conversations with the students, it appeared that the students had internalized years of failure in school, and without the confidence in themselves as thinkers they were very open to the safe routine of workbooks. In addition, prison, with its system of rewards and punishments (the ultimate of which was meted out by the parole board), contributed to students' willingness to accept a rote method of learning. By the fall of 1987, after almost two years of trying, I wanted to quit.

While I was wrestling with whether or not to leave teaching, the ABE teacher resigned; the Educational Supervisor then asked me to teach the class for four months until a new teacher could be hired. This offer was unexpected and unprecedented, since prisoners are permitted only to be aides to civilian teachers. I saw the opportunity to try to implement my vision of education, and I took it, as I felt it would allow me to define the approach to literacy education for the class as a whole, rather than as a side project.

The Education Supervisor, as an educator, was supportive of a problem-posing approach. He knew of my graduate work and was willing to take a risk with me. In allowing me to teach the class, the prison authorities had to balance their personal interest in my ideas about education with the system's policy of limiting an inmate's level of responsibility and influence over other inmates, along with concern not to threaten the civilian teachers' job security and status.[6] According to prison authorities, the decision was possible because it was limited in time, and I would officially remain in the position of teacher's aide to the other ABE teacher who worked with students at a tested reading level of K-3.[7]

The Issue of AIDS Enters the Classroom

The most important challenge facing me was to create a reading class in which concerns that had meaning to the women would "drive" the learning process. The issue of AIDS opened this possibility. In September 1987, the ABE reading class watched a television show on the National AIDS Awareness Test. At that time, AIDS was still largely an issue prisoners did not discuss, although it was deeply affecting their lives. Close to 20 percent of incoming women inmates tested positive for the HIV virus (New York State Commission on Correction, 1988). Women lived in a state of anxiety over whether they might be HIV positive and whether to take the test. Many women had used intravenous (IV) drugs, and many had lovers or spouses who still did. Women were sisters, mothers, daughters, and homemakers for people with AIDS. Here, women shared cooking areas, showers and toilets, and a life together. People were scared—scared of each other, scared for their lives. The stigma that AIDS carried reenforced a sense of guilt and shame that the women already felt as prisoners pronounced "guilty" by the courts and society. There was a fear of just being associated with AIDS. This fear created both a collective silence and a desperate need to talk.

During the television show, I noticed that the women were riveted to the screen, trying to write down information, their voices sounding out rapidly staccato, one after another: "How do you spell 'pneumonia'?" "How about 'disease'?" "And 'infection'?" "What's an antibody?" "What do they mean, 'immune system'?" "Spell 'protection,' 'hemophiliac'." While they tried to hold on to the meaning of new terms, I went to the blackboard to write down all the words they were calling out. AIDS was a powerfully emotional issue; a new sense of urgency entered the classroom.

That night I focused on everything I had learned but, until then, been unable to implement. I prepared a vocabulary worksheet, an activity that was familiar to the women. While the words were typically drawn from a textbook list for children at different grade levels, the words on this list came from the

AIDS show. The women studied avidly, learning words far above their difficulty level in their workbook lists. Some words were conceptually familiar but difficult to spell, such as *transmit, doctor, disease, patient,* and *pneumonia;* some led to learning new concepts, such as *immune system, antibody,* and *hemophiliac.*

In addition to the vocabulary, I asked three questions that were on all of our minds: *What are the pros and cons of taking the AIDS test and how do you feel about it? If you tested positive would/should you tell somebody and who would you tell? What do you think would be a good program for AIDS here at Bedford Hills?* These questions created an environment in which the students related to real life emotional and social issues; they began addressing problems that they faced both individually and communally. I asked the women what they thought.

"I don't want to take the test. I'm scared to find out. I used needles."

"You have to tell your lover, otherwise you might hurt her."

"I don't even know what the test tells you, do you?"

"I'm not worried now, but what about when I go home? My man, he's been with women while I'm here. Even though he says he hasn't, he's like any other man. I know the real deal."

"I shot up with some people and now they're dead. I don't want to know and then again I do."

Everyone participated. The women speaking to one another turned their orderly rows into an informal circle. I also talked, feeling my commonality with the women because I too had feelings about testing, safe sex, and fears of rejection. I also felt our differences as women spoke about IV drugs in their lives and decided to speak to these differences, making explicit the fact that I didn't know about IV drugs and wanted to know more. This was the first of many times that I would try to make the differences in our backgrounds a point for exchange. In that first discussion, I began to change my role as teacher: I was a prisoner, exploring shared problems; a facilitator, guiding learning and discussion; and a person with specific information I wanted to learn and impart.

Soon, women began to write about personal experiences with AIDS, and even brought unsolicited writings to class. For example, Lucia wrote:

> My friend died from AIDS last year. . . . Since then I've been scared. This is a disease that they haven't found the medicine for. I would like to be one of those persons from the big laboratory to help find the medicine for those people who have AIDS. I'm trying not to think about the disease, but I have a brother and a sister and they are into drugs. They say they don't use anybody's syringe, but still I'm afraid.

Lucia had never written anything in class and had difficulty writing in her native Spanish, as well as in English. When she presented her piece, she was sharing a hidden secret about her family, her fears and her dreams, as well as asking for help in English and writing. The drive to express her intense feelings had led her to take real risks in her writing and use of English.

With reading centered on AIDS-related materials, the women contributed to the curriculum, something that had not happened previously. They brought in newspaper articles and pamphlets to share with the class, which I developed into reading lessons. One day Juana, who was about to transfer to the GED class, came to me holding pages of paper tightly in her hand. She said, "I've written something; it's a story, maybe the class would like it." She had a look of triumph on her face, and a triumph it was! Juana's story, called "Chocolate and Me," was about a relationship between two women in jail, one of whom had AIDS.[8] When she read it, the women listened intently as they felt their own lives being described by one of their class members, and clapped enthusiastically when it was over. Juana worked on it, learning the concept of paragraphs, struggling with sentence structure and spelling. Then I typed it, made copies, and developed a reading lesson from it. The class felt proud that one of their members had written something that they were studying. This was the first of many times that the women's own writings became the reading materials for our class.

Writing a Play: Building on the Strengths of an Oral Tradition

During this time, I proposed to the class that we write our own play.[9] I had several goals: to develop literacy through the process of creating a play in which women would be communicating important thoughts and feelings; to broaden literacy ability through studying the genre of a play and integrating the language forms of reading, writing, talking, and listening; and to develop the strengths of working in cooperation with others.

We began by talking about what a play is, learning about the elements of plot, character, conflict, dialogue, and setting. I gave out vocabulary worksheets with words related to theater. We read plays from a literacy program facing issues similar to those in our own community.[10] This encouraged us: if another basic literacy class could write a play about issues of housing, health, and drugs, then we, too, could write such a play. When one woman asked, "What should the play be about?", another responded, "It should be something about us, our lives." This was one more step by participants in gaining confidence that their own life experiences were significant. When it came time to decide on a focus, the women chose AIDS, because we were increasingly involved with it in class.

During the next weeks, the conflicts around which to base the plot emerged from our real questions and anxieties about AIDS: Should a person take the HIV test or not? If she tests positive, should she tell her parents? Her lover? The work on the play allowed women to reflect on their day-to-day experiences, and the play changed along with their reflections. One day Elena said, "A friend of mine told me last night that she just tested positive. She's supposed to go home in four months. She had so many dreams—traveling, having kids—now those dreams have all gone down the drain. Maybe I shouldn't push so hard for testing."

Jackie added, "Yeah, I agree, here I am in the play, pushing Anna to take the test, but I'm scared. I'm not ready to deal with it; I know I'm not, and I bet I'm not the only one." From this discussion, the group decided to make the dialogue in the play less pressured toward taking the test.

As we improvised dialogue around each conflict, plot and characters slowly developed. When it was time to create a script, two or three people followed each person's spoken words and wrote down whatever they could. We then pieced the entire dialogue into a whole. Finally we put all the scenarios on the blackboard and made choices as to the sequence of action.

The theater framework allowed participants to try out different resolutions to conflict, to experience the emotions they most feared, and to learn from the process. During one rehearsal, we focused on the woman who was the counselor in the play. "Try to get into it more, try to really put yourself into it," the women coached and pushed. Suddenly Teresa burst into tears. "I think I'm afraid," she said, "afraid to put myself in it completely because then it makes it real, and I guess no matter how calm I seem to all of you, really I'm afraid to think about AIDS." Women went to her and hugged her. After that moment, she did put herself more into the acting and was more open about her experiences and fears.

Work on the play further molded my changing role as teacher. The women urged me to take a part in the play. For a moment I hesitated, wondering if it was appropriate for a teacher to do that. Then I laughed at myself, realizing I was feeling afraid I might lose my authority. Taking the part strengthened my teaching, as I identified with the women in working on a shared problem.

Theater gave the Hispanic and African-American women an opportunity to build on a strong oral tradition. They were able to use their own language, dialects, informal speech, and body language. Some of the women who had the greatest problems developing their reading and writing were outstanding in the development of dialogues and acting. The theater process accentuated the strengths of some women, while valuing the strengths of each as language, communication, reading, and writing all developed.

A Community Develops in the Classroom

The students' growing consciousness of themselves as part of a community, first in the classroom and then in the prison, became a positive factor in literacy development. The classroom had been a place in which each person individually felt locked into her own sense of failure. "I hate being in this class, people think it's for dummies. Maybe it is," Anna had said. No one wanted to be identified with being in the ABE class, "the lowest spot on the totem pole," just as no one wanted to feel like they were part of the prison.

But as people began to talk about their fears and questions concerning AIDS, something changed in the classroom. A sense of community, an awareness of common experiences, and a feeling of support began to grow. The most emotional moment reflecting this came when Lucia shared with the class that she had just found out that her brother was hospitalized with AIDS. I wrote in my journal:

> When Lucia came back into the classroom, people said they were sorry and wanted to be there for her. Elena suggested that Lucia write about her feelings. So Lucia spent the rest of the class writing about what is happening with her brother.

When people arrived at class in the morning, they now spoke with each other differently, with an openness, a sense of identification, and growing trust. As one woman wrote, "In our class we talk about a lot of things and learn a lot of reading. Sometimes we talk about real things that make our tears come out. . . ."

The support for one another expressed itself in the classroom in many ways. For example, when a woman got sick, everyone made a card for her; when a woman made parole, people had a celebration for her. The class organized a Christmas party, something that had never before happened in an ABE class. The most significant articulation of community occurred when we were picking a title for the play. When someone said, "Let's call it *Our Play* because it is about us," there was enthusiastic agreement. That sense of there being an "us" had never existed before, and the title expressed a pride in the "us" that had emerged.

ABE class members carried this ethos of support beyond the class and into the prison population. Word began to get out that the ABE class was talking about AIDS in a supportive way; other prisoners now sought out women in the ABE class as confidantes on their living units. One day Ching came to class and said to me, "A woman on my floor found out she has AIDS and tried to kill herself. I'm the one person she told. I know why she tried. She came to me, I'm the person she talks to." Ching's eyes filled with tears. I saw then that the knowledge that the ABE class was accumulating was also bringing with it awesome responsibilities.

The feeling of community influenced literacy ability, as well as intellectual and emotional growth. People took risks in reading and writing because they were no longer afraid. They felt less ashamed of themselves and were willing to express their thoughts more freely. As they brought increasingly complex reading materials to class and began to teach one another, recognizing that each one could teach as well as learn, a tentative grouping of learners and teachers emerged. One of many examples of this occurred when the women were preparing for a spelling test. "I'll help Jamie," said Ms. Edna, who was seventy years old. They worked for a while, and then Ms. Edna brought the test over to me. They had gotten 100 percent on it. They were beaming at their mutual success.

A growing social awareness laid the basis for the next critical leap: the desire to change the conditions that were causing problems. "What can we do with everything we're learning?" Jackie asked. "People are coming to me, asking me things," Alicia added. Instead of seeing AIDS as an individual problem, people began to see it as a common one, and one they could work on together. First the women worked on an article for the school journal, hoping to share what they had learned. I took the class through the process of writing a composition, focusing on what they wanted to say about AIDS. After five hard-working sessions, the article, *Alert to Aids,* was done, and was published not long after with all the class members' names on it. Although the feeling of community had first grown inside the class, it now extended beyond the class into the prison as a whole. The women continued to use their developing literacy skills to make a difference. *Our Play* became the means of accomplishing this.

Are We Really Learning to Read and Write?

The transformation that was taking place in the classroom challenged participants' notions about what counts as education. In place of filling out multiple choice questions from workbooks, the women were learning from their own experiences and reading materials that did not have "yes" or "no" answers. The range of literacy activities was far beyond those normally carried out in the ABE class. Yet, it was not an easy transformation, and not everyone was comfortable with the process. The students had questions, and so did I. Randy said, "I feel I've learned a lot about AIDS, I'm learning to write a composition, I'm reading lots of articles, and I'm actually writing a play, but I'm just not sure I'm really learning." Many women wanted a clear sense of right and wrong answers. The workbooks had provided this, as well as a sense of progress because of the movement through the book and from one level to the next. Some women did not like working in groups. Others wanted to know whether their progress would show up on the test scores.

During the work on the play, one woman playing a major role did not do as well on the quarterly TABE test as she had hoped. She announced that she was quitting the play to go back to the workbooks. Everyone wanted her to come back to the play and eventually she did, with renewed commitment. However, I knew that I had to take her concerns seriously, and that they were shared by others. I, too, was worried about whether this work would give them the needed test preparation.

During this period, when I encountered both a variety of student resistance and my own insecurities as a relatively new teacher of literacy, I asked myself whether I was imposing on the women an educational approach that I thought was best for them, but that they didn't want. Perhaps my views were linked to the differences in my background. Would it give them adequate test preparation? With time, the range of reading materials, the explosion of writing, and the students' engagement and personal growth all made me more confident about my approach. And now, having established a meaning-driven context within the classroom, I was able to begin focusing on problem areas. I took readings and developed lessons similar to those in the workbooks. This, I felt, would allow the women to feel a relationship between the past and the new learning experiences. I tried to develop a better balance between group and individual work, spending time with each person on specific areas of need. Many of the women needed work on both the sound symbol relations and the basic structure of English language. Finally, I developed lessons on test-taking skills.

Performing the Play: Empowerment Within a Prison

By mid-December of 1987, we were ready to put on the play. We were all nervous. AIDS was still a subject associated with fear and stigma. Those who were taking the risk to open up a hidden subject were not seen by either themselves or other inmates as potential educators, because they were in the lowest level academic class.

The play was performed six times, and each time the audience reacted beyond all dreams. It brought into the open fears, questions, and issues in a safe social setting, breaking the silence so that people could together begin to deal with the epidemic. Women cried as a father rejected his daughter, moving his chair away from her after she told him she had tested positive. Yet the tears were mixed with embarrassed laughter, because they knew that they, too, might move away from someone whom they thought to have AIDS. When a woman told her lover she had tested positive, there was a dead silence as people waited for the lover's reaction. Everyone was able to identify with one of the women or the other; they were living through what they themselves might face. When the support group in the play came together for the last scene and told each other of the good and of the difficult reactions they had gotten from family and friends, the audience stood up and cheered, feeling the strength that came from people supporting each other.

After several performances, we held discussions with the audiences about what could be done to deal with the crisis of AIDS here at Bedford Hills. The audience asked for support groups and a program to be built like the one depicted in the play. Members of the prison administration came to watch one of the performances. The superintendent requested that the class put on the play for the civilian counselors in the prison, and the class made a video of it.

Several months later, a group of women separate from the ABE class, including myself, formed an organization for peer education and counseling called AIDS Counseling and Education (ACE). The ACE Program has created a major difference in attitudes, medical care, mental health, knowledge, and support in the prison around AIDS-related issues.[11] It uses the video of *Our Play* to help women deal with the emotional issues that AIDS raises.

After the play, the ABE class did its first evaluation of their learning experience, another step in the women's self-consciously helping to mold their own education. The Education Supervisor, who facilitated the evaluation, asked,

"What did the work in the AIDS unit accomplish for you?" The answers included, "Writing skills, vocabulary, recognizing words, spelling, how to write a play, learning about conflicts and resolutions."

"Learning about AIDS."

"How to put on a play and how to act."

"How to respect people's feelings, how to speak louder, and how to express our feelings."

"I liked the counseling group because it involved counseling each other."

"We gave people a message, we helped people."

"The play brought a level of emotions, awareness to help learn."

"I feel wise, learning how other people feel."

"The play gave me a mirror to look at my own life."

I believe that these quotes reflect how the women in the ABE class felt empowered in different ways, both as individuals and as a group. The classroom experience allowed individuals to understand their own lives more clearly. Their self-concept changed from being poor learners to people who could teach others. Although the process had begun with one peer educator, myself, the participatory problem-posing approach generated many others, as women taught one another in the classroom, and as the ABE class educated the population through informal discussions and writing the play. A sense of efficacy and agency developed for all of us—myself as teacher, the women in the class as students, and all of us as prisoners. As a group, the class knew that they had made a major contribution to the entire prison population by breaking the silence about AIDS, using their growing literacy ability to do so. The play had helped to create conditions whereby an ongoing program developed. Three years later, I asked one of the ABE class participants in *Our Play,* who is presently a member of ACE teaching others about AIDS, how she felt about her experience in the ABE class and the play. She said to me:

> The play made people more aware. Some people didn't want to face it, some people went around judging people that have AIDS. The play helped change that. I felt good about myself. I didn't know what AIDS was before I came to Bedford. It made me feel good that I'm educated and how I can help educate others. I grew in the process, that was a step, and a step makes for progress.

The Model Repeats: A Multicultural Community Expresses Itself

Was the intense student involvement during the unit on AIDS tied only to the issue of AIDS, or was it linked to the new way of teaching? Clearly AIDS was an issue of great emotional urgency, and it did provide the initial energy to transform the educational approach. Once the ABE class openly embraced the issue of AIDS and owned it as a shared human problem instead of as a badge of guilt, then, paradoxically, the very issue that led to oppressing and denying people their humanity became a vehicle of transformation and hope. As women freed themselves from the dehumanization of stigma and prejudice, proclaiming their own self-worth and humanity, an energy was created that drove the learning process, the desire for knowledge, the confidence to create.

Once the women had experienced a literacy education that focused on issues of importance, they wanted it to continue. Fundamentally, it was the educational approach that had provided the glue to overcome the fragmented reality that is debilitating to prisoners and teachers alike. Fragmentation was overcome when the learning process tapped into the whole person, and when a sense of community was created so that people felt committed to each other, as well as to broader goals.

An indication of the power of such an educational approach occurred when the new teacher was hired and reestablished the individualized, basic skills model, sending all of us—students and myself—back to the workbooks and multiple-choice questions. I felt a sadness, almost as if there had been a death of a fragile new life. The students evidently felt the same way and, as the weeks went by, many of them complained to the teacher and to administrators, asking for a return to teaching in which their ideas and issues mattered. This active role of ABE students requesting a certain type of education was unprecedented at Bedford Hills.

The AIDS unit had generated enough support for a participatory approach that not only the education supervisor, but also higher prison authorities were interested in seeing it continue in some form. The new teacher, who was troubled by declining attendance, and was also open to the problem-posing approach, agreed to let me teach the class two out of five days, during which time he would be present in the classroom. This arrangement left him in authority, yet gave credence to my work.

The model repeated itself as the ABE class explored other thematic units over the next year. In one called "Mothers and Daughters," we explored our mothers' lives, our relationship to them as daughters, and our own role as mothers. In another, we explored issues of personal experiences and values with money. Finally, for a six-month period, we took on a major project—writing a handbook for incoming inmates, entitled *Experiences of Life: Surviving at Bedford Hills.*

For two days a week, the class became a writers' workshop. It began with the women, myself included, sharing what was on our minds the first night we arrived in prison. Then we brainstormed about what we had known, feared, and wondered about prison life in Bedford Hills before arriving here. I found writings by other prisoners about these concerns and used them as the basis for structured reading lessons. They triggered intense writing, from several sentences to several pages, until enough material was created for the book. The chapters included, "Advice for How to Survive in Prison," "Coming from Another Country," "Being Pregnant in Bedford Hills," and "Mothers and Children."

The exploration of each new issue deepened participants' sense of themselves and of shared realities. Out of the cumulative experience of feeling our commonality as prisoners and women, a trust developed that made it possible for us to explore our cultural, racial, ethnic, and linguistic differences. Literacy acquisition interacted with the exploration of cultural identity. One among many examples of this occurred when it came time to edit the handbook. We looked at the different forms of language that were found in the writings of the women in the handbook: Standard American English, informal speech, Black English, and slang. For the first time, many women heard that the Black English, which always had been corrected as "wrong," was a dialect reflecting a culture.

The class had a long discussion about what style of language to use for the handbook. Some wanted it to be in Standard American English because they felt that new women coming in should see that the ABE students knew the standards of accepted grammar. Other women wanted to leave some of the informal language or slang and Black English dialect in order to facilitate communication with the new women. A Chinese woman proposed a solution: to leave it in the style that the particular woman had written if she wanted, but to explain in the beginning of the book that the decisions about language had been a conscious, educated choice. Thus, the readers would know that the ABE students knew enough to distinguish between and to choose different types of language. This was how it was done.

Prisoners as Educators

As a prisoner teaching, I experienced a shifting of roles and identities. I was an inmate, reminded of that reality by a twenty-to-life sentence and the day-to-day experiences of being strip-searched after a visit, separated from my son, and locked down; yet, at times I felt myself to be a teacher in training, headed for an identity as an educator, occasionally asked by another inmate, "Are you a teacher or a prisoner?", until they noticed my green pants and gave me a knowing nod. In my role as educator, teachers would sometimes speak to me with respect, almost as a peer; some were genuinely excited about the work and supported my educational growth. Yet there was an ambivalence about me as an educator. One example can be seen in the words of a teacher who was familiar with the quality of the AIDS work, yet who introduced me as her "inmate clerk." At times I would be a translator, negotiating between two worlds. Then the reality of control and limits would bring everything back into focus. Although there was a shifting of roles, I found that the primary tendency of the system was to define me as prisoner. It was always a struggle to transcend the limitations of that role.

To what extent was the participatory approach tied to a prisoner being the one teaching? In the class evaluation, the women addressed this issue, responding to the Education Supervisor's question, "How was Kathy's teaching like past teachers or different from them?" The women responded, "In the past a teacher was always just a teacher, but she (Kathy) was both part of it and also a teacher."

"She was learning also. She was also like a counselor."

"Teachers never participated in learning, past teachers taught 'what to do,' not 'how to'." The Education Supervisor asked, "Could a civilian do it, not just a prisoner?" One woman said, "Yes, but they would have to be sympathetic to the group and have to pick up on the vibes. It wouldn't happen as fast, have to build rapport, that takes time." To the question, "How do you build rapport?", someone responded, "Show care, speak what you're about, you open up to us. we'll open up to you, forget that you're a civilian."

There was a strength in the peer education process, of a prisoner teaching prisoners. It allowed for a shared exploration of issues that became the basis of literacy curriculum development. Additionally, as a prisoner I shared the powerlessness felt by the students and had a deep stake in creating a participatory learning process, in which we as prisoners were ourselves making decisions, taking on problem-posing and problem-solving.

Yet the very strength of the peer education process was also its weakness in the prison context. Although most of the prison administrators with whom I dealt expressed personal enthusiasm toward the educational approach I was using, they also expressed a dilemma when the question of whether I could actually teach arose: how could they permit me real responsibility as an educator without giving me too much responsibility as a prisoner? How could such an empowering group process be initiated by prisoners without it becoming a threat to security?

Future Prospects

The paradox of education is precisely this—that as one begins to become conscious, one begins to examine the society in which one is being educated. The purpose of education, finally, is to create in a person the ability to look at the world for oneself, to make one's own decisions, to say to oneself this is black or is white, to decide for oneself whether there is a God in heaven, or not. To ask questions of the universe, and then to learn to live with those questions, is the way one achieves one's own identity. But no society is really anxious to have that kind of person around. What societies really ideally want is a citizenry which will simply obey the rules of society. (Baldwin, 1988, p. 4)

If creating a liberating education is difficult and paradoxical within the society at large, as James Baldwin writes, then it is all the more so within a prison, an institution of authoritarian control. Yet, after a year-and-a-half of utilizing a problem-posing approach in the classroom, there was change. The experience was so positive that it moved not just inmates, but also some teachers, educational administrators, and some prison officials towards supporting more of this kind of teaching.[12] This support led me to ask: could a problem-posing approach to literacy become an ongoing part of the educational programs in the prison? Was the experience simply a chance occurrence, or was it consonant enough with the prison goal of rehabilitation to imagine extending it to involve more classes and more inmates as peer educators?

Three education supervisors agreed to work with me on a proposal to implement a problem-posing curriculum more widely. We addressed the question: Who were the most appropriate people to do the teaching? We agreed that inmates would bring particular strengths to the process, namely that of identification with the learners. Moreover, a program using peer educators meant extending the rehabilitative process beyond the students in the literacy classes to those women with higher educational backgrounds. In this prison alone, more than one hundred women are either in college or have bachelor degrees; therefore the potential number of literacy peer educators was large, and developing teaching skills, carrying out work that required self-reliance, and contributing to the broader community was clearly within the concept of penal rehabilitation.

The final proposal involved training peer educators from among prisoners to work four hours per week in every basic education class, using a problem-posing curriculum developed in cooperation with the students. The Superintendent approved the program and productive meetings began with education administrators, teachers, and interested peer educators. Then, midway through the planning period, the prison Administration disapproved it.

Both the support and the withdrawal of support for the peer education program can only be understood as aspects of the broad contradictions among the primary prison goals of control, punishment, and deterrence, and that of rehabilitation. These conflicting goals manifest themselves in many ways, including what type of behaviors are rewarded or sanctioned, the perspective towards inmates, and different education models. How this contradiction is resolved at any moment in time depends on specific conditions. In this case, a number of conditions as diverse as personnel and social climate changed between the time of approval and disapproval: 1) The key education supervisor, who was the critical link between the teachers and our group of inmate peer educators and who supported the program, left the prison for another job; 2) The New York State financial crisis led to education cutbacks, and teachers were laid off. I knew from conversations with teachers and administrators that this increased anxiety among remaining teachers about their jobs made them more resistant to, and threatened by, inmates teaching or even inmates playing an active role in their own learning; 3) There was an increasing tendency towards law and order policies and attitudes within the society with concomitant social-service cutbacks. The general political climate was more antagonistic towards prisoners, inmate initiative, and program innovation. The prison administration reacted to all these factors by canceling a program involving inmates' critical thinking and initiative.

The current education crisis facing most prisons illustrates the impact of these conflicting goals. Prison populations are swelling due to drug-related crimes—in New York State, they have grown from 35,000 to 55,000 since 1985, when crack became a driving force in crime, and prison officials estimate that 75 percent of the inmates are incarcerated for drug-related offenses (Browne, 1991). The need for basic education programs has grown with the population increase.

Conversely, the budget cutbacks in education mean elimination of classes taught by civilian teachers. The first layoffs at Bedford Hills, in January 1991, led to the elimination of the ABE class for those inmates reading at the K-3 level and also of the ESL class; the GED class has also suffered significant cutbacks. Between 1989 and 1993 the number of academic and vocational teachers was cut from 25 to 9. The crying need for educational services could be alleviated by allowing inmates to be peer educators and by using participatory methods in which learners actively work on problems they face. Yet prison authorities are reluctant to allow such a problem-posing curriculum to develop or to allow inmates to teach classes. In short, while prison administrators may talk about providing an education for rehabilitation, they rarely do what is necessary to make it happen.

These contradictory needs and goals are integral to the structure of the prison system and, as such, cannot be transcended. At the same time, however, they frame the conditions under which struggle can occur; the very existence of these contradictions offers possibilities for change.[13]

Prisons, like other societal institutions, contain cracks and openings for change—conflicting goals and policies, a diversity of people, changing historical directions. At Bedford Hills, due to a particular combination of these variables, it became possible to create a liberating form of education that lasted for several years. This experience is now an immutable part of the educational history at Bedford Hills, a basis upon which to build.

The enormous expansion of prison populations suggests that prisons mirror and are part of a larger social crisis. This connection is reflected in the words of one New York State Department of Corrections spokesperson who said that prisons "probably give out more high school equivalency diplomas than ninety percent of the high schools in the state. Why do people have to come to prison to learn to read and write and get drug treatment?" (Browne, 1991). Human potential, which will be wasted or encouraged, is crowding into prisons. The challenge that problem-posing education raises in prison is part of a larger challenge facing the entire society: will social problems be dealt with by measures of control from above or through mobilization and education from below?

Conclusion

One never knows what improved literacy ability in itself will do for women in prison. One person may gain in self-esteem, while another will make practical improvements in letter writing, filling out forms, or reading to her child. For some, the ability to compete in the job market may increase, but indications are that for most it will not. For the adults with whom I work, the kinds of improvements necessary to increase job opportunities involve great effort over an extended period of time.

What if one embeds literacy acquisition in a broader education that has at its heart problem-posing, critical thinking and acting on shared problems? How might that affect people's personal growth, family relationships, jobs, and their ability to create the lives they want? Although the answer to this clearly depends on many unknowns, these are questions I have asked myself as I have thought about the struggle to build a problem-posing approach and about the women with whom I work and live.

One story in particular illustrates the complexity of this issue. When Anna was here, she participated fully in the AIDS unit, in the play, and in every successive unit during the year-and-a-half that the educational program existed. She, as much as anyone, felt empowered by the entire experience. When Anna went home, she started by getting a job in a flower shop. When the father of her children came out of prison, she made a decision to go back to him in spite of their problems with drugs, because he offered economic and emotional security. Soon afterward she became pregnant and, during her pregnancy, her husband began seeing another woman. Anna went back to drugs. She was rearrested on a parole violation and came back to Bedford Hills for eight months before going home again.

When Anna was in the play and learning to read and write, while also learning about AIDS, this approach to education seemed like the answer. There were moments when I felt that the human potential and creativity that were emerging in the classroom would allow the women to take on the world, or at least in their own lives, and remake them to fit their dreams. Then, when Anna came back and told me her story, I felt the crushing limitations of even the most positive educational experience in light of what Anna and other women face, including personal scars and the need for social and economic changes.

As educators, we are often forced to accept more limited results than we envision in our hopes and dreams. The success of a short-term literacy program, one that meets our best vision, cannot be measured by one set of tangible standards; the social forces are too complex. Thus, despite Anna's return to prison, I believe that her learning experience and that of the others in the ABE class affirms an approach to teaching literacy based on the lives and experiences of the women themselves. Anna and the others so often have spoken with great pride of what they read and wrote, of the things they learned and taught to others. The participatory approach encouraged a feeling of their own worth and capacity. Although it contains no guarantees, it does offer a powerful hope, because it involves the full potential of participants. Lucia, who is among the many who have not returned to prison, said before she left, "I never thought I would be doing this. I never even did it on the street. I never thought I would act in a play and here I am reading everything. I can go home to my kids and say, 'I've done something!'"

Notes

1. This quote is a verbatim statement taken from an interview with an ABE student with whom I worked. Some of the quotes in the article come from similar interviews, while others come from my own journal entries. Although this article was written when almost all of the women quoted had already left prison on parole, or had transferred to a different prison, I was able to get in touch with the majority of them to tell them that I was doing public writing and to get their permission to use material about or by them. Because some of the women consented to have their real names used and others preferred to remain anonymous, I used fictitious names throughout. The one exception is Juana Lopez, who previously had material written for the ABE class that was published using her real name.

2. The prisoners in Bedford Hills Correctional Facility are overwhelmingly Black and Hispanic women, mothers, undereducated in a formal sense, frequently poor, and usually single heads of households. The ethnicity of the general prison population in New York State prisons is 50 percent Black, 31 percent Hispanic, and 19 percent White. (The United States population as a whole is 12 percent Black and 7 percent Hispanic.)

The ethnicity of those prisoners with serious reading problems, that is, those under the 5.0 reading level, is 54 percent Black, 37 percent Hispanic, 9 percent White, and 5 percent other. In terms of the education levels of the women who enter the New York State prison system, 18 percent read below a fifth-grade level; 16 percent have math skills below a fifth-grade level; 77 percent dropped out while in high school; and 63 percent do not possess a high school diploma (Nuttall, 1988).

Seventy-three percent of the women in Bedford Hills are mothers (Division of Program Services, 1992), and the majority were single heads of households (Humphrey, 1988). One study showed that over half the women in prisons have received welfare payments during their adult lives (Craig, 1981); in a National Institute of Corrections study of men and women, 80 percent of those who were employed before arrest made less than a poverty-level salary (Bellorado, 1986).

Forty-four percent of the women in Bedford Hills Correctional Facility were convicted of a drug offense; however, the warden at Riker's Island, which is the largest feeder jail to Bedford Hills, estimates that drugs underlie the incarceration of 95 percent of the female inmates there (Church, 1990). Lastly, in a study done at Bedford Hills in 1985, 60 percent of respondents said they had been victims of abuse (sexual, physical, or emotional) (Grossman, 1985).

3. Recent examples of women's prisons in which repressive measures such as extreme isolation or sexual abuse have been documented include the underground prison in Lexington, Kentucky, and the Shawnee Unit in Maryanna, Florida.

4. In addition to the basic education programs, some of these programs include: The Parenting and Foster Care Programs of the Children's Center, where women learn about issues related to being mothers; the Family Violence program, where women examine violence in their personal lives and some of the social values and roles that permit or even encourage such violence; the AIDS Counseling and Education (ACE) program, where women have struggled to build a community of support around AIDS-related issues and have trained themselves to become peer educators and counselors; and the four-year college program run by Mercy College, where women can earn bachelor degrees.

5. The Department of Education of the New York State Department of Correctional Services defines literacy by using a combination of grade level and functional competency definitions. The functional competency definition was crystallized into a Life Skills curriculum (Nuttall, 1983). However, in the three-and-a-half years during which I was involved in the ABE class, the Life Skills curriculum was not put into practice except in an occasional lesson.

6. A recent policy statement of the New York State Department of Correctional Services states, "Although the Department has been reluctant to place inmates in positions where they might possibly acquire influence or authority over other inmates, we have used inmates as teacher's aides and vocational aides and in recent years have begun to employ them as pre-release peer counselors and ASAT aides" (Division of Program Services, 1991, p. 3). This statement is comparable with the long-standing practice of not permitting inmates to teach academic classes, but of encouraging them to do one-on-one tutoring, either as a teacher's aide or volunteer tutor.

7. In the summer of 1987, the ABE class was divided into two classes defined by level K-3 and level 3-6. I was working with the 3-6 level, and it was this class that I was offered to teach. Beginning with the winter of 1991–1992, the K-3 teacher was laid off, and once again there is one ABE class, level K-6.

8. Juana's story, "Chocolate and Me," was published by the PWA Coalition in *Surviving and Thriving with AIDS: Collective Wisdom*, vol. I (1988).

9. The sources of the suggestion and the guidance in using theater with literacy instruction were Dr. Ruth Meyers, my graduate study mentor, who worked with the Creative Arts Team (CAT), a professional educational theater company in residence at New York University, and Klaudia Rivera, who at the time was Director of the Community Language Services Project of the Adult Learning Center at LaGuardia Community College, where literacy and theater work was developed.

10. The plays were written by different classes of the Community Language Services project (CLS) of the Adult Learning Center at LaGuardia Community College in 1986, under the coordination of Klaudia Rivera, coordinator of the program.

11. For more information about the ACE Program see J. Clark and K. Boudin (1990), "A Community of Women Organize Themselves to Cope With the AIDS Crisis: A Case Study From Bedford Hills Correctional Facility," and K. Boudin and J. Clark (1991), "A Community of Women Organize Themselves to Cope with the AIDS Crisis: A Case Study from Bedford Hills Correctional Facility."

12. In December 1987, Educational Supervisor Rob Hinz wrote about my teaching after the completion of the AIDS unit: "Her use of Dr. Freire's theoretical work on praxis combining thought and action in a dialectical approach to the teaching of reading to adults has had remarkable results. The women with whom she was working are technically classified as technically illiterate, yet she was able in three months to provide classroom instruction on AIDS . . . and to, using the vehicle of a play, have these women writing and reading while at the same time boosting their self-image and confidence."

In the spring of 1988, the prison authorities gave permission for the ABE class video to be shown at an ABE conference of educators in New York City, with a presentation of the teaching methods done by Klaudia Rivera.

In the winter of 1988–1989, the Bedford Hills Correctional Facility Education Department sent a copy of the ABE class handbook to Albany as an example of an education product.

13. An example of how the contradictory needs and goals present opportunities for change is reflected in a recent development in the New York State Department of Correctional Services. The enormous increase in the prison population has created the need for a greatly increased work force inside the prison. Looking toward inmates to partially meet this need has led to a reformulation of a philosophy about inmates: "In keeping with our new emphasis on training inmates to meet the needs of the Department and encouraging and recognizing individual inmate responsibility, it is now our intention to make even greater use of properly trained and qualified inmates. We plan to establish new job titles of 'Inmate Program Associates.' The Program Associates will work in such areas as classrooms, orientation, pre-release, libraries, and counseling" (Division of Program Services, 1991, p. 3). It is too soon to know how this new philosophy will actually manifest itself.

Works Cited

Altwerger, B., Edelsky, C., & Flores, B. M. (1987). Whole language: What's new? *The Reading Teacher, 41,* 144–145.

Anderson, R. C. (1985). Role of the readers' schema in comprehension, learning and memory. In H. Singer & R. B. Ruddell (Eds.), *Theoretical models and processes of reading* (3rd. ed., pp. 372–384). Newark, DE: I.R.A.

Baldwin, J. (1988). A talk to teachers. In R. Simonson & S. Walker (Eds.), *The Graywolf Annual Five: Multi-cultural literacy.* St. Paul, MN: Graywolf Press.

Bellorado, D. (1986). *Making literacy programs work: Vol. I. A practical guide for correctional educators* (Grant No. FZ-7). Washington, DC: U.S. Government Printing Office (Stock No. 027-000-1293-1).

Boudin, K., & Clark, J. (1991). A community of women organize themselves to cope with the AIDS crisis: A case study from Bedford Hills Correctional Facility. *Columbia Journal of Gender and Law, 1,* 47–56.

Bransford, J. D. (1985). Schema activation and schema acquisition: Comments on Richard Anderson's remarks. In H. Singer & R. B. Ruddell (Eds.), *Theoretical models and processes of reading* (3rd. ed., pp. 385–397). Newark, DE: I.R.A.

Browne, A. (1991, February 10). Cuomo: Release nonviolent cons. *The Daily News,* pp. 3, 24.

Burkhart, K. W. (1976). *Women in prison.* New York: Popular Library.

Church, G. J. (1990). The view from behind bars [Special Issue: Women: The road ahead]. *Time,* pp. 20–22.

Clark, J., & Boudin, K. (1990). A community of women organize themselves to cope with the AIDS crisis: A case study from Bedford Hills Correctional Facility. *Social Justice, 17* (2).

Craig, G. M. (1981, July). The development of literacy/conscientization program for low-literate women in prison. *Dissertation Abstracts International, 42,* p. 68. (*University Microfilms No. 81-12, 793*)

Division of Program Services. (1991). *Division of Program Services action plan.* New York: New York State Department of Correctional Services.

Division of Program Services. (1992). *Female cluster program services action plan.* New York: New York State Department of Correctional Services.

Ellowitch, A. (1983). *Women and the world of work.* Philadelphia: Lutheran Settlement House Women's Program.

Fingeret, A. (1984). *Adult literacy education: Current and future directions.* Columbus: Ohio State University, National Center for Research in Vocational Education.

Freire, P. (1970). *Pedagogy of the oppressed.* New York: Seabury Press.

Freire, P. (1974). *Cultural action for freedom.* Cambridge, MA: Harvard Educational Review (Monograph Series No. 1).

Goodman, K. (1973). Psycholinguistic universals in the reading process. In F. Smith (Ed.), *Psycholinguistics and reading.* New York: Holt, Rinehart & Winston.

Goodman, K. (1985). Unity in reading. In H. Singer & R. B. Ruddell (Eds.), *Theoretical models and processes of reading* (3rd. ed. pp. 813–840). Newark, DE: I.R.A.

Grossman, J. (1985). *Domestic violence and incarcerated women: Survey results* (Prepared by New York State Department of Correctional Services; administered in July 1985 to female inmate population at Bedford Hills Correctional Facility). New York: Department of Correctional Services.

Humphrey, C. (1988). *Female, new court commitments (1976–1987).* New York: Department of Correctional Services.

Hunter, C., & Harman, D. (1979). *Adult illiteracy in the United States: A report to the Ford Foundation.* New York: McGraw Hill.

Juana. (1988). Chocolate and me. In *Surviving and thriving with AIDS: Collective wisdom* (vol. 1). New York: PWA Coalition.

Knowles, M. (1984). *Androgeny in action.* San Francisco: Jossey-Bass.

LaBerge, D., & Samuels, S. J. (1985). Towards a theory of automatic information processing in reading. In H. Singer & R. B. Ruddell (Eds.), *Theoretical models and processing of reading* (3rd ed., pp. 689–718). Newark, DE: I.R.A.

New York State Commission on Correction. (1988). *Acquired immune deficiency syndrome: A demographic profile of New York State inmate mortalities 1981–1987.* New York: Author.

Nuttall, J. H. (1983). *Reducing inmate illiteracy in New York State.* New York: Department of Correctional Services.

Nuttall, J. H. (1988). *An update of illiteracy in New York's correctional system.* New York: Department of Correctional Services.

Smith, F. (1973). *Psycholinguistics and reading.* New York: Holt, Rinehart & Winston.

Sullivan, L. E. (1990). *The prison reform movement: Forlorn hope.* Boston: Twayne.

I would like to acknowledge the invaluable role of Ruth Meyers who, as my mentor during my graduate program, helped shape the thinking, practice, and interpretation of experience described in this article. I am grateful to Klaudia Rivera, who shared with me her own experience in adult literacy education and also played an important role in the use of theater in literacy work. I owe a special debt to Elsa Auerbach and Bill Ayers, who took considerable time and effort editing the many drafts of this article and who helped inform its content and style. I wish to acknowledge the contributions of Susan Kessler, Paul Mattick, Rose Paladino, Margaret Randall, Ruth Rodriguez, Ann Seidman, and Ruth Wald, each of whom raised critical questions of content and organization. I want to thank the numerous women from Bedford Hills Correctional Facility, both prisoners and civilian employees, who took the time to read the article and who brought the particular perspective of people who were living and/or working inside a prison. Finally, I owe a special debt to the women in the ABE class and to the group of twelve prospective peer educators, without whom the educational process would not have been possible.

12

Integrating Disability Studies into the Existing Curriculum
The Example of "Women and Literature" at Howard University

Rosemarie Garland Thomson

Editors' Note: In this chapter, Rosemarie Garland Thomson achieves such an analysis at a historically black university through "disability." Thomson argues that disability is a useful category of analysis for all of our courses. She invites her students at Howard University "to consider how gender, class, and disability bisect racial groupings and to interrogate the very process of social categorization according to physiological or psychological characteristics." She focuses on the social construction of disability, politicizing the categories of "disabled" and "ablebodied," and examines the cultural processes that produce such distinctions. Her literature course, subtitled "Human Variation and the Politics of Appearance," examines feminine beauty, body image, appearance norms, and the beauty industry in American culture, using historical figures like Marilyn Monroe as well as women's magazines, autobiographical essays by disabled women, Toni Morrison's *The Bluest Eye,* and Alice Walker's *The Color Purple.*

As a white woman with a quite visible physical disability who is a professor at a historically black university, I envision my role to be introducing complexities into my students' tendency to see race as the primary, if not exclusive, focus of individual and group identity. The centrality of racial history, issues, identity, and community to many of the humanities and social science courses at Howard, as well as the predominant black presence, foster a strong sense of black solidarity among our students. Yet, at the same time, Howard's almost exclusively black student and majority black faculty population also afford the kind of safe atmosphere where distinctions among the black community can be examined without the kind of recourse to minimizing differences in order to establish black solidarity that sometimes prevails at predominantly white institutions. My job at Howard is to invite students to consider how gender, class, and disability bisect racial groupings and to interrogate the very process of social categorization according to physiological or psychological characteristics. While many of my colleagues balance race with gender and class analyses, introducing disability as a category of social analysis is rare. Disability studies is simply not a part of the general educational currency at Howard or at most other institutions. The salience of race as an analytical category at my university seems to me to both obscure and invite an examination of disability as a parallel yet distinct social identity based in corporeal or mental differences. The hyper-awareness of racial considerations often overshadows or minimizes other forms of what I call socially constructed "corporeal otherness" even while it serves as a model for examining those same forms of cultural marginalization. What I intend to discuss here is how I attempt to introduce disability studies—disability consciousness, if you will—in the context of a sustained focus on racial difference and to a lesser extent on gender distinctions.

In the broadest sense, my aim in teaching disability studies is to complicate the received "we" and "they" conception that implies both a victim/perpetrator and a normal/abnormal relationship between the disabled and the nondisabled. To do so, I probe the categories of "disabled" and "nondisabled," questioning their interpretation as mutually exclusive groups who are sorted according to bodily or mental traits. I emphasize the social aspect of disability, its relativity to a standard that is culturally determined, rather than its physical aspect, precisely because our traditional account of disability casts it as a problem located in bodies rather than a problem located in the interaction between bodies and the environment in which they are situated. In short, this pedagogical goal requires moving disability from its traditional medical model interpretation and placing it into a minority model understanding. It means not describing disability in the language of inherent physical inferiority or medical rehabilitation but instead adopting the politicized language of minority discourse, civil rights, and equal opportunity so as to invoke such historical precedents as the Black Civil Rights Movement and the Women's Movement. In other words, by focusing on the social construction of disability, by framing disability as a cultural reading of the body that has political and social consequences, and by invoking a politics of positive identity, I hope to facilitate understanding and identification across identity groups rather than guilt and resentment. Such an approach is intended to relativize and politicize both the categories of "disabled" and "able-bodied" while casting a critical eye on the cultural processes that produce such distinctions.

Yet, the kind of curricular refashioning that enables me to teach courses in disability studies is not easily accomplished. It is often not feasible or timely to convince institutions to offer new courses whose titles include the term "disability" because it is difficult to classify them. Administrations wish to know where they fit in the traditional scheme of the disciplines and categories: does disability belong to the humanities, to sociology, to special education, to health or science? More problematic yet, how broad an appeal might such courses have? Disability sometimes seems at first glance like a tangential or narrow field of inquiry, one that would attract only a special population. Although I would argue that disability studies should be a humanities course which, most appropriately, satisfies a diversity requirement, it can be arduous to reframe institutionally what might have been previously perceived as a health course so that it can be understood as minority studies or cultural studies. To diffuse this logic and its accompanying resistance, I propose that we teach disability studies as an integrated part of all the courses we design, just as many of us have begun to consider race, gender, and class issues as fundamental aspects of all disciplines and subjects of inquiry. Indeed, as the disciplines of women's students and ethnic studies have learned, such categories sometimes foster the assumption that these are the only arenas where racial or gender concerns are appropriately addressed. One of the goals of disability studies should be, then, to knit disability as a category of analysis into all of the courses in which we examine the workings of culture, especially courses that address issues of representation, identity, subjectivity, or the political implications of ideology.

In such a spirit, I integrate disability issues into all the courses I teach as an English professor. By way of example, I will discuss here how I infuse disability studies into a particular undergraduate humanities course called "Women in Literature" that I teach regularly at Howard. I intend to show here, first, examples of material from various disciplines that are not explicitly labeled "disability studies" but which can nevertheless be marshaled to elucidate the way that disability, along with other stigmatized identities, operates in Western culture. Second, I will suggest how literary and cultural analysis might be enlisted to reveal the ways that social relations produce the cultural distinctions of disability, race, gender, as well as class. Third, I will reflect on student responses to the material and the approach.

In all my teaching, rather than focusing exclusively on disability as the sole form of social otherness under consideration, we simultaneously investigate the bodily based social identities of race, ethnicity, gender, and sexual orientation as parallel but distinctive social categories whose function is, among other things, both to differentiate and in some cases to stigmatize individuals on the basis of corporeal differences. By intertwining analyses of a range of identities culturally constructed from bodily traits and behaviors, I encourage students to draw comparisons among them as well as mobilize their own varied experiences of differing types of social marginalization or oppression. Thus, my aim is not to privilege disability identity, but rather to probe the sociopolitical and psychological aspects involved in a matrix of often overlapping forms of social identity which rest on a premise of irreducible corporeal difference.

Even though the course I am assigned to teach at Howard is entitled "Women in Literature," I subtitle it "Human Variation and the Politics of Appearance" with the intention of linking political subordination to the cultural valuing and devaluing of bodies on the basis of their appearance. Centering our inquiry on appearance enables us to discuss not only the system of standards upon which social discrimination draws, but to consider how appearance norms contribute not only to racism but to other forms of social oppression as well. In order to scrutinize simultaneously race, gender, class, and disability, the course undertakes as its primary subject a critical examination of feminine beauty. Since the politics of appearance along with its value system, "beauty," encompass multiple forms of social marginalization, all students can identify with the issues in one way or another. In this way, ableism becomes one variation of a general form of social discrimination rather than an issue that the nondisabled students might think has nothing to do with them.

By focusing on beauty as an oppressive cultural ideology perpetuated and enforced by a wide range of institutions and received traditions, we are able at the outset to diffuse any simple split between those who could slip into the normative position in regard to our topic and those who are outside of it. There is no "we" or "they" when it comes to issues of appearance and beauty. It is quickly apparent that feminine beauty is a personal issue for all the students, even the men. Because the course fulfills a university humanities requirement, it draws from a range of ages and the students who enroll represent a wide variety of academic interests and experiences. The majority of students are women, some of whom are sympathetic to and familiar with feminism, some of whom are resistant to assertions of any cultural or historical gender differences, and most of whom are curious about investigating an academic subject that seems so close to lived experience. Men usually comprise ten to fifteen percent of the class. Some of the men are feminists themselves or quite interested in women's issues, while often a handful of the men seem vociferously hostile to the course's persistent focus on the female position. Most students are from middle-class or black elite backgrounds, while some are from the inner-city and are working class or from the working poor. Although virtually all the students are black, they represent a rich diversity of cultural backgrounds— African-American, African, Caribbean, Southern rural, Northern urban, Western U.S., mixed race and nationality—as well as a wide range of notions of what it means to be black. The only confident generalization I can make about black students is that they are black, a social identity which signifies diversely for them.

All the students seem quite eager to discuss and examine beauty standards, body-image issues, women's changing social position, questions of identity and community, and especially relations between men and women (a point I will return to later). Indeed, the course's greatest challenge is managing coherent, focused discussions which draw on personal stories yet retain an analytical edge. I nevertheless explicitly introduce the feminist assertion that the personal is political so as to encourage sharing personal observations and experiences both in class as well as in the daily reading response journals students are required to keep. What critically and personally scrutinizing beauty eventually allows us to explore is the ways in which cultures saturate bodies with meanings, an essential concept for understanding the disabled category. Along with illuminating how bodies are interpreted within societies, interrogating beauty also encourages students to flush out the value systems and the power dynamics that underpin those interpretations.

At the beginning of the course almost all students rather uncritically assume that beauty is a somewhat fixed property of the female body. Although many students recognize the historical and cultural relativity of appearance standards, they tend to see beauty as an absolute physical quality free from political implications or relations of power. Many students are willing to challenge impossible beauty norms, but few have taken their critiques beyond the arena of personal adequacy or inadequacy. Beauty, they often feel, is something corporeal that one has or does not have—just like a disability. But whereas having a disability seems a disadvantage, having beauty seems an advantage. Few students have considered the disadvantages of beauty. Thus, we further probe the operation of beauty and disability to see the parallels and to uncover the social relations that govern enforcement of bodily norms. What I try to develop is a global critique of appearance norms which at once transcends and draws from students' individual relationships with their bodies and their personal negotiations with beauty demands.

One successful way to do this, I have found, is to shift our attention to beauty's mutually constituting opposite, "ugly," which under scrutiny yields up the recognition that while beauty may not initially seem oppressive, the attribution of its flip side, ugliness, is indeed disempowering—a point I will return to later. Introducing ugliness makes it easier to denaturalize beauty, to show that it is a series of practices and positions that one takes in order to avoid the stigmatization of ugliness. I accomplish this by introducing and juxtaposing two historical figures to the class: one woman who epitomized beauty, Marilyn Monroe, and another woman who epitomized beauty's opposite—not just ugliness, but freakdom. She is Saartje Bartmann, the nineteenth-century African woman known as "The Hottentot Venus," whose body, which was normal in her own culture, differed so much from the European standard that she was recruited into English and French freak shows. By recognizing how constructed Marilyn's beauty was—the hair dye and makeup, the photo techniques, the cosmetic surgery, the name change—and how vulnerable it made her to its transience as well as its exploitation, the students see that beauty is not only a set of practices but that its empowerment is quite limited if not actually detrimental, as Marilyn's biography illustrates so well. What Marilyn and Saartje have in common is that their bodies were displayed for profit before audiences in ways that were not necessarily beneficial to them but that were dictated by the culture's need to articulate formally its standards for the female form.

While the students' response to Saartje Bartmann's display as an exoticized, sexualized freak is uniform disgust and outrage, their responses to Marilyn Monroe are usually more varied and complex. Juxtaposing the exploitative display of a white woman and a black woman invites, of course, a consideration of race and its accompanying power dynamics. The students who reveal great hostility toward Marilyn as the figure of perfect white beauty that has been held up to them as forever unattainable are generally softened and their judgment is legitimated by Gloria Steinem's analysis of the star's miserable life. Other students clearly admiringly identify with Marilyn, expressing sympathy that her life was not the fairy tale that they imagined beauty would confer. Regardless of whether they adore or despise her, students generally find shocking the pathology and liability of Marilyn's beauty. For the most part, they are unaware of the ways that beauty is mediated by cultural presentation: they assume that what they see is the natural, unreconstructed woman and that beauty delivers fulfillment. Most students are also astonished that white women try to reconfigure their bodies because they depart from beauty norms. They are very aware of the disparity between female bodies of African heritage and the stylized contemporary white beauty standard, but many do not realize that European female bodies usually cannot conform to the impossible ideal either. For example, students frequently express interest and surprise when I reveal my own conviction about the inadequacies of my hair, which is straight and limp. This sometimes creates a complex dynamic in which students identify across race with white women on the basis of shared gender experience even as they recognize white women's relative privilege within beauty culture's hierarchy of bodies. What they witness is an affirmation of what they already know but which cultural pressures mute: that a satisfying life is not so simply linked to looking right. This, of course, lays the groundwork for examining the body's social context and suggesting that the disabled body does not necessarily produce misery.

In order to denaturalize and politicize beauty culture, at the outset of the course we critically view a number of advertisements to catalogue the qualities of beauty which are so hyperbolically and relentlessly choreographed in the pages of women's magazines. With a little guidance, students adeptly and zealously read the images, compiling a stunningly uniform and narrow profile of acceptable body traits for women which include—among others—hairlessness, odorlessness, a prepubescent slimness and youth, softness, whiteness, thick wavy hair, as well as psychological characteristics such as passivity and self-consciousness. While the students are keenly aware of the racist implications in the ads' celebration of European physical features and of thinness, they have not usually thought through the role of women's bodies as spectacles in a consumer society that accords males the role of spectator and actor—a relationship that is writ large, if subtly, in advertising. Analyzing the images and reading theoretical critiques—such as John Berger's *Ways of Seeing,* an exploration of the social relation between the male spectator and the female spectacle in European oil painting—reveals for students a dynamic, in this case gendered and racialized, in which one role is to look, judge, and act while the other role is to be gazed upon, measured, and passive. They begin to understand here that the usually disembodied, usually male figure who has the power to define and to evaluate is seldom pictured in these ads, but that the woman presenting herself before the gaze is displayed for his approval and explication. Such critiques provide the students with explanatory vocabularies which they tend to wield in their journals and essays as they discuss their lives. Often they write authoritatively of spectators and spectacles, of gender and racial systems, and of social constructions.

While the class is certainly a feminist analysis of how beauty operates as sexism, it at the same time illustrates the more general process of how the body is the arena where asymmetrical power relations are acted out. This sets us up for discussing how the categories of normal and abnormal so fundamental to disability oppression are products of a social relationship in which one kind of person has the power to judge and to assume normativeness, while another must submit to judgment. The overwhelmingly female class is thus able to make a leap of identification between themselves as women, particularly black women, and people who have disabilities: they come to understand that the process of objectification that is a part of the ideology of feminine beauty is related to the process of objectification that is part of being considered disabled. Just such a dynamic between the defining subject and the defined object produces the traditional interpretation of physical disability as abnormality or inferiority. Examining this relationship allows us to uncover the power relations involved in the gaze not only in terms of gender and race, but also to relate that concept to "the stare" that is a specific form of social oppression for people with disabilities. The evaluating gaze of the male upon the female can be seen as parallel to the evaluating gaze of the "ablebodied" upon the disabled. One of the students' favorite readings, Alice Walker's autobiographical essay "Beauty: When the Other Dancer is the Self," specifically links disability to the politics of appearance as well as to the matrix of race, class, and gender. This essay interrelates Walker's becoming blind with her loss of femininity and worth and then chronicles how she regained a valued self image. Like the Marilyn Monroe story, this particularized narrative is popular with students because it manifests in an individual life the points that the cultural analyses explicate.

The course also highlights several cultural sites where ambiguity exists between beauty and disability to suggest that the coercive valuing of certain body types over others is what lies at the heart of both disability and beauty oppression. The first of these intersections is the nexus where prescriptions for beauty result in bodily transformations that amount to "disabilities." Discussing such historically and culturally varied practices as corseting, foot binding, clitorectomies, anorexia, and cosmetic surgery reveals to us the cultural relativity of the concept of disability, for such practices are understood in one context as the achievement of beauty or social acceptability and in another context as precisely the kind of bodily transformation that is taken to be a "disability." We particularly focus on cosmetic surgery because it is the practice for normalizing the (usually female) body that seems the least exotic, distanced, or pathological to modern American sensibilities. Indeed, many of the students accept the confessional mode I invite with the reading response journals to reveal anoretic or bulemic tendencies or admit to having considered cosmetic surgery to "improve" their looks or to "correct" what beauty has told them are their deficiencies. Because studies indicate that black women are generally more comfortable with their bodies than white women and generally suffer less frequently from eating disorders, I am surprised that many of my students disclose how inadequate they—often secretly—imagine their bodies to be, how tormented they are by these convictions, and how willing they would be to alter painfully their bodies to fit the standards. My suspicion is that the studies are measuring class differences more than race differences and that my students are responding to middle-class pressures to conform to beauty norms that underclass women, who are perhaps more alienated from mainstream requisites, might be spared.

Through framing cosmetic surgery as part of the beauty industry and ideology, students can recognize that the surgical normalization of the female body to meet cultural standards of beauty is parallel to the coercive "corrective" procedures that disabled people are often subjected to in order to reform their bodies to meet norms that they defy. Some of the images and discourse we examine are articles and ads on cosmetic surgery that are featured in women's magazines. Critically studying this marketing language enables students to understand how uniform the appearance standard is and how constructed it is even as it masquerades as natural and effortless. Perhaps most interesting is that with both disability and beauty the naturally occurring body is mutilated in order to conform to a standard that is presented to us as "regular" or "normal." Just as rhinoplasty and liposuction sculpt the "ugly" nose or the "fat" hips to the standard contours beauty dictates, surgeons "reconstruct" the disabled body and fit it with myriad prosthetics—often only to police life's physical variations, ones that are apparently so intolerable within contemporary American culture. It is this tyrannical concept of "normal," serving as it does capitalism, white supremacy, and patriarchy, that I want the students to come to question.

Mounting such a comprehensive cultural critique creates some pedagogical dilemmas I am not sure I successfully negotiate. By attacking beauty standards, even if I let the material speak for me, I risk implying that the students are complicit in their own oppression. What floats palpably in the classroom—coming from many sources—is the accusation of false consciousness, the suggestion that the students themselves are being castigated for their participation in beauty practices. More problematic yet is the logic inherent in the critique that caring about men is consorting with enemy. I try to address this problem directly by discussing the concept that there is no place outside acculturation for anyone to be, that we all want to be attentive to our appearance even as we try to avoid being in thrall to it. We talk much about placing ourselves in relation to beauty norms in ways that we can live with. Nevertheless, indictments erupt in class discussions that I try at once to defuse and to play out. The intense hair debate, provoked predictably by Alice Walker's witty and highly politicized essay about "oppressed hair," always provides a forum which at least exposes this dynamic even if we never resolve it. The discussion about what it means and whether or not a black woman should straighten her hair is highly charged with defensiveness, accusations, and humor, serving as a conduit to examining identity politics, the racism inherent in beauty standards, and the politicization of personal practices. The ever inconclusive hair question perhaps best illustrates the complexity of these issues.

Another dynamic that requires scrutiny is what I call coercive agreement. Most students' response to the concept of disability as a site of oppression is that they have never thought about it before. Many quickly and profoundly make the connections I hope to establish with race and gender, while some seem to unreflectively adopt an overly sympathetic attitude that I suspect may be in deference to me because I have a disability and am the teacher. This coercive agreement is one of the hazards of advocating in the classroom for a group to which you belong. Such a situation is one reason I prefer invoking as many manifestations of corporeally justified oppressive social relations as I can to analyze the larger processes at work.

One of the liveliest and most polarized of these instances always occurs around the issue of "fat," which lies in a zone somewhere between ugliness and disability, and is often the conduit through which female students come to personally identify with the social stigmatization that accompanies disabilities. While being overweight can constitute a functional disability, the students are quick to see that the social condemnation attached to being obese is usually far more detrimental than the impairment involved. Furthermore, the students' own struggle with our cultural tyranny of slimness enables them to recognize that bodily aberration is relative to a cultural and historically specific standard that serves particular interests, such as the cosmetic or fashion industries, for example. Again, autobiographical essays—Roberta Galler's about being disabled and Carol Munter's about being obese—are read together so that students can compare the subjective experiences of both women. As I mentioned before, my students seem to respond with greater understanding and interest to the identifitory and personalizing mode of the individual life story presented in the subjective voice than they do to theorizing or historical surveys. While each writer concludes that society rather than their bodies needs to change, Munter's movingly account of the denigration of her body because it is fat presents an idea new to most students, who, of course, have internalized the script of blaming the overweight person rather than the impossible standards the culture of beauty demands. Yet, frequently arguments erupt in class when some students frame fat as unhealthy, undisciplined, and inexcusable excess while others fiercely defend themselves or friends and family as victims. Fat—which I point out legally constitutes a disability—is the subject most often mentioned in the reading response journals. It is remarkable how freely some students assail obese people in ways they would never openly denigrate people with disabilities, on the assumption that obesity can be altered by an act of will. The class never reaches consensus on this point or on the lively argument of whether it is appropriate for black women to straighten their hair. Nevertheless, the juxtaposition of disability and fat oppression emphasizes that often the cultural context surrounding and defining our bodies, not our bodies themselves, creates problems for us—and that this context rather than our bodies requires alteration.

To complement the autobiographical accounts and to move the issue of appearance from the individual body into the larger context of social relations and value systems that support power dynamics, we read as well excerpts from historical critiques of those systems such as Naomi Wolf's *The Beauty Myth,* Gerda Lerner's *The Creation of Patriarchy,* Simone de Beauvoir's *The Second Sex,* Elizabeth Spelman's *Inessential Woman,* and bell hooks's *Black Looks: Race and Representation.* Some students find the accounts of the systematic nature of sexist oppression to be a revelation that frees them from a sense of individual failure for their own insecurities as women, while others resist accounts of patriarchy as having so much historical force and precedence. One of the most persistent sentiments among many students—both male and female—is the myopic and rather defensive conviction that women of this generation are fully liberated from the residue of sexism, that the problems are simply gone. It is interesting that students tend to recognize the enduring presence of racism, while insisting that society no longer limits women. Perhaps this is an important enabling progress narrative that should not be questioned; on the other hand, it risks denial and naivety. One of my most difficult challenges is to facilitate a comprehensive critique of systematic racism, sexism, and ableism while still encouraging empowerment and exploring modes of resistance.

So in order to expose the systematic nature of oppression without suggesting that it inevitably overwhelms individual agency, the first part of the course delineates the complex workings of oppression while the second part explores potential strategies of opposition. Because the course "Women in Literature" is offered as an English as well as a humanities course, literary analysis occupies a central place. To this end, we read two novels which place at the center of their social critiques the institution of feminine beauty as it is inflected with racial, class, and gender considerations. First is Toni Morrison's *The Bluest Eye,* a powerful novel which presents how the inextricable, institutionalized forces of racism, sexism, and classism combine to enact the tragic destruction of a young, black girl, abetted by the often unwitting complicity of the very community that might have saved her. The second is Alice Walker's novel *The Color Purple,* which provides a prescription for combatting the complex matrix of forces which attribute "ugly" to certain female bodies. While Morrison's is a descriptive account of the tragic political and personal consequences precipitated by what I am calling "the ideology of beauty," Walker's account offers students an optimistic paradigm for resistance and transformation. Morrison's novel is a tragedy which demonstrates the complexity and relentlessness of oppression and Walker's novel is a comedy (not a funny story but a painful tale with a happy ending) which details the triumph of a woman over those same crushing forces. Taken together, the two novels constitute the dual aspect of cultural critique: a complex articulation of the problem in its multiple material manifestations and a speculative strategy for resistance.

As preparation for reading the assigned novels and autobiographical writings, we thoroughly discuss the issue of representation, stressing the ways that representation shapes the reality that it supposedly reflects. We examine the political and ethical consequences of literary representation by reading Susan Sontag's study *Illness as Metaphor,* which elaborates the metaphorical uses of tuberculosis in the nineteenth-century and cancer in the twentieth century in order to suggest the negative consequences that these modes of cultural representation hold for people who have the diseases. Sontag's classic analysis thus allows us to use the representation of disability as a vehicle to understand the representation of race in Morrison's novel.

The juxtaposition of *The Bluest Eye* and *The Color Purple* form the center of the course. Around each novel are clustered the analytical or historical essays and the shorter biographical readings (all of which are listed at the end of this essay) so that Morrison's and Walker's narratives act as individualized testimonies to the concepts the course is designed to examine. The particularization of the issues that the novels accomplish gives the students a sense of reality and immediacy about the ways that the politics of appearance function in the complexity of lived experience. Moreover, their journals, discussions, and essays suggest that the students are able to identify often in profound ways with the two central characters, Pecola and Celie, on the basis of their being judged as "ugly." What Morrison's novel allows the students to understand is that "ugliness" is not located in any objective physical criteria but instead in the ideological systems of denigration that produce "ugliness" as a condition of racism, sexism, and classism, not as a property of a particular body. Yet the students seem to find most compelling the emotional involvement they establish with the characters, the personalization of social and political issues that narrative and identification make available to them. My intention is to devastate them with Morrison and uplift them with Walker, for Celie transforms the sentence of ugliness not through Prince Charming nor cosmetic surgery nor weight loss nor any of the traditional prescriptions for female self-creation. Instead, Walker's Celie transfigures from ugliness not into beauty, but into personal empowerment catalyzed by female community, meaningful work, economic independence, sexual sovereignty, and loving recognition of others. Women in the class respond particularly favorably to *The Color Purple* because, I think, it enables them to imagine themselves escaping social judgments of their bodies.

When the class seems adept at articulating this transformation, I use it as an opportunity to move among racism, sexism, and disability by differentiating between what I call the traditional "narrative of overcoming" and another story

I term the "narrative of resistance," both of which are common disability narratives. Although both narratives are affirmative and perhaps related, an essential distinction needs to be made. The conventional "narrative of overcoming" suggests that one's body is the recalcitrant object that must be surmounted, often either by some physical or psychological feat of rehabilitation or by a spiritual transcendence of the anomalous body. In contrast, the "narrative of resistance" claims rather than transcends the body, rejecting the traditional pronouncement of its inferiority and asserting the right of that body to be as it is. The notion of "resistance" thus locates the disabled or otherwise disapproved body within a cultural environment in which norms create deviance while the concept of "overcoming" places the deviance within the body deemed aberrant.

If on the one hand the novels act as touchstones for an identifying understanding, on the other hand they also arouse the most profound resistance among students. In both Morrison's and Walker's novels a simplistic reading suggests that the women are victims and the men are perpetrators. Although I offer ample textual evidence that no easy polarity between innocent women and guilty men is supported by the texts, the subjects of incest and rape that the novels explore always spark discussions in which some students usually take entrenched positions which pit men against women. The conflict that is sometimes fueled is exacerbated by the issue of racial solidarity and is shot through with suggestions of betrayal on both sides. Sometimes in class discussions, a great deal of hostility between men and women emerges that I must try to process sensitively and equitably. There are also always resistances to the critique of beauty that follow the logic that to reject beauty standards is to reject men. In every class, I feel that some students leave with the conviction that the course is essentially anti-male, no matter how much I attempt to present complexity and draw parallels among racism, sexism and ableism. The journals indicate that a few students choose to see beauty as innocent and me as a curmudgeon. Most often, some of the men hold this view, perhaps because they are emotionally identified with the male characters in the novels rather than with the women or perhaps because beauty is less anxiety provoking for them.

In conclusion, I need perhaps to offer a caveat concerning the position I have advocated so unequivocally here. It is important to recognize the limitations of the methodology that underlies the course that I am describing. By relating a variety of forms of social stigmatization, one risks failing to make clear the specificity, the distinct character, of each form. In comparing the disability category with race or gender systems, one must be vigilant not to conflate them so as to suggest that racial categorization, for example, is the same thing as disability, but simply in another form. The distinguishing aspects of disability such as physical pain, impairment, onset and origin, social milieu, specific economic concerns, and the like must not be erased by the move toward embracing a minority model. Nor should we fall into the simplistic equation I often hear either that "everybody has a disability of some sort" or that "being a woman (or black) is a disability." Comparing various forms of marginalized identities also risks invoking unproductive attempts to determine a hierarchy of oppression. I try with varying degrees of success to shift discussions of who suffers more than whom into examinations of complexity, interrelatedness, and uniqueness. While it is useful and illuminating to make comparisons and seek out underlying similarities among stigmatizing processes, it is equally important to particularize each identity so as to address precisely how it works in the world and how its attribution affects the persons involved.

Course Readings and Works Cited

Alexander, Elizabeth. "Cuvier." *The Venus Hottentot.* Charlottesville: University of Virginia Press, 1990. 3–7.

Bass, Alison. "When the Mirror Reflects a Distorted Self-Image." *Boston Globe* 21 October 1991: 27–29.

Berger, John. *Ways of Seeing.* London: BBC and Penguin Books, 1972. Chapter 3, 45–64.

Caputi, Jane E. "Beauty Secrets: Tabooing the Ugly Woman." *Forbidden Fruits: Taboos and Tabooism in Culture.* Ed. Ray Browne. Bowling Green: Popular Press, 1984. 36–55.

Clements, Marcelle. "The Mirror Cracked." *New York Times Magazine* 15 September 1991: 71–73.

Davis, Kathy. *Reshaping the Female Body: The Dilemma of Cosmetic Surgery.* New York: Routledge, 1995.

de Beauvoir, Simone. *The Second Sex.* Trans. and Ed. H. M. Parshley. New York: Vintage Books, 1952. xv–xxiv.

Galler, Roberta. "The Myth of the Perfect Body." *Pleasure and Danger: Exploring Female Sexuality.* Ed. Carole S. Vance. Boston: Routledge & Kegan Paul, 1984. 165–172.

Gould, Stephen J. "The Hottentot Venus." *The Flamingo's Smile: Reflections in Natural History.* New York: W.W. Norton, 1985. 291–305.

hooks, bell. *Black Looks: Race and Representation.* London: Turnaround, 1992.

Lakoff, Robin. "Beauty and Ethnicity." *Face Value: The Politics of Beauty.* Boston: Routledge & Kegan Paul, 1984. 245–276.

Lerner, Gerda. *The Creation of Patriarchy.* New York: Oxford UP, 1986. 212–243.

Lorde, Audre. *Zami: A New Spelling of My Name.* Freedom, CA: The Crossing Press, 1982.

Morgan, Kathryn Pauly. "Women and the Knife: Cosmetic Surgery and the Colonization of Women's Bodies." *Hypatia* 6.3 (Fall 1991): 25–53.

Morrison, Toni. *The Bluest Eye.* New York: Washington Square Press, 1970.

Munter, Carol. "Fat and the Fantasy of Perfection." *Pleasure and Danger: Exploring Female Sexuality.* Ed. Carole S. Vance. Boston: Routledge & Kegan Paul, 1984. 225–231.

Piercy, Marge. "Hello Up There." *To Be of Use*. New York: Doubleday, 1969. 93.

———. "A Work of Artifice." *To Be of Use*. New York: Doubleday, 1969. 75.

———. "Unlearning Not to Speak." *To Be of Use*. New York: Doubleday, 1969. 97.

Sontag, Susan. *Illness as Metaphor*. New York: Farrar, Straus, and Giroux, 1977.

Steinem, Gloria. "The Body Prison." *Marilyn*. New York: New American Library, 1986. 137–154.

Wade, Cheryl Marie. 1995. "I Am Not One of The." *Sinister Wisdom* (1987). Reprinted in *Radical Teacher* 47.

Walker, Alice. *The Color Purple*. New York: Washington Square Press, 1982.

———. "Oppressed Hair Puts a Ceiling on the Brain." *Living by the Word: Selected Writings, 1973–1987*. San Diego: Harcourt Brace Jovanovich, 1988. 69–74.

———. "Beauty: When the Other Dancer Is the Self." *In Search of Our Mothers' Gardens*. New York: Harcourt Brace Jovanovich, 1983. 384–393.

———. "Finding Celie's Voice." *Ms.* December 1985: 71–96.

Wolf, Naomi. "The Beauty Myth." *The Beauty Myth: How Images of Beauty Are Used Against Women*. New York: William Morrow, 1991. 9–19.

Young, Iris Marion. "Breasted Experience." *Throwing Like a Girl and Other Essays in Feminist Philosophy and Social Theory*. Bloomington: Indiana UP, 190–209.

———. "Women Recovering Our Clothes." *Throwing Like a Girl and Other Essays in Feminist Philosophy and Social Theory*. Bloomington: Indiana UP, 177–187.

13

The Other "F" Word
The Feminist in the Classroom
Dale Bauer

Editors' Note: Facing resistance to feminism by some students and faculty who propose teacher "neutrality" in the classroom, Dale Bauer identifies the particular goals of a feminist teacher. She argues that "political commitment—especially feminist commitment—is a legitimate classroom strategy and rhetorical imperative. The feminist agenda offers a goal toward our students' conversions to emancipatory critical action." To counter student resistance, Bauer draws on the work of Ira Shor and Paulo Freire to foreground dialogics in the classroom, but emphasizes the importance of Kenneth Burke's idea of education as persuasion. Bauer advocates feminism "as a matter of persuasion, as a 'rhetorical turn'" that invites social action, and she insists that the feminist teacher must offer a language of resistance and identification.

Evaluating Feminist Teachers

The best of our writing is entangled in the messiness of our experience.

—Nina Auerbach

In just about half of a colleague's teaching evaluations (twelve of twenty-six evaluations) from two first-year composition and introduction to literature sections, she read objections to her feminist stance, especially her discussions of feminism and pedagogy. Most of the objections came from students who insisted that the classroom ought to be an ideologically neutral space free from the instructor's interests and concerns. The following samples, copied verbatim, suggest the drift of the students' complaints:

> I feel this course was dominated and overpowered by feminist doctrines and ideals. I feel the feminist movement is very interesting to look at, but I got extremely bored with it and it lost all its punch & meaning because it was so drilled into our brains.

> I also think you shouldn't voice your "feminist" views because we don't need to know that—It's something that should be left outside of class.

> I found it very offensive that all of our readings focused on feminism.

> Feminism is an important issue in society—but a very controversial one. It needs to be confronted on a personal basis, not in the classroom. I didn't appreciate feminist comments on papers or expressed about a work. This is not the only instructor—others in the English Dept. have difficulties leaving personal opinions out of their comments.

As one of those other instructors who have "difficulties" leaving that other "f" word, feminism, out of my classroom, I am troubled by the easy separation these students insist upon between the private or personal and the public space. Precisely because they insist on this separation, our first task should be to show how the personal is public. Perhaps the last quote is the most telling: feminism is a social issue; the classroom, however, is removed from society. Social issues are not to be publicized, either to know the issues, to engage them, or to challenge the issues in the process. Rather, established truth, as Paulo Freire has told us, is to be banked. The students fear more than anything a perceived intellectual bankruptcy in the classroom. For this student, the classroom is a place of absorption, but it should not be a social arena.

Another student articulates a fear of gendered subjectivity:

> My professor has one distinct and overburying [sic] problem. She is a feminist and she incorporates her ideas and philosophy into her grading scale. If you do not make women sound superior to men or if you make women sound inferior, despite the belief of the writer, she will grade lower. I think the University should investigate this class and compare the scores of the males in the class with the females. It is my belief that among males that we are getting lower grades because of our sex.

The instructor in a personal note to me glossed this evaluation as follows: "The closest I can come to 'mak[ing] women sound superior' is to require that all essays be written in inclusive language." This evaluation is striking for two reasons. First, the metaphor of detection and investigation, of eradicating gender difference in the classroom, indicates many students' beliefs about classroom neutrality. Second, and perhaps more important, it represents the fear of gender issues invading the public world of the classroom during an era in which it is necessary for most students to insist on rationalizing intellectual labor. For most feminists, there is no separation between the outer world and the inner word, let alone between politics and intellectual work.

This second issue concerns feminism as a topic of intellectual and academic value. In the students' complaints, I hear a suggestion, echoed by some of my colleagues, that feminism is not a discipline, that gender issues are based on perspectives unsuitable for the labor of the intellectual. Consider the following student comment: "I think works should be more well-rounded without a continual stress on feminism." "Well-rounded" and balanced are set off against "feminism"—that locus of imbalance, fanaticism, eccentricity. "Continual stress" comes out of the perception of aggravation. The irony in the student comments, however, arises from a cultivated distance from the authority in the classroom; here an authority identified with an alien, radical, and threatening political position. On this point, I am persuaded by Suzanne Clark's articulation of literary studies as part of the continuum of rhetorical studies: "Feminist writing . . . breaks down the distances established by irony and provokes rhetorical responsiveness—the dialectic of resistance and identification that can then lead to critical thinking" (10; see Paine's definition of critical thinking 538–39).

How can a feminist rhetoric constitute this dialectic in the classroom? In the student comments I quoted above, there is an often overwhelming insistence on individualism and isolation; they also insist on the alienated work of the classroom, even if the professor holds forth the goal of collaborative learning in contrast to a traditional sense of knowledge as mechanized or routinized labor (see Paine 559). The students (responding here to feminism) labor at developing a critical distance to avoid participating in "the dialectic of resistance and identification" crucial not only to teaching and critical thinking, but also to political responsibility. Interrogating her students on the understanding of indoctrination, Gayatri Spivak addresses this problem in her recent book, *In Other Worlds*. She challenges her students' acceptance of the split between "moral speculation" and decision making. Spivak sees this separation as rendering them "incapable of thinking collectively in any but the most inhumane way":

> Suppose an outsider, observing the uniformity of the moves you have all sketched in your papers, were to say that you had been indoctrinated? That you could no longer conceive of public decision-making except in the quantified areas of your economics and business classes, where you learn all about rational expectations theories? You *know* that decisions in the public sphere, such as tax decisions, legal decisions, foreign policy decisions, fiscal decisions, affect your *private* lives deeply. Yet in a speculative field such as the interpretation of texts, you feel that there is something foolish and wrong and regimented about a public voice. (99)

What Spivak notes as the public-private split in the academy is fostered by the teaching of decision-making policy as a science, as corporate policy. Decision making in the realm of ethics and values (the stuff of the humanities classroom) is still conceived as intensely intimate, insular, isolated from what we see as the public voice of politics, business, and multinational capitalism.

Why this resistance to collective moral and ethical rhetoric? How do we move ourselves out of this political impasse and resistance in order to get our students to identify with the political agenda of feminism?

My response, like Ira Shor's and Freire's, is to foreground dialogics in the classroom. This strategy uses one kind of mastery, feminist and dialogic in practice, against another, monologic and authoritarian. I am working from the notion that the classroom is a place to explore resistances and identifications, a place also to explore the ambiguous and often ambivalent space of values and ethics. That is not to say that we return to the politics of the personal, a politics often mired in contradiction and confusion. The contradictions that the feminist encounters in the classroom—as outlined in *Gendered Subjects*, for instance, by the collaborators on "The Politics of Nurturance"—reveal the internalized patriarchal structures and our resistances to them (see Pheterson's definitions of internalized oppression and domination 141).

Consider the collective claim about ambivalence in "The Politics of Nurturance": "As a result of our successes in the system, we are more deeply and passionately ambivalent about the intellectual life than our students can be" (13). I focus on this sentence because I sense that our students are often more deeply ambivalent about commitment than we, their instructors, are—in part because we realize that commitment is the only survival tactic and in part because we have more experience in dealing with confusion about several, often contradictory allegiances. My students seem often quite unambiguously committed to "the system"; their ambivalence is buried deeply, already reconciled. In recognizing their unacknowledged ambivalence, feminists must teach a way not of reconciling this division but of fostering the critical urgency born out of it.

Fostering that ambivalence does not mean leaving students in a void or teaching critical thinking without a critical alternative to dominant social norms. In effect, we teach ethics as a kind of counter-indoctrination, a debriefing, to privatizing personal ethics. One of my own evaluations in a first-year composition course brought the lesson home: "[The teacher] consistently channels class discussions around feminism & does not spend time discussing the comments that oppose her beliefs. In fact, she usually twists them around to support her beliefs." In my defense, I would say, following Charles Paine (563), that we must accept our own roles as rhetoricians. On the student's behalf, I would argue that his or her recognition of the rhetorical agenda of the class— to foreground feminism as a classroom strategy—is sophisticated and aware. That is, the teacher is responsible for clarifying the agenda of the classroom, the student for challenging that agenda. Each agent—whether teacher or student—is responsible as citizens for ethical choices, although those choices often involve contradictory positions. Because agency involves a complex intersection of historically conditioned practices, discourses, and customs or habits, choice is never unambivalent or easy or unmediated. Students may ask, is it possible—or even desirable—to occupy an unambivalent position, to assume an identity without crisis? Gender complicates one's position, and this gendered mode of identifying is political: it rejects biological essence in favor of rhetorical choice. Gender identification, then, becomes a set of choices that signify the marking or signing of one's body in the world. The ambivalent space of this signing (a double participation in the imaginary and the symbolic) should not always be read negatively. Rather than opposing the public and private voices or opposing masculine and feminine, we need to see how to negotiate that opposition in order to speak a multiplicity of voices into the cultural dialogue.

With this in mind, I dispute the analysis of the feminist teacher's position the authors of "The Politics of Nurturance" offer. They suggest that the feminist teacher is nurturer, mother:

> Our students see us as something more, or certainly something other, than simply their teachers. We are, inescapably, also their mothers—necessary for comfort but reinforcing a feared and fearful dependency if such comfort is too easily accepted. But we are also, in part, their fathers—word-givers, truth-sayers—to the extent we incorporate what Dinnerstein calls the father's 'clean' authority in our female bodies. (14)

This distinction between mother and father roles, like the one between public and private invoked in the student evaluation comments, belies the positive ambivalence students feel about the confusion of familial roles and authoritative spaces which occurs in the feminist classroom. The Oedipal model doesn't hold up.

While the feminist classroom is not "the place where the cultural split between mother and father may be healed" (18), the authors' strategy to articulate the unconscious is nevertheless on target. For the feminist classroom is the place where the cultural split can be investigated for its effect in the conscious and unconscious processes which make ambivalence a part of radical pedagogy. This is why I find Gregory Jay's "The Subject of Pedagogy: Lessons in Psychoanalysis and Politics" useful in determining the unconscious processes of resistance (and, by implication, identification) in teaching: "There is a 'pedagogical unconscious' . . . informing the educational performance, and what we resist knowing is intricately tied to our constitution as social subjects" (789). Where there is no ambivalence, there is no dialogue (see Fine 165). Where there is no dialogue, there is no dialectic of resistance and identification.

One way to tap into this urgency is to offer something else in the place of the resistance that critical pedagogy offers. It is not enough to foster critical thinking: we need to suggest something in the place of what we tear down when we ask students to resist cultural hegemony (see Bizzell and Clark). Cultural optimism, what Henry Giroux criticizes as the pedagogy of "positive thinking" (123–25), is too broad: nonetheless, we need an antidote to cultural criticism's and critical pedagogy's negativity.

In short, I would argue that political commitment—especially feminist commitment—is a legitimate classroom strategy and rhetorical imperative. The feminist agenda offers a goal toward our students' conversions to emancipatory critical action (see Paine 564).

Private into Public Discourse: A Rhetoric of Conversion

To refuse the task of building a critical language is to refuse to re-invent oneself collectively outside the atomized and privatized self and liberal (possessive) individualism of the dominant culture.
—Peter McLaren and
Michael Dantley

Nina Auerbach's "Engorging the Patriarchy" is one narrative of conversion or, rather, "unconversion" into feminist agency. This conversion emerges from a rejection of the authoritative word—the word of former Governor Reagan's mandate to the Cal State System where Auerbach first taught after graduate school—to be "drearily functional and nothing more" (233). Auerbach sees her first years as an assistant professor as a period in which she was "*unconverted*—into a loss of faith—forced to see (and sometimes to implement) the ways in which books betrayed experience" (233). Her realization is a matter of transforming the outer word—what she resists in the dominant culture, in Reagan's California—into an internally persuasive word which "converts" her into feminism. The process of turning the outer word (that is, received cultural and social opinion) into an inner speech (her political self-declaration) is even clearer in Auerbach's following claim: "I became a feminist critic at the University of Pennsylvania because my department assumed I already was one" (234). This may seem backward, but this is more often the case than not: we do not declare ourselves feminist critics and then change our critical orientation to the world. Rather by virtue of our ideologies, our words, we are marked and judged by the community around us as feminists. Similarly, we do not transform students and then change their critical orientation to the world. Rather, the process of self-identification is more complex and more fruitful than an easy declaration of their resistance to hegemony.

I use Auerbach's confession as a paradigm for the pedagogical model to break down resistances and offer identifications in the classroom (see Emerson 33). The question is, how do we make the word respond to our own intentions in a feminist pedagogy? How do we make our authority as feminist rhetors available to our students for their language and thus contravene their resistance? In asking our students to deconstruct dominant ideology, "we exercise authority over them in asking them to give up their foundational beliefs, and at the same time, we give them nothing to put in the place of these foundational beliefs because we deny the validity of all authority, including, presumably, our own" (Bizzell 14). So goes Pat Bizzell's argument for the current trend in critical studies. But a feminist—or identificatory—rhetoric is an appropriate form of classroom authority, a conception of authority designed to promote "collective participation in the rhetorical process" (Bizzell 16, 18). At the base of this is the conviction that all signs are social; all language, therefore, is ideologically charged and can unite us rather than divide us socially. Language has a material reality that goes beyond individual differences and is culturally shared, although every shared language means negotiation and commitment. We are in line, then, in the classroom to negotiate the gap of understanding between our students' experience and our own, a gap which often seems insurmountable (Emerson 36–37). Negotiating this stance is often the hardest for the feminist rhetor. But it's clear that there is no way not to accept this authority: anything less ends up being an expressivist model, one which reinforces, however inadvertently, the dominant patriarchal culture rather than challenges it.

My emphasis on feminist rhetoric relies on Kenneth Burke's formulation of education as persuasion. Advocates of radical pedagogy often use the term "identification" without understanding its rhetorical base or, more important, how to employ identification in the classroom. Burke's *Rhetoric of Motives* provides this compelling political (indeed, personal) identification with an ideological stance: "In accordance with the rhetorical principle of identification, whenever you find a doctrine of 'nonpolitical' esthetics affirmed with fervor, look for its politics" (28). Why not apply this claim to the pedagogical situation itself? Whenever we hear students or colleagues affirming the "'nonpolitical' esthetics" of the classroom, look for its political consequences. For Burke, education is persuasion, making a rhetorical identification possible with the position (even of difference and conflict) from which we speak. Burke distinguishes between realistic and idealistic identifications. In realistic identification, persuasion compels social action. The idealistic identification occurs when the powerful identify with someone less powerful. Feminists yearn for the latter—when we can hope for a change in patriarchal attitudes—but work within the former, a realistic identification with those oppressed. Like Burke, I hold out for the magic of the idealistic identification, but I work in the classroom and in criticism for the realistic identification.

In "Identification and Consubstantiality," Burke puts the case for an ethics of motives based on the rhetoric of identification:

> A is not identical with his colleague, B. But insofar as their interests are joined, A is *identified* with B. Or he may *identify himself* with B even when their interests are not joined, if he assumes that they are, or is persuaded to

believe so. . . . Similarly, two persons may be identified in terms of some
principle they share in common, an 'identification' that does not deny their
distinctness. (20–21)

Burke rightly suggests that division is implied in identification since without it
there would be no need for the rhetorician to work to achieve community.
Again, Burke's *Rhetoric of Motives:* "But put identification and division am-
biguously together, so that you cannot know for certain just where one ends and
the other begins, and you have the characteristic invitation to rhetoric" (25).
Burke goes on to label rhetoric as a *"body of identifications"*—a multiplicity of
situations, stances, positions (26). It is up to the ideological critic, therefore, to
show how these positions contradict each other and, in practical terms, demand
a choice. "Belonging" is rhetorical (28). In this sense, we can think of feminism
as a rhetorical criticism, an act by which we teach students how to belong, how
to identify, as well as how to resist.

   Finally, Burke writes about the relationship of identification as an awareness of contingent joining and separating with another. Thus, Burke implies
that identification allows for another voice to be in sync but not to erase difference: "to begin with *identification* is . . . though roundabout, to confront the implications of *division.* . . . If men were not apart from one another, there would
be no need for the rhetorician to proclaim their unity" (22). The implications of
this claim are at least twofold for feminist criticism: the feminist can work toward social change by suggesting identificatory readings rather than (or only)
resisting ones (as I will discuss later). Opposition creates the necessity of
rhetoric, of resistance and identification. Burke argues that political conditions
call for a powerful identification with others, but those same conditions esca-
late "the range of human conflict, the incentives to division. It would require
sustained rhetorical effort, backed by the imagery of a richly humane and spontaneous poetry, to make us fully sympathize with people in circumstances
greatly different from our own" (34). Burke's humanism aside, his argument
brings to the fore the divisiveness of a culture which we, as radical teachers of
English, try to overcome.

   When we ask our students to identify with a political position offered in
class or to identify with us as the most immediate representative of that political stance, we are asking them to give allegiance to an affinity or coalition politics that often competes with or negates other allegiances they have already
formed (see Alcoff 423, 431). We ask them to recognize identity—and politics—as social constructions. But without that critical tension between internally persuasive words and externally authoritative rhetoric, we have no hope,
nor offer any, for radical social change. Thus, paradoxically, I affirm the students voicing their concerns against feminism in their teaching evaluations:
that voicing shows that their feminist teachers (who bravely offered their evaluations for my study) brought their students into some conflict with their pre-

viously held norms. In short, there is no natural or essential identification, but only one forged from rhetorical situations and political awareness. In that case, in the classroom, we are not presenting objective categories of political affiliation but a rhetorical context of modes or bodies of identifications.

In teaching identification and teaching feminism, I overcome a vehement, even automatic, insistence on pluralistic relativism or on individualism. I teach how signs can be manipulated, appropriated, and also liberated. Coming to consciousness of any kind is the recognition of the social signs we all internalize and inherit, inevitably against our will. As Auerbach explains, her coming to consciousness as a feminist meant for her becoming aware of the ideological signs she represented for others. Feminism, then, proved to be both social (her interaction with her colleagues "marking" and "de-signing" or, better yet, "resigning" her to her oppositional stance) and psychological, since her internally persuasive voice resulted in her rejection of another social category: the "good" mother and caretaker/teacher.

Auerbach uses her social de-signation as feminist in order to open up the question of cultural politics with her students. She works, then, from the notion that there is no individual stance that would be alien to her but that the classroom is thoroughly social, a locus of many voices, often conflicting, always in flux. In her words:

> No doubt all beginning teachers identify with their students rather than with their colleagues, and I did too. Trying to negotiate the den of vipers which the Cal State English Department looked like to me at that time, I saw myself in my students, and I saw myself for the first time. . . . Like my students, I tried to learn to be blandly affable and to keep my mind in the closet, my unorthodox scholarly writing a secret. . . . I was converted into subservience. (233)

The "answers" about feminism don't come from "within"; but, as Auerbach notes, we designate ourselves through our dialogue with others and with ourselves. In advancing the dialogue within herself, Auerbach hopes to affect the one with her students.

Whose signs we articulate as part of our internally persuasive speech make all the difference. As I see it, the dialogue in the feminist classroom helps clarify the contradictions between what we all have internalized as part of a patriarchal unconscious and a resistance to those assumptions. As feminist rhetors, we supply an authoritative word about potential sites of identification and of resistance to patriarchy.

Ultimately, we don't think "feminism" until we have the sign-system to do so. Our task, then, is to make this speech readily available and heard—sometimes over and against the social objections of others. As Pat Bizzell argues in "Orators and Philosophers in English Studies, or, The Rhetorical Turn Versus Schemes for Cultural Literacy," we need the oratorical perspective of feminism, what she aligns with the anti-foundationalist theoretical concerns of

English studies. "We have nothing to study but the matter of persuasion, in other words ideologies, the kind of value orators have always dealt with" (6). I want to advocate feminism as a matter of persuasion, as a "rhetorical turn."

Narration and Social Change

So far, critical pedagogy has generally slighted the problem of identification; excellent studies like Giroux's, McLaren's, Weiler's, and Shor and Freire's are filled with narratives of students' resistance to hegemonic forms. There are few or no narratives about the identification students have with, say, antiracist, anti-sexist, or antihomophobic politics. The process comes down to articulating social change in the literature classroom so that it strikes a middle ground between optimism and pessimism. The feminist teacher must offer a language of resistance and identification: both are confessional forms—direct addresses—designed as rhetorical invitations to the reader. They invite participation in narratives, in the literature we teach (see Warhol).

How do we draw out and discuss those resistances to theory, to feminism? I do so by compelling students to work through them in literature by confronting fears and values mediated by the form of fiction. Let me explain how I use Pat Barker's *Blow Your House Down* (1984) as one example of breaking down cultural stereotypes. This novel about working-class British women, many of whom have turned to prostitution because of the 1974 coal strike and the failing British economy, is ostensibly a detective/murder mystery, but it eventually explodes our expectations about the genre as well as about violence against women. A prostitute-killer is loose, and the first three sections of the novel, each one from the perspective of a different woman, detail responses to arbitrary violence against women. In the first, Brenda explains how she became a prostitute when her first husband left her and how difficult it is to give up life on the streets: "It was hard to say really why you stuck with it. Money, friends, habit—and of course it was easy, if you were ever short, if you ever needed anything, it was always there" (63–64). Kath's section, the second, leads up to her murder, after Kath has lost her boys and daughter to the social welfare system. In the third part, Jean avenges that murder, along with the murder of Carol, her own lover.

Each section also raises questions about these women's relations to their clients, to the dole, to dominant cultural morality, to capitalism in general. The final section, Maggie's, begins with another act of random violence, this time against a "respectable" woman who works in a chicken factory rather than on the streets. Like Maggie, the students must come to terms with a violence against women which is random and senseless and which finally makes the victim more victimized by the neighbors and the police than by the assailant. She is suspected of "asking for it," if only because she takes a shortcut home from work on Friday night after her weekly drink with her colleagues: "you needed a drink, you needed something to swill the blood and guts away, and make you fit to face the world" (177). Another sort of victimization occurs in the novel: like the prostitutes, Maggie is "cut"—interrogated about the events of the attack and then shunned by her neighbors. Maggie comes to feel as though her neighbors were, in her terms, "enjoying it too": "They read the papers, they tried to read *between* the lines, and the same questions were there. *What does he do to them? How much did he do to her?* It was all very exciting, having a victim living in the same street" (193). The spectacle of violence perpetuates the rationalization of that violence.

This is a confusing novel for many students, in part because of the explicit economics of prostitution (there is no point of view from which the sexual encounters that occur appear anything other than economic and quotidian). But the students are willing enough to accept the violence against the prostitutes since part of their job, the students reason, is an acceptance of risk. What they are not prepared to accept is the violence against Maggie, the wife and mother, whose shortcut home endangers her life. Maggie has not "asked for it," nor is Maggie's profession morally suspect. Because of this rupture of generic and moral expectations, the students are led to question their assumptions about violence against women. There is no rationale or logic to violence: the only logic behind violence, they learn, is patriarchal power.

Barker historicizes that violence: her novel calls into question women's expectations of violence both in the home and outside of it. The women debate what to do about the recent prostitute killings going on:

> And there were all sorts of ideas flying around. "Always get out of the car." "Never get out of the car." "Take the numbers." "Work in pairs." "Don't bend down." "Don't turn your back." "Don't suck them off." Load of rubbish. I never did any of it. I did start carrying a knife and then I thought well, you dozy cow, you're just handing him the weapon. So after that I didn't bother. (17)

In rehearsing the contradictory advice about dealing with violence on the streets where she works, Maureen reveals the mystification of male violence, no less frightening because it is random and aleatory.

After her attack, Maggie's heterosexual marriage is no longer a safe place, nor is the master bedroom. She comes to expect violence from Bill in the same way that the prostitutes anticipate it on the streets. As Elaine says, "'the way I look at it, if you're living with a bloke he's gunna hit you about something'" (105). Maggie's experience of violence leads her to a rejection of the alienated work in the chicken factory and a moral confusion, one of the only positive effects of her encounter with what Barker terms the "abyss" of violence:

> Their own bedroom. She knew every mark on the wallpaper, every creak of the floorboards, every bump and sag in the mattress. It ought to've been completely safe, but it wasn't. She found herself listening for Bill's footsteps on the stairs.

This was something she couldn't understand. As long as she could *see* Bill, as long as he was in the same room with her, she was alright. But if he was behind her, or in a different part of the house, she started to worry. It wasn't fear exactly, but she needed to know what he was doing. . . .

But she was left with a feeling that the road back to 'normal' might be longer than she had wanted to believe. (186)

Maggie also comes to understand that her middle-class notions about violence—that it happens only to women who provoke men, women who work on the streets—are illusory. Both Jean's and Maggie's sections suggest what happens when women cannot comprehend violence according to "rational" categories. Violence, in Barker's text, is not a masculine construction: rather, it is symbolic, available to both men and women and destructive to both. Barker provides a middle-class audience with an identificatory model in Maggie, a model to explore in class discussions of ethics.

Because this text raises so many questions about class and gender, it opens up as topics of discourse values and assumptions which have been naturalized in dominant culture. These classes, indeed perhaps feminist pedagogy and rhetoric in general, end ambivalently: these disrupted values or assumptions are not occasions for reconstituting consciousness into clear categories of good faith feminism and bad faith—or, worse, good and bad politics. Having access to a common language is only a first step: speaking languages of difference is another.

My final appeal is to Kenneth Burke's *Rhetoric of Motives* and the call for rhetorical criticism:

Education ("indoctrination") exerts such pressure upon [the student] from without; [students complete] the process from within. If [they do] not somehow act to tell [themselves] what the various brands of rhetorician have told [them], [the] persuasion is not complete. Only those voices from without are effective which can speak in the language of a voice within. (39)

As feminist rhetors, our task is to make compelling the wider implications of the feminist dialogue in the classroom. Because my voice in the classroom is one in competition with other voices speaking for the students' allegiance, the most pernicious voice that reinforces the split between public and private, I would do well to be aware of the rhetorical situation of the classroom—of the necessity for a mastery that is not oppressive, of an authoritative voice that is not the only authority.

Works Cited

Alcoff, Linda. "Cultural Feminism versus Post-Structuralism: The Identity Crisis in Feminist Theory." *Signs* 13 (Spring 1988): 405–36.

Auerbach, Nina. "Engorging the Patriarchy." *Historical Studies and Literary Criticism.* Ed. Jerome J. McGann. Madison: U of Wisconsin P, 1985.

Barker, Pat. *Blow Your House Down.* New York: Ballantine, 1984.

Bizzell, Patricia. "Orators and Philosophers in English Studies, or, The Rhetorical Turn Versus Schemes for Cultural Literacy." *College English.*

Burke, Kenneth. *A Rhetoric of Motives.* New York: Prentice, 1950.

Clark, Suzanne. "Feminism, Poststructuralism and Rhetoric: If We Change Language, Do We Also Change the World?". CCCC paper. March 16, 1989.

Culley, Margo, Arlyn Diamond, Lee Edwards, Sara Lennox, and Catherine Portuges. "The Politics of Nurturance." *Gendered Subjects.* Eds. Margo Culley and Catherine Portuges. Boston: Routledge & Kegan Paul. 1985: 11–20.

Emerson, Caryl. "The Outer Word and Inner Speech: Bakhtin, Vygotsky, and the Internalization of Language." *Bakhtin.* Ed. Gary Saul Morson. Chicago: U of Chicago P, 1986: 21–40.

Fine, Michelle. "Sexuality, Schooling, and Adolescent Females: The Missing Discourse of Desire." *Harvard Educational Review* 58 (February 1988): 29–53.

———. "Silencing in Public Schools." *Language Arts* 64 (February 1987): 157–74.

Giroux, Henry. *Schooling and the Struggle for Public Life.* Minneapolis: U Minnesota P, 1988.

Jay, Gregory S. "The Subject of Pedagogy: Lessons in Psychoanalysis and Politics." *College English* 49 (November 1987): 785–800.

McLaren, Peter, and Michael Dantley. "Leadership and a Critical Pedagogy of Race: Cornel West, Stuart Hall, and the Prophetic Tradition." *Journal of Negro Education.*

Paine, Charles. "Relativism, Radical Pedagogy, and the Ideology of Paralysis." *College English* 51 (October 1989): 557–70.

Pheterson, Gail. "Alliances between Women: Overcoming Internalized Oppression and Internalized Domination." *Reconstructing the Academy: Women's Education and Women's Studies.* Eds. Elizabeth Minnich, Jean O'Barr, and Rachel Rosenfeld. Chicago: U Chicago Press, 1988: 139–53.

Shor, Ira, and Paulo Freire. *A Pedagogy for Liberation: Dialogues on Transforming Education.* South Hadley, MA: Bergin & Garvey, 1987.

Spivak, Gayatri Chakravorty. *In Other Worlds.* New York: Methuen, 1988.

Warhol, Robyn R. *Gendered Interventions.* New Brunswick: Rutgers UP, 1989.

Weiler, Kathleen. *Women Teaching for Change: Gender, Class & Power.* South Hadley, MA: Bergin & Garvey, 1988.

14

Researching the Minimum Wage
A Moral Economy for the Classroom

Vara Neverow-Turk

Editors' Note: Drawing on Dale Bauer's essay, Vara Neverow-Turk acknowledges the political nature of all literacy instruction, reminding us that even asking for an essay on students' summer vacations is not value-free. She takes the freshman comp research paper beyond library research and clichéd subjects to student inquiry into social agencies and social problems like welfare and poverty. During the semester she describes, her students studied what it would be like to live on the minimum wage. This approach heightened their awareness of, and changed their views about, "the poor." In a society that celebrates wealth and demonizes the poor, such a course can be counterhegemonic, that is, inviting solidarity with rather than contempt for those at the bottom.

Writing and research assignments in a composition class may seem politically inert but are not. Even the trivial is ideological. Writing about one's summer vacation, that quintessential cliché of composition instruction, is inherently political since it must necessarily elicit sensitive socioeconomic information about the writer, information that can scarcely be considered value-free. Ironically, the numerous assaults on what has recently been termed the "neo-Fascism of the left" (Camille Paglia qtd. in Stanfill 24) and "illiberal education" (D'Souza 51) have inadvertently revealed the severely ideological intent of all pedagogies. This backlash against so-called "political correctness" has made glaringly explicit the extent to which every cultural practice is a political practice. In fact, thanks to current conservative retrenchment, one need not any longer justify the claim that writing is always already a political act.

Certainly, the writing assignment to be discussed here, an assignment which requires students to research and report on what it would be like to live on minimum wage, is not really any more political than a more traditional research assignment on, say critical perspectives on *Hamlet* or the effects of television on children; it is simply more obvious about its political content because it involves an inquiry into economics rather than literature or culture.

As this assignment suggests, my approach to teaching composition is openly political in that I choose, for pedagogical reasons, to focus writing classes on social issues. I take this socially-oriented approach to the teaching of writing not because I regard writing as form without content but because I find that my students squirm when I deal with rhetorical issues and research techniques in isolation. While I find the detailed analysis of rhetorical structures fascinating, the majority of my students regard this exercise as a form of torture. By contrast, they find discussion of social concerns intellectually engaging and thus, because they are engaged, they perform better rhetorically. Like Toni-Lee Capossela, whose article, "Students as Sociolinguists: Getting Real Research from Freshman Writers," proposes a controlled content for the teaching of researched writing, I think that students respond more confidently to the guided research situations created by thematically focused courses. Because I think of my composition classes as courses in which students are given access through their writing assignments and class discussion to the concept of citizenship, to the idea of political responsibility, to the realization that they can make a difference in the world, I emphasize issues that will generate social concern. During the course of a typical semester, my students read several utopian texts (the works I've used include Margaret Atwood's *The Handmaid's Tale,* George Orwell's *Nineteen Eighty Four,* Marge Piercy's *Woman on the Edge of Time,* and B. F. Skinner's *Walden Two).* The students write papers based not on the traditional "literary" aspects of the readings but on the social issues the texts raise. I also require the students to write letters of protest (the students select their own targets, topics, and political positions), to present oral reports on social action groups of their own choosing, and to do extensive research on a social problem (again, the students determine for themselves what problem to investigate and how to approach the problem).

Since many composition class research assignments based on social problems elicit the all-too-familiar moralizing on subjects ranging from the merits of capital punishment to the horrors of child abuse (illustrated by verbatim transcription of accounts of abuse too painful to read), I encourage students to focus their research on the agencies that address the problems. A student writing a paper on drug abuse might evaluate the efficacy of government policies in the war against drugs or the procedures of a local drug treatment facility, while a student writing a paper on dying with dignity might visit a hospice or research the right-to-die movement.

The specific assignment that I focus on in this article was designed to involve students in researching, analyzing, and reporting on the living situation of an individual earning the minimum wage. The students were not being asked to look at the larger sociopolitical context of the minimum wage, only at the impact of this wage ceiling on an individual wage earner. My students (like most college students?) typically believe in the American Dream and are also convinced that the working poor, the homeless, welfare recipients, prostitutes, and other members of the underclass have ready access to numerous alternative life choices and that their existing circumstances can be easily corrected if, for example, they would only work harder or stop having so many children whom "we" have to support. For these students, it is quite a revelation to compare their own affluence, however modest, with the financial strain of living on minimum wage.

The students whose responses I will discuss did the assignment at the end of the semester as their final paper. They were to present their findings orally to the class and then submit their finished essays for grading. As I had hoped, the class seemed intrigued rather than dismayed when I described the task (several told me later that even some of their parents had been interested in the project and their findings). The students immediately began to consider how they might go about accumulating the necessary information and together we generated a list of the concerns they would have to address (it would also have been possible to have the students do this task in groups).

The brainstorming process was itself an excellent exercise in classification. The obvious things were listed first. Everyone mentioned food, shelter, and clothing but most quickly realized that they might not be able to afford to eat regularly at McDonald's, might not feel safe living in the neighborhoods where they could afford housing, and might have to adjust their ideas about what to wear and where to buy it.

As the list evolved, the students realized that if they had to make ends meet on the state minimum wage (in this state, the minimum wage is currently $4.25, or $170 a week before taxes) their lives would be radically altered. Things they took entirely for granted like transportation, telephone service, heat, dry cleaning, entertainment, health care, even education itself, began to look like luxuries. When the class agreed to add the variable of a dependent child to the calculations, the prospects seemed even grimmer.

Having completed this preliminary list of basic needs and wants, we moved on to discussing how the students would determine what living on minimum wage would be like. They decided that they would have to consult newspaper listings for jobs and for apartments or rooms for rent. They planned to find out the expense of transportation to and from their workplaces, price furniture at thrift shops, make shopping lists and go to supermarkets to calculate the cost of food and other necessities. Most of them realized that they could never afford to purchase or maintain a car and its insurance payments. Several students suggested that they would want to contact social service agencies and determine their eligibility for government subsidies.

The students had a month to complete the project and were permitted to work in teams if they wished. On the final day of class, the students presented their findings. Most of the reports were interrupted by comments and questions because everyone in the class was an expert on the topic and had something to say about the other students' work. Staying out of the red on an annual pre-tax income of $8840 was a tough proposition and sometimes personal idiosyncrasies and oversights in budgeting created a good deal of giggling. For example, very few of the students had remembered to include laundry costs in their calculations and only a few thought to figure in the cost of such common items as toilet paper, toothpaste, deodorant, shampoo, soap, and detergent.

One student's list of the clothing he thought he would need included a couple of pairs of jeans, some socks and underwear, and a few shirts. He didn't seem to realize that he might need a coat even though it gets pretty cold in New England in January. The same student elicited shrieks of delighted laughter from his peers when he read his weekly grocery list which everyone said sounded like the shopping list for a party. The list included a case of beer (he was under the drinking age), two bags of potato chips, two pounds of cold cuts, four loaves of bread, two cans of soup, and a two-pound jar of peanut butter. However, his estimate of a weekly expenditure of $35.00 on food was completely accurate based on his purchases (assuming that he bought primarily generic products). Some students hadn't done their research as thoroughly as they might have and were soundly criticized by their peers for estimating that food would cost only $50 a month; some were teased for extravagances such as allocating $40 a month for "beauty supplies" or $50 for phone bills.

Many students had some difficulty finding listings of full-time jobs that paid minimum wage. The obstacle was that most unskilled jobs in the state pay $5.00 an hour, a wage that would bring in $200 before taxes every week. When I give the assignment again, I may ask students to calculate the different effects of an annual salary of $8,840 vs. one of $10,400. Most minimum-wage jobs did offer medical and dental benefits (with high deductibles and no family coverage) as well as sick-leave and vacations.

In a class of nineteen students, there were two returning students, both of whom, for different reasons, were more politically and socially conscious than the others in the class. One was an African-American woman from Little Rock, Arkansas, a Republican, who was a founding member of the local chapter of the NAACP; the other was an Italian-American, male Vietnam veteran. The rest of the class were traditional-age students. Of seventeen traditional-age students, twelve were women and five were men. Most students at this university are from Italian-American Catholic backgrounds. Most are first-generation college students from second-generation immigrant families. The majority of the students are going to a state university because they can't afford a private university.

They are mostly young women who plan to have careers in the helping professions. Few students in the class had given any thought to the circumstances of those less affluent than themselves prior to that semester.

The African-American woman responded to the assignment by crafting a fiction which traced the misfortunes of a Black woman and her child when they moved to New Haven from the deep South. The woman in the student's story had been told she could get a job that paid a good deal more than she currently made as a farm worker if she moved North. Because she was not used to earning so much money or to coping with the higher cost of living, she failed to budget for rent and food and within a few weeks had to go on welfare. However, she had not been a state resident for a full six weeks and consequently was not eligible for welfare. As a result, she had to beg her neighbors for food and go without heat or hot water in her apartment. Eventually, after humiliating encounters with the welfare agency, which demanded to know, prior to awarding benefits, the name and whereabouts of her child's father, she decided to return to the South.

In an equally experimental vein, the Vietnam veteran imagined a Rip Van Winkle tale of a hippie who fell asleep in 1968 and awoke in 1990 to a new era of homelessness and destitution in which the war against poverty had become the war against the poor. Both of these fictions were firmly based on economic facts which the students had gathered through interviews, library research, and phone calls to government agencies.

The most sophisticated and thorough responses to the assignment were submitted by two young women who worked together on the project, producing interrelated but very different essays. Both, perhaps significantly, came from families that had faced fairly severe financial hardship. One of the young women mentioned that she and her three siblings had been raised single-handedly by her mother after her father had deserted them. The family had received a government subsidy in commodities and she recalled having "eaten a *lot* of grilled cheese sandwiches" as a child. The other young woman's father had himself grown up in a family that was on welfare. He escaped the welfare syndrome, but his five sisters did not and they now have daughters who are themselves on welfare to support their dependent children.

Together, these young women had contacted virtually every social service agency in the area. They called Housing and Urban Development and found out that they were eligible for rent subsidies. When they mentioned this in the class, however, the Vietnam vet, who is a recipient of various subsidies, asked them if they knew what the waiting period would have been, indicating that normally it was three years. The young women had also found out that they would be better off financially if they were single mothers. If they each had a dependent child, they would be eligible for a modest day-care subsidy (about half of what day care normally costs), for the government food subsidy for women with infants and children, and for a heat subsidy. Further, they priced and found adequate day-care services that served children lunch and kept them a full work-

day, they applied for minimum wage jobs, and they looked for and found af-
fordable apartments that would accept HUD funds.

All the students in the class agreed that living on minimum wage would be
extremely difficult, and all acknowledged that they would have to make great
sacrifices and great psychological adjustments if they were ever to have to cope
with those circumstances. Some stated outright that, for them, it would be impossible—and given the way that they had budgeted their income, they were
right. Several of the students said that they could understand why people turned
to crime to support themselves and their families. Many of the students admitted that they had never before realized that they were spoiled. They confessed
that it had never occurred to them that they hadn't really earned their brand new
cars, their summer vacations at their parents' beachfront homes, their refriger-
ators bulging with food, their VCRs, computers, and washing machines, or
their college education.

In addition to encouraging a degree of social awareness, the assignment
encouraged students to apply their research skills outside the classroom by calling agencies, contacting landlords, comparing prices, budgeting income, planning meals, arranging for day care, looking for a full-time job, and scheduling
commitments. These unconventional research forays also developed the students' survival skills. The methods of gathering and analyzing data that students
employed in completing this assignment went well beyond the narrow scholarly challenge of finding library sources and exposed them to interdisciplinary
tactics for accumulating information. Further, the assignment required the
students to use specialized documentation formats to cite the interviews, pamphlets, government forms, newspaper listings, and other sources of information
they consulted in the process of doing the assignment.

But why give such an assignment at all? Is it even appropriate to raise such
issues in a composition class? Although some would certainly say no, and say
so emphatically, the stereotype of a traditional writing class as a service course
devoted solely to the mastery of academic discourse has long since been challenged and modified. While not every composition teacher practices a radical
pedagogy, Paulo Freire's model of a revolutionary classroom that transcends
the "'banking' concept of education in which the scope of action allowed to the
students extends only as far as receiving, filing, and storing the deposits" (58)
has had a palpable impact on composition instruction. Even the emphasis on
writing as process which has become a convention of composition teaching
resonates with Freire's claim that "[k]nowledge emerges only through invention and re-invention" (58).

Certainly composition courses with agendas are becoming more and
more commonplace. The college classroom is increasingly seen as a valid
context for open political engagement. Dale Bauer, for example, rejects the
definition of the classroom as "an ideologically neutral space free from the instructor's interests and concerns" (385) and argues instead that "political commitment . . . is a legitimate classroom strategy and rhetorical imperative" (389).

Indeed, she sees the classroom as "a place to explore resistances and identifications, a place also to explore the ambiguous and often ambivalent space of values and ethics" (387). This revisioning of the classroom challenges the view that pedagogy ought to be apolitical and calls attention to the dominant culture's investment in the educational process (Ohmann; Sledd).

I should emphasize, however, that while I teach writing with a political agenda, I do not overtly force that agenda on my students nor do I grade them on whether their writing is politically correct by my standards. I recognize the tremendous power that the instructor wields over the student through both the medium of grades and the sheer authority of the classroom hierarchy, and I do not want to abuse that power. When I say that I do not force my politics upon my students I mean that I encourage them to argue for the political positions they hold and to do so persuasively, even passionately. This engagement with conflicting ideas is stimulating and exhilarating for most students for it tries their rhetorical mettle and gives them the opportunity to defend their positions against their opponents' viewpoints. I would prefer that my students discover the contradictions in their positions (and mine) through questioning and argument rather than through intimidation and enforcement. When one of my students said somewhat ruefully after the course was over and the grades submitted, "I didn't expect Composition 101 to be Social Conscience 101," I was gratified, for he tempered the quip by thanking me for having encouraged him to think about social problems he had previously dismissed without investigating their origins and their implications. If the ability to analyze a problem, to plan and execute a project, to think critically about complex issues, and to gather evidence to support an argument or demonstrate a point is part of what we want to teach in composition classes, then this type of assignment offers a model for engaging students in a process of inquiry that they themselves acknowledge as worthwhile. This assignment and others like it foster a sociocultural literacy that goes beyond the academy.

Works Cited

Atwood, Margaret. *The Handmaid's Tale*. Boston: Houghton Mifflin, 1986.

Bauer, Dale M. "The Other 'F' Word: The Feminist in the Classroom." *College English* 52 (Apr. 1990): 385–396.

Capossela, Toni-Lee. "Students as Sociolinguists: Getting Real Research from Freshman Writers." *College Composition and Communication* 42 (Feb. 1991): 75–79.

D'Souza, Dinesh. "Illiberal Education." *The Atlantic Monthly* Mar. 1991: 51–79.

Freire, Paulo. *The Pedagogy of the Oppressed*. Trans. Myra Bergman Ramos. New York: Continuum, 1982.

Ohmann, Richard. *English in America: A Radical View of the Profession*. New York: Oxford UP, 1976.

———. "Literacy, Technology, and Monopoly Capital." *College English* 47 (Nov. 1985): 675–89.

Orwell, George. *Nineteen Eighty Four.* New York: New American Library, 1949.

Piercy, Marge. *Woman on the Edge of Time.* New York: Fawcett, 1986.

Skinner, B. F. *Walden Two.* 1948. New York: Macmillan, 1976.

Sledd, Andrew. "Readin' Not Riotin': The Politics of Literacy." *College English* 50 (Sept. 1988): 495–508.

Stanfill, Francesca. "Woman Warrior: Sexual Philosopher Camille Paglia Jousts with the Politically Correct." *New York* 4 Mar. 1991: 22–31.

15

Community Service and Critical Thinking

Bruce Herzberg

Editors' Note: While Neverow-Turk positions her students as researchers of social agencies, Bruce Herzberg has his students working in social agencies as part of a service-learning program at Bentley College. Herzberg proposes that service learning helps create social conscience among students, lessening their prejudices, as they identify with their clients. But he is concerned that students primarily regard the social problems they witness as personal, instead of searching for systemic explanations. As a critical teacher, he raises questions to his students about social structures, ideology, and justice through his service-based composition course. In this article, he traces the experience of students who volunteered to tutor at a homeless shelter from their initial fears and prejudice to their understanding of social causes. He wants his students to not only question and analyze the world, but to imagine how they can transform it.

"Capitalism with a human face," said our new provost, Phil Friedman. This was the way he hoped the United States would model capitalism for the new democracies in eastern Europe. It was, therefore, a motto for what the students at Bentley College, a business school, should be learning. My English Department colleague Edward Zlotkowski challenged the provost to put a human face on the students' education by supporting a program that would make community service part of the curriculum. Friedman agreed and Zlotkowski took on the massive job of linking courses with community agencies. At first, the projects were simple: Students in writing courses visited soup kitchens and wrote up their experiences. Later, as the service-learning program developed, students in accounting classes helped revise the accounting procedures of nonprofit community-service agencies and audited their books for free. Students in marketing and business communication designed advertising and public relations materials to improve the distribution of agencies' services. And the students in one freshman composition class—mine—learned to be adult literacy tutors and went weekly to a shelter in Boston to offer their help.

There are many obvious benefits, to students and to the agencies and individuals they serve, from service learning. Many students become eager volunteers after the ice is broken by class projects and they see where they can go, how they can help. A surprising number of the students in my class, for example, did some volunteer work in high school, but would not be likely to do so in college—in a new city, without contacts—were it not for the liaison provided by service learning. Most agencies are eager for new volunteers.[1] And of course, the students perform real and needed services. Faculty members, too, report a new sense of purpose in their teaching. This is, perhaps, most striking at a school like Bentley, where students are not only majoring in business but often seem to have fallen into the narrowest view of what that means, adopting a gray and jaded image of the businessman, scornful or embarrassed by talk of social justice and high ideals. Edward Zlotkowski describes his teaching efforts at Bentley in the years before he founded the service learning program as attempts "to help my students break out of the intellectual and moral miasma in which they seemed to me to wander."

I should interject here that the idea of service learning did not originate at Bentley. There are well-developed community service projects at several colleges and universities. Stanford has made extensive use of service learning in freshman English courses. And Campus Compact, an organization of college presidents that promotes public service in education, has been in existence since 1985. The observations I have made about the venture at Bentley are echoed in reports from other schools.

There is a good deal of evidence from our program that service learning generates a social conscience, if by that we understand a sense of the reality and immediacy of the problems of the poor and homeless along with a belief that people in a position to help out should do so. Students report that their fears and prejudices diminish or disappear, that they are moved by the experience of helping others, and that they feel a commitment to help more. This is a remarkable accomplishment, to be sure.[2] But it is important to note that these responses tend, quite naturally, to be personal, to report perceptions and emotions. This is where my deepest questions about service learning lie.

I don't mean to belittle the kind of social awareness fostered by service learning, especially with middle-class students. Students in business courses are discovering real applications of their knowledge in the organizations they serve. More importantly, they are learning that they can use their knowledge not only to get jobs for themselves but also to help others. But what are they learning about the nature of the problems that cause these organizations to come into existence? How do they understand the plight of the people who need these services? I worry when our students report, as they frequently do, that homelessness and poverty were abstractions before they met the homeless and poor, but now they see that the homeless are people "just like themselves." This, they like to say, is something that could happen to them: They could lose their jobs, lose their houses, even take to drink.

Here, perhaps ironically, is a danger: If our students regard social problems as chiefly or only personal, then they will not search beyond the person for a systemic explanation. Why is homelessness a problem? Because, they answer, so many people are homeless. The economy is bad and these individuals lost their jobs. Why are so many people undereducated or illiterate? Because they didn't study in school, just like so-and-so in my fifth grade class and he dropped out. Community service could, as my colleague Robert Crooks puts it, "work in a larger way as a kind of voluntary band-aiding of social problems that not only ignores the causes of problems but lets off the hook those responsible for the problems."[3] Campus Compact director Susan Stroud voices the same kind of concern: "If our community service efforts are not structured to raise the issues that result in critical analysis of the issues, then we are not involved in education and social change—we are involved in charity" (3).

I agree. I don't believe that questions about social structures, ideology, and social justice are automatically raised by community service. From my own experience, I am quite sure they are not.

Such questions can and should be raised in a class that is engaged in a community service project. Here, too, there is no guarantee that students will come to see beyond the individual and symptomatic. But that is what I wish to discuss at greater length. I don't see why questions like these cannot be raised in any course in the university, but if there are prime locations, they would be (and are, at Bentley) courses in economics, political science, sociology, and composition.[4] The connection to composition is by no means obvious. It is all too easy to ask students to write journal entries and reaction papers, to assign narratives and extort confessions, and to let it go at that. A colleague reported overhearing a conversation between two students: "We're going to some shelter tomorrow and we have to write about it." "No sweat. Write that before you went, you had no sympathy for the homeless, but the visit to the shelter opened your eyes. Easy A."[5] Even for those whose awakening is genuine, there is reason to doubt that the epiphany includes an understanding of the social forces that produce and sustain poverty, illiteracy, discrimination, and injustice. There is little evidence that students spontaneously gain critical self-consciousness—an awareness of the ways that their own lives have been shaped by the very same forces, that what they regard as "choices" are less than matters of individual will. Writing personal responses to community service experiences is an important part of processing the experience, but it is not sufficient to raise critical or cultural consciousness.

Writing about the actual experience of doing community service, then, does not seem to me to be the primary work to be done in a composition course like mine. Instead, we study literacy and schooling and write about that.[6] At this point, I need to explain some of the mechanics of the course, but I will keep it short.

Students are invited to be in this project and we have had no difficulty raising enough volunteers from the pool of incoming students. I have run the project in a one-semester version, but the two-semester sequence that I will describe here is far better. During the spring semester, the students are also enrolled together in a section of introductory sociology.[7] In the fall semester, the students are trained to be adult literacy tutors, and in the spring semester they do the actual tutoring.

The composition course is not devoted to literacy tutoring, but rather to the study of literacy and schooling, as I have mentioned. This is an important distinction: We do not set out to study teaching methods or composition pedagogy. The students learn some of the teaching methods they will need in tutor-training sessions that take place largely outside of class time. But in the class itself, our goal is to examine the ways that literacy is gained or not gained in the United States and only in that context do we examine teaching theories and practices.

During the fall semester, we read Mike Rose's *Lives on the Boundary* and a number of selections from *Perspectives on Literacy,* an anthology edited by Kintgen, Kroll, and Rose. In the spring semester, we read Kozol's *Savage Inequalities* and more of the essays in *Perspectives on Literacy.* The students write many summaries of sections of these books as well as several essays drawing on what they learned from them. In the spring semester, they write research papers on topics that arise from our studies.

Toward the end of the fall semester, the students have about ten hours of tutor training designed to sensitize them to the problems and attitudes of illiterate adults as well as to provide them with some teaching materials and methods. These sessions focus on the need to respond to the concerns of the learners and to understand the learners' reasons for seeking literacy education. The sessions also help the tutors generate ideas about teaching materials and how to use them. While the tutoring is going on, we devote some class time each week to questions about how to handle interpersonal problems or obtain appropriate teaching materials.

In the 1992–93 session, the sociology professor and I took the students to the shelter at the beginning of the spring semester for an orientation session. The following week, the students returned to the shelter without us and started the actual tutoring. At the start, the students were naturally apprehensive about tutoring adults in a shelter. Most of them had done some volunteer work before, but not in settings like that. They were very nervous when we actually went to the Pine Street Inn. We left Bentley's clean, well-lighted suburban campus and drove the ten miles into downtown Boston after dark, parked under the expressway, and went past a milling crowd of men into a dreary lobby. We watched the men being checked with a metal detector while we waited for John Lambert, the director of the shelter's education program. The students clumped together around Dave, a football player. Dave wrote in his field notes that he was conscious of this attention and that it made him even more nervous than he already was.

We went upstairs for our orientation, stepping over some sleeping men stretched out on gym mats in the dining hall. Upstairs, we met a number of men who had been working with volunteer tutors. The students later said that they were impressed by the effort that these men were making to try to improve their lives. They did not seem attentive, though, to the analysis offered by the shelter's assistant director, who explained that while the shelter provided critically needed services, it also undermined any sense of independence the residents might have. Their self-esteem seemed to be under constant attack by all the social institutions they came in contact with, including the shelter itself. When I brought it up in class, the students had little memory of this discussion. On their first visits to the shelter, they were simply more concerned with negotiating the immediate physical and psychic environment. Soon, however, they became accustomed to going to the shelter. Two or three of the boys in the class, including big Dave, did not get learners right way and instead walked around the shelter, visiting with the residents and trying to recruit them into the literacy program. Some of the girls did this on occasion, too. The students were irritated that they did not have learners but eventually realized that their presence in the shelter was a valuable advertisement for the literacy program.

The learners' needs are various: Some are almost completely illiterate, some are schizophrenic, a few need ESL teaching, some read well but need help with higher-order skills. Many of the learners come irregularly; many are easily distracted. One woman is pregnant, another is ridiculed by her boyfriend for needing help with phonics. One young woman is prevented by her mother (who also lives at the shelter) from taking tutoring because, the mother insists, she doesn't need it. But many of the students developed excellent tutoring relationships and all learned how to draw on their own resources both psychologically and pedagogically.

The students tended to see their learners, quite naturally, as individuals with personal problems—alcoholism and drugs, mental breakdown, family disintegration, or some nameless inability to concentrate and cope. It is quite easy to see these problems as individual ones. Very few of the students ever became indignant about what they saw. They hoped to help a few people as much as they were able. They would like to know if there is a "cure," but they don't regard that as a realistic hope. What I want to focus on here is how difficult my students find it to transcend their own deeply-ingrained belief in individualism and meritocracy in their analysis of the reasons for the illiteracy they see.

They do become indignant when we discuss *Lives on the Boundary,* which describes the ways that schools systematically diminish and degrade culturally disadvantaged students, or when we read *Savage Inequalities,* which tells about the structural inequities in the funding of public education and the horrible consequences of that inequity. The students are indeed distressed by systemic discrimination against poorer people and disenfranchised groups. In their responses to these books, it is clear that they understand the class discrimination inherent in tracking and the effect of tracking on self-esteem. But they do not seem to see this discrimination in the lives of their learners. One reason, perhaps, is that the learners themselves regard their situations as personal problems. They, too, have imbibed the lessons about individualism and equal opportunity. The traces have been covered over. Thus, in order to understand that they are in the presence of the effects they have been reading about, the students must also understand—viscerally if not intellectually—the nature of what Gramsci called hegemony: the belief that one participates freely in an open and democratic system and must therefore accept the results it produces. They must see, in other words, that the people in the shelter believe the same things that they, the students, do—that there is equal opportunity to succeed or fail, to become literate or remain illiterate. They need to analyze the way that schools and other institutions, like the shelter itself, embody those beliefs.

Here is a passage from *Lives on the Boundary*. We spent a lot of time with this:

> American meritocracy is validated and sustained by the deep-rooted belief in equal opportunity. But can we really say that kids like those I taught [as a Teacher Corps volunteer] have equal access to America's educational resources? Consider not only the economic and political barriers they face, but the fact, too, that judgements about their ability are made at a very young age, and those judgements, accurate or not, affect the curriculum they receive, their place in the school, they way they're defined institutionally. The insidious part of this drama is that, in the observance or the breach, students unwittingly play right into the assessments. Even as they rebel, they confirm the school's decision. They turn off or distance themselves or clam up or daydream, they deny or lash out, acquiesce or subvert, for, finally, they are powerless to stand outside the definition and challenge it head on. . . . [T]he children gradually internalize the definition the school delivers to them, incorporate a stratifying regulator as powerful as the overt institutional gatekeepers that, in other societies, determine who goes where in the educational system. There is no need for the elitist projections of quotas and exclusionary exams when a kid announces that he just wants to be average. If you want to insist that the children Joe and Monica and the rest of us taught had an equal opportunity in American schools, then you'll have to say that they had their equal chance and forfeited it before leaving the fourth grade. (128)

Elsewhere in *Lives on the Boundary*, Rose speaks sensitively about the difficulties freshmen have with academic discourse, a discourse "marked by terms and expressions that represent an elaborate set of shared concepts and orientations" (192). Rose himself is a brilliant stylist of academic discourse, as the passage I've quoted reveals. Rose advises that students need many opportunities to become comfortable with this discourse, and I take his advice seriously. There is much that my students cannot fathom in his book, many references to abstractions and complex terms (such as "incorporate a stratifying regulator as powerful as the overt institutional gatekeepers"), so we spend time talking and writing about important passages like this.

"American meritocracy is validated and sustained by the deep-rooted belief in equal opportunity." This sentence is a complete stopper. My students consistently claim that they have never heard the word "meritocracy" before. Once defined, though, the idea is perfectly obvious to them: of course those who are smartest, most talented, and work hardest rise to the top. What else? "Equal opportunity" is also initially difficult for them—not because it is unfamiliar but because it never seemed to require definition or reflection. This is not the first place in *Lives on the Boundary* that the students have encountered a challenge to the idea of equal opportunity: The challenge is both implied and explicitly stated many times. Yet, even 128 pages into the book, their first reaction is to regard this sentence as a positive statement about a noble ideal, an American virtue. It costs them a great effort to see that Rose is saying that one false idea is sustained by another, that the very words "validated and sustained" carry a negative connotation, that "deep-rooted belief" means self-deception. It costs them more than intellectual effort: It means a re-evaluation of the very deep-rooted beliefs that Rose is discussing here. It means seeing that Rose is talking about their beliefs and criticizing them.

When Job, the righteous man, loses his property, his children, and his health, he angrily questions the belief that God is just and gives people what they deserve. He lashes out at his friends, the false comforters, who steadfastly maintain that the good are rewarded and the wicked punished (and thereby imply that Job is suffering for some sin). Yet Job is in a terrible dilemma. He is frustrated and angry, convinced that the comforters are wrong, yet unable to explain his situation—for he believes precisely the same thing the comforters believe. When a belief is deeply-rooted, alternatives are inconceivable.

How do my students abandon their comfortable belief in equal opportunity and meritocracy? Did they not deserve, did they not earn their place in school and society? They have the greatest respect for Mike Rose and want to believe what he says, but it isn't easy. As education critic Colin Greer says, traditional historians of education "mistake the rhetoric of good intentions for historical reality" and persist in believing, against all evidence, that schools are the instruments of social change (4). We can hardly fault students for clinging to such a belief. We ran into a similar problem discussing a passage earlier in Rose's book:

> We live, in America, with so many platitudes about motivation and self-reliance and individualism—and myths spun from them, like those of Horatio Alger—that we find it hard to accept that they are serious nonsense. (47)

Here, too, we had worked on the definition of "individualism" and the negative connotations of "platitudes" and "nonsense." The students never heard of

Horatio Alger. After I explained about Alger, Lynne told us, without the least self-consciousness and without comment, that her grandfather came from Italy without a cent and became a success in America all on his own, without help from anybody.

In their fall semester papers, the students tested out the ideas they were learning about systemic discrimination through schooling. They were very tentative about this at first. Kyle wrote:

> In America today, we find that how an individual will do in school is often dependent upon what economic class they come from. Through studies of literacy, experts have found that there are different levels of success in school among individuals of diverse socioeconomic backgrounds. . . . Children of (the) middle- and upper-class are able to attend better schools and have greater access to books and other reading materials. Therefore, they tend to feel more comfortable with the material in school while lower-class children, whose parents are not so well off in terms of money, are more inclined to be insecure. In addition, in situations where parents of poor children have had low levels of education, there is a good possibility that their children will also have low levels of education. While at the time the situation is reversed with children of well-to-do parents.

These ideas are clearly unfamiliar to Kyle, and so he needs to repeat them holding onto the possibility of individual differences. "Experts" have discovered this injustice—it is not immediately accessible to experience. The parents of lower-class children are not so well off "in terms of money"—though they may, I think Kyle implies, have good intentions.

It is difficult, as I have said, for my students to understand these ideas, let alone deal with them critically. In the spring semester, for example, while we were studying Kozol's *Savage Inequalities,* a book that describes and decries the differences between well-funded suburban schools and their decrepit and overcrowded counterparts in the cities, Lynne (who told us about her grandfather) suggested that the students in south Chicago's schools were probably just not personally motivated to do school work, like the kids in their high school who flunked. Several students murmured in agreement, though when I challenged her, several others expressed dismay about Lynne's assumptions. Lynne is not a conservative ideologue. As with the comments about her grandfather, she was simply being unselfconscious. Her comments helps us see how hard it is to understand the social nature of experience and to accept the idea of structural injustice.

In an essay called "Critical Teaching and Dominant Culture" in *Composition and Resistance,* a volume of essays on critical teaching, Cy Knoblauch describes his attempts to bring his students to some consciousness of the injuries of class. He tells how his students were unmoved by "The Lesson," Toni Cade Bambara's story about poor black children visiting F.A.O. Schwartz. Knoblauch quotes a student response that he characterizes as typical: "If you strive for what you want, you can receive it." As Knoblauch cogently argues, the goal of critical pedagogy is to help students see and analyze the assumptions they make in comments like these. Still, it takes a lot of time and work to do this and Knoblauch is honest enough to say that he did not have the success he wished for.

Time and work were on our side, though, in the literacy-tutoring project—we had two semesters of composition, a sociology course, and the project itself. At the time that Lynne made her comment about Chicago schoolkids, the students had been tutoring at the Pine Street Inn shelter for several weeks. There was, apparently, nothing automatic or instantaneous about that experience that helped them understand Rose or Kozol. The community service experience doesn't bring an epiphany of critical consciousness—or even, necessarily, an epiphany of conscience. The effect was slow and indirect. In time, the students began to realize that the people at Pine Street were *not* like them. They did not, finally, conclude that "this could happen to me." Though they were not allowed (by the wise rules of the shelter and good sense) to quiz their learners on their personal lives and histories, they had learned enough about the learners' family distress and social isolation, their disconnection from community, lack of individual resources, and reliance on charitable institutions and the effects of those conditions on their self-images—to realize that "this could happen to me" is a shallow response.

The tutoring, as best we could determine, appeared to be productive for the learners at the shelter. In many ways, the best help that tutors can provide in such a setting is to come regularly and respond sensitively to the learners' concerns. The learners are coming to the literacy program at the end of what is typically a long series of personal and social failures, and though they expect—and often demand—a school-like experience again, the tutors are there to humanize it as much as they can.

The final research papers for the composition course show a growing sophistication about the social forces at work in the creation of illiteracy. Students visited nursery school classes to see how children learn, returned to their own high schools to find out what happened to the kids who flunked, corresponded with convicts in prison-education programs. In his paper, "The Creation of Illiteracy through Tracking," Dave (the football player) writes, "Tracking tends to maintain or amplify differences in socioeconomic status, the opposite of 'equalizing' these differences as schools should." Schools can't be held responsible for prior economic discrimination, Dave argues, but they must be held accountable for reinforcing it. Kevin borrowed several history textbooks used over the last ten years in the Waltham High School, counted the number of pictures and other references to African-Americans and compared them to the number of pictures and similar references to whites, analyzed the images, and tried to imagine what a black student would learn about American culture from an education in Waltham, Massachusetts (Kevin is white). Our friend Lynne asked how school systems with the money to do so were addressing the needs of disadvantaged students. She concludes that "the systems with the extra money to spend on special programs are not facing these types of problems." She points out that there is no lack of information about how to spend this money well and describes the settled and unreflective attitudes about schools and teaching that prevent the adoption of new methods.

Some students referred to their tutoring experience in their papers. Mark, for example, noted the kind of knowledge his learners sought—sentence-diagramming and algebra—and commented that their frustrating search for credentials, fostered by traditional (and failed) schooling, had left them without job skills on the one hand and with an artificially low sense of their own abilities on the other. Most of the students did not, however, incorporate the tutoring experience in the research papers they wrote for my class. This was as it should be: The goal of the course was not, as I have explained, to facilitate the tutoring experience, but to investigate the social and cultural reasons for the existence of illiteracy—the reasons, in other words, that the students needed to perform the valuable service they were engaged in. In that sense, the tutoring project was constantly present in our class. In the sociology course, the students used their visits to Pine Street more directly as the object of field observations and analysis.

The effort to reach into the composition class with a curriculum aimed at democracy and social justice is an attempt to make schools function the way Dave and my other students want them to—as radically democratic institutions, with the goal not only of making individual students more successful, but also of making better citizens, citizens in the strongest sense of those who take responsibility for communal welfare. These efforts belong in the composition class because of the rhetorical as well as the practical nature of citizenship and social transformation.

What the students' final papers show, then, is a sense of life as a communal project, an understanding of the way that social institutions affect our lives, and a sense that our responsibility for social justice includes but also carries beyond personal acts of charity. This is an understanding that has been very rare among Bentley students. Immersed in a culture of individualism, convinced of their merit in a meritocracy, students like those at Bentley need to see that there is a social basis for most of the conditions they take to be matters of individual choice or individual ability. As Kurt Spellmeyer says, "the university fails to promote a social imagination, an awareness of the human 'world' as a common historical project, and not simply as a state of nature to which we must adjust ourselves" (73). Students who lack this social imagination (most of them, according to the study Spellmeyer cites) attribute all attitudes, behavior, and material conditions to an individual rather than social source. Students will not critically question a world that seems natural, inevitable, given; instead, they will strategize about their position within it. Developing a social imagination makes it possible not only to question and analyze the world, but also to imagine transforming it.

Notes

1. A successful program requires a great deal of coordination between the school and the community agencies. Individual teachers working on their own to arrange contacts will find the task exhausting and daunting. While many agencies welcome short-term volunteers, some cannot. Literacy tutoring, for example, requires consistency over time, so that tutors can establish a relationship with the learner. In short, the school-agency ties must be well developed before the students show up. I don't wish to discourage such programs, but to suggest that good planning can prevent many problems and frustrations. See Cotton and Stanton, "Joining Campus and Community through Service Learning," in *Community Service as Values Education.*

2. The advocates of service learning assume that values must be taught in college. I'm comfortable with that assumption and won't try to make the case for teaching values or critical consciousness here. The question of whether to teach values at all is by no means settled. It has been raised persistently as a general question in education and it has been a topic of hot debate in composition studies. Patricia Bizzell argues cogently for the importance of teaching values in *Academic Discourse and Critical Consciousness.* C. H. Knoblauch and Lil Brannon's *Critical Teaching and the Idea of Literacy* is a recent and valuable contribution. Maxine Hairston dissents in "Diversity, Ideology, and Teaching Writing." Paulo Freire, Henry Giroux, and Ira Shor have long been advocates of teaching values through the development of critical consciousness. And I have something to say about the issue in "Composition and the Politics of the Curriculum."

3. Crooks goes on: "Let me hasten to say that by 'those responsible' I mean all of us, who through direct participation in institutional actions, policy-making, ideas, attitudes, or indirectly, through silence and compliance, offer support to pervasive economics, social, political, and cultural systems that produce the kinds of problems that community service addresses."

4. At some universities, the theology department is the primary location for these courses. Georgetown University, Boston College, and Marymount College link community service to theology courses on injustice and social responsibility, for example.

5. I reported this conversation to Zlotkowski, who responded that he believed that many students remained defensive about the fact that they really did have their eyes opened. In anonymous student evaluations that have no effect on grades, he finds a predominance of sincere reports of changed attitudes.

6. The courses in the Stanford program tend to focus on writing to or for the agency being serviced. Such projects are undertaken at Bentley by more advanced classes. See *Let 100 Flowers Bloom* for a description of Stanford's rationale. A high-school writing course in which students work as literacy volunteers is described by Norma Greco in "Critical Literacy and Community Service: Reading and Writing the World."

7. The benefits of "clustering" courses are described in *Learning Communities* by Faith Gabelnick et al. When students are co-registered in two or more courses, instructors can develop common themes, draw on material taught in each other's courses, explore shared readings from different perspectives, and have some common writing assignments. While my students were working on their writing with me and doing their tutoring at the shelter, in the sociology course they were learning about the effects of social and institutional forces on the formation of identity. Their final research papers were submitted in both courses.

Works Cited

Bizzell, Patricia. *Academic Discourse and Critical Consciousness.* Pittsburgh: U of Pittsburgh P, 1993. 277–95.

Cotton, Debbie, and Timothy K. Stanton. "Joining Campus and Community through Service Learning." *Community Service as Values Education.* Ed. Cecilia I. Delve et al. San Francisco: Jossey-Bass, 1990.

Crooks, Robert. "Service Learning and Cultural Critique: Towards a Model for Activist Expository Writing Courses." Conference on College Composition and Communication, San Diego, CA, March 1993.

Friedman, Phil. "A Secular Foundation for Ethics: Business Ethics and the Business School." *EDP Auditor Journal* 2 (1989): 9–11.

Gablenick, Faith, Jean MacGregor, Robert S. Matthews, and Barbara Leigh Smith, eds. *Learning Communities Creating Connections Among Students, Faculty, and Disciplines.* San Francisco: Jossey-Bass, 1990.

Greco, Norma. "Critical Literacy and Community Service: Reaching and Writing the World." *English Journal* 81 (1992): 83–85.

Greer, Colin. *The Great School Legend: A Revisionist Interpretation of American Public Education.* New York: Basic, 1972.

Hairston, Maxine. "Diversity, Ideology, and Teaching Writing." *CCC* 43 (1992): 179–93.

Herzberg, Bruce. "Composition and the Politics of the Curriculum." *The Politics of Writing Instruction: Postsecondary.* Ed. Richard Bullock and John Trimbur. Portsmouth, NH: Boynton, 1991. 97–118.

Kintgen, Eugene R., Barry M. Kroll, and Mike Rose, eds. *Perspectives on Literacy.* Carbondale: Southern Illinois UP, 1988.

Knoblauch, C. H. "Critical Teaching and Dominant Culture." *Composition and Resistance.* Ed. C. Mark Hurlbert and Michael Blitz. Portsmouth, NH: Boynton, 1991. 12–21.

Knoblauch, C. H., and Lil Brannon. *Critical Teaching and the Idea of Literacy.* Portsmouth, NH: Boynton, 1993.

Kozol, Jonathan. *Savage Inequalities.* New York: Crown, 1991.

Let 100 Flowers Bloom: Community Service Writing Curriculum Materials Developed by the Stanford Freshman English Program. Stanford U, n.d.

Rose, Mike. *Lives on the Boundary.* New York: Free, 1989.

Spellmeyer, Kurt. "Knowledge Against 'Knowledge.'" *Composition and Resistance.* Ed. C. Mark Hurlbert and Michael Blitz. Portsmouth, NH: Boynton, 1991. 70–80.

Stroud, Susan. "A Report from the Director." *Campus Compact* Fall 1992: 3–4.

Zlotkowski, Edward. "Address to the Faculty of Niagara University." Niagara, NY, April 1993.

16

Teaching the Political Conflicts
A Rhetorical Schema

Donald Lazere

Editors' Note: Donald Lazere presents an ambitious rhetorical scheme through which students can reflect politically about their world. Lazere struggles with the ethics of critical teaching, in search of a method that introduces students to ideological analysis without imposing his politics on them. He presents a rhetorical model for researching the ideology of texts in freshman composition. His goal is for students to recognize and critique political positions and biases. Lazere's "rhetorical schema" and attached appendices concretely "teach the political conflicts," a method advocated by Gerald Graff. Lazere also suggests that writing courses can be part of the reorientation of English toward cultural studies through a rhetorical approach.

During the 1990–91 academic year, reports erupted into the national press about attempts at the University of Texas at Austin and the University of Massachusetts at Amherst to address controversial political issues such as racism and sexism in freshman writing courses. One reason these attempts provoked disputes, within their own English departments as well as publicly, is that little basis has been established within the discipline of composition delineating either a theoretical framework or ethical guidelines for dealing with political controversies in writing courses. While I do not have the local knowledge necessary to judge the particular conception and implementation of the courses at Austin and Amherst, I want briefly to address the larger theoretical issues and then go on to outline my own model for incorporating critical thinking about politics in writing courses, an approach which has evolved over some twenty-five years of college teaching and a decade of presenting workshops based on this model.

Overviews

Under the opposition of Maxine Hairston and other critics to courses like those at Austin and Amherst lie not only quarrels with politicizing writing instruction but broader theoretical assumptions and emphases that have dominated the profession for most of the last three decades—assumptions that I believe have imposed crippling restrictions on our field. The major emphasis in theory, courses, and textbooks has been on basic writing and the generation and exposition of one's own ideas, to the neglect of more advanced levels of writing that involve critical thinking in evaluating others' ideas (particularly in the public discourse of politics and mass media)—i.e., semantics, logic and argumentative rhetoric, and their application to writing critical, argumentative, and research papers and other writing from sources. The consequence of these dominant attitudes has been a failure of responsibility in the English profession to emphasize those aspects of composition that bear quite legitimately on the development of critical civic literacy—a failure that has contributed by default to the present, universally deplored state of political illiteracy, apathy, and semantic pollution by public doublespeak in America.

Obviously, I endorse the theoretical conceptions of courses like those at Austin and Amherst. But I also share the concern of critics that such courses can all too easily be turned into an indoctrination to the instructor's particular ideology or, at best, into classes in political science. This concern has certainly been warranted by the tendency of some leftist teachers and theorists to assume that all students and colleagues agree—or *should* agree—with their views, rather than formulating their approach in a manner that takes respectful account of opposing views. My own political leanings are toward democratic socialism, and I believe that college English courses have a responsibility to expose students to socialist viewpoints because those views are virtually excluded from all other realms of the American cognitive, rhetorical, semantic, and literary universe of discourse.[1] I am firmly opposed, however, to instructors imposing socialist (or feminist, or Third-World, or gay) ideology on students as the one true faith—just as much as I am opposed to the present, generally unquestioned (and even unconscious) imposition of capitalist, white-male, heterosexual ideology that pervades American education and every other aspect of our culture.

I assert, then, that our primary aim should be to broaden the ideological scope of students' critical thinking, reading, and writing capacities so as to empower them to make their own autonomous judgments on opposing ideological positions in general and on specific issues. And it is just this aim that justifies introducing political issues in writing courses, within a *rhetorical* framework quite different from anything students are apt to encounter in political science or other social science courses. My concept of that framework consists of a version of what Gerald Graff advocates in literary theory as "teaching the conflicts"—introducing as explicit subject matter the issues of political

partisanship and bias, as examples of the subjective, socially constructed elements in perceptions of reality and of the way ideology consciously or unconsciously pervades teaching, learning, and other influential realms of public discourse, including news reporting, mass culture, and of course political rhetoric
itself. (By addressing these issues, *through a distinctively rhetorical approach,*
writing courses can also become a vital part of the reorientation of English
toward cultural studies.)

Part of my theoretical intention here is to indicate ways in which partisan political positions—like my own favoring socialist views on economic
matters or those on sexism and racism emphasized in the courses at Austin and
Amherst—can be introduced within a rhetorical schema that is acceptable to
teachers and students of any reasoned political persuasion. In this way, I believe
the left agenda of prompting students to question the subjectivity underlying
socially constructed modes of thinking can be reconciled with the conservative
agenda of objectivity and nonpartisanship. This approach obliges teachers to
raise in class the question of their own partisan biases and how they can most
honestly be dealt with in pedagogy and grading; I have found that students are
immensely relieved at being able to discuss this taboo subject openly, to come
to an open accord with the instructor about what guidelines are most fair, and
to evaluate the instructor's fairness at the end of the course accordingly.

The most economical way of concretizing my rhetorical position and tacitly answering likely objections to it is to provide an outline of the schema's
central components in the form of four units of study that can be integrated into
a writing course such as the one I teach as my department's second term of
freshman English, a course devoted to argumentative and source-based writing
and the research paper.[2] These units coincide with the preliminary stages of
researching and writing a term paper on a topic of current public controversy,
a paper which consists of a rhetorical analysis of sources expressing opposing
ideological viewpoints on the topic. The units provide a pedagogical context
for seven appendices, which form the substantive core of the schema. The appendices provide the kind of guides to locating and analyzing partisan sources
that have only recently started to show up in writing textbooks (e.g. Mayfield
236–63), and I hope my version will prompt other writers to incorporate them
in textbooks, as I am doing myself in a textbook in progress.

If, as is almost inevitable, I sometimes let my own partisanship bias my
presentation, I think that, far from discrediting my general intention, this will
only illustrate and validate it. An implicit message of my approach to teaching
political conflict is that any effort to construct such a schema is itself bound to
be captive, in some measure, to the partisan biases it sets out to analyze. The
only possible way to transcend these biases is refinement through dialectical
exchanges with those of differing ideologies. So much the better, then, if readers who find fault with my definitions, interrelations among ideological positions, or predictable lines of partisan rhetoric can suggest modifications that
will bring the schema closer to the difficult ideal of acceptability to those of any

reasoned ideology; I regularly modify and update it myself in response to student suggestions in class. I hope that my beginnings here will prompt ongoing professional debate on these points and thereby help bring such debate into the forefront of composition theory.

The content of this scheme and the four course units it is keyed to do not dictate any particular pedagogical model. Nor do their emphases on specific subject matter related to politics contradict the current emphasis in the profession on the writing process; on the contrary, the sequence of topics and assignments shows how process instruction can be extended to critical thinking, reading, and writing about political subject matter, while the appendices constitute a heuristic for the process of working the analysis of partisan rhetoric into an outline for the term paper.

As a final introductory note, I need to respond to the concerns of Hairston and other critics that writing instructors are venturing out of their own field of expertise when they address political issues. The level at which these issues are analyzed in a course like the one I describe here is that at which they are addressed, not in scholarly studies, but in political speeches, news and entertainment media, op-ed columns, general-circulation journals of opinion, and other realms of public discourse to which everyone is exposed every day. The political vocabulary and information covered here are no more specialized than what every citizen in a democracy should be expected to know, even before taking a college argumentative and research writing course. Indeed, two of the main points that must be stressed throughout such a course are the difference in levels of rhetoric between public and scholarly treatment of political issues and the need for students to take more specialized courses to gain deeper knowledge of these issues. Students *can* learn in writing classes, though, to develop a more complex and comprehensive rhetorical understanding of political events and ideologies than that provided by campaign propaganda and mass media—or, for that matter, by most social science courses, whose emphasis is empirical rather than rhetorical. Higher education in composition as well as literature has the unique, Emersonian mission of bringing to bear on current events the longer view, the synthesizing vision needed to counteract the hurriedness, atomization, and ideological hodgepodge that debase our public discourse as well as our overdepartmentalized curricula and overspecialized scholarship.

Four Units for Teaching Political Conflicts

Political Semantics

This first topic in the schema can be integrated into a standard argumentative and research writing course with a review, within a General Semantics perspective, of definition, denotation, and connotation. This review provides a context for discussion of racism and sexism through study of selections from the large body of writings analyzing the role of definition and connotative language in the social construction of racial and gender identity, and of other issues in which control of definitions functions as a form of social power. Analysis of readings with opposing viewpoints on race and gender can focus on the semantic intricacies involved in current disputes over "political correctness," limits on free speech, tolerance of intolerance, and "reverse discrimination."

The unit continues with study of the problems of subjectivity involved in defining political terms, including the way partisan biases color our perception of these terms' meaning, through ambiguous or selective definitions, unconcretized abstractions, connotative associations and slanting, etc. Students are assigned to look up in one or more dictionaries the following terms: "conservatism," "liberalism," "libertarianism," "radicalism," "right wing," "left wing," "fascism," "plutocracy," "capitalism," "socialism," "communism," "Marxism," "patriotism," "democracy," "totalitarianism," "freedom," and "free enterprise." Then they bring their different dictionaries to class and read aloud the multiple and varying definitions for each word. In this way, students learn that understanding these terms and using them accurately in spoken or written discourse are complicated, not only by each dictionary's giving several meanings for each word but by differences among various dictionaries (and from one edition to another of the same dictionary—a nice lesson in historical subjectivity). Furthermore, even the largest unabridged dictionary fails to cover the almost infinite number of senses in which "liberal," "conservative," "socialist," "communist," and "Marxist" are used throughout the world, or the equally immense diversity of political factions which identify themselves with each of these ideologies. In America alone, a conservative may be a Menckenian aristocrat, a Donald Trump-type corporate capitalist, a Moral Majority populist, a Ku Klux Klanner, a member of the Libertarian Party, etc. And yet our mass media chronically use *conservative* either without any definition at all or as a simplistic label, as though it had one and only one meaning. Many Democratic and Republican Party politicians consciously evade any consistent definition of their ideology in an unscrupulous attempt to woo the widest possible constituency; hence they almost inevitably must resort to doublespeak.

This dictionary exercise can point up another widespread semantic confusion in our public discourse, the false equation of political terms like "democracy," "freedom," "justice," "patriotism," and "dictatorship" with words referring to economic systems—"capitalism" or "free enterprise" and "socialism." One must again go beyond dictionary definitions to address the problematic relation between these political and economic terms, for partisans of varying ideologies posit differing connections between, say, freedom and democracy on one hand and capitalism and socialism on the other. In Appendix Six, I have attempted to present my own definitions of these relations as objectively as possible, but, as I make clear to students, scholars whose ideological convictions differ from mine might take issue and present a quite different set of definitions. Indeed, the larger rhetorical question (a vital one for both class exercises and theoretical inquiry by English scholars) is whether it is possible to arrive at definitions of these terms and relationships that can be agreed on by partisans of all differing ideologies.

Next, the writer seeking accuracy of definition needs to key these political terms to a spectrum of positions from far right to far left in the United States and the rest of the world (see Appendix Two). Rather than speaking of "the liberal *New York Times,*" one should explain and document the sense and degree of liberalism referred to. "Liberal" in relation to what other media? One might clarify the label by placing the *Times* to the left of *Time* but to the right of *The Nation.* The whole range of American news media—along with politicians and parties, individual journalists and scholars, and even figures in popular entertainment (like Clint Eastwood and Jane Fonda, Donald Duck and Doonesbury,[3] Madonna and Bruce Springsteen, "Dallas" and "Roseanne")—can be placed on this spectrum in such a precise way that their political identity can be agreed on to a large extent by those of every ideological persuasion. In distributing Appendix Two to students I make it clear that this is a very general overview that necessarily involves over-simplifications and some debatable placements, and that this schema needs regular updating due to shifts in the positions of countries, individual politicians, writers, and periodicals. Recent upheavals in the Communist world have compounded semantic complexities: left-wing has been equated historically with Communism as a political ideology, but if "left-wing" is defined as opposition to the status quo, does that make those trying to overturn the status quo in Communist countries leftists or rightists? (During the 1991 attempted coup in the Soviet Union, my students, in tracking American news media, found that they most often designated the Communist hard-liners "right wing" and "conservative.")

Extending the right-to-left spectrum worldwide serves to call students' attention to the parochially limited span of ideology represented by the poles of the Republican and Democratic parties and of "conservatism" and "liberalism" that define the boundaries of most American political, journalistic, scholarly, and cultural discourse. Factions and positions that are considered liberal in the United States, for example, usually stay well within the limits of capitalist ideology, thus are considerably to the right of the labor, social-democratic, and communist parties with large constituencies in most other democratic countries today. (A politician or position labeled "moderate" in the United States is considered right-wing from today's European perspective, while many American "radicals" would be "moderates" in Europe. Similarly, many "ultra-conservatives" in American terminology appear "moderate" in comparison to fascistic countries.) Therefore, in order to expose themselves to a full range of ideological viewpoints, students need to seek out sources excluded from the mainstream of American discourse, though such sources may be hard to find in many communities. The most prominent of these ideologies in a worldwide perspective are democratic socialism and libertarian conservatism (both of which favor political freedom), communism and fascism (both of which are opposed to democracy and freedom but are nonetheless strong presences in today's world and therefore need to be studied and understood through their own spokespeople and not just through the distorting filters of second-hand accounts).

Throughout this unit, and the rest of the course, the instructor needs to indicate the parameters of this kind of rhetorical analysis and the need for students to expose themselves, in history, political science, or economics courses, to more systematic analysis of ideologies and the way they have actually been implemented throughout the world.

Psychological Blocks to Perceiving Bias

The psychological factors that lead student writers and readers into partisan or biased arguments are an essential aspect of critical thinking and argumentative rhetoric that is inadequately emphasized in most conventional approaches to composition. (The growing body of recent scholarship applying the psychology of critical thinking "dispositions" and of cognitive and moral development to composition is useful theoretical and pedagogical background here; see my "Critical Thinking in College English Studies.") This unit—keyed, along with the following one, to Appendices Five through Seven—focuses on the most common psychological blocks to critical thinking that students should watch for in their sources for their term paper, as well as in themselves while reading and writing on these sources, and in their teachers in this and other courses. These blocks include culturally conditioned assumptions (which frequently emerge as hidden premises in arguments), closed-mindedness, prejudice and stereotyping; authoritarianism, absolutism, and the inability to recognize ambiguity, irony, and relativity of point of view; ethnocentrism and parochialism; rationalization, wishful thinking, and sentimentality. (Despite its brevity and simplicity, Ray Kytle's *Clear Thinking for Composition* is the most useful textbook I know on these blocks.)

The topic of prejudice provides a further occasion for consideration of opposing viewpoints on racial, sexual, and class bias. To avert a one-sided approach to these charged issues, it may be best to introduce them through psychological studies like Allport's *The Nature of Prejudice,* Rokeach's *The Open and Closed Mind,* or the developmental principles of Perry and Kohlberg and their feminist critique in Gilligan. In regard to subjectivity in political ideology in general, the beginning point here can be the hypothesis that many students have lived all their lives in a parochial circle of people who all have pretty much the same set of beliefs, so that they are inclined to accept a culturally conditioned consensus of values as objective, uncontested truth. (Most of the students at my school are middle-class whites, so middle-class ethnocentrism is the focus of study; this and other units of the course might need to be adjusted to differing pools of students.) Students need to become aware that what they or their sources of information assume to be self-evident truths are often—though not always—only the opinion or interpretation of the truth that is held by their particular social class, political ideology, religion, racial or ethnic group, gender, nationality and geographical location, historical period, occupation, age group, etc. Furthermore, we are all inclined to tailor our "objective" beliefs to the shape of our self-interest; consequently, in controversies where our interests are involved, we are susceptible to wishful thinking, rationalization, selective vision, and other logical fallacies. (A basic example of semantic cleans and dirties is that "biased" is a word that always applies only to arguments favoring the other side; we instinctively label arguments that confirm our own biases as "impartial," "well-balanced," "judiciously supported with solid research.")

Modes of Biased and Deceptive Rhetoric

While authorities used as sources, such as scholars, professional researchers or journalists, public officials, and business or labor executives can—or should—be expected to have a more informed viewpoint than students on specialized subjects, students should be made aware that authorities are not immune from numerous causes of subjective bias. This unit, then, addresses modes of biased or self-interested arguments in sources, as well as of outright deception—another aspect of rhetoric inadequately addressed in many conventional composition and argumentation courses and textbooks that regard fallacious reasoning mainly in terms of impersonal, formal reasoning and unintentional fallacies. A more realistic approach to contemporary public discourse necessitates a systematic study of possible causes for bias (and the predictable rhetorical patterns they produce—see Appendix Seven) in conventional sources of information—including political partisanship, conflicts of interest, sponsored research and journalism, special pleading, and other forms of propaganda and pure lying that have come to be known as public doublespeak. The growing influence during the past twenty years of books and articles produced by scholars in research institutes like those in Appendix Three, whose sponsors—frequently foundations representing corporations or political lobbies with special interests in the subjects studied—calls for particular attention to the possible biases of such scholars.

Useful textbooks and teachers' guides for this unit include the works cited by Schrank, Harty, Lazere, Rank, Dieterich, and Lutz. The latter two were published by the NCTE Committee on Public Doublespeak, whose *Quarterly Review of Doublespeak* and annual Doublespeak and Orwell Awards are equally valuable classroom resources. These can be supplemented by comparative analysis of current issues of periodicals devoted to criticism of bias in media, such as *Extra!, Propaganda Review,* or *Lies of Our Times* on the left, versus *AIM Report, Repap Media Guide,* or *MediaWatch* on the right.

The next point to be made is that every ideology—political, religious, etc.—is predisposed toward its own distinct pattern of rhetoric that its conscious or unconscious partisans tend to follow on virtually any subject they are reading, writing, or speaking about. Critical readers need to learn to identify and understand the various ideologies apt to be found in current sources of information. Having done so, they can then to a large extent anticipate what underlying assumptions, lines of argument, rhetorical strategies, logical fallacies, and modes of semantic slanting to watch for in any partisan source. (See Appendices Five through Seven.)

This is not to say that partisan sources should be shunned. Indeed, a clear-cut, well-supported expression of a partisan position can be more valuable than a blandly non-partisan one. Nor does partisanship in a source necessarily go along with biased or deceptive reasoning. One must judge a partisan argument on the basis of how fully and fairly it represents the opposing position and demonstrates why its own is more reasonable. Some partisan authors or journals are highly admirable on this score (and students should be encouraged in their papers to cite such examples, not just fallacious or deceptive ones). Others, unfortunately, predictably repeat the same one-sided, doctrinaire line year after year, whatever the subject, and they are to be read, if at all, with one's bias calculator close at hand.

Locating and Evaluating Partisan Sources

The foregoing discussion units culminate in an assignment, for the preliminary stages of the term paper, of an annotated bibliography and working outline, designed to locate and analyze articles and books with opposing partisan viewpoints on the chosen topic (Appendix One). These exercises can help prevent students from simply picking *American Spectator* or *In These Times,* a book published by Arlington House or Monthly Review Press, or a report from American Enterprise Institute or the Institute for Policy Studies off the library shelf to use as a source and quoting it as gospel, without a critical understanding of the sponsor's habitual viewpoint. Following this procedure enables students to replace categorical assertions in their papers with statements like these:

> Barbara Ehrenreich, writing in *Democratic Life,* a journal of the Democratic Socialists of America, presents a socialist analysis of the effects of Reaganomics on the gap between the rich and poor in the United States.

> Ed Rubenstein, in the conservative *National Review,* refutes statistics presented by leftists like Ehrenreich claiming that Reaganomic policies have widened the gap between the rich and poor.

Student writers can then go on to explain how the source's general ideological viewpoint applies to the particular issue in question, to analyze the rhetorical/ semantic patterns accordingly, and to evaluate the source's arguments against opposing ones. In this way they can get beyond the parochial mentality of those who read and listen only to sources that confirm their preconceptions while deluding themselves that these sources impartially present a full range of information.

Lest this approach be misconstrued as an invitation to total relativity or scepticism, students are asked in the conclusion to their term papers not to make a final and absolute judgment on which side is right and wrong about the issue at hand, but to make a balanced summary of the strong and weak points made by each of the limited number of sources they have studied, and then to make—and support—their judgment about which sources have presented the best-reasoned case and the most thorough refutation of the other side's arguments. Grading for the paper and the course, then, becomes a matter of evaluating the quality of students' support for their judgments—regardless of what those judgments may be.

Conclusion

English faculties correctly resist attempts to make composition a "service course" providing only the technical skills needed for writing in other disciplines; however, composition can and should be a service course in the sense of fostering modes of critical thinking that are a prerequisite to studies in other disciplines—preeminently the social sciences—and to students' lifelong roles as citizens. To reiterate, this does not mean that composition should be turned into a social science. Nor does this conception of composition duplicate recent efforts to incorporate writing instruction within social science courses and other disciplines. Writing across the curriculum is a laudable enterprise, but it is not the same thing as what I am advancing, a program for studying political issues squarely within the discipline of English and through its distinctive humanistic concerns. By thus breaking through the arbitrary disciplinary constrictions that have diminished the scope of composition scholarship in recent decades, we can begin to restore the study of composition to its classical role as the center of education for citizenship.

Appendix One
Assignment for an Annotated Bibliography and Working Outline

Turn in ten bibliographical entries, on five leftist and five rightist sources, including at least one magazine article and one book or monograph report from the left-wing publishers and one article and book or report from the right-wing publishers in Appendices Three and Four. Annotate the sources according to the following guidelines, and develop them into a detailed working outline keyed to citations of these entries.

1. Identify author's political position, using clues from affiliation with a particular research institute, book publisher, journal of opinion, party, or organization, and—more importantly—from arguments s/he presents that exemplify the glossary terms and the particular patterns of political rhetoric in Appendices Six and Seven; give enough quotes (or highlighted photocopies) to support your identification. In cases where the author is not arguing from an identifiable position but only reporting facts, indicate which position the reported facts support, and explain how. (Note: some newspapers, magazines, etc., have an identifiable political viewpoint in general, in their news and op-ed orientation, but also attempt to present other views at least some of the time; e.g., the *LA Times* is predominantly liberal, but often carries conservative op-ed columns, letters, etc. So you shouldn't assume that any article appearing in such a periodical will automatically have its predominant viewpoint; look for other identity clues.)

2. Apply to each source the "Semantic Calculator for Bias in Rhetoric" (Appendix Five), along with the more general principles of rhetorical analysis studied in this course.

Appendix Two (A)
Political Spectrum*
(Ca. 1980s)

Left Wing ← → Right Wing

	Dictatorship		Political Democracy, Freedom		Dictatorship	
	Communism	Socialism		Capitalism	Plutocracy	Fascism
	USSR	Nicaragua (Sandinista)	Sweden	France	USA	Chile (Pinochet)
	China	Chile (Allende)	Denmark	Italy	Japan	Philippines (Marcos)
	Cuba		Norway	W. Germany		South Africa
	North Vietnam			Spain		El Salvador
	Cambodia			Canada		Nicaragua (Somoza)
	North Korea			England		South Vietnam
						South Korea
						Taiwan
						Nazi Germany
						Fascist Italy
						Franco Spain
						Fascist Japan

American Parties

Democratic   Republican

Libertarian

*This version reflected the world spectrum in the mid-1980s. Regular updatings are, of course, necessary, and recent upheavals in the Communist world in particular necessitate major revision on the extreme left.

The politics of Middle Eastern countries are too complex a mix of left-wing and right-wing forces to schematize here. For example, Iran under the Shah was a plutocratic dictatorship allied with the U.S.; under the Ayatollahs it is another variety of right-wing dictatorship, a theocratic one, but is allied with some Communist and left-wing Arab forces.

Appendix Two (B)
American Media and Commentators from Left to Right

Media (Left to Right)

People's World	*The Nation*		*NY Times*	*Time*	*New American*
The Guardian	*In These Times*	*LA Times*	*Wash. Post*	*US News &*	*Plain Truth*
	Mother Jones	*NY Review*	*Newsweek*	*World Report*	*Wash. Times*
	Extra!			*Readers Digest*	*(Insight)*
	Village Voice				
	The Progressive	*Atlantic*	*New Republic*	*Wall St. Journal*	
	Z Magazine	*New Yorker*	*Harper's*	*Commentary*	
	Tikkun PBS	documentaries	*Reason*	*American Spectator*	
	Pacifica Radio NPR		CBS news	Most newspapers, local TV & radio	
			NBC, ABC news	*National Review*	
			Lehrer News Hour	McLaughlin Group	
			60 Minutes		

Commentators (Left to Right)

Alexander Cockburn	Eric Alterman	James Steele		George Will	Pat Buchanan
Edward Said	Gore Vidal	Michael Kinsley		Chas. Krauthammer	Phyllis Schlafly
Noam Chomsky	Barbara Ehrenreich	Anthony Lewis		William Safire	Pat Robertson
Edward Herman	Jesse Jackson	Tom Wicker		Evans & Novak	Paul Harvey
Jeff Cohen	Todd Gitlin	Richard Reeves		Henry Kissinger	Jerry Falwell
Norman Solomon	Robert Scheer	Bill Moyers		Irving Kristol	Rush Limbaugh
Julianne Malvaux	Betty Friedan	Seymour Hersh		Norman Podhoretz	John Leo
Katha Pollitt	Gloria Steinem	David Halberstam		Midge Decter	Cal Thomas
Jesse Jackson	Molly Ivins	Woodward & Bernstein		Jeane Kirkpatrick	Don Imus
Bernie Sanders	Irwin Knoll	Ted Koppel		William F. Buckley	Dinesh D'Souza
Paul Wellstone	James Weinstein	John K. Galbraith		Michael Novak	
Michael Moore	Ralph Nader			Milton Friedman	
William Greider	Victor Navasky			Thomas Sowell	
	Roger Wilkins				
	Cornel West				
	Michael Lerner		Murray Rothbard (libertarian)		
	Donald Bartlett		Douglas Bandow (libertarian)		
			Virginia Postrel (libertarian)		

Appendix Three
Political Orientations of Publishers & Foundations

Book Publishers

Liberal or Socialist

Pantheon
Monthly Review Press
South End Press
Praeger
Beacon Press
Seabury/Continuum Books
International Publishers
Pathfinder Press
Routledge
Methuen
Schocken
Bergin & Garvey

Conservative or Libertarian

Arlington House
Freedom House
Brandon Books
Reader's Digest Books
Greenhill Publishers
Laissez-Faire Books (Libertarian)
Paragon House

Research Institutes and Foundations

Liberal or Socialist

Institute for Policy Studies

Center for Responsive Law
(Journal: *Public Citizen*)

Public Interest Research Groups

Common Cause
(Journal: *Common Cause*)

Brookings Institute

Institute for Democratic Socialism
(Journals: *Democratic Left,
Socialist Forum*)

Center for the Study of Democratic
Institutions (Journal: *New
Perspectives Quarterly*)

Conservative or Libertarian

American Enterprise Institute
(Journal: *Public Opinion*—not
Public Opinion Quarterly)

Center for Strategic and
International Studies

Hoover Institution (Stanford)

The Media Institute

Hudson Institute

Heritage Foundation (Journal:
Policy Review)

Olin Foundation
Scaife Foundation
Cato Foundation (Libertarian:
Cato Journal)

Appendix Four
Current General Periodicals

This is a partial list intended to supplement, not replace, the more accessible, mass circulation newspapers and magazines, most of which have a center-conservative to center-liberal orientation.

American Scholar	Quarterly	Left-conservative
American Spectator	Monthly	Center-to-left conservative
Atlantic Monthly	Monthly	Center-liberal
The Black Scholar	Quarterly	Socialist
Chronicles of Culture	Monthly	Left-conservative
Commentary	Monthly	Center-conservative
Commonweal	Bi-weekly	Left-liberal Catholic
Conservative Digest	Monthly	Center-to-right conservative
Dissent	Bi-monthly	Socialist to Center-liberal
Foreign Affairs	Quarterly	Center-conservative to right-liberal
The Guardian	Weekly	Socialist
Harper's	Monthly	Center-liberal to left-conservative
Human Events	Weekly	Center-to-right conservative
Insight (Washington Times)	Weekly	Center-to-right conservative
In These Times	Weekly	Socialist
Modern Age	Quarterly	Center-conservative
Mother Jones	Monthly	Socialist to left-liberal
Ms.	Monthly	Center to left-liberal
The Nation	Weekly	Socialist to left-liberal
National Review	Bi-weekly	Center-conservative
New American	Bi-weekly	Right-conservative (formerly *American Opinion*)
New Guard	Quarterly	Center-conservative
New Politics	Quarterly	Socialist
New Republic	Weekly	Right-liberal to left-conservative
New York Review of Books	Bi-weekly	Center-liberal
New York Sunday Times	Weekly	Center-liberal to left-conservative

New Yorker	Weekly	Left-to-center-liberal
People's World	Daily	Community Party USA
Progressive	Monthly	Socialist to left-liberal
Public Interest	Quarterly	Left-to-center-conservative
Public Opinion	Monthly	Center-conservative
Reason	Monthly	Conservative libertarian
Rolling Stone	Bi-weekly	Center-liberal
Social Policy	Bi-monthly	Left-liberal
Socialist Review	Quarterly	Socialist
Tikkun	Bi-monthly	Left-liberal
Utne Reader	Bi-monthly	Digest of liberal journals
Village Voice	Weekly	Left-liberal
Washington Monthly	Monthly	Center-liberal to left-conservative
World Press Review	Monthly	Digest of diverse foreign viewpoints
Z Magazine	Monthly	Socialist

Appendix Five
A Semantic Calculator for Bias in Rhetoric*

1. What is the author's vantagepoint, in terms of social class, wealth, occupation, ethnic group, political ideology, educational level, age, gender, etc.? Is that vantagepoint apt to color her/his attitudes on the issue under discussion? Does she/he have anything personally to gain from the position she/he is arguing for, any conflicts of interest or other reasons for special pleading?

2. What organized financial, political, ethnic, or other interests are backing the advocated position? Who stands to profit financially, politically, or otherwise from it?

3. Once you have determined the author's vantagepoint and/or the special interests being favored, look for signs of ethnocentrism, rationalization or wishful thinking, sentimentality, and other blocks to clear thinking, as well as the rhetorical fallacies of onesidedness, selective vision, or a double standard.

4. Look for the following semantic patterns reflecting the biases in No. 3:

    a. Playing up: (1) arguments favorable to his/her side,

    (2) arguments unfavorable to the other side.

b. Playing down (or suppressing altogether):

(1) arguments unfavorable to her/his side,

(2) arguments favorable to the other side.

c. Applying "clean" words (ones with positive connotations) to her/his side.

Applying "dirty" words (ones with negative connotations) to the other.

d. Assuming that the representations of his/her side are trustworthy, truthful, and have no selfish motives, while assuming the opposite of the other side.

5. If you don't find strong signs of the above biases, that's a pretty good indication that the argument is a credible one.

6. If there *is* a large amount of one-sided rhetoric and semantic bias, that's a pretty good sign that the writer is not a very credible source. However, finding signs of the above biases does not in itself prove that the writer's arguments are fallacious. Don't fall into the *ad hominem* ("to the man") fallacy—evading the issue by attacking the character of the writer or speaker without refuting the substance of the argument itself. What the writer says may or may not be factual, regardless of the semantic biases. The point is not to let yourself be swayed by words alone, especially when you are inclined to wishful thinking on one side of the subject yourself. When you find these biases in other writers, *or in yourself,* that is a sign that you need to be extra careful to check the facts out with a variety of other sources and to find out what the arguments are on the other side of the issue.

*This guide derives from Hugh Rank's "Intensify-Downplay" schema, various forms of which appear in Rank (*Persuasion, Pitch*) and in Dieterich.

Appendix Six
A Glossary of Political Terms and Positions

Left wing and right wing (also see Appendix Two):

"The left wing" (adjective: "left-wing" or "leftist") is a broad term that includes a diversity of parties and ideologies (which often disagree among themselves but usually agree in their opposition to the right wing) including liberals, nearest the center of the spectrum, and—progressively toward the left—socialists and communists (the latter two are also sometimes called "radical").

"The right wing" (adjective: "right-wing" or "rightist") is a broad term that includes a diversity of parties and ideologies (which often disagree among themselves but usually agree in their opposition to the left wing) including libertarians, nearest the center of the spectrum, and—progressively toward the right—conservatives, ultra-conservatives, plutocrats, and fascists.

Leftists tend to support:	*Rightists tend to support:*
The poor and working class	Middle and upper class
Labor, consumers, environmental and other controls over business	Business, management, unregulated enterprise
Equality (economic, racial, sexual)	Inequality (economic, racial, sexual)
Civil and personal liberties	Economic liberty; controls on personal liberties (e.g., sexual conduct, abortion, obscenity, drugs)
Cooperation	Competition
Internationalism	Nationalism (primary loyalty to one's own country)
Pacifism (exception: Communists)	Strong military and willingness to go to war
Questioning of authority—skepticism (exception: Communism is authoritarian)	Acceptance of authority, especially in military, police, and strong "law and order" policies
Government spending for public services like education, welfare, health care, unemployment insurance	Government spending for military, subsidies to business as incentive for profit and growth
Progressive taxes, i.e. greatest burden on wealthy individuals and corporations	Low taxes for wealthy individuals and corporations as incentive for investment ("supply-side economics" or "trickle-down theory")
Religious pluralism, skepticism, or atheism	Religious orthodoxy

Capitalism:

An economic system based on private investment for profit. Jobs and public services are provided, and public needs met, to the extent that investment in them will predictably result in a return of capital outlay. In its principles capitalism does not provide any restrictions on extremes of wealth and poverty or of social power, but its advocates (especially pure, libertarian capitalists) believe that the workings of a free market economy, unrestricted by government controls or regulation, will minimize social inequity.

Capitalism is not a political system; in principle, a capitalist economy can operate under either a democratic government or a dictatorship, as in plutocracy or fascism—see Appendix Two (A).

Socialism:

An economic system based on public investment to meet public needs, provide full employment, and reduce socioeconomic inequality. In various models of socialism, investment and industrial management are controlled either by the federal government, local governments, workers' and consumers' cooperatives, a variety of community groups, etc.

Socialism is not a political system; in principle, a socialist economy can operate under either a democratic government or a dictatorship, as in Communism—see Appendix 2 (A).

Communism:

With lower-case "c": Marx's ideal of the ultimate, future form of pure democratic socialism, with virtually no need for centralized government.

With upper-case "C" as in present-day Communist Parties: A socialist economy under undemocratic government. Historically, Communists have manipulated appeals to left-wing values like socioeconomic equality and worldwide cooperation in order to impose police-state dictatorship and military aggression.

Plutocracy:

Rule by the rich. A capitalist economy under undemocratic government.

Fascism:

A combination of capitalist and socialist economies under an undemocratic government. Historically, fascists have manipulated appeals to conservative values like patriotism, religion, competitiveness, anti-communism, respect for authority and law and order, traditional morality and the family, in order to impose police-state dictatorship.

Fascism typically is aggressively militaristic and imperialistic, and promotes racial hatred based on theories of white (or "Pure Aryan") supremacy and religious persecution of non-Christians. It glorifies strong authority figures with absolute power.

Conservatives, Liberals, and Socialists in America:

In the American context, conservatives are pro-capitalist. They believe the interests of business also serve the interests of labor, consumers, the environment, and the public in general—"What's good for General Motors is good for America." They believe that abuses by businesses can and should be best policed or regulated by business itself, and when conservatives control government, they usually appoint businesspeople to cabinet positions and regulatory agencies without perceiving any conflict of interest therein.

American liberals believe that the interests of business are frequently contrary to those of labor, consumers, the environment, and the public in general. So although they basically support capitalism, liberals think business abuses need to be policed by government regulatory agencies that are free from conflicts of interest, and that wealth should be limited.

American socialists, or radicals, believe even more strongly than liberals that the interests of business are contrary to the public interest; they believe that capitalism is basically an irrational and corrupt system where wealthy business interests inevitably gain control over government, foreign and military policy, the media, education, etc., and use the power of employment to keep the workforce and electorate under their control. They think liberal government reforms and attempts to regulate business are usually thwarted by the power of business lobbies, and that even sincere liberal reformers in government offices usually come from and represent the ethnocentric viewpoint of the upper classes. The socialist solution is to socialize at least the biggest national and international corporations, as well as the defense industry, and operate them on a nonprofit bias, and to place much higher taxes on the rich, so as to reduce the power of wealthy corporations and individuals.

Appendix Seven
Predictable Patterns of Political Rhetoric

Leftists will play up:	*Rightists will play up:*
Conservative ethnocentrism, wishful thinking, and sentimentality, rationalizing the selfish interests of the middle and upper class and America abroad	Leftist "negative thinking," "sour grapes," anti-Americanism, and sentimentalizing of the lower classes and Third World rebellion
Right-wing bias in media and education	Left-wing bias in media and education
Conservative rationalization of right-wing extremism and foreign dictatorships allied with US (e.g., El Salvador, South Vietnam); rightists' use of "Communism" as scapegoat for rebellion against right-wing extremism	Leftist rationalization of Communist dictatorships or guerillas (e.g., Nicaragua, North Vietnam) and wishful thinking in leftists' denial of Communist influence in anti-American rebellions

| US military strengths, selfish interests of the military and defense industry; right-wing scare tactics about the Russians or other adversaries being ahead | Russians' or other adversaries' military strengths; manipulation of leftist "doves" by Communists et al.; left-wing scare tactics about nuclear war |
| Rip-offs of taxpayers' money by the rich; luxury and waste in private industry and the military | Rip-offs of taxpayers' money by the poor; luxury and waste by government bureaucrats; selfish interests and inefficiency of labor, teachers, students, etc. |

Notes

1. I have developed this argument in "Literacy and Mass Media" and *American Media and Mass Culture.*

2. I have incorporated this approach in *Composition for Critical Thinking,* a monograph-length description of a model for a two-term freshman English course; the same pedagogical approach tacitly informs "Mass Culture, Political Consciousness, and English Studies" and its development in *American Media and Mass Culture,* explicitly in the introduction and readings on critical pedagogy in the concluding section, "Alternatives and Cultural Activism."

3. For analyses of implicit ideological viewpoints in comic books, see the two chapters from *How to Read Donald Duck,* by Ariel Dorfman and Armand Mattelart, and "From Menace to Messiah: The History and Historicity of Superman," by Tom Andrae, reprinted in *American Media and Mass Culture.*

Works Cited

Allport, Gordon. *The Nature of Prejudice.* Reading: Addison-Wesley, 1979.

Dieterich, Daniel, ed. *Teaching About Doublespeak.* Urbana: NCTE, 1977.

Gilligan, Carol. *In a Different Voice: Psychological Theory and Women's Development.* Cambridge: Harvard UP, 1982.

Graff, Gerald. *Professing Literature: An Institutional History.* Chicago: U of Chicago P, 1987.

Hairston, Maxine. "Required Writing Courses Should Not Focus on Politically Charged Issues." *Chronicle of Higher Education* 23 January 1991: B2–3.

Harty, Sheila. *Hucksters in the Classroom: A Review of Industry Propaganda in Schools.* Washington: Center for the Study of Responsive Law, 1979.

Kohlberg, Lawrence. *Essays on Moral Development: Volume 1, The Philosophy of Moral Development.* San Francisco: Harper and Row, 1981.

Kytle, Ray. *Clear Thinking for Composition.* New York: Random House, 1986.

Lazere, Donald. *American Media and Mass Culture: Left Perspectives.* Berkeley: U of California P, 1987.

———. *Composition for Critical Thinking: A Course Description*. Rohnert Park, CA: Center for Critical Thinking and Moral Critique of Sonoma State U, 1986. ERIC, 1986. ED 273 959.

———. "Critical Thinking in College English Studies." ERIC Digest, 1987.

———. "Literacy and Mass Media: The Political Implications." *New Literary History* 18 (Winter 1987): 238–55. Rpt in *Reading in America: Literature and Social History*. Ed. Cathy Davidson. Johns Hopkins UP, 1989. 285–303.

———, guest editor. "Mass Culture, Political Consciousness, and English Studies." *College English* 38 (Nov. 1977).

Lutz, William A., ed. *After 1984: Doublespeak in a Post-Orwellian Age*. Urbana: NCTE, 1989.

Mayfield, Marlys. *Thinking for Yourself: Developing Critical Thinking Skills Through Writing*. 2nd ed. Belmont, CA: Wadsworth, 1991.

Perry, William. *Forms of Intellectual and Ethical Development in the College Years*. New York: Holt, 1970.

Rank, Hugh. *Persuasion Analysis: A Companion to Composition*. Park Forest: Counter-Propaganda P, 1988.

———. *The Pitch*. Park Forest: Counter-Propaganda P, 1982.

Rokeach, Milton. *The Open and Closed Mind*. New York: Basic, 1960.

Schrank, Jeffrey. *Deception Detection*. Boston: Beacon P, 1979.

———. *Snap, Crackle, and Popular Taste: The Illusion of Free Choice in America*. New York: Dell, 1977.

17

Students (Re)Writing Culture

James Berlin

Editors' Note: This chapter from Jim Berlin's posthumously published *Rhetorics, Poetics, and Cultures* (1996) offers two cultural studies courses in critical literacy. One course, Codes and Critiques, is an approach to critical literacy informed by semiotics. Students investigate the meaning of daily experiences through a variety of texts. They examine the cultural codes embedded in texts drawn thematically from advertising, work, play, education, gender, and individuality. He invites students to see texts as "terministic screens" (to use Burke's phrase) through which meaning is conveyed in the social construction of the self. The other course, The Discourse of Revolution, similarly emphasizes decoding and deconstruction as rhetorical methods, but focuses on texts and contexts in England during the time of the French and Industrial revolutions at the end of the eighteenth century. Changes in economic, social, political, and cultural conditions produced the competing rhetorics and conflicting ways of reading and writing reality. Berlin presents these two courses as possibilities for helping students "become better writers and readers as citizens, workers, and critics of their cultures."

I would now like to turn to concrete descriptions of the kind of classroom activities I am recommending. I want to outline two courses: a lower division offering entitled "Codes and Critiques" and an upper division class called "The Discourse of Revolution." Both are designed to involve students in an equal share of writing and reading, with student responses at the center of classroom activity. The two courses also insist on a balanced inclusion of poetical and rhetorical texts. In short, they are intended to challenge the old disciplinary binaries that privilege consumption over production and the aesthetic over the rhetorical. Both sets of concerns should be at the center of critique. I am, of course, especially interested in resisting the hierarchy of specialization that has separated the teaching of writing from the teaching of reading. My proposals for English studies thus encourage a professoriate as confident in teaching the ways of text production as it now is in dealing with certain forms of textual interpretation.

There are a number of qualifications I want to make in offering these course outlines. Most important, I do not wish to present them as anything more than possibilities. Their purpose is finally illustrative rather than prescriptive. I hope that teachers will find in them suggestions for developing course materials and activities appropriate to their own situations. These descriptions accordingly include considerable summary of course materials and their methods of presentation. I do want to emphasize, however, that the center of each course is the response of students to the materials and methods considered. Since this response varies dramatically from group to group and instructor to instructor, I will not try to capture the exact dimensions of any one classroom. Instead, I will simply sketch some of the conflicting reactions I have encountered. I should also note that the range of activities recommended for a refigured English studies can best be seen by considering both course descriptions. In other words, neither should be considered by itself a comprehensive suggestion of classroom possibilities for instruction in critical literacy.

Course One: Codes and Critiques

This course focuses on reading and writing the daily experiences of culture, with culture considered in its broadest formulation. It thus involves encounters with a wide variety of texts, including advertising, television, and film. The course is organized around an examination of the cultural codes—the social semiotics—that work themselves out in shaping consciousness in our students and ourselves. Since I devised the syllabus for this course to be shared with teaching assistants in my mentor groups at Purdue, and since my report here is based on our shared experience over the past four years, I will use the first-person plural in referring to the effort. I would also like to thank those teaching assistants for their generous cooperation.

We start with the personal experience of the students, with emphasis on the position of this experience within its formative context. Our main concern is the relation of current signifying practices to the structuring of subjectivities—of race, class, sexual orientation, age, ethnic, and gender formations, for example—in our students and ourselves. The effort is to make students aware of cultural codes, the competing discourses that influence their positioning as subjects of experience. Our larger purpose is to encourage students to negotiate and resist these codes—these hegemonic discourses—to bring about more democratic and personally humane economic, social, and political arrangements. From our perspective, only in this way can students become genuinely competent writers and readers.

We thus guide students to locate in their experience the points at which they are now engaging in negotiation and resistance with the cultural codes they daily encounter. These are then used as avenues of departure for a dialogue. The course consists of six units: advertising, work, play, education, gender, and individuality. Each unit begins by examining a variety of texts that feature competing representations of and orientations toward the topic of the unit. Here I will describe some of the main features of the unit on work. The unit provides a sampling of attitudes toward work from a broad range of perspectives. These include selections from Benjamin Franklin's "The Way to Wealth," Studs Terkel's *Working* (1985), Richard Selzer's *Mortal Lessons* (1976), William Ouchi's *Theory Z: How American Business Can Meet the Japanese Challenge* (1981), Adrienne Rich's poetry and her "Conditions for Work: The Common World of Women," and Toni Cade Bambara's fiction and her "What It Is I Think I'm Doing Now." The unit also includes films and videotapes of television programs that are useful treatments of work in the United States. The important consideration here is not only the texts in themselves, but the texts in relation to certain methods of interpreting them.

The course provides students with a set of heuristics—invention strategies—that grow out of the interaction of rhetoric, structuralism, poststructuralism, semiotics, and cultural studies. While those outlined here have been developed as a result of reading in Saussure, Pierce, Levi-Strauss, Barthes, Gramsci, Raymond Williams, Stuart Hall, and others, an excellent introduction for teachers and students can be found in John Fiske's *Introduction to Communication Studies* (1990) and Diana George and John Trimbur's *Reading Culture* (1992). In examining any text—print, film, television—students must locate the key terms in the discourse and situate these terms within the structure of meaning of which they form a part. These terms, of course, derive from the central preoccupations of the text, but to determine how they work to constitute experience, students must examine their functions as parts of coded structures—a semiotic system. The terms are first set in relation to their binary opposites as suggested by the text itself. (This follows Saussure's description of the central place of contrast in signification and Levi-Strauss's application of it.) Sometimes these oppositions are indicated explicitly in the text, but more often they are not. Students must also learn that a term commonly occupies a position in opposition to more than one other term.

For example, we sometimes begin with an essay from the *Wall Street Journal* entitled "The Days of a Cowboy Are Marked by Danger, Drudgery, and Low Pay," by William Blundell (10 June 1981, A1+). This essay is most appropriate for the unit on work, but its codes are at once so varied and so accessible to students that it is a useful introduction to any unit. The reading strategy employed once again involves looking at the text successively within its generic, ideological, and socioeconomic environment.

Students first consider the context of the piece, exploring the characteristics of the readership of the newspaper and the historical events surrounding the essay's production, particularly as indicated within the text. The purpose of this analysis is to decide which terms probably acted as key signifiers for the original readers. The essay focuses on the cowboss, the ranch foreman who runs the cattle operation. The meaning of *cowboss* is established by seeing it in binary opposition both to the cowboys who work for him and the owners who work away from the ranch in cities. At other times in the essay, the cowboss is grouped together with the cowboys in opposition to office workers. Through the description of labor relations on the ranch, the cowboys are also situated in contrast to urban union workers, though the latter are never explicitly mentioned. Finally, the exclusively masculine nature of ranching is suggested only at the end of the essay, when the cowboss's wife is described in passing as living apart from the ranch on the cowboss's own small spread, creating a male–female domain binary. All of these binaries suggest others, such as the opposition of nature–civilization, country–city, and cowboy–urban cowboy. Students begin to see that these binaries are arranged hierarchically, with one term privileged over the other. They also see how unstable these hierarchies can be, with a term frequently shifting valences as it moves from one binary to another—for example, cowboy–union worker but cowboss–cowboy. It is also important to point out that this location of binaries is not an exact operation and that great diversity appears as students negotiate the text differently. Their reasons for doing so become clear at the next phase of analysis.

In this phase, students place these terms within the narrative structural forms suggested by the text, the culturally coded stories about patterns of behavior appropriate for people within certain situations. These codes deal with such social designations as race, class, gender, sexual orientation, age, ethnicity, and the like. Students analyze, discuss, and write about the position of the key terms within these socially constructed narrative codes. It is not too difficult to imagine how these narrative codes are at work in the binaries indicated above. Students can quickly detect the narratives that cluster around the figure of the cowboy in our culture in this essay—for example, patterns of behavior involving individuality, freedom, and independence. These narratives, however, are simultaneously coupled with self-discipline, respect for authority (good cowboys never complain), and submission to the will of the cowboss. Students usually point out the ways these narratives are conflicted while concurrently reinforcing differences in class and gender role expectations. Of particular value is to see the way the essay employs narratives that at once disparage *Wall Street Journal* readers because they are urban office workers while simultaneously enabling them to identify with the rugged freedom and adventure of the cowboys, seeing themselves as metaphorically enacting the masculine narrative of the cowboss in their separate domains. In other words, students discover that the essay attempts to position the reader in the role of a certain kind of masculine subject. They can then explore their own complicity and resistance in responding to this role.

In doing so, students situate these narrative patterns within larger narrative structures that have to do with economic, political, and cultural formulations. Here students examine capitalist economic narratives as demonstrated in the essay and their consequences for class, gender, and race relations and roles both in the workplace and elsewhere. They look, for example, at the distribution of work in beef production, with its divisions between managers and workers, thinkers and doers, producers and consumers. They also consider the place of narratives of democracy in the essay, discussing the nature of the political relations implied in the hierarchies of terms, persons, and social relations presented. It should be clear that at these two narrative levels considerable debate results, as students disagree about the narratives that ought to be invoked in interpreting the text, their relative worth as models for emulation, and the degree to which these narratives are conflicted. In other words, the discussion that emerges from the use of these heuristics is itself conflicted and unpredictable.

Thus, the term as it is designated within a hierarchical binary is situated within narratives of social roles. These roles are then located within more comprehensive narratives of economic and political formations in the larger society. The point of the interpretation is to see that texts—whether rhetorical or poetic—are ideologically invested in the construction of subjectivities within recommended economic, social, and political arrangements. Finally, this hermeneutic process is open-ended, leading in diverse and unpredictable directions in the classroom. This is one of its strengths, since it encourages open debate and wide-ranging speculation. Students arrive at widely variant readings, and these become the center of discussion.

The course is also designed to introduce students to methods for interpreting the cultural codes of television—methods based, in this case, on the work of John Fiske. In particular, we give students the first chapter of Fiske's *Television Culture* (1987), in which he offers a method for analyzing television codes closely related to the heuristic the students call upon in interpreting printed texts. This method involves three interconnected interpretive moments. As Fiske explains, the raw materials of television are always encoded by social codes that consist of "appearance, dress, make-up, environment, behavior, speech, gesture, expression, sound, etc." (5). These form the codes of what he labels "Level one: REALITY." These materials are in turn encoded electronically by technical codes that include "camera, lighting, editing, music, sound" (5). These technical codes "transmit the *conventional representational codes,* which shape the representations of, for example: narrative, conflict, character, action, dialogue, setting, casting, etc." (5). The technical and conventional representational codes form the codes of "Level two: REPRESENTATION." Both reality and representation are in turn "organized into coherence and social acceptability by the *ideological codes,* such as those of: individualism, patriarchy, race, class, materialism, capitalism, etc." (5).

In this segment of the course, then, we invoke Fiske's method as a guide to "reading" two situation comedies with which the students are usually familiar. *Family Ties* and *Roseanne,* for instance, have worked quite well. Students view selected episodes during the unit on work to learn to analyze television codes as well as to gather evidence for their essays on the cultural organization of work and its place in forming subjectivity in their lives. Students learn to see these domestic comedies not as simple presentations of reality but as representations—that is, coded constructions—of an imagined reality. These two programs are especially useful in the work unit because they can be regarded as attempts to present family experience from the points of view of two different class positions.

Family Ties aired from 1982 to 1989, leaving at the peak of its popularity. The show centered around the Keatons, an upper-middle-class family of five living in an unnamed urban area in Ohio. The parents are successful professionals. Stephen, the father, is a manager at a PBS television station, and Elise, the mother, is an architect. The children are Alex, 17 when the show began, Mallory, 15, and Jennifer, 9. Over the course of the show's run, Alex and Mallory went on to college, but both continued to live at home. One of the recurring themes of the show was the conflict between the parents, who were sixties political activists and Peace Corps members, and Alex, who is a political conservative motivated by the drive to be rich.

Roseanne began in 1989. The Connor family, the show's central focus, is lower middle class, living in a moderately priced neighborhood in a Chicago suburb. Both parents have experienced job disruptions. Dan, the father, was originally a self-employed building contractor taking on small jobs. He eventually realized his dream to own his own business by opening up a motorcycle shop. Later, the business went under. Early on in the series, Roseanne—the mother—worked as a waitress at a department store in a local shopping center, but she too loses her job. With the help of a gift from her mother, she opened up a sandwich shop with her sister. The business was eventually bought out, though she now works there as a waitress. The children are Becky, who eloped and moved to Wisconsin, but has recently moved back home with her husband; Darlene, away at college; and D.J., a early teenage son.

Students begin by writing descriptions of the physical settings of the homes and the characteristic dress of the characters depicted in the two programs. The point of this exercise is for students to recognize that the sets and costumes are created by the producers of the shows. They are not simply video copies of actual homes and people (except for the external shots of the neighborhood in *Roseanne*). The sharp contrasts in the two households lead to a discussion of social class and its relation to work, income, and ideology. Some of the differences between the attitudes and behavior found in the two households are the result of simple economics. For example, the action in the two dramas most commonly takes place in the kitchen, the center of domestic life in television sitcoms. The sizes of the two kitchens and the cost of the appliances obviously involve a disparity in income and expenditures. At the same time, the differences in the decor of the two houses are not exclusively a matter of money spent. Often, a sense of taste related to class affiliation rather than finance is at issue. For example, in one series of *Roseanne* episodes, the wife in an upper-middle-class family that moved in next door found the Connor family quite beneath her. The contrast between the decor of the two houses, identical twins architecturally in a tract-like neighborhood, became an issue, and the Connors clearly identified the taste of their neighbors with elitism and snobbery. In other words, the Connors decorated their house in a manner that simultaneously made them feel comfortable and asserted their class loyalty.

Problems the families in the two sitcoms encounter each week are often related to their incomes, job stability, and class. Both families, for instance, have faced decisions about college education for their children. The question for *Family Ties* revolved around finding colleges suitable to the interests and aptitudes of Alex and Mallory. Money was never a major concern, and in one episode Mrs. Keaton visited expensive private schools with her daughter. For the *Roseanne* household, Becky's hard-won success in high school and her plans to go away to college led to cruel disappointment when her parents lost their jobs. In fact, her eloping was a direct result of this turn of events. This contrast is especially worth considering because of its relation to gender codes across classes. Mallory is presented as a person more interested in clothes and dating than in school. Indeed, she is often made to appear shallow and thoughtless. Despite this, her parents are surprised when she indicates she does not want to go to college, planning instead to work in a women's clothing store in the hope that she will eventually have her own shop. Her parents applaud her entrepreneurial spirit, but finally convince her to try college for one year while using the clothing store dream as a back up. Becky, on the other hand, sees marriage as her only alternative to college. This class contrast is especially apparent when one is aware that in an earlier episode, Mallory also eloped with her inarticulate working-class boyfriend (who, for her parents, is redeemed because he is a talented artist), only to abruptly change her mind in the office of the justice of the peace. The differing gender codes that operate in the two social classes are clearly at issue here.

Students usually conclude that the two shows were the products of different economic times. *Family Ties* prospered during the eighties, when economic success for those at the upper income levels was a reality. This program spoke for this successful group. *Roseanne* is a production for a time when the concentration of wealth depicted in *Family Ties* has reached such glaring disproportions that we now speak of the income of the "bottom ninety percent" of the population. This realization on the part of students, however, is an important discovery. They begin to understand that television's presentation of the family and the place of work in it are related to popular perceptions of "the real," "the normal," and "the everyday." In other words, the family the largest segment of the television audience chooses to watch is a function of its self-perception, and this in turn is as much related to its conception of what it would like to think is true as to what in fact exists. After all, the Keaton family in *Family Ties* in the mid-eighties represented a small proportion of families in the United States. Then, as now, less than 20 percent of the workforce consisted of college graduates, and much less than 10 percent enjoyed the apparent Keaton income. Indeed, *Roseanne* presents a family experience much closer to the daily lives of the overwhelming majority of Americans, past or present. In other words, most of those who viewed and enjoyed *Family Ties* were more like the Connors than the Keatons, yet they obviously derived pleasure from their weekly watch.

This leads to a discussion of subject formation, television, and cultural codes. As the students describe their responses to the two programs, explaining the pleasures of the text they experience in watching them, it becomes apparent that many women in the class do not enjoy watching *Roseanne*. While some men in the class find it entertaining, most women do not. As class members discuss their preference for *Family Ties,* they begin to consider the different subject positions the two shows attempt to create for the audience. The students obviously prefer the version of work and family life they are asked to endorse in viewing the Keatons. Moreover, they do so even after acknowledging that the genuine conflicts addressed in the program are usually avoided or ignored rather than resolved. Mallory offers challenges to her parents, but she always, often inexplicably, does what her parents think best. Alex rebels, but he does so in a socially approved manner, working hard to be rich. The adverse consequences of his extreme selfishness are never addressed; indeed, in the ingratiating actor Michael J. Fox's hands, ruthlessness is made charming. The students realize that neither the superficiality nor the dishonesty of *Family Ties* interferes with their pleasure in the half-hour presentation. Instead, they continue to find the characters attractive—a response to which I must also confess—since both parents and children display characteristics that the students admire in manners, dress, and general behavior. Stephen and Elise are professionals who approach work, parenting, and play in the successful manner that most beginning students at my institution find worthy of emulation. No problem is too hard for them to solve, even if the solutions cannot stand the light of close analysis. The program offers a fulfillment of most of my students' dreams for themselves as college graduates and professionals. Although the dreams may not be intellectually convincing, they offer an imaginary fulfillment of desire.

This realization leads, in turn, to a consideration of the ways conflicts in cultural codes are typically resolved in television programs, *Roseanne* included. *Family Ties* was indeed notable for addressing serious family problems, most obviously those that result from the clashes between parents and children on such issues as marriage, education, and careers. The program also considered crises at the workplace, with Elise being pursued by a young suitor and Stephen experiencing the difficulty of pleasing a demanding boss. Yet *Family Ties* was no less distinguished for its easy resolution of these difficulties. The lesson of most episodes was that there was no problem that could not be overcome by two or more family members simply sitting down at the kitchen table next to the Zinn range and talking it out. In other words, the program tended to present the upper-middle-class professional nuclear family as in itself the answer to all of life's problems—an extension, one student noted, of the Reagan administration's contention about the place of the family in resolving economic and social problems. Of course, *Roseanne* is not immune to this impulse. For example, the economic problems that the Connor family once faced were resolved by a sizeable financial gift from Roseanne's mother, a move made to punish Roseanne's father for his marital infidelity. The point of this discussion, then, is not to privilege one program over the other. Instead, its purpose is to understand the pleasures of television in their relation to the imaginary resolution of conflicts and the fulfillment of cultural expectations. To enjoy the artificial working out of genuinely serious economic, class, gender, and age conflicts within a thirty-minute television program is not a problem. To expect that these difficulties can be solved in the same manner in our own experience is quite another matter.

This segment on television most usefully ends with a final consideration of the medium's effects in shaping subjectivity among viewers. Students are encouraged to discuss the manner in which they negotiate and resist the cultural codes championed in the programs they watch. No one would argue that students are unwilling dupes of television. But they are not impervious to its seductions either. The larger question students are entertaining, of course, is the role of culture in shaping them as the subjects of their experience and their role as critical agents in a democratic society. Here they can explore their reasons for preferring the version of work and family found in one or the other program, investigating the class, gender, race, religious, and ethnic codes that they have been encouraged to enact. The purpose is neither to reject nor to celebrate their customary manner of responding to important experiences. The purpose is to become reflective agents actively involved in shaping their own consciousness as well as the democratic society of which they are an integral part. Unlike classrooms that insist that each student look within to discover a unique self, this course argues that only through understanding the workings of culture in shaping consciousness can students ever hope to achieve any degree of singularity. By exploring television programs and their dialectical relation to viewers in the operation of subject formation, students begin to come to terms with the apparatuses of culture as they create consciousness.

A final segment of the course as we have taught it has focused on film, calling in particular on the method offered in Graeme Turner's *Film as Social Practice* (1993). Like Fiske's method, it has considerable structural similarity with the heuristic the course teaches for decoding printed texts, combining a structuralist analysis of film as narrative with a poststructuralist ideological critique—a similarity that students readily recognize and find useful. Drawing upon Levi-Strauss's contention that cultural codes are based on a set of binary oppositions imaginatively resolved in their ruling mythologies, Turner argues that films too are organized around a set of binaries embodied in a narrative that attempts to reconcile them. Poststructuralist ideological critique, however, goes beyond the analytical identification of binaries that narratives seek to reconcile—the characteristic strategy of Levi-Strauss's structuralism—by investigating the political and rhetorical effects of such narrative resolutions, what meanings they make available and what meanings they suppress. This is the move that distinguishes poststructuralism from structuralism, the move to problematize precisely those binary oppositions whose symbolic resolution gives narratives their sense of conventionalized closure.

Since the conflicts and contradictions a film addresses can never be totally resolved—or can be resolved imaginatively but not actually—the narrative will always result in some measure of ambiguity and ambivalence, some surplus of meaning that exceeds narrative resolution. In other words, the narrative will always carry within it traces of the conflicts and contradictions that resist the resolutions of the ruling mythologies. Moreover, since a film is located within a set of more or less determinable but changing historical influences, the ways in which its conflicts as well as their resolutions are read by viewers change over time. By way of example, Turner traces the changes the James Bond character underwent after 1960 in print and film in response to changing historical conditions (as discussed by Tony Bennett and Janet Woollacott 1987). Films are seen as responses to historical contexts, and the meanings that viewers find in them are a function of this context as much as the film itself. Thus, the binary conflicts that an audience discovers in a film as well as the resolution of these conflicts are as much a product of the historical conditions of the audience as of the elements of the film. Furthermore, the interpretive act is situated in ideological conditions, in representations of what really exists, what is good, and what is possible.

We thus ask students to locate the binary oppositions they see working in a film and to determine the kind of resolution of them the narrative movement of the film achieves. From this analysis, they can infer the ideological leaning of the film—that is, what they take to be its preferred reading. Here again, their responses are usually nowhere near unanimous. As Turner points out, films are texts that do not lend themselves to uniform readings. The divergences that do emerge, however, are not always as radically opposed to each other as they might at first appear. Still, these differences must be encouraged and entertained. I would like to outline the way this method can unfold in considering two recent films: *Other People's Money* and *Roger and Me.*

Other People's Money, released in 1991, is based on a mid-eighties off-broadway play by Jerry Sterner. Students usually situate the film as a product of the late eighties, when the merits of unbridled free enterprise were called into question by the consequences of the doings of Wall Street financial wizards. The plot involves an attempt to launch a corporate takeover by one Lawrence Garfield, the wealthy owner of an investment firm (played by Danny DeVito). The founding company of this diversified corporation, New England Wire and

Cable, is losing money, while the corporation as a whole is solidly in the black. The result is that the corporation is worth much more than the face value of its stock. Garfield plans to win major control of the corporation, close down New England Wire and Cable, sell the land on which it is built, and clear a hefty profit as the stock then rises to its true value. He is opposed by the son of the late founder of the wire and cable company, Andrew Jorgensen (known as "Yorgy" and played by Gregory Peck), who runs his father's operation as a family business. Jorgensen is determined to fight Garfield, confident that eventually his company will once again make money. He is accordingly persuaded to request the assistance of Kate Sullivan, a partner in a prominent Wall Street legal firm and daughter of his longtime friend, fellow worker, and, perhaps, lover. Sullivan (played by Penelope Ann Miller) agrees to lead the effort to stop the takeover, even though she and Jorgensen clearly do not get along with each other. Meanwhile, Garfield falls in love with her, and there is some indication as the film unfolds that the feeling may be reciprocated.

The major issues at stake in the film's preferred narrative are articulated in the climactic scene in which Jorgensen and Garfield give stirring speeches defending their positions at a stockholders' meeting. Jorgensen stands for the corporation as paternal family, with managers industriously caring for the welfare of workers and the community as a whole. Closing down New England Wire and Cable would destroy the small Rhode Island town in which it is located, and Jorgensen would rather operate at a loss than do this, waiting for the day when the demand for his product will increase. Garfield stands for the corporation as generator of profits, concerned only with making sure that investors receive a maximum return on their investment. Only through constantly increasing profits can corporations truly serve the interests of the larger society, he argues. In the end, Garfield wins, as the stockholders vote with him and he assumes control of the corporation. In the closing scene of the film, however, negotiations between Sullivan and Japanese businessmen are presented in dumb show, and we finally learn that a Japanese corporation wants to hire the firm to build wire-constructed safety air bags for the auto industry. The workers will buy back the plant from Garfield, and Sullivan and Garfield will handle the negotiations, opening the possibility, of course, that they will get together romantically.

Students have little difficulty uncovering binary oppositions at play in the film. As they do so, however, they also discover that these binaries are both unstable and frequently contradictory. For instance, in the early part of the film, there is the constant juxtaposition of scenes between Manhattan and the plant in Rhode Island—the glamor, hard polish, and technology of the one against the mundane, quaint, and primitive charm of the other. These scenes seem to establish a city–country binary, and Jorgensen later reminds Sullivan of the clean air they enjoy as the two of them have a smoke on the spacious front porch of his quaint, hillside country home after Thanksgiving dinner. The shots of the plant, however, reveal a smoking industrial quagmire of pipes and tubes and dilapidated buildings. While the plant was shot in the most picturesque of manners, using color settings that cast it in nostalgic golds and browns, the facility was clearly an ancient, outdated steel foundry. One wonders just how clean the air can be. The country–city, nature–culture binary does not seem consistent.

This sort of visual binary that eventually results in contradiction is reproduced as the students consider gender and class codes. As is all too clear, both Jorgensen and Garfield are unapologetic sexists in their attitudes and behavior. Jorgensen must be tactfully persuaded to seek Sullivan's advice, and then he ignores it in forcing a stockholders' vote that she has insisted he will probably lose. Garfield's blatant sexual advances toward Sullivan are less offensive than they might be only because DeVito's impish charm is able to make them humorous in their unexpected bluntness and crude candor. (On their first meeting, he suddenly proposes they get together to sweat between satin sheets.) The film seems to ask us to see Sullivan as the feminist who reconciles the old capitalist order with the new, but she does so without influencing the blatant sexism that is at the heart of both. She is also the agent in saving the workers' jobs, but the sharp criticism of both Jorgensen and Garfield that this implies—if they're so smart, why didn't they think of this alternative?—is left unexplored. The conclusion even points to the conflicted response to the Japanese presented in a number of scenes; they are both admired for their success and resented for competing so effectively with the United States.

The film's treatment of social class is typical of most Hollywood productions of the eighties in that workers are simply not allowed to speak for themselves. When asked to look for the workers' stance on the conflicts offered, students have no difficulty concluding that the company's employees are given no voice in the negotiations. Even worse, they are presented as totally dependent children who must be protected by the patriarch Jorgensen. They are center-screen only at the opening when they are shown entering the plant, a little later when a family-like photograph of all the employees is being taken, and again near the end when they are portrayed outside the hall where the stockholders' meeting is being held, listening intently to loudspeakers broadcasting the speeches of Jorgensen and Garfield. The only speaking part a worker is given involves a frightened man asking Jorgensen in a childlike manner to reassure him that everything will be all right despite the takeover bid. Jorgensen, of course, does so in the soothing tones a father uses with a frightened child. The patriarchy displayed in the gender relations in the film is thus extended to the treatment of workers. Garfield shares in this attitude, adding contempt to arrogance as he wonders aloud while entering the crowded plant site for the stockholders' meeting why the workers always bring their children to their demonstrations, doing so while he dismissively looks at them beating on his limousine windows.

This leads to *Roger and Me*. This 1989 film is on its face a documentary dealing with the lives of auto workers losing their jobs as a result of General Motors plant closings in Flint, Michigan. But this film speaks for workers and is finally a stinging and artfully presented denunciation of corporate capitalism. Indeed, the managerial class presented in relatively glowing terms in *Other People's Money* is here held up to vicious ridicule. The film thus serves a number of functions in the dialectical thinking students must undertake in addressing cultural codes. The film attempts to depict some of the grim realities of the capitalistic process that Garfield so blithely ignores. (Indeed, Garfield explicitly states that stockholders owe workers nothing, since workers have never done anything for stockholders except demand higher wages. For Garfield, as for Adam Smith, the system works best when each of us selfishly pursues our own individual interests.) In Flint, no Japanese firm miraculously appears to create new jobs for workers. Michael Moore, the film's creator and narrator, examines the catastrophic results of a corporation abandoning a city to seek higher profits elsewhere. Indeed, the recurring image in the film is the eviction of family after family from their homes by the county sheriff, their possessions ungraciously stacked up next to the street. At the same time, an analysis of the binary oppositions inscribed in the film reveals in them the same sort of instability and contradiction we saw in the other film. *Roger and Me* is as ideologically loaded as *Other People's Money,* and just as unsuccessful at resolving the conflicts and contradictions it presents as its counterpart.

The ideological reading of the narrative strategies of the two films, then, is designed to make students suspicious of easy resolutions of complex social, economic, and political problems. Texts should be understood in terms of what they omit as well as what they include, and they should be situated within their historical context. In a broader sense, motivating students to become critical readers and writers of film and television is meant to equip them to make more intelligent decisions in their public and private experience, particularly since they are encouraged to see the inescapable relation of the personal and the political. The two films offer comforting ideological narratives, but neither finally can be accepted at face value. Any successful response to the conflicts and contradictions they locate must include the dialectical interaction of both points of view.

I should also mention at this point that we have experimented with students producing their own short videotaped productions. The point of doing so is to enable them to see the immensely complex coding system involved in producing the effect found in even the most pedestrian television program. Students begin to discover firsthand how difficult it is to generate the effects of the real found in a professionally televised event. Perceiving television from the point of view of the producer encourages students to recognize the manufactured character of television programming, the manner in which it is constructed rather than simply recorded. Groups of three or four students who produce their own five-minute news program or an account of a sporting event come to view television from the point of view of production as well as consumption. Situated within a course emphasizing cultural critique, this effort makes students better readers of video texts.

After some experience with written and video texts, students apply these heuristics to their personal experiences to analyze in essay form the effect of an important cultural code on their lives. The students select the topic and content of the essay, but they do so within the context of the larger theme of each unit. Thus, in the unit on work, students choose some feature of their work experience or their observation of cultural codes regarding work—in the media, for example—that has been of particular personal significance. The students then locate points of conflict and dissonance in the cultural codes discovered, along with their ideological predispositions. They are not expected to attempt a resolution of these conflicts, a matter usually much more complex. Students commonly choose to write about their experiences in part-time jobs while in high school. For example, they have considered the differences in treatment accorded men and women or African American and white workers, discussing these disparities in terms of cultural codes regarding race and gender within a particular work context. A number of women who grew up in agricultural communities have discussed the unfair constraints imposed on them in performing farm work, prohibitions that seemed to them arbitrary and irrational. Many students have written about their experiences in fast-food restaurants, discussing the conflicting class, race, and gender codes that were subtly as well as overtly enforced. Most students have deplored the dissonance manifested in these codes, but others have attempted to justify them as economic or cultural expedients needed for a smoothly functioning social order. Since drafts of student essays are always shared with other class members, however, unreflective generalizations about the inevitability of class, race, gender, or age behavior never go unchallenged.

Students become accustomed to debate and disagreement in this course as they explore a diversity of cultural codes. The differences in their ways of negotiating and resisting these codes become quickly apparent, as when, for instance, they discuss both their direct subversions of work rules and their less confrontational avoidance of them. The important consideration is that the students situate the personal actions they invoke within race, class, gender, sexual orientation, ethnic, and age codes and then locate these codes within larger economic and social narratives. In this way, they begin to understand the coded nature of their daily behavior, and they begin to become active, critical subjects rather than passive objects of their experience.

As students develop material through the use of the heuristics and begin to write initial drafts of their essays, they discuss the culturally coded character of all parts of composing—from genre to patterns of organization to sentence structure. Students must learn to arrange their materials to conform to the genre codes of the form of the essay they are writing—the personal essay or the academic essay, for example. (The production of a video news story enables an encounter with still another kind of genre code, this one visual and aural.) These essay genres conform to socially indicated formal codes that students must identify and enact and of course carry great consequence for meaning. A given genre encourages certain kinds of messages while discouraging others. Next, at the level of the sentence, stylistic form comes into play, and the student must again learn to generate sentence structures and patterns of diction expected in the genre employed. Students must engage in sentence combining and sentence generating activities. It is important that students be made aware of the purposes of these codes, both practical and ideological. In other words, expecting certain formal and stylistic patterns is not simply a matter of securing "clear and effective communication." As most writing teachers realize, most errors in grammar and spelling do not in themselves interfere with the reader's understanding. The use of *who* for *whom,* for example, seldom creates any confusion in reference. These errors instead create interferences of a social and political nature.

Finally, I would like to restate a point on the interchangeability of reading and writing made earlier. In enacting the reading and writing process, students learn that all experience is situated within signifying practices and that learning to understand personal and social experience involves acts of discourse production and interpretation, the two acting reciprocally in reading and writing codes. Students discover that interpretation involves production as well as reproduction and is as constructive as composing itself. At the same time, they find out that the more one knows about a text—its author, place of publication, audience, historical context—the less indeterminate it becomes and the more confident the reader can be in interpreting and negotiating its preferred reading. Similarly, the more the writer understands the entire semiotic context in which he or she functions, the greater the likelihood that the text will serve as an effective intervention in an ongoing discussion. After all, despite the inevitable slippages that appear in the production and interpretation of codes, people do in fact regularly communicate with each other to get a great variety of work done successfully. At the same time, even these efficacious exchanges can harbor concealed or ignored contradictions. These contradictions are important for the reader and writer to discover, because they foreground the political unconscious of decision making, a level of unspoken assumptions often repressed in ordinary discourse.

Again, an important objective of this course is to prepare students for critical citizenship in a democracy. We want students to begin to understand that language is never innocent, that it instead constitutes a terrain for ideological battle. Language—textuality—is the terrain on which different conceptions of economic, social, and political conditions are contested, with consequences for the formation of the subjects of history, the consciousness of the historical agent. We are thus committed to teaching reading and writing as an inescapably political act, the working out of contested cultural codes affecting every feature of experience. This involves teachers in an effort to problematize students' experiences, requiring them to challenge the ideological codes students bring to college by placing their signifying practices against alternatives. Sometimes this can be done cooperatively, with teachers and students agreeing about the conflicts apparent in a particular cultural formation—for example, the elitist and often ruthlessly competitive organization of varsity sports in high schools. Students can thus locate points of personal resistance and negotiation in dealing with the injustices of this common social practice. At other times, students and teachers are at odds with each other or, just as often, the students are themselves divided about the operation and effects of conflicting codes. This often results in spirited exchange. The role of the teacher is to act as a mediator while ensuring that no code, including his or her own, goes unchallenged.

Course Two: The Discourse of Revolution

I would like now to describe a course for college juniors and seniors that might be called "The Discourse of Revolution." Once again, I describe one possibility, an example rather than a definitive model. As I indicated in the last chapter, the moments at which large changes in economic, social, political, and cultural conditions take place most clearly demonstrate the conflicts between different conceptions of reading and writing practices, of poetics and rhetorics. This course is organized around a consideration of signifying practices and their relation to subject formation within the contexts of power at one of these important moments in political and textual history, focusing on texts and their contexts in England during the time of the two revolutions at the end of the eighteenth century—roughly between 1775 and 1800. Once again, the heuristic to be employed in examining both rhetorical and poetical discourse requires looking at each text in its interacting generic, ideological, and socioeconomic environments. At each level, the reader attempts to locate the conflicts and contradictions addressed, resolved, ignored, or concealed with a view to considering their significance to the formation of subjects and to the larger culture. In the case of literary texts, the unique historical role of the aesthetic is a special concern. I should add that I have in mind a teacher who is familiar with, although not necessarily an expert in, the period under study.

The course begins with a consideration of the concrete economic, social, and political events of the period. Students read in the history of the time. The version I have found most useful is Michel Beaud's *A History of Capitalism* (1983), especially chapter three, "The Century of the Three Revolutions (Eighteenth Century)." Beaud establishes in clear detail the complex interactions of four major economic and political events of the century, events especially evident in the period being considered. These events are at the center of the development of mercantile capitalism and the beginnings of industrial capitalism.

The first of these events was the extension of England's colonial domination and worldwide trade through the development of merchant capitalism. The construction of a banking system that made possible the financing of commercial expansion was crucial. England began the export of coal and wheat, became a transport center for the traders of other countries, and established itself as a warehouse center for goods traveling through the Americas, the Indies, and Europe. The cultivation of international economic exchange led to an increasing supply of primary products—such as tea, sugar, and cotton—and a corresponding enlargement of manufacturing due to new market outlets for textiles and other manufactured products. Beaud is especially effective in tracing the role of slavery in the establishment of England's economic success. This trading cycle involved the selling of English guns in Africa that were used to kidnap and enslave Africans. The slaves were then sold to the colonies as cheap labor for the production of cotton, tobacco, and sugar. These materials were then returned to England for processing, manufacture, and export. Since England also built the ships involved in this trade and provided the seaports for warehousing and exchange, it is not difficult to see the reasons behind its great economic growth in the eighteenth century.

The second element in the rise of England as an economic and political power had to do with the enclosure acts and the modernization of agriculture. The enclosure acts appropriated land that had historically been used by the common people to supplement their meager wages. With the enclosure acts, the use of this land was restricted to the major land owners in a district. At the same time, landed gentry and aristocrats developed new farming techniques that increased yields and profits. These techniques improved efficiency and lessened the need for workers. The combination of the enclosure acts and the loss of work to new farming techniques created a surplus labor force that could be called upon by the newly developed manufacturing enterprises of the cities.

This availability of labor was central to the third major element in the development of England's economic growth. The scientific spirit and the techniques applied to production led to a series of inventions that grew upon one another. These inventions ranged from the development of machines for the rapid production of textiles to the introduction of steam power in mills. Such new manufacturing enterprises hired the workers who had been displaced from rural areas by the enclosure acts and scientific farming. Finally, the additional capital made available by commerce and agriculture paid for the construction of more mills.

All of this led to increased production and an extension of wage payment. Since worker struggles intensified, the state interceded on behalf of the monied interests in a series of protectionist measures, establishing policies designed to suppress worker revolts. In 1769, for example, to destroy machines or the building in which they were housed was designated a felony offense, punishable by death. Government troops were used to break up worker riots in Lancaster in 1779 and Yorkshire in 1796. By 1799, laws were enacted to prohibit workers' associations formed to press for better wages, reduced working days, and the improvement of working conditions. This suppression of the working class was undertaken by an emerging power bloc made up of the new bourgeoisie and the old aristocracy. Ultimately, these two groups called upon a shared version of culture and taste to provide a common ground for their economic and political alliance. In a nation of some 6,000,000 people, the electorate was made up of 450,000 men consisting of lawyers, local notables, well-to-do farmers, clergy, and university professors. Parliament thus represented the interests of these groups.

Once students have read and discussed Beaud, they move on to contrast his account of these events with the account offered in Linda Colley's *Britons: Forging the Nation, 1707–1873* (1992). While Colley details the interaction of the economic, social, and political developments found in Beaud's account, she places them within a different narrative frame. Rather than foregrounding economic activity as the most important influence in the events of the eighteenth century, Colley argues for the primacy of the political. For her, the story of this period is the reaction of the Britons to military threats from abroad, especially France. These threats, she argues, were most responsible for forming a national identity and encouraging a complex range of social and economic as well as military responses. She is especially interested in tracing the effects of these threats on forming a national identity. Thus, she places significant features of national behavior between 1707 and 1837 within a narrative organized around two major themes. Colley explains:

> What made these themes, mass allegiance on the one hand and the invention of Britishness on the other, so central during this 130-year long period was a succession of wars between Britain and France. Prime powers on sea and on land respectively, the whale and the elephant as Paul Kennedy styles them, they were at war between 1689 and 1697, and on a larger scale and for higher stakes between 1702 and 1713, 1743 and 1748, 1756 and 1763, 1778 and 1783, 1793 and 1802, and, finally, between 1803 and the Battle of Waterloo in 1815. And these were only the most violent expressions of a much longer and many-layered rivalry. (1)

Colley thus deals extensively with the two revolutions central to this course and in doing so presents an especially rich analysis of their consequences for gender, class, and race formations and relations. One purpose of studying her account next to Beaud's is to examine the effects of different narrative frames on the interpretation of specific historical events. This experience is also meant to encourage students to look for similar contrasts in the interpretation of rhetorical and poetic texts. Students thus arrive at conclusions about the place of narrative frames in understanding historical events and the role of writing and reading practices in influencing these frames.

Having looked at different narrative accounts of the larger historical events of the period, students go on to examine the changes in publication practices and the reading public that appeared in response to the emerging economic and political conditions. Although somewhat dated, Ian Watt's "The Reading Public and the Rise of the Novel" in *The Rise of the Novel* (1957) is still useful.

This can be supplemented by student reports on J. Paul Hunter's *Before Novels* (1990), Isabel Rivers's collection *Books and their Readers in Eighteenth-Century England* (1982), and Bridget Hill's *Women, Work, and Sexual Politics in Eighteenth-Century England* (1989). These provide an overview of the production, distribution, and consumption of printed texts during this period. They are especially effective in charting transformations in the social structure, particularly in the formation of the new middle class. Reading and writing were being redefined along class lines, and the specialization of these activities for different groups became commonplace. Reading became an activity undertaken for pleasure, a pursuit of leisure, as well as for the purposes of knowledge and moral improvement. Written texts became commodities for entertainment, to be exchanged in the growing market economy. This encouraged a new group of writers, since it was possible for a select few to earn a living by the profits from their writing, even though wealthy patrons still bore the costs of publishing many books in the period. Changes in publishing were also related to transformations in the role of women in all classes at this time. Shifting economic and social conditions created new opportunities for women's independence as well as new forms of repression. Their role as producers and consumers in the expanding reading public was especially important.

Again, the purpose of asking students to undertake this work is to prepare them to consider the ways in which the signifying practices in texts were working to form subjects, to create particular kinds of consciousness, along the lines of gender, class, race, age, sexual orientation, and related categories. As students will quickly discover, the texts they encounter respond to these subject formations and the contradictions and conflicts they create, doing so both openly and in covert and unconscious ways. Students can thus examine the power conflicts and contradictions among classes and among individuals as they are revealed in the texts of this period. These conflicts can then form the basis for large and small group discussions as well as for individual and collaborative written responses, considerations that call for a comment on the pedagogical procedures to be followed in the classroom.

As I indicated earlier, authority should be shared as much as possible. While the teacher sets up the syllabus, maps out a diverse body of readings, and offers methods for responding to them, students should have a choice in activities, assume leadership roles in instruction, and participate in an ongoing dialogue on the issues explored. All texts cannot be read in their entirety. Thus, small groups of three or four students should present their interpretation of a particular text to the class, explaining such matters as the rhetorical patterns they see at work, the narratives inscribed in the text, and the ideological loyalties they discover. They will, of course, also seek the conflicts and contradictions these narratives ignore or resolve in unconvincing ways, paying particular attention to the class, race, and gender roles at issue and their relation to larger socioeconomic proposals. Such encounters commonly lead to disagreement as students arrive at different interpretations, often even as they use similar interpretive categories in reading. Here the productive nature of reading can be explored, particularly the possibilities for a variety of formulations of a common text. Disagreement is to be expected as the students observe the diverse ideological positions of the texts they read.

Class members should also, of course, be involved in text production. They should keep journals, prepare position papers for the class, and even imitate and parody the materials of the late eighteenth century in an attempt to understand the methods of signification called upon and their relationship to economic, social, political, and cultural constructions. They should self-consciously pursue particular rhetorical devices, devices chosen because of their effectiveness in making a case. In other words, the rhetorics and rhetorical texts of the late eighteenth century must be seen in terms of their differences from contemporary constructions as well as their similarities. Students will learn that producing different utterances about a single event commonly involves producing different meanings. On average, class members should thus prepare about five pages of typewritten text every three weeks or so and a larger term project on a problem of special personal interest. Meanwhile, their journals, written in three half-hour sittings weekly, can serve as commentary on the class's activities and the students' experience in developing new reading and writing strategies. Of course, the journal also acts as a private forum for considering issues raised in the class.

Students begin their encounter with primary texts by considering the rhetorical treatises that present in detail the conflicting norms for communication being debated during the time under study, beginning with John Ward's neoclassical Ciceronian rhetoric *A System of Oratory* (1759). Ward's book is important because it represents one of the more prominent discussions of the rhetorical forms preferred by ruling groups during most of the century. This book can be followed by the new rhetorics that articulate the signifying practices, subject formations, and economic and political conditions favored by the emerging bourgeoisie and their aristocratic allies, such as George Campbell's *The Philosophy of Rhetoric* (1776) and Hugh Blair's *Lectures on Rhetoric and Belles Lettres* (1783). Both Campbell and Blair were Scottish clerics and university professors, Campbell at Marischall College, Aberdeen, and Blair at Edinburgh, where he was Regius Professor of Rhetoric and Belles Lettres. The two rhetorics were extremely popular, with Blair's going through 130 editions in England and America, the last in 1911. Both are grounded in Scottish Common Sense Realism, and while Campbell's is the more rigorously philosophical of the two, Blair's is notable for its relation to Adam Smith's lectures on rhetoric delivered at the University of Glasgow when Blair was a student, as well as for its readable style.

These rhetorics of the emerging bourgeois order must be considered not only in relation to the positions they replaced, but also in relation to those competing with them for primacy. Two of these that are especially worth considering because they offer a rhetoric designed for the new gender designations of the period are Hannah More's *Strictures on the Modern System of Female Education* (1799) and Catherine Macaulay's *Letters on Education* (1790). While both are primarily concerned with the unique conditions of education for girls, both also consider rhetoric. More and Macaulay were themselves members of the new middle class of women writers, offering at once encouragement and implicit criticism of the patriarchal rhetorics of Blair and Campbell. Mary Wollstonecraft's *Vindication of the Rights of Woman* (1792), on the other hand, presents rhetorical principles designed to directly counter the patriarchal ideology of the emerging middle class.

In examining the sections of these rhetorics selected by the teacher—or, as often happens, by a student group working collaboratively—class members should interrogate the texts in a particular way. This does not mean, I should caution, that only one method of reading should be tolerated in the class. No one expects students to abandon their customary methods of interpreting texts. Indeed, old and new hermeneutic strategies should interact in the students' reaction to the text, and this interaction should become a part of the ongoing class discussion as well as written assignments.

Students should first determine the recommended subject position of the interlocutor portrayed in the rhetoric along with the corresponding subject position indicated for the audience. In other words, students must determine who is allowed to speak and who is allowed to listen and act on the message of the speaker. The object is to analyze the features of these two interacting subject formations. After all, a rhetoric is primarily a device to train producers of discourse. During the time under study, however, rhetorics became as interested in advising audiences as interlocutors. Indeed, Blair's text is the first I know that argues that it is also intended for people who will never have to speak or write but are interested in text interpretation. Blair may be referring to the new class of women readers who were a part of an identifiable reading public but whose access to textual production was limited—except, of course, for a few members who were engaged in certain literary genres. Indeed, women were attending classroom lectures at Edinburgh at this time, although they were not allowed formal matriculation. Once again, issues of class and gender emerge as the rhetorics define the characteristics of the expected interlocutor and audience.

Students should also examine the rules for evidence these rhetorics display, a concern that deals with questions of epistemology and ideology. In other words, they should locate principles for discovering the available means of persuasion, principles that distinguish true from untrue knowledge, indicating what counts as real and what is ephemeral, what is good, and what is possible. The inductive rhetorics of Campbell and Blair, authorizing certain bourgeois conceptions of nature and human behavior, can thus be distinguished from the deductive and vaguely aristocratic rhetoric of Ward, on the one hand, and the feminist, communal, and egalitarian rhetoric of Wollstonecraft, on the other.

Last, students should determine the manner in which language is conceived in each rhetoric, considering its relation to knowledge and its role in

bringing about agreement and disagreement. As in their work on subject formations, students will see here the play of class, gender, race, sexual orientation,
ethnicity, age, and similar designations in determining what can and cannot be
communicated. Of course, the contrasting and contradictory recommendations
of the varied rhetorics in all of these matters should constantly be studied in
their differing relations to power formations.

Having considered these more or less theoretical treatises, students turn
their attention to actual rhetorical texts that addressed the revolutions that were
at the center of the period. (I want to thank Mark Gellis for the suggestions for
this section provided in his doctoral dissertation "Burke, Campbell, Johnson,
and Priestly: A Rhetorical Analysis of Four British Pamphlets of the American
Revolution.") These texts represent various ideological positions, roughly corresponding to those in the rhetorical texts examined. The rhetorics taken up
earlier were inspected for their presentation of the subject of the address, the
subjects addressed, the rules of knowledge to be invoked, and the relation of
language to all of these. Exploring rhetorical texts involves applying the differing formulations of these elements to the conflicting representations of revolution offered. The purpose is to relate the versions of subjects, communities
(audiences), and language to actual narrative interpretations of experience. In
other words, the ruling conceptions of each argument should be examined as
they unfold in the narrative presentation of events and their principle actors in
the portrayal of revolution. The genre of the text here becomes important, as
students determine the formal patterns of the argument—inductive, deductive,
emotional, ethical—and the way a particular rhetoric indicates they are to pro-
ceed. Style, of course, is also of concern here, as the characteristic choices in
diction and syntax are related to rhetorical and ideological commitments.

One of the more accessible devices for enabling students to deal with narrative patterns is Kenneth Burke's dramatistic scheme (1966). It conceives of
the formation of plot in terms of the relations among scene, act, agent, agency,
and purpose. Students can with little difficulty locate the elements of the presentation that fall into each category and then determine their relative importance in the plot design of the text. In turn, the plot can be situated within
ideological predispositions that Burke locates in certain configurations of the
interacting elements. It can then be related to larger socioeconomic patterns.

A good first case to take up is George Campbell's pamphlet arguing
against the American Revolution, *The Duty of Allegiance* (1777). This can be
followed by Edmund Burke's contrary treatment of the American Revolution
in *A Letter to the Sheriffs of Bristol* (1777). The contrast is intended to encourage an exploration of the different rhetorical devices used in the defense of different positions, but students should also pay careful attention to the conflicting representation of historical events both texts address. In other words, while
Campbell and Burke often agree on the details of an important incident, they
usually disagree about its causes and consequences. Next up might be Burke's
Reflections on the Revolution in France (1790), along with Wollstonecraft's *A*

Vindication of the Rights of Men (1790), a work written to rebut Burke, and *A Vindication of the Rights of Woman* (1792). These might be followed, in turn, by a discussion of Thomas Paine's *The Rights of Man* (1791–1792) and, finally, selections from Olaudah Equiano's *The Interesting Narrative of the Life of Olaudah Equiano or Gustavus Vassa, the African* (1789). The last is a memoir that reveals vividly the cruelties of slavery as related by one of its victims, a person stolen from Africa and enslaved in 1756, eventually to be located on a plantation in Virginia. After being sold to a Philadelphia businessman, Equiano was able to save enough money to buy his freedom and move to London in 1766. The book is a valuable firsthand account of a gifted writer's experience of the inhumanity of slavery, told in the style of high Augustan Humanism.

At this point, the class turns to a sharply contrasting set of signifying practices, practices themselves marked by difference. The second half of the course, that is, is devoted to sampling the variety of poetics and poetic texts that the period produced. Here the effort is to see the intense conflict over poetic forms that appeared at this time and the relation of these differences to economics and politics. It is common, for instance, for students in courses dealing with English Romantic poetry to be told about the instantaneous and extraordinary departure of the poetical methods of Wordsworth and Coleridge from the work of their predecessors. In this course, however, students are asked to read a variety of the texts appearing during the last quarter of the eighteenth century to test the adequacy of this proposition. In the process, they will arrive at—or at least have to consider—alternative formulations that certainly seem more attentive to the actual events and practices of the time. In other words, students will examine a range of poetic texts to realize the remarkable variety in the different forms appearing and to locate the relation of these varieties to literary, ideological, and socioeconomic developments.

This section of the course begins with readings in poetic theory and criticism. Samuel Johnson represents a useful starting point, since he is commonly thought of as the representative figure of the third quarter of the century—a proposition, incidentally, that will be challenged in this section of the course. Students should read *Rasselas* (1759) and selections from the "Preface to Shakespeare" (1765) to see a prominent conception of the nature of poetry and the role of the poet in the life of the society appearing at this time. (I realize these selections appear a bit before the period considered, but their contrastive value in these later discussions justify their selection.) Once again, students should read with a view to locating the rhetorical elements of the act of poetic production and reception, discovering the notion of the subject of creation and interpretation, the epistemological and ideological guides for determining the matter and method of poetic texts, and the signifying practices to be preferred. These texts will, of course, reinforce certain notions of economic, political, and cultural constraints encountered in the rhetorical texts read earlier, with the category of the aesthetic a key concern. Students must locate the preferred formal properties of the poetry encouraged, including diction, syntax, and metrical patterns as well as generic formulas. They will discover that certain kinds of subject matter, themes, and narrative paradigms are preferred as well.

Johnson can be followed by selections from Burke's *Philosophical Enquiry into the Origins of Our Ideas of the Sublime and the Beautiful* (1757) and Archibald Alison's *Essays on the Nature and Principles of Taste* (1790). While Burke's essay is years prior to the period considered here, it was continually influential, as evidenced by Alison's treatment of the beautiful and sublime. Students might also consider statements by Campbell on poetics, particularly the taxonomy in which he makes poetry a lower subdivision of persuasive oratory, and statements by Blair, who devotes the largest part of his *Lectures on Rhetoric and Belles Lettres* to poetic texts. Students should also read selections from Maria Edgeworth's *Letters for Literary Ladies* (1795). Although Edgeworth is concerned with novelists as well as poets, her perspective on the unique strengths and weaknesses of women artists is instructive. Finally, the class might read Wordsworth's "Preface to *Lyrical Ballads*" (1800).

The overall effect of examining these disparate comments is to familiarize students with the remarkably divergent statements on poetry offered at this time. Furthermore, when they turn to the poetry itself, students are likely to find diversity even greater than they had anticipated. They might best begin with the canonical texts, those most likely to display features considered in the most prominent critical statements, such as Johnson's *The Vanity of Human Wishes* (1749). This poem appeared long before 1775, but it once again enables discussion of some of the salient thematic, narrative, and formal features of a major strand of eighteenth-century verse. Students can readily locate the classical influences; the conventional devices favored, including the couplet; and the abstract, specialized poetic diction preferred in this genre. They should also consider the satiric intention and the devices used to achieve it. This poetry of the urbane and the urban might then be contrasted with the canonical poetry of the countryside. Particularly worth considering is George Crabbe's *The Village* (1783). This work depicts the dark side of rural life from the point of view of an unfriendly observer of the lower orders while following many of the expected conventions of the Augustan pastoral genre. Crabbe was encouraged by both Burke and Johnson, the latter offering revisions of portions of *The Village*. This can be followed very usefully by a selection from William Cowper's *The Task* (1785), an English Georgic poem with mock epic tones reflecting on the daily experience of country life before the French Revolution and including comments on such topics as the cruelty of war and slavery. *The Task* is especially noteworthy since by 1800 it had sealed its author's reputation as the most famous poet of England.

The next group of poems I recommend consists of works that were well regarded in their own day but which have failed to make it into the contemporary canon. The authors of these texts were self-consciously responding to the work of the canonical poets of the first group. The important difference is that they were writing from the unique perspective of women, sometimes in an attempt to align themselves with what they saw to be their male counterparts, sometimes in open opposition to them. Their readers, it should be noted, were often the same as those of the male poets of the age, a middle-class group that probably included at least as many women as men.

One of the most successful was Hannah More, a poet praised by Johnson but commonly denounced by Coleridge, Southey, and DeQuincey. More was conservative in art and politics while arguing for more equitable—but not equal—relations between women and men. She also included in certain poems attacks on the horrors of slavery. Anna Seward was considered in her own day one of the outstanding poets of the 1780s. She openly opposed Johnson's poetic and wrote verse that was praised by Wordsworth, but she remained politically conservative, eventually denouncing the French Revolution. Anna Leatitia Barbauld displayed a remarkable complexity in her poetics and politics. She was a part of the Johnson circle but a supporter of the French Revolution and a strong opponent of slavery. She was also an acquaintance of Wordsworth, Coleridge, and Southey, and her subject matter includes the ordinary concerns of common people—as in "Washing Day" and "To the Poor." She often cannot, however, escape the diction and syntax of an earlier time. Helen Maria Williams was also a part of the Johnson circle but Boswell dropped the "amiable" he had used to describe her in his *Life of Johnson* because of her support of the French Revolution. Williams represents a genuine departure in the form and themes of her poetry, so much so that Wordsworth dedicated his first published poem to her (Lonsdale 1989, 413–14). Mary Robinson was a successful actress and poet who, despite public censure for her personal life—at one point she was the contractual mistress of the Prince of Wales—was one of the most highly regarded and frequently published poets of her day. Her poetry displays the radical themes and, occasionally, the forms that were the counterparts of her politics and her defiance of conventional norms. She is an especially keen observer of the subtleties as well as obvious injustices of the class structure in the city. Finally, Phyllis Wheatley, an American slave educated by her master, published *Poems on Various Subjects, Religious and Moral* in 1773 during a trip to London with her master's son. She was later freed, but died in poverty and obscurity in 1784. Wheatley's poetry offers the rich contrast of a slave's perspective couched in the form and language of neoclassic and eighteenth-century religious verse.

These poets can be followed by a set of writers representing the emergence of the working class in literary circles, a group sometimes referred to as the "plebeian poets" or "peasant poets." Gustav Klaus's *The Literature of Labour: Two Hundred Years of Working-Class Writing* (1985) and Donna Landry's *The Muses of Resistance: Laboring-Class Women's Poetry in Britain, 1739–1796* (1990) are good introductions to this topic. These poets' appearance is related to the increase in education among workers due to the Charity Schools and Sunday Schools, but their rise to prominence at this time is largely attributable to the support of patrons.

Anne Yearsley was among the best known of the peasant poets, and Eliza-beth Hands among the most highly regarded. Yearsley was promoted in her ca-reer by Hannah More, although her patron never felt it appropriate that she at-tempt to make a living as an author. Yearsley's *Poems on Several Occasions* (1785) was published with the support of a subscription raised by More, but by its fourth edition in 1786 the poet found it necessary to append an "Auto-biographical Narrative" defending herself from More's attempt to manage her finances. She also published "Poem on the Inhumanity of the Slave Trade" (1788) and collections entitled *Stanzas of Woe* (1790) and *The Rural Lyre* (1796) as well as a novel and a play and some political pamphlets. Yearsley's poetry examines the class and gender conflicts that marked her life, moving be-tween conventional themes and techniques and political and formal boldness. As Landry (1990) notes, her later poetry places her somewhere "between civic poet and social dissident" (122). Elizabeth Hands's single volume of verse, *The Death of Amnon. A Poem. With an Appendix: Containing Pastorals, and Other Poetical Pieces,* was published in 1789. Its title piece is a skillful comic satire in the manner of Swift presented from the perspective of a feminist social critic. Hands is probably the most resourceful of the peasant poets, fluent, as Landry puts it, in "the English literary tradition yet bold enough to mock it, paying homage to the fathers yet reworking pastoral verse forms in a feminizing way" (186). Hands brilliantly turns the conventions of the genres she calls on against the themes they traditionally forwarded, using her class and gender position to challenge dominant conceptions—even if she cannot finally resist a conserva-tive stance.

James Woodhouse and Robert Bloomfield were peasant poets who suffered under the burden of being thought of as the embodiment of the untutored, nat-ural genius. Woodhouse's *The Life and Lucubrations of Crispinus Scriblerus* (written in 1795 but not published until 1896) provides an autobiographical account of the difficulties of the self-educated, working-class poet, a figure treated at once as a celebrity and a freak. Woodhouse's relationship to Eliza-beth Montagu, his patron, parallels that of Yearsley in its bitter disputes. Rob-ert Bloomfield's *The Farmer's Boy* (1800) was a critical success and widely read. It offers a personalized account of the social life of rural England, in-cluding a critique from the perspective of the loyal peasant. Bloomfield and Woodhouse both reveal in their poetry the clash of competing styles in form and theme, as the language and experience of the worker in the field contend with the conventions of the Georgic pastoral celebrated in the parlors of polite society.

Finally, I like to have the class turn to selections from Wordsworth and Coleridge's *Lyrical Ballads* (1798 and 1800), especially the preface from the 1800 edition. This collection and the statement of its principles of composition, of course, have long been considered revolutionary departures in the history of English letters—a status most often grounded in the language of binary opposition, with a coherent version of Romanticism put up against a coherent version of Neoclassicism. The introductory remarks on the Romantic period in *The Norton Anthology of English Literature,* for example, are not unusual. Here the romantics are at every turn praised for their departures from their benighted predecessors. While the last age of poets looked to the outer world and favored the epic and drama, we are told, the new poetry looked to the inner world in a celebration of the lyric. Against the ordinary experience of daily public life, the Romantics offered imaginative vision and the autobiographical. The poet as the observer of public manners is replaced by the poet as prophet. Rules and decorum are supplanted by feeling and spontaneity and original and organic forms. A mechanistic conception of nature is challenged by a natural world of divine force. Rural scenes are now to be frequented for their spiritual character, and the rustic and the commonplace are preferred to the city and its quest for novelty. In place of the common sense, order, and middle path of the neoclassical is proffered the radically individual, the creative, the imaginative, the infinite. Finally, the apocalyptic vision of the Bible is extended to history as the French Revolution is seen by some to be the fulfillment of human destiny in the establishment of a perfect order on earth.

It will require little effort on the part of students to see that these generalizations do not always square with their experience of the texts of this period. The students' final project might thus be to critique these simple binaries, testing the adequacy of them when measured against their own estimates. For instance, Margaret Anne Doody's *The Daring Muse: Augustan Poetry Reconsidered* (1985) challenges the accuracy of these generalizations for even the earliest Augustans. Students can thus try to account for the valorizing of a certain set of writing and reading practices as the basis of a literary canon and the attendant attribution of these characteristics almost exclusively to Wordsworth and Coleridge. *The Norton Anthology,* for example, claims that in "his democratization of poetry," Wordsworth was "more radical than any of his contemporaries. He effected an immense enlargement of our imaginative sympathies and brought into the province of serious literature a range of materials and interests which are still being explored by writers of the present day" (10). This passage will not ring true to students who have read noncanonical texts of the era.

This critique also encourages an equally significant observation: canon formation involves a discussion of our own discursive practices, our own loyalties in rhetoric and poetic. Indeed, the Preface to the *Lyrical Ballads* can be read as a rhetoric, a statement about signification in its broadest sense that forwards certain arguments for the character of discourse in politics and economics as well as poetry. As students examine it from this perspective, the central place of Wordsworth and Coleridge in the Romantic literary canon may suggest an attempt to recuperate in them certain kinds of ideological assertions. The poetry and criticism of *Lyrical Ballads* can be placed in relation to many of the most fundamental convictions of today's professional middle class about the existent, the good, and the possible, particularly in its insistence on the efficacy of the sovereign subject in economic and political action.

By the end of the course, students will have examined in detail the role of signification in forming our understanding of events. In considering the competing representations of the two revolutions, they will have explored the varied formulations that differing generic, ideological, and socioeconomic frames encourage. The case of the American Revolution is especially useful, since it offers interpretations widely at odds with those students customarily encounter this side of the Atlantic. The rhetorical analysis encouraged in the class assists students in arriving at judgments about the relative value of each. They also should at least begin to realize the role of the reading and writing practices of a particular moment in influencing decision making and action, including their own. This realization will be most potent, perhaps, for poetic texts, which the course seeks to present as important historical forces in consciousness formation, addressing significant personal and political issues, a central part of the play of power in historical conflicts. Students should come to see, in other words, that those texts that continue to be read are chosen as much for their uses to the disputants in these conflicts as for their reputed aesthetic value. The qualities of the aesthetic are variously defined across time, and they always appear in relation to other valued cultural codes.

Finally, I would again emphasize that the course described here is meant to be open-ended. Students should be encouraged to come to their own conclusions, the only provision being that they be prepared to support them and have them challenged. As I emphasized in the last chapter, students should be regarded as subjects of their experience, not empty receptacles to be filled with teacher-originated knowledge. This will make for a diversity of discoveries and for disagreement in discussion. Such activity, however, is to be expected and even fostered. It is a part of students actively becoming agents of change in a democratic society. Students in this kind of course are at every turn asked to challenge accepted wisdom and to come to their own positions about the issues under consideration. In addition, the reading and writing practices that the course encourages will further their ability to enter public dialogue, to master the operations of signification in the distribution of power. Students in such a course should thus become better writers and readers as citizens, workers, and critics of their cultures.

18

Freirean Pedagogy, Cultural Studies, and the Initiation of Students to Academic Discourse

Raymond Mazurek

Editors' Note: Ray Mazurek, like Lazere, Bauer, and Berlin, addresses the thorny issue of politics in critical pedagogies. In the beginning of his teaching career, he was reluctant to express his left politics in his teaching. However, after reading Paulo Freire, Richard Ohmann, and Ira Shor, Mazurek began to experiment with linking media studies, academic discourse, and social critique in his composition courses. Mazurek advocates teaching academic discourse, but with a cultural studies approach that provides a "recognition of the students' subjectivity, and [an] analysis of the social production of cultural meaning by powerful institutions which help construct that subjectivity." According to Mazurek, cultural studies provides "one of the best opportunities for furthering the original aims of Freirean approaches to composition." Through a Freirean method, he elicits keywords, photos (pictorial codes), and generative themes from his students to engage their subjectivity. He concludes with ways teachers can respond to student resistance to critical pedagogy. Like Bauer and Lazere, Mazurek sees rhetoric's focus on civic discourse as a useful foundation to justify and enable critical comp courses.

Cultural studies offers to teachers in the 1990s some of the same attractions that Freirean pedagogy offered in the 1960s and subsequent years: the hope of engaging students in critical reflection on generative issues that are simultaneously of great public significance and personal resonance. However, like Freirean pedagogy in North America, cultural studies is difficult to put into practice.

Freirean pedagogy, itself a contested term, has often been identified with a nonauthoritarian approach that would empower students, validating their own voices, while furthering an implicit critique, gradually developed, of the cultural and political institutions that disempower them. However, as Donald Lazere has argued in a recent essay in *College English,* nonauthoritarian pedagogy has in North America succeeded especially well with students in elite universities who are "already socialized to the elaborated codes implicit in such methods" (17), and less well with upwardly mobile working-class students and others in non-elite colleges. Such students are often in need of initiation into the codes through which the university (and the white-collar institutions which employ university graduates) operates before they can comfortably engage in critique. A similar paradox is at work when we consider cultural studies and its relation to the non-elite students who make up the vast majority of those in college writing classes. Cultural studies can be alienating and abstract for students from families that lack "cultural capital," students who need work in basic strategies of writing and analysis and who are sometimes suspicious of the apparent "intrusion" of complex content areas into the writing courses which they believe that they desperately need. But I believe that it is precisely these students who have the most to gain from studying the sources of much of their own subjectivity in the mass media.

In recent years, I have experimented with both Freirean pedagogy and cultural studies in my composition classes, and I believe that cultural studies—particularly an analysis of the mass media—provides one of the best opportunities for furthering the original aims of Freirean approaches to composition. Within the mass media lie "generative themes," topics that embody central contradictions in contemporary ideology and whose exploration can lead to critical reflection and point to political empowerment. It is interesting to note that while Lazere advocates cultural studies—along with explicit instruction in the elaborated discourse of the academy and a deemphasis on nonauthoritarian methods such as the "open classroom"—as an alternative to the Left's emphasis on Freirean pedagogy in North America, he has not seemed to notice the close connection between the possibilities of media analysis (and the exploration of the social construction of subjectivity it implies) and the original Freirean project. Moreover, there is also another connection, for cultural studies is part of the complex, sometimes oppositional discourses of academic culture, and initiation of students (whose consciousness is often rooted in popular culture) into the contemporary academic styles of interpreting and writing about culture is in a sense a reapplication of the original Freirean project for overdeveloped societies in a postmodern age.

Recently, the project of initiating students into academic discourse has been critiqued as too narrow a focus for composition courses by scholars such as Patricia Bizzell, who was once a key advocate for the idea that the initiation of students to academic discourse might produce a sort of Freirean critical consciousness. Like Lazere, Bizzell points out that there is no *necessary* connection between academic discourse and critical consciousness. She also argues that "in the present political emergency . . . we should be trying to do something more than teach academic discourse, namely to help students acquire the language using abilities that will be of most use to them as citizens" ("Argument" 15). Bizzell wishes to distance herself from the notion of academic discourse as a neutral technique that will automatically lead to political insight regardless of content, and she argues against the idea that Freirean pedagogy, academic discourse, or indeed "*any* critical method could automatically lead to a left-oriented view of the socio-political world without any ideological arguments having to be made" (*Academic Discourse* 20–21). However, while I share these reservations, as well as her "dream of what democratic discourse might be" ("Argument" 15), I see a closer connection than Bizzell currently seems to between this dream and the academic sites and discourses that might foster it. Universities are conflictive sites of power which often underwrite the status quo, but they are also places where traditions of critical thought create space for arguments about values and self-reflective analyses of power. As one of my older students, who had just completed six years in the much more restrictive atmosphere of the U.S. Navy, recently put it, where else but in the university do people have so much time and freedom to pursue social questions in depth? While it would be, as Bizzell claims, a serious mistake to impose academic discourse "on all students at all costs with total disregard for whatever knowledge they might bring to school from other discourse communities" (*Academic Discourse* 27), the sophisticated literacy offered by academic discourses is nevertheless "highly advantageous . . . for effective opposition to the dominant culture in today's society" (Lazere 14), especially for many of the students at state universities. Moreover, cultural studies is itself an essentially academic discourse, however much it attempts to study the broader culture or contribute to the creation of a democratic culture by providing powerful tools for understanding society and producing critical discourses for various political ends.

Cultural studies offers a potential way out of the confusion that some of us have felt about the introduction of content and the role of politics in composition courses, a confusion that (at least in my own case) was sometimes increased by commitments to nonauthoritarian pedagogy. I offer the following discussion of my own experience as a potentially instructive example, for I believe that it contains many elements shared by others—at least by some of us on the institutional margins of the profession, who began our careers as (somewhat radical) literary scholars but who have accepted jobs with heavy commitments to composition.

For the first decade during which I worked as a full-time college teacher at several non-elite state universities, I kept my work in composition (the bulk of my teaching) compartmentalized and virtually segregated from my academic writing (on the ideological implications of literary texts), from my teaching of literature (where exploration of issues such as race, class, and gender played an important role), and from my political activism (chiefly anti-intervention work on Central America during the Reagan presidency). Composition was a baffling, sometimes fulfilling world of daily labor, in which I had had little instruction but many years of practical experience. In Stephen North's terms, I was a "practitioner," proud of rolling up my sleeves and doing some of the hardest work in the department, perhaps fulfilling my blue-collar origins. I stole a good idea here and there (mostly from expressivists such as Peter Elbow and Ken Macrorie), but mostly just blundered along trying to improve students' writing and provide them with a little intellectual challenge. I included works such as Studs Terkel's *Working* and Frederick Douglass's *Narrative* in my writing courses to provide such a challenge, but presented them with an inductive approach that asked the students to write about the works before we had discussed them extensively in class, and I was usually hesitant about exploring my own controversial interpretations in detail. In argumentative papers and rhetorical analysis, we drifted into politics, but I felt somewhat self-conscious expressing my views (almost always far to the left of the students'). Strangely, this self-consciousness rarely intruded in literature classes, where it seemed perfectly natural to analyze the class conflicts underlying the literature of the 1930s or the causes of the Vietnam War. Since I thought of composition as "writing instruction" and "individual expression" rather than as a full-fledged field, my views seemed out of place in writing classes.

In 1989 I received tenure, and freed from the necessity of churning out literary articles, I began to think more seriously about composition, its politics, and how I should teach it. I began rereading texts on radical pedagogy and English studies that I had had a cursory knowledge of before: Freire's *Pedagogy of the Oppressed,* Ira Shor's *Critical Teaching and Everyday Life,* and Richard Ohmann's *English in America* and *Politics of Letters.* I started revising my teaching of composition, gradually becoming reconvinced, as I had long suspected, that my previous hesitation about the "intrusion" of politics was also a politics, acquiescing to the trivialization of instruction in writing and rhetoric. Nevertheless, I was hesitant about the place of content (i.e., books) in composition courses. I believed that composition courses should provide the intellectual challenge of other introductory college courses, but "reading" had always seemed to confuse students, who wrote best about their own experience. My sense of the parameters of composition as a field was a muddled combination of current-traditionalism, linguistics, expressionism, and concern for audience. Working at a branch campus of a state university where there was little interest in composition studies as a research area and little reward for exploring new areas (there was pressure to publish, but that almost precluded spending research time outside one's traditional "field" while writing toward tenure), I felt that I had to invent composition as a field virtually on my own even though I had taught primarily composition, full-time, for almost a decade, and although that decade was the 1980s, not the 1960s. I mention these details about my situation because I believe that the micropolitics of English departments—and the marginalization and isolation of those who teach composition—are vitally important to any analysis of the role of politics in a larger sense in composition studies. (Given this marginalization, it is no accident that the majority of teachers in composition classes have generally been women, and narratives such as Lynn Bloom's "Teaching College English as a Woman" offer vivid testimony to the consequences of the dual denigration of female scholars and the writing instruction they have typically provided. Some of the more extreme conditions that Bloom describes have improved. Yet composition as a field, and those who teach it (women and men), is *still* considered second-rate and invisible, like the students in the courses, and I suspect that this is more true at the non-Ph.D.-granting institutions, where the vast majority of practitioners and students labor, than at the research institutions, where the majority of composition scholars—who define the field—work.)

When I tried to apply Freirean pedagogy, it was in a way that reflected my uncertainty about the content of composition courses. Since expressionist theories dominated my thinking, that content seemed to lie somewhere in the students' own minds, and had to be invented out of their own experience. Expressionist composition theory was consistent with both my literary orientation and my radical politics. As Todd Gitlin has pointed out, the radical politics of participatory democracy, forged in Students for a Democratic Society and the Student Nonviolent Coordinating Committee in the 1960s but with a lasting influence on the Left, were dominated by a mystique of personal expression (163–66). In addition, the idea of rhetoric as personal expression has a consistent appeal to young students in contemporary society, though it is merely a starting point that needs to be worked through. Thus, the attraction of Freirean theory for me lay partly in its movement from personal expression to an awareness of the social, and the version of Freirean pedagogy I developed reflected my roots in expressionism (for a critique of expressionism, see Berlin, *Rhetoric and Reality* and "Rhetoric and Ideology," and Bauer).

Selecting for my first comprehensive "experiment" a sophomore writing course ("Writing in the Social Sciences") where many of the students were education majors, I introduced Freire as both a topic for discussion and a source of the pedagogy for the class, assigning the second chapter of *The Pedagogy of the Oppressed,* with its famous critique of the banking concept of education, and supplementary readings. I tried to guide the class through a reduplication of Freire's method (a word I use cautiously) as developed in his early literacy classes in Brazil: searching for generative themes, the issues in the class most urgently in need of critical reflection; codifying or representing those themes; and decoding or reflecting on them (for a discussion of this process, see Freire, "Education"; for discussions of Freirean pedagogy for North Americans, see Freire and Shor, as well as Tompkins.)

I began with an in-class writing, asking students what ideas and/or experiences drew them to their major fields (almost all were in education or the social sciences), what issues they wished to explore at the university, and what goals they wished to attain after leaving college. After writing for forty minutes (half the period), I asked them to introduce themselves, saying as much or as little from their initial writings as they chose. On the second day, I returned the papers without comment, pointing out to them that I had *read* the essays and did not wish to critique them at this stage, and that reading their writing for content would always be more important to me than critiquing it, though I would do that also. I then asked them to circle the three words most resonant with meaning, for them, intellectually or emotionally, in their essays, to write briefly about why the words were resonant, and to suggest possible topics for the course's required long paper based on their reflection (the keywords exercise was derived from a somewhat different use of keywords in Freirean pedagogy by Finlay and Faith). In small groups, the students discussed why their words were resonant and tried to discover possible writing topics that grew out of the words, reporting their ideas to the class as a whole. For the first week, I tried to stay in the background as much as possible, as Ira Shor recommends when working with students who have known primarily teacher-centered classrooms.

In the second week, I introduced Freire's ideas, asked them to read the "banking education" section from *Pedagogy of the Oppressed,* and reproduced the class's complete list of resonant words and possible topics. I then gave an assignment, asking the students to find an article, picture, or (preferably) both that "represented" or codified some of the class's resonant words, and to briefly explain the relationship between the words and the "representation." It took a little time to clarify this: I was asking them to assume that significant intersubjective tendencies were revealed in the resonant words, and that these could lead us to issues worth exploring together. I was not asking them to continue to work with their own words to explore issues of personal interest, which was how many students wanted to interpret the assignment. Rather, I was suggesting that the class might uncover "generative themes" for exploration and decoding, in a way modelled roughly on Freire's Brazilian literacy experiments, which we had discussed in class. This naturally led to a discussion of ideological perspectives. I supplemented reading from Freire by assigning an interview with Frances Moore Lappe that had appeared in the *The Progressive,* suggesting that her definition of the political arts—"the exercise of judgment, listening, dialogues, reflection, evaluation, and the constructive expression of anger" (qtd. in Blanchard and Watrous 36)—paralleled Freire's. (Curiously, the more conservative students were much more hostile to Lappe's ideas than to Freire's. Perhaps he seemed more safely exotic; perhaps they felt safe with Freire's notion that the student's own voice was an important starting point for knowledge and could thus forgive him for his radicalism.) We also began an assignment on the political slant of an article in the news, and began reading a textbook, *Writing in the Social Sciences,* and I suggested that our own experiment with their resonant words modelled what social scientists tried to do. This suggestion was confusing to them, as most of the students were sophomores with little theoretical background in the social sciences, which they tended to define as fields designed to help other people.

The most common words the class (20 students, 18 of them women, all of them white) chose were *helping/help* (on 6 lists), *teaching/teaching methods*

(6), *caring* (2), *communication* (2), *life, life/death* (2), *experience* (2), and *politics* (2). From their representations and explanations of the resonant words, I chose four to copy for class discussion. These I placed in a sequence, forming a sort of visual narrative, which I taped to the blackboard on the days when we discussed them. The first was a picture of Greg LeMond, the cycling champion, with a short write-up describing his struggle to achieve; the second was a picture of a homeless black man, sleeping in rags on the floor. (Also in the picture, but not showing up in my original xerox of it, was a young child with a teddy bear, curled up beside the man. Providing a better copy on the second day of discussion added to the controversy this picture generated.) The third showed parents, teachers, and police having a discussion in a school library as part of an education program in a local school, and the fourth was the widely circulated picture of triumphant Berliners on top of the Berlin wall. Each of these was accompanied by a short essay, discussing identification with self-achievement, the need to help the homeless, the need to deal with the problem of drugs, or the need to consider the worldwide impact of the changes in Eastern Europe.

Class discussion centered on the homeless issue, and on the relation between the first two representations. Debate and disagreement grew between those who looked at achievement as something that reflected the individual's efforts and worth and those who looked at social problems such as homelessness as the result of forces beyond individual control. Two writing assignments grew out of the discussion: first, a simple invitation to continue the discussion in an essay, and later, a second essay asking them to do so again, this time bringing in documented evidence that illuminated the discussion (most chose the more obvious news sources, but one student interviewed a homeless man). Not all students became engaged in the discussion, but some became very engaged. The most vocal student was a man in his twenties who was a political science major and ardent Reagan supporter; the most controversial paper referred to the class's resonant words to attack his position, saying:

> The reason that I was really shocked to hear the negative opinion about the homeless in class was because of the class we were in and the list of words that we gathered and said were important to us. Some of these words were: *helping, caring, society, communicating, teaching, learning, feelings, education, hope, influence,* and *life.* I think that anyone in our class who said that the homeless are lazy and just want to be that way, should take another look at our list of resonant words. All these words deal with helping people, but in our discussion, some people put the homeless down like a disease.

Another student, following a similar line of argument, wrote:

> One of the class's resonant words was *helping,* but how many are only interested in helping those on a similar social level as their own? Helping middle-class children carries more prestige than working in a shelter for the homeless.

One advantage of having begun with the generative words was that they provided a way of referring back to the contradictory ideas and feelings (the ideology and "structures of feeling," as Raymond Williams might say) with which the class began their exploration. To further class discussion and link it to our study of writing, I copied as many papers as possible, anonymously or with their names, as students permitted.

In our discussions, I repeatedly asked why the first two pictures generated so much more discussion than the others and why the identification of some students with the first picture was so strong. I encouraged them to consider the way social constructions (widely circulated images and ideas, the culture's resonant words) of achievement appealed to them in contrast to social representations of the Other. One student pointed to the resemblance of the LeMond picture to an advertisement; another wrote about all the help LeMond had received, in his supposedly individual achievement, from sports medicine, support crews, sponsors, and so on. I introduced my own interpretations of their ideas, summarizing what was happening in their discussions, suggesting that the culture had encouraged them to construct images of themselves as autonomous self-achievers and thus to blame those who did not achieve in a supposedly meritocratic society that worked to benefit the wealthy and disempower the poor. I also pointed out that in my own college years, the representations that evoked the least comment from them (especially the Berlin Wall with its image of revolution) would have provoked the most, and that if I had to name the story told by their representations, I would describe it as a narrative about the relation of public and private, self and other, about their own entrapment in public constructions of the private on the one hand and unrealized possibilities of social change on the other. But there was never consensus in the class, and my own remarks were (I think rightly) a bit to the side of what was happening. In ways that parallel the experience Tompkins describes, the class became its own audience for part of that semester to a degree I had not witnessed before, acknowledging and accommodating the positions of others and questioning their own, but remaining locked in ideological divisions they could not completely explain.

The second part of the semester, in which we worked on individual long papers, lacked the energy or engagement of the first, and I've never repeated this experiment in exactly the same way, for reasons similar to those Lazere gives in his critique of Freirean pedagogy. As Lazere suggests, Freirean pedagogy and other democratic learning methods have a positive value, yet in classes for non-elite students, "it must be kept in mind that these students are at a disadvantage compared to those at elite universities in their level of pertinent cultural literacy and familiarity with academic codes, so that compensatory time must be spent in these realms that unfortunately conflicts with the time available for Freirean pedagogy" (19). In my experiment, I included discussions of rhetorical principles and effective writing, especially in the last part of the course, but I came away feeling that more needed to be done to integrate rhetorical considerations more fully into the syllabus (which I intentionally invented as I went along, although students were aware of the major writing assignment from the beginning). This criticism is hardly an insurmountable one—it is always possible to include more or less explicit instruction on writing principles, and generating the desire to write for a real audience is far more difficult than providing a little structure when needed. However, too much energy (my own and the students') had gone into inventing the course and finding the themes to explore. Similar results might have been achieved had we discussed materials that had been previously chosen by the instructor. As it was, I selected the representations and their narrative arrangement anyway, and thus I implicitly suggested an interpretation of their ideological perspective from the beginning. Similarly, too much of the analysis of the representations as social constructions depended upon my analysis; it may have been more useful to read discussions of the social construction of self in advertising and to test those ideas against the students' own experience and resistance.

More recently, I have attempted to adopt a cultural studies approach to composition, influenced by the work of James Berlin, Diana George, John Trimbur, and others. However, it was my experience the second time that I attempted to use Freirean pedagogy, in the spring of 1991, that convinced me to use more structured approaches to cultural critique. That semester was dominated by the Gulf War, the occasion of a personal crisis for so many of us on all sides of the issue. Teaching two sections of "Writing in the Social Sciences" in January of 1991, I lacked the energy to go through the stages of exploring generative themes; I started the course in more or less the same way but ignored the resonant words and focused on finding topics for common exploration. One of the topics that emerged was the war, but there our discussion was frozen. Near the beginning of the semester, my picture and some of my remarks appeared on the front page of the local newspaper as part of the coverage of a Washington demonstration against the war; suddenly I was at the center of controversy and under suspicion, along with the rather strange Freirean ideas I had introduced but not fully developed. Neither of these two classes was as satisfactory as the first, though the section that finally selected the Gulf War as one of its common topics worked better than the class that steered away from it, probably because the section was able to more fully explore the issue and its hostility toward the instructor. In that class, however, dialogue did not have the free range that existed in the earlier semester. Students who were for the war allowed their names to appear on papers; other students expressed doubts but did not want papers copied; one young woman wrote strongly in opposition but insisted her paper be copied anonymously. Discussion on the topic was stifled, as only one person (the instructor) was really willing to voice opposition (and I, too, was feeling the pressure of the McCarthyite atmosphere in the community and the nation). Most students chose to write on something safer, and everyone, myself included, was relieved to get to the more traditional elements of the course, such as the long report on individually chosen topics.

The conditions that semester were probably unique, though they made apparent some of the problems of the pedagogy I had adopted. Inventing the content of the course through Freirean methods had proved to be a laborious process which I abandoned under pressure, and I was left with a set of controversial issues without a way of relating them to the deeply felt, often contradictory ideas and emotions which underlay the controversy. Probably there was no way to do this—no easy way—with a topic such as the Gulf War. But a further problem was the degree to which the pedagogy was implicit, and fell back into an expressivist mode, where we (teachers and students) expressed views on the Gulf War with no mediating ground. As Dale Bauer has noted in her discussion of the parallel problems of feminist pedagogy, expressivism, with its rigid separation of public and private, "reinforces, however indirectly, the dominant patriarchal model rather than challenges it" (390). A goal of feminist pedagogy, in contrast, "like Ira Shor's and Freire's, is to foreground dialogics in the classroom. This strategy uses one kind of mastery, feminist and dialogic in practice, against another, monologic and authoritarian" (387). In the minds of many of the students in my 1991 classroom, I had become the latter kind of monologic authority, especially for those in the section that did not choose to pursue the war as a topic for writing and thus did not have a chance to engage in the kind of negotiation of differences that Bauer advocates. A focus on texts which presented conflicting positions, and an exploration of rhetorical, academic, or cultural codes as ways of articulating and producing those positions, would have provided better ways of dealing with controversy. As it was, too much of the controversy and the pedagogy existed within the students and the instructor; too little in the analysis of texts and practices that had a material, intersubjective existence between them.

In "Writing and the Social Sciences," I now focus on contrasts between the presentation of the problem of literacy in popular media and in books such as Mike Rose's *Lives on the Boundary,* and on different styles of academic social science as represented by Rose's humanistic, ethnographic approach (which my students like) and more traditional empirical social science works such as William Julius Wilson's *The Truly Disadvantaged* (which my students find intimidating). The course attempts to introduce students to some of the different approaches to social issues produced within popular and academic discourses— knowledge which inexperienced students being initiated to those disciplines need. Students write rhetorical analyses of contrasting works, as well as critiques of the writer's ideas, before doing some independent research. However, it is very important that the works are selected for their exploration of "generative themes." For most of my students, the problem of literacy and their own difficulty initiating themselves to the alienating discourses of college is a central issue, for they have been portrayed (or "written") as insufficiently literate or capable by popular culture, by many of their teachers and professors, and by themselves; they have learned negative interpretations of themselves and of the academic discourse which they have rarely been invited to join. Issues of class, ethnicity, pedagogy, and power (the issues Rose and Wilson raise) are central to the way students have learned these perceptions of the university. They often perceive Rose's story as not unrelated to their own, and find Wilson more alien (in his race, for most of my students are white, but more significantly in his empirical and impersonal style), but both writers provide critical discourses which challenge their perceptions and beliefs.

The social-science writing course I have constructed is a formidable one, especially for sophomores who have had as little explicit instruction in writing on discourses other than personal experience as some of them have had in previous courses. It is a challenge to provide enough self-affirming exercises to mitigate the difficulty some of these students have with writing about and analyzing complex texts and relating these to their own lives. The political controversies of the course, however, are as much in the reading as in the instructor's and students' consciousness, and the social production of that consciousness through education and social class is itself the central issue. Curiously, the antagonism between the students and myself has been transformed from an opposition to my political views to an antagonism toward the difficulty of the course. Lazere notes a similar paradox, the "irony . . . that when leftist teachers, including myself [Lazere], try to present students with an honest account of the necessity—and difficulty—of critical education, students perceive *us* as the coercive authority figures, in contrast to the permissive mainstream culture" (14).

A similar antagonism often emerges in my freshmen writing courses, which in recent years have usually focused either on the topic of academic initiation and education (using Rose in ways similar to those described above), on the mass media, or on both. Recently, I have developed a freshmen writing course centered on the theme of "Media, Self, and Culture," in which students move from (1) an essay on their personal experiences and goals to essays which ask them (2) to analyze the cultural meanings of advertisements, (3) to write a response to one of the essays on culture in the reader, and (4) to complete a longer paper on an issue presented in the news while also taking account of the way the rhetoric of different news media influences the presentation of content. Because the assignments are challenging for non-elite students, four summaries and exploratory writings on the readings are also required (and graded, however liberally, so these short assignments are taken seriously); there is also ample time for revision of up to two essays and/or submission of a fifth essay during the last three weeks of the semester, which are entirely devoted to workshop sessions. The readings (mostly from George and Trimbur's *Reading Culture*) present interpretations of such topics as rap music, advertising, the "baby bust" generation of the late 1980s, and the news. Bill Moyers's 1989 PBS video series, *The Public Mind,* provides an excellent video supplement. The sections on advertising and generations, especially, provide some of the same insights into the social construction of self and other as were attempted by my earlier Freirean experiments, and the analysis of the news provides a rudimentary analysis of the social construction of ideology.

Students often resist the ideas and insights in the reading, and I find that it is difficult to provide sufficient time for reading, analysis, writing, and critique on one topic before moving on to another. It is never easy to give students' resistance enough time and room to be recognized, heard, challenged, and redeveloped. But this problem exists in every composition pedagogy based in critical thinking in the fullest sense, recognizing that dialogue is, in Lappe's words, one of the "political arts." The cultural studies course I have developed has the advantage of providing explicit instruction in rhetoric (the papers include an expressive essay, an analysis, a response for a hostile audience, and an evaluation/research paper), time for revision and work on basic literacy, recognition of the students' subjectivity, and analysis of the social production of cultural meaning by powerful institutions which help construct that subjectivity. Thus, the course moves the project of critique away from the question of specific issues (though those get raised in the process) and toward the question of the social construction of consciousness (though some parts of that question, such as who constructs whose consciousness, and for what ends, remain highly controversial). Similarly, the responsibility for critique no longer resides exclusively within the teacher, but also in the theories and interpretations being examined, theories which are closely aligned with contemporary conceptions of rhetoric as a field. For study of the mass media is simultaneously the study of the most powerful means of persuasion in the culture and the most powerful source of ideas in the "public mind." If college rhetoric courses should focus on public discourse, as has been often suggested, then the study of mass media should be a key part of those courses, for the mass media (especially television) are at the center of the public discourse of late-twentieth-century culture; they are also the key sources of the *invention* of our students' ideas, which cannot be adequately explained by expressive theories.

Fears that cultural studies courses like my own might constitute the imposition of "political correctness" upon students are naive. Some of the best papers in the "Media, Self, and Culture" course have been written by women who became interested in the power of the mass media to construct negative gender stereotypes; other students have written strong essays developing their resistance to the idea that their values are shaped by the mass media. In her research paper, one of the best students in the class used ideas presented by the conservative columnist George Will (one of the required readings) to analyze what she perceived as the unfairly pro-choice slant in the coverage of abortion demonstrations, even though she clearly knew that my own sympathies lay elsewhere. Her paper was hardly unique in its presentation of ideas which directly opposed my own. While I can hardly claim to be as successful as I would like to be, I seek to create an atmosphere where students like her feel free to write against the grain of my own politics, as well as one where I feel free to critique her position. To try to foreclose the possibility of such a dialogue is to underestimate the resources of both students and teachers.

Cultural studies provides some resolution to the dilemmas radical teachers like myself sometimes experience regarding sharing their political viewpoints with students. For if the focus of the course is on "rhetoric" in the broadest sense—on the social processes and conflicts which produce ideas and discourses—rather than on specific issues perceived only as "content" to be written about, then the instructor's views do not seem as individual, odd, or intrusive. Heated controversies will still occur, between students and instructor and among students, but the rhetorical focus provides a mediating ground. Individual choices as to how much of one's thinking to reveal on issues are still complicated, unsettling choices, for students as well as teachers, choices that must be made in response to the urgencies and pressures of specific pedagogical moments.

Notes

I wish to acknowledge the help and influence of several friends and colleagues who have had a considerable influence on my thinking about composition pedagogy: Regina Rinderer of Delta College, who first introduced me to the work of Paulo Freire when we both taught at Southern Illinois University in Carbondale; Mike Riley, my colleague in the hinterlands of English Studies at the Berks Campus of Penn State, who has developed his own somewhat different cultural studies composition approach, centered on Bill Moyers's *The Public Mind;* and Jim Berlin of Purdue University, who generously gave of his time to discuss his ideas on composition and cultural studies when I visited Purdue during my sabbatical in the fall of 1990.

Works Cited

Bauer, Dale. "The Other 'F' Word: The Feminist in the Classroom." *College English* 52 (1990): 385–96.

Berlin, James. "Composition and Cultural Studies." *Composition and Resistance*. Ed. C. Mark Hulbert and Michael Blitz. Portsmouth, NH: Boynton/Cook, 1991. 47–55.

———. "Rhetoric and Ideology in the Writing Classroom." *College English* 50 (1988): 477–93.

———. *Rhetoric and Reality: Writing Instruction in American Colleges 1900–1985*. Carbondale: Southern Illinois UP, 1987.

———. "Rhetoric, Poetic, and Culture: Contested Boundaries in English Studies." *The Politics of Writing Instruction*. Ed. Richard Bullock and John Trimbur. Portsmouth, NH: Boynton/Cook, 1991. 23–38.

Bizzell, Patricia. *Academic Discourse and Critical Consciousness*. Pittsburgh: U of Pittsburgh P, 1992.

———. "Argument, Community, and Knowledge." *Diversity: A Journal of Multicultural Issues* 1 (1992): 9–23.

Blanchard, Bob, and Susan Watrous. "An Interview with Frances Moore Lappe." *The Progressive* (February 1990): 34–37.

Bloom, Lynn. "Teaching College English as a Woman." *College English* 54 (1992): 818–25.

Elbow, Peter. *Writing with Power.* New York: Oxford UP, 1981.

Finlay, Linda Shaw, and Valerie Faith. "Illiteracy and Alienation in American Colleges: Is Paulo Freire's Pedagogy Relevant?" *Freire for the Classroom.* Ed. Ira Shor. Portsmouth, NH: Boynton/Cook, 1987. 63–86.

Freire, Paulo. *Education for Critical Consciousness.* Trans. Myra Bergman Ramos. New York: Continuum, 1973.

———. *Pedagogy of the Oppressed.* Trans. Myra Bergman Ramos. New York: Continuum, 1989.

Freire, Paulo, and Ira Shor. *A Pedagogy for Liberation: Dialogues for Transforming Education.* South Hadley, MA: Bergin and Garvey, 1987.

Friedman, Sharon, and Stephen Steinberg. *Writing and Thinking in the Social Sciences.* Englewood Cliffs, NJ: Prentice-Hall, 1989.

George, Diana, and John Trimbur, eds. *Reading Culture.* New York: Harper-Collins, 1992.

Gitlin, Todd. *The Sixties: Years of Hope, Days of Rage.* New York: Bantam, 1987.

Lazere, Donald. "Back to Basics: A Force for Oppression or Liberation?" *College English* 54 (1992): 7–21.

Macrorie, Ken. *Uptaught.* New York: Hayden, 1970.

Moyers, Bill. *The Public Mind: Image and Reality in America.* Directed by Gail Pellett. Alexandria, VA: PBS Video, 1989.

North, Stephen. *The Making of Knowledge in Composition: Portrait of an Emerging Field.* Portsmouth, NH: Boynton/Cook, 1987.

Ohmann, Richard. *English in America: A Radical View of the Profession.* New York: Oxford UP, 1976.

———. *Politics of Letters.* Middletown, CT: Wesleyan UP, 1987.

Rose, Mike. *Lives on the Boundary: The Struggles and Achievements of America's Underprepared.* New York: Macmillan, 1989.

Shor, Ira. *Critical Teaching and Everyday Life.* Boston: South End, 1980.

Tompkins, Jane. "Pedagogy of the Distressed." *College English* 52 (1990): 652–62.

Trimbur, John. "Cultural Studies and Teaching Writing." *Focuses* 1.2 (1988): 5–18.

Williams, Raymond. *Marxism and Literature.* New York: Oxford UP, 1977.

Wilson, William Julius. *The Truly Disadvantaged: The Inner City, the Underclass, and Public Policy.* Chicago: U of Chicago P, 1987.

About the Editors

Ira Shor has a dual appointment as Professor of English at the City University of New York Graduate School and at the College of Staten Island. His *Critical Teaching and Everyday Life* was the first booklength treatment of Freirean literacy in the United States. He worked with Paulo Freire for a number of years and coauthored with Freire his first "talking book," *A Pedagogy for Liberation*. Shor, whose most recent book is *When Students Have Power*, speaks widely around the country. He grew up in the working class of New York City.

Caroline Pari is Assistant Professor of English at Borough of Manhattan Community College, CUNY. She received her Ph.D. from CUNY, specializing in Composition and Rhetoric, Women's Studies, and nineteenth-century women's writing. Pari has contributed to *Teaching Working Class,* edited by Sherry Linkon, and *Composition/2000,* edited by Michelle Hall Kells and Valerie Balester. She is a native of Queens, New York, and lives there with her husband.